Pro .NET Best Practices

Stephen D. Ritchie

Pro .NET Best Practices

Copyright © 2011 by Stephen D. Ritchie

ISBN-13 (pbk): 978-1-4302-4023-5

ISBN-13 (electronic): 978-1-4302-4024-2

Trademarked n ames, logos, an d images may app ear in this book. Rather than us e a trademark s ymbol with every occurrence of a trademarked name, logo, or ima ge we use the names, logos, and images only in a n editorial fashion and to the benefit of the trademark owner, with no intention of infringement of the trademark.

The use in this publication of trade names, tr ademarks, service ma rks, a nd s imilar terms, ev en if th ey a re not identified as such, is not to be ta ken as an expres sion of opinion as to whethe r or not they are subject to proprietary rights.

While the advice and information in this book are believed to be true and accurate at the date of publication, neither the authors nor the editors nor th e publisher can accept any legal responsibility for any errors or o missions that may be made. The publisher makes no warranty, express or implied, with respect to the material contained herein.

President and Publisher: Paul Manning
Lead Editor: Jonathan Hassell
Technical Reviewer: Paul Apostolescu
Editorial Board: Steve Anglin, Mark Beckner, Ewan Buckingham, Gary Corne ll, M organ Ertel, Jonathan Gennick, Jonathan Hasse ll, Robe rt Hutchin son, Mich elle Lowman, Jame s Markham, Mat thew Moodie , Je ff O lson, Jeffrey P epper, Douglas Pu ndick, Be n Renow-Clarke, D ominic Shakeshaft, G wenan Sp earing, Matt Wa de, Tom Welsh
Coordinating Editor: Annie Beck
Copy Editor: Elizabeth Berry
Compositor: Bytheway Publishing Services
Indexer: SPI Global
Artist: SPI Global
Cover Designer: Anna Ishchenko

Distributed to the book trade worldwide by Springer Scie nce+Business Media New York, 233 Spring Street, 6th Floor, New York, NY 10013. Phone 1-800-SPRINGER, f ax (20 1) 348 -4505, e-mail orders-ny@springer-sbm.com, or v isit www.springeronline.com.

For information on translations, please e-mail rights@apress.com, or visit www.apress.com.

Apress and friends of ED book s may be purchased in bulk f or academic, corporate, or promo tional use. eBoo k versions and licenses are also available for most ti tles. For more information, reference our Special Bulk Sales–eBook Licensing web page at www.apress.com/bulk-sales.

Any source code or other supplementary materials ref erenced by the author i n this te xt is av ailable to re aders at www.apress.com. For detailed inf ormation about how to lo cate y our book's source code, go to http://www.apress.com/source-code/.

This book is dedicated to my family.
To my wife, Robin
To my daughters, Dianna and Jessica
To my stepsons, Devin and Wyatt

Thank you for all your love, support, and encouragement.

Contents at a Glance

Contents

About the Author

Stephen Ritchie has been writing software professionally for over 20 years. He works as a software development consultant at Excella Consulting in the Washington, D.C. area. His passion for following best practices goes back to the college chemistry lab and an almost fanatical devotion to getting things absolutely, precisely correct. The intervening years of developing software professionally have taught him to appreciate the value of experience, practical know-how, and continuous learning. Today, Stephen is the .NET best practices steward at Excella Consulting, working with .NET project teams to facilitate and sort out the helpful practices from the unhelpful ones, the practicable from the impracticable, and the sounds-good from the it-really-is-good practices and principles.

About the Technical Reviewer

Paul Apostolescu has worked for over a decade in the computer and software security industry and architected products ranging from kernel-level security to applications for enterprise security continuous monitoring. He is a Microsoft Certified Solutions Developer and holds various other security certifications.

Acknowledgments

I want to thank my family, Robin, Dianna, Jessica, Devin, and Wyatt. They have been very supportive and have encouraged me to write this book. I want to thank my parents for all that they have done to raise and support me.

I want to thank the team at Apress for all their excellent work. I want to thank Jonathan Hassell, my acquisitions editor, for helping to get this book started and encouraging its success. Thank you to Matthew Moodie, the developmental editor, for your guidance and support. Thank you to Annie Beck, the coordinating editor, for your hard work and for keeping the whole project moving forward. Thank you to the copyeditor, Elizabeth Berry, who improved the quality and readability of the text. Thank you to all the other people who worked behind the scenes to make this book possible. I especially want to thank Paul Apostolescu for his insightful and helpful technical review; it is very much appreciated.

Thanks to my colleagues at Excella Consulting for their help and support. Through my work with the Excella Centers of Excellence and as a .NET best practices steward for the firm, I know that I work with some of the finest consultants and developers. I appreciate all that I have learned and will continue to learn through our combined efforts, shared knowledge, and continued collaboration.

I want to acknowledge the developers, bloggers, writers, and mentors who teach and communicate to other .NET developers. Their experience and expertise is an invaluable resource for the whole .NET community. Many professional developers, like me, benefit greatly from your efforts. Thank you.

Introduction

Pro .NET Best Practices is a book that was primarily written for professional software developers who want to bring new and different .NET practices to their teams and organization. The phrase *best practice* is a handy way to describe widely-used practices and generally-accepted standards that many .NET developers in many organizations have found to be good and effective practices. Because best practices cannot work in every situation, the book encourages you to sort out what may or may not work well for your situation.

The adoption of new and different practices is a central theme of this book. Consider the four levels at which best practices are embraced:

- *Individual*: You or any individual adopts better practices to increase personal and professional productivity, quality, thoroughness, and overall effectiveness.

- *Group*: The team adopts better practices to be more industrious together, avoid problems, achieve desired results, improve interpersonal relationships, and work more effectively with other teams.

- *Organization*: Your company, agency, or firm adopts better practices to bring more positive outcomes to the organization, attract and retain employees, satisfy end-user expectations, and make stakeholders happy.

- *Profession*: Better practices are widely adopted and become generally-accepted standards, patterns, and principles that bring alignment to software development and benefit to all that follow them.

In an ideal world, best practices are quickly adopted at all four levels. However, this is not realistic for many of the reasons discussed in this book's early chapters. Pragmatists know that they usually cannot control all four levels within their current circumstances and can only influence a few. And so they work within their span of control and spheres of influence. As you read this book, think about adopting better practices within those areas you can control and positively shaping those areas that you do influence.

Pro .NET Best Practices is a practical reference on the best practices that you can apply to your .NET projects today. You will learn standards, techniques, and conventions that are realistic and helpful to achieving results. The book covers a broad range of practices and principles with an emphasis on tools and technologies for

- Automated testing

- Build automation

- Continuous integration

- Code analysis

To get warmed up, you can turn to the sample .NET best practices scorecard in Appendix B. If you take the time to score your current project, what might the score tell you about where things currently stand? Hopefully, completing the scorecard prompts these kinds of questions:

- What are the best practices you want to see adopted? Why are they important to you? Do you foresee any obstacles or barriers?

- What practice on the scorecard should you, your team, or your organization focus on first? Do you prioritize practices that offer greater efficiencies or help to prevent problems?

- How would you revise the scorecard to make it fully apply to your current situation? What practices would you add to the list? What practices would you remove?

- Once you have the scorecard that is right for you, how often would you reassess it? Is yearly too infrequent? Is weekly too intrusive and demotivating?

Adopting best practices is an initiative that is guided by having relevant objectives and a way to track progress. Put together the right scorecard, based on your situation. Track it regularly and use the overall score as a gauge that indicates and validates your continuous improvement.

> *If I find 10,000 ways something won't work, I haven't failed. I am not discouraged, because every wrong attempt discarded is another step forward.*
>
> Thomas Edison

The complex problems in life require iterative solutions. Edison knew that patience and perseverance are an inventor's competitive advantage. The same is true for best practices. It is better to take an iterative and incremental approach to adopting new and different practices. Be patient with it, stick to it, and have fun with it.

Who This Book Is For

This book is for anyone who has a stake in bringing better practices to software development.

Developers

As a developer, you have personal practices that make you an effective software developer. Are there new and different practices that could make you a more effective developer? This book offers realistic, practicable, and truly helpful best practices. The early chapters focus on the benefits, relevance, and purpose behind adopting best practices. The later chapters focus on technologies, tools, and techniques that bring greater effectiveness. The final chapter examines the influence of biases and aversions and how you can overcome these obstacles to adopting better practices.

Team Leaders

As a team leader, you see the team develop software through their current practices. Could the team perform better and achieve better outcomes with new and different practices? You can expect that this book will offer you pragmatic advice on how to implement suitable best practices likely to be followed by project members. You learn how to get best practices started and keep them from falling out of practice. You learn how to gain support for following best practices from all stakeholders by recognizing and overcoming biases, highlighting the gap between current results and desired results, and demonstrating the value of following best practices.

How This Book Is Structured

Pro .NET Best Practices presents the topics to provide reasonable breath and go into depth on key practices. For example, the chapter on code analysis looks at both static and dynamic analysis, and it goes into depth with FxCop and StyleCop. The goal is to strike the balance between covering all the topics, discussing the widely-used tools and technologies, and having a reasonable chapter length.

Chapters 1 through 5 are focused on the context of new and different practices. Since adopting better practices is an initiative, it is important to know what practices to prioritize and where to uncover better practices within your organization and current circumstances.

- Chapter 1 shows how to choose new and different practices that are better practices for you, your team, and your organization.

- Chapter 2 draws out ways to uncover better practices in the areas of .NET and general software development that provide an opportunity to discover or learn and apply better practices.

- Chapter 3 presents practical advice on how to get team members to collaborate with each other and work toward a common purpose.

- Chapter 4 describes specific practices to help with quantifying the value of adopting better development practices.

- Chapter 5 provides you with practices to help you focus on strategy and the strategic implications of current practices.

Chapters 6 through 9 are focused on a developer's individual practices. These chapters discuss guidelines and conventions to follow, effective approaches, and tips and tricks that are worth knowing. The overarching theme is that each developer helps the whole team succeed by being a more effective developer.

- Chapter 6 helps sort out the generalized statements, principles, practices, and procedures that best serve as.NET rules and regulations that support effective and innovative development.

- Chapter 7 is an informal review of the C# language's power both to harness its own strengths and to recognize that effective development is a key part of following .NET practices.

- Chapter 8 describes many specific practices to improve test code, consistent with the principles behind effective development and automated testing.

- Chapter 9 discusses using build automation to remove error-prone steps, to establish repeatability and consistency, and to improve the build and deployment processes.

Chapters 10 through 12 are focused on supporting tools, products, and technologies. These chapters describe the purpose of various tool sets and present some recommendations on applications and products worth evaluating.

- Chapter 10 presents the continuous integration lifecycle with a description of the steps involved within each of the processes. Through effective continuous integration practices, the project can save time, improve team effectiveness, and provide early detection of problems.

- Chapter 11 provides an overview of many static and dynamic tools, technologies, and approaches with an emphasis on improvements that provide continuous, automated monitoring.

- Chapter 12 is a comprehensive list of testing frameworks and tools with a blend of commercial and open-source alternatives.

The final chapter, Chapter 13, is about the aversions and biases that keep many individuals, teams, and organizations from adopting better practices. You may face someone's reluctance to accept or acknowledge a new or different practice as potentially better. You may struggle against another's tendency to hold a particular view of a new or different practice that undercuts and weakens its potential. Many people resist change even if it is for the better. This chapter helps you understand how aversions and biases impact change so that you can identify them, cope with them, and hopefully manage them.

Appendix A provides a list of resources organized by topic. Many of the resources are either referenced throughout the book or are good sources for further reading. Either way, once you are ready to tackle a .NET practice area, this appendix is a good way to delve into the details.

Appendix B provides a scorecard for you to use while evaluating and tracking best practices. As discussed earlier in the Introduction, this scorecard is a starting point for your ongoing initiative to bring better practices to .NET development.

Prerequisites

To follow along with the examples in this book, you need the following:

- A good working knowledge of the .NET Framework 4.0 and the C# language

- Microsoft Visual Studio 2010. Many examples in the text refer to features of the Professional, Premium, or Ultimate editions of Visual Studio 2010. A few code samples work with Visual Studio 2010 Express.

- Many samples use Microsoft SQL Server Express, but other versions should work fine. Some use the database that comes with the MVC Music Store tutorial, available at mvcmusicstore.codeplex.com.

- NUnit version 2.5.10 or later, available at nunit.org.

- Moq version 4.0.0 or later, available at code.google.com/p/moq.

- FxCop version 10.0 or later. I wrote a blog post that describes how to extract the FxCop 10.0 setup program from the *Microsoft Windows SDK for Windows 7 and .NET Framework 4*. With the FxCopSetup.exe file, you can run the installer on your development machine or build server. See http://ruthlesslyhelpful.net/2011/06/09/liberate-fxcop-10-0/.

- StyleCop version 4.5.25 or later, available at stylecop.codeplex.com.

Many other tools and technologies are presented and discussed throughout the book. Information on obtaining those specific applications is provided at the time the topic is discussed.

Downloading the Code

This book includes source code that is available for download. The source code illustrates the practices described in the book. It is *not* production code. You can download the code at www.apress.com by searching for and going to the detail page of *Pro .NET Best Practices*. On the book's detail page is a link to the sample code compressed into a ZIP file. You can use a utility like 7-Zip (7-zip.org) or WinZip to uncompress the code.

For more detailed information, go to http://www.apress.com/source-code/.

Contacting the Author

Stephen can be reached through

- Excella Consulting: www.excella.com

- E-mail: stephen.ritchie@excella.com

- LinkedIn: www.linkedin.com/in/sritchie

- Blog site: ruthlesslyhelpful.net

CHAPTER 1

Ruthlessly Helpful

The phrase "best practices" is sometimes difficult to accept. "Best practices" is really a concept that has become a part of the software development vocabulary; however, the phrase can be troublesome because not every *best* practice is clearly a *better* practice for all situations. In fact, a practice that improves one situation might worsen another situation. For that reason, this book avoids the phrase "best practices" and favors "ruthlessly helpful practices." That phrase embodies the idea that a ruthlessly helpful practice for you might not be right for others, which is fine. It embodies an attitude of healthy skepticism, situational relevance, and judgment. In this chapter, you learn just what that phrase means, how it relates to selecting practices, and how to apply that attitude to those areas that you feel need improvement.

The word *ruthless* serves as a contrast to the passion and bias in the word *best*. Best is a superlative; there is nothing better than the best. That word is often used to press the point that no other practice needs to be considered. Some use it to shut down discussion and debate. In reality, every new and different practice needs to be carefully considered. To be ruthless, you must discount the biased arguments and zealous opinions. You want to select practices that are right for you and your team.

The word *helpful* tries to put the focus on results and positive outcomes. In the end, a new and different practice represents a change that must show results. The results could be in fewer problems or faster problem resolution. The results could be improvements in delivery, quality, and relationships. The results could be in greater job satisfaction. You want to select practices that get results for you and your team.

The most important takeaway of this chapter is that this entire book is about how to choose new and different practices that are better practices for you, your team, and your organization. Feel free to call them *best practices* or *ruthlessly helpful practices* but, in the end, you ought to see them as the practices that are entirely appropriate to you.

COMMENTARY

Selecting the best practice from among the many good practices is not easy. In fact, making hard decisions and dealing with dilemmas is a challenge for many projects. One technique I have learned to avoid is listing out the pros and cons. I rarely find that this approach gets to the heart of the decision. The list does not present a clear choice or direction. When selecting a new or different practice I focus on two questions:

- Is the practice not good enough to apply in this situation?

- Is the practice too good to pass up in this situation?

The first question attempts to exclude the practice because the situation is not right, the risks are too great, or the benefits are too marginal. The second question attempts to include the practice because it addresses current problems, has few risks, or the likely benefits are significant. This approach seems to make the decision less difficult and resolves the dilemmas that many practices present. The right choice becomes clear and better practices are adopted.

As a developer on a large, multiyear software development project, I observed a curious phenomenon. Every couple of weeks, a consultant would spend the afternoon talking to the developers about the problems we were experiencing. This consultant came to be known as "the professor" and the meetings were known as the "drive-by" meetings. Most of the professor's advice left the team confused and uncertain. We were rarely able to put the advice into practice. It all seemed very theoretical and not very appropriate to our situation. Some of what we did try either did not work or seemed to make things worse. What struck me as curious was that our team was in trouble, yet we spent a lot of time listening to and considering these unrealistic and impractical suggestions. Today I know that better practices prove themselves through application and results, and I insist on seeing both.

On an earlier project, I had a very challenging programming assignment. I was given a set of detailed specifications and tasked with implementing them. The document was very difficult to read and the information extremely complex. I went to the business analyst who wrote the specifications to see if he would explain them to me. That started out as a big mistake. He was arrogant, condescending, and hostile. At one point, he said the material was so straightforward that even a five-year-old could understand it. For some reason, what he said got me to thinking and I said, "I need you to explain it to me like I am a five-year-old."

The analyst stopped and thought for a minute. Suddenly, his whole demeanor changed. He went to the board and started explaining everything from the beginning. He gave me an overview of the requirements. As he explained things, I took notes and asked relevant questions. Whenever he went too deep or too technical, I would repeat that I needed him to explain it to me like I'm a five-year-old. Today, I find it a ruthlessly helpful practice to ask a business analyst to explain requirements that I do not understand in the most simplistic terms.

Practice Selection

This book presents standards, techniques, and conventions that many professional .NET developers would agree are very good practices. People with different experiences or expertise might believe there are better practices. A ruthlessly helpful practice represents a point-of-view and an assertion that following the given practice is both sensible and beneficial. Common sense dictates that having a set of sound, helpful practices in place today is more useful than spending a lot of time researching and selecting the best practice. It is important to have an efficient way to select new and different practices that focus on improving outcomes.

In the book *Rapid Development*,[1] Steve McConnell provides a list of 27 best practices. In addition to that list, the book provides tables of many best practice candidates and a summary of best practice

---

[1] Steve McConnell, *Rapid Development* (Redmond, WA.: Microsoft Press, 1996).

evaluations. This is a very comprehensive treatment of the topic of best practices. For commercial software development organizations looking to adopt best practices across the board this approach is a great way to organize the initiative. In *Rapid Development*, the evaluation of best practices includes five criteria:

- Potential reduction from nominal schedule
- Improvement in progress visibility
- Effect on schedule risk
- Chance of first-time success
- Chance of long-term success

Steve McConnell's analysis is very complete and clear. However, as that book notes, you need to determine what practices are appropriate for your team and your organization. This is not an easy task.

Based on the principle of triage, this section provides a way of selecting better practices for the individual, the team, and the organization. You are encouraged to use the following four criteria to guide your thinking when evaluating a practice:

- *Practicable:* Is the practice realistic and feasible in your situation?
- *Generally-accepted and widely-used:* Is the practice commonly used, understood, and documented?
- *Valuable:* Is the practice expected to solve problems, improve delivery, increase quality, or mend relationships?
- *Archetypal:* Is there a clear model with examples to follow?

The reason these criteria are helpful is that they are each indispensable and decisive factors. A practice that cannot be put into practice on a project is not a better practice for that project. Think of these criteria as a way to triage a new and different practice. Better than a list of pros and cons, this set of questions helps to discard best practices that are not right for a given situation. These factors also help to focus your attention on those practices worth pursuing.

Practicable

A ruthlessly helpful practice must be realistic and feasible. One reason a new practice may not be realistic is that the team is not ready to adopt the new practice. For example, continuous deployment requires that the deployments are automated. If the team has not established the practice of automated deployment then advocating for continuous deployments is unrealistic. Select a new practice appropriate to a near-term goal that is within the team's capabilities. Identify the obstacles to implementing those practices and focus the effort on addressing feasibility. In this example, once the practices related to automated deployments are well established then the team is open to discussing continuous deployments as a realistic next step. Assess every new and different practice against what is doable within the team and the organization.

Pointing to a lack of practicality is one way that change is opposed. Once a better practice is seen as realistic and feasible it is important to take the next step and apply the practice. Practical application demonstrates what the new and different practice involves and gives people hands-on experience using the practice. For example, it is not enough to advocate or mandate that unit tests be written. Developers need to be shown practical examples of how to write proper unit tests. The practical application ought to focus on five topics: expectations, standards, resources, acceptance, and consequences.[2] Table 1-1 provides the practical application topics and a description for each. In addition, this table provides an example for each topic by using the practice of unit testing as an example.

Table 1-1. Practical Application Topics

Topics	Description	Example for Unit Testing
Expectations	Specify the desired results in terms of objectives, timelines, quantity, and quality.	Write the unit tests to ensure the code-under-test works as intended. Write test methods for every class method. Create a test case for each logic branch. Test the boundaries and exceptions.
Standards	Include policies, procedures, principles, and conventions. Discuss no-no's and failure paths.	Use a specific testing framework. Use a specific mocking framework. Follow the naming convention. Use a specific test method layout. Only have one primary assertion per test method.
Resources	Provide ways to get assistance, books, websites, and internal standards documents.	The team leader is available to help with writing unit tests. Use a specific set of recommended unit testing books. Specific examples to follow are provided.
Acceptance	Provide guidelines for acceptable performance. Describe monitoring and metrics. Explain how reviews are conducted.	Code is not complete until the tests are written. The test code coverage percentage must meet a threshold. The test code is reviewed. Retrospectives include talking about test code. Input on unit testing is provided during performance reviews.
Consequences	Describe the logical benefits. Explain the benefit to teamwork. Explain how appreciation and recognition naturally follow.	Unit testing makes debugging easier. Potential problems are found earlier. Other developers can easily understand the code-under-test. Other developers see how their changes impact another area of the system.

These five topics help eliminate vagueness and engage self-supervision. Individuals clearly see that the new practice is backed up by information that supports their ability and motivation to put the change into practice. In many situations the application of a practice falls down because of a deficiency in one of these subjects. Without acceptance and accountability the practice is irregular and inconsistent. Without resources, developers often do not know how to get started or can get stuck.

Working through these five topics also reveals self-imposed limitations and skepticism. The hidden obstacles that are based on implicit assumptions are drawn out for discussion. For example, a common assumption is that time spent unit testing will reflect poorly on a developer's productivity. That concern can be addressed directly by explaining how unit test coverage and test code review are now part of the change in how a developer's productivity is measured.

---

[2]Adapted from Stephen R. Covey, *Principle Centered Leadership* (New York: Summit, 1991).

Generally Accepted and Widely Used

A ruthlessly helpful practice is based upon more than just a good idea. Adopting a better practice that is a good idea for one team or organization is certainly commendable. However, if a practice applies only to a specific set of circumstances and is counter-productive in another set of circumstances then it cannot become a widely accepted practice. General adoption is important. Widely used practices have broad application that either reveals that the practice is helpful in many circumstances or describes the situations where the practice is not helpful. For example, in a high-trust environment, where communication and cooperation are good, adopting Agile practices is often successful. In contrast, in a low-trust environment, where there is very little trust and a lot of finger pointing, adopting Agile practices can lead to missed expectations and a lot of bad outcomes. Agile is only a better way of developing software for teams and organizations that share the values and honor the principles outlined in the Agile Manifesto.[3] When the preconditions exist, generally-accepted and widely-used practices are useful to those project teams that are ready to benefit from the improved practices. The circumstances and preconditions for common practices are better understood and more extensively discussed, which allows you to decide if the practice is appropriate and beneficial to your situation.

The more projects that have adopted a practice the more experience there is to support the practice. You should get a sense of how widely a practice is adopted. The difficulties and objections that block the practice's effectiveness are better understood and documented, and you can benefit from this experience and information. As practitioners write books and blog postings a lot of thought goes into how to properly apply the practice. These are often important retrospectives. Many times the practice starts as an experimental approach that develops into a more generalized approach with deeper understanding and more support.

Take, for example, the practice of continuous integration (CI), which started with discussions about automated builds and a master build script.[4] The automated build server brought down the latest code and ran a build script, making it easier to find integration problems early. Today there are many CI server products that are widely used to run the master build, automate tests, perform code analysis, and automatically deploy the software. Clearly, early adoption of CI practices was beneficial to those projects. The risk for other projects, however, was that early CI practices could have caused significant diversions and distractions. Now that CI is a generally-accepted and widely-used practice the disruption is minimal and the benefits are quickly realized.

Taking a conventional approach has a few additional benefits. One such benefit is in attracting and hiring new developers that have experience and skill in that practice area. Another is that conventional approaches tend to have stronger management support and are easier to gain buy-in from the team members. Overall, generally-accepted and widely-used .NET practices and principles allow you to benefit from the knowledge and experience of others.

Valuable

A ruthlessly helpful practice must show value with respect to achieving desired results. Value is subjective. What one developer values in a given situation is not what another values in a totally different situation. For the developer with complete, clear, and consistent requirements the time spent in an exhaustive review meeting is wasted. For the developer struggling with overly complex requirements, adding in that review meeting to remove unnecessary or overly complex requirements is very valuable. In the second case, the desired result is to help the developer cope with over-specification. This practice helps to achieve that desired result. The key concept is to look at the results the individual,

---

[3] The Manifesto for Agile Software Development: `http://agilemanifesto.org/`.
[4] The original CI article: `http://martinfowler.com/articles/originalContinuousIntegration.html`.

the team, or the organization is currently getting. If you want better results, a change is needed. Any practice that provides more or better desired results is a more valuable practice.

Take some time to consider what the team *needs* in order to achieve desired results. For example, a developer who is trying to resolve a defect might need the steps to reproduce the defect or some other missing information. If defects that cannot be reproduced are a systemic problem for a project, a valuable change in practice improves the situation. That practice might regularly provide better steps to reproduce a defect, or involve changing the developer's debugging environment. You ought to value new and different practices by finding the important needs and addressing them.

The gap between the current results and the desired results is another source of value. For example, the team leader might like it if the developers started to follow coding standards. Assuming the coding standards are sensible and beneficial, the team leader wants to find a way to enforce the coding standards. The practice of code analysis, described in Chapter 11, is helpful in this regard. Specifically, the StyleCop tool helps developers adhere to a coding standard and provides a way to automate monitoring. You ought to value new and different practices by finding ways to get the results you would like and wish for.

Archetypal

A ruthlessly helpful practice must provide clear examples that serve as a model to follow. Concepts are usually not enough for individuals and teams to follow. Most developers want and need examples that turn the concepts into real and actionable information. By providing examples, new and different practices communicate the specifics of how to implement the practices. As a team leader, it is important that you find or develop the archetype for team members to follow. The act of creating the archetype helps iron out and prove out the approach by narrowly focusing on any specific impediments.

As an example, let's once again look at the practice of continuous integration. The first step to creating the archetype is selecting a CI server. Chapter 10 provides a list of CI servers worth evaluating. The next steps might involve installing the CI server software, establishing the version control settings, writing the build script, and setting up the notification mechanisms. A narrowly focused test-bed project proves out the CI practice to establish for others a way to learn and understand how all the pieces come together. This project also provides a way to conduct walkthroughs and tutorials aimed at demystifying the continuous integration practices.

One of the greatest benefits of an archetype is that it concentrates on isolating and removing obstacles. The archetype is tangible proof that skeptics cannot deny. For every raised objection or imagined barrier there is now a proven resolution. Because moving from the current status quo to a new and improved situation often requires a tangible demonstration, the archetype helps move toward better practices. In the example of the CI server, general questions like notification options or security or cost are answered with specific examples that allow people to see the new practice both modeled in the proper way and in terms they can appreciate.

Before endorsing a better practice or implementing a new practice, spend some time putting together a prime example that demonstrates the practice. If the practice is ruthlessly helpful then you ought to find that the archetype is complete and clearly supports the practice.

Target Areas for Improvement

There are many ways to improve software development. Some managers suggest an improvement in development costs by having the programming done offshore. That decision can have huge negative implications to delivery, quality, and relationships. In fact, these three aspects are at the source of worsening or dysfunctional software development. A very common complaint is that projects fail to deliver a software product that meets the business need. Others include poor quality and late delivery.

A ruthlessly helpful practice focuses on targeting one of three important areas for improvement:

- Delivery

- Quality

- Relationships

Within each of these target areas there are two general ways by which to show improvement. One is by addressing and reducing problems and the other is through initiative and creativity. Solving problems can generally be thought to include detecting, diagnosing, addressing, and reducing problems. In most situations, it is a lot easier to see problems. People are aware of problems and are willing to acknowledge that an issue is a problem. Innovation can generally be thought to include initiative, novel approaches, ideas, and creativity. Innovation brings change and change is not always easy or welcomed. Consider new and different practices as either solving problems or bringing innovation. People find it less risky to adopt better practices that solve problems. Better practices that innovate frequently offer greater long-term rewards and advantages.

A ruthlessly helpful practice shows improvement by helping to resolve problems with less total effort. For example, a change in practice might help a developer debug, isolate, and diagnose a problem faster. Figure 1-1 is a conceptual diagram that illustrates the impact of better practices on the total effort spent on problems. In the early stages of the project, significant time and effort is devoted to dealing with questions, issues, delays, defects, and other problems. After a few sprints, better practices reduce the total effort devoted to dealing with problems. Later on, introducing additional better practices further improves the situation. Less effort dealing with problems means more time to devote to other important matters. This is growing capability through better problem solving.

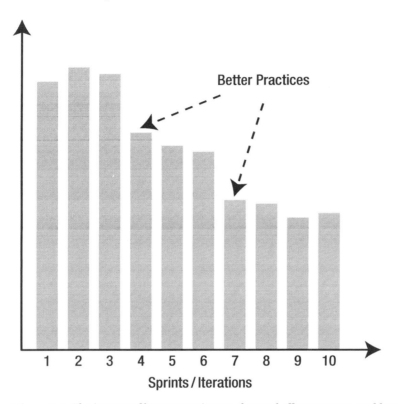

Figure 1-1. *The impact of better practices on the total effort spent on problems*

A ruthlessly helpful practice might show improvement through innovation. For example, a new practice helps a developer write code more efficiently. This means the developer can implement new features faster. Figure 1-2 is a conceptual diagram that illustrates the impact of better practices on the productivity in achieving desired results. In the early stages of the project, results are produced during each sprint. The team believes the productivity can increase with better practices. A new or different practice increases productivity and more is accomplished. Later on, additional changes to practices continue to improve productivity. This is growing capability through innovation.

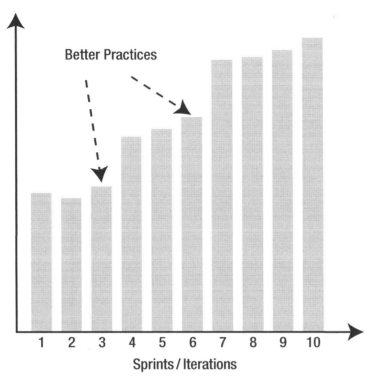

Figure 1-2. The impact of better practices on productivity in achieving desired results

Delivery

A ruthlessly helpful practice takes the current delivery situation and improves it. Productivity and efficiency are improved. The ability to meet milestones and deadlines is improved. The team can accomplish more with the same or fewer resources. These are ways that better practices improve delivery, which come from better problem solving and innovation.

One thing that often slows down delivery is the time it takes to find and fix problems. The quicker a problem is identified and properly resolved, the greater the capacity to deliver. For example, an important part of unit testing is boundary analysis. As part of unit testing a method, boundary analysis reviews and carefully considers the parameters of the method. A series of test cases ensures that the method works properly under a wide range of expected and unexpected parameter values. In addition, the test code arranges the class-under-test into many expected and unexpected conditions before the method is called. The goal of boundary analysis is to find problems as early as possible by testing the limits of the method-under-test. The developer anticipates potential problems as part of writing the code. The developer makes sure that exceptions are handled properly. This practice reveals potential problems for the developer to address proactively. These are practices that improve delivery by identifying and addressing problems early and efficiently.

Another way a practice can improve delivery is through innovation. Developer productivity tools are an excellent example of how new approaches have increased the developer's capacity to deliver. Many years ago the integrated development environment (IDE) brought together the code editor, compiler, linker, and debugger in what was a new and innovative way of rapidly connecting the source code to the running code. Before the IDE, there was a significant lag time between when code was written and when it was executed. For most developers this delay inhibited productivity. Today the Visual Studio IDE is commonly used and helps developers deliver better software faster. Productivity tools, such as ReSharper and Visual Studio 2010 Productivity Power Tools, offer a wide array of productivity enhancements that further improve a developer's capacity to deliver.

Quality

A ruthlessly helpful practice takes the current quality situation and improves it. The system's fitness-of-purpose, structural quality, or both can be improved by better practices. As with other areas of improvement, the change for the better comes through better problem solving, innovation, or both.

A major quality problem is the introduction of a regression bug, which is a defect that had been found and fixed but is turning up again. The quality perception of the software is damaged by a regression bug. The trust relationship between testers and developers is also hurt. Any practice that prevents regression bugs from making it to the testers solves this particular problem. An example of a solution is the writing of an automated test that verifies that a resolved issue remains resolved. The practice involves writing test code for each and every defect that is reported. The developer assigned to fix the defect must start by writing an automated test that reproduces the defect. The defect is resolved by making sure that this test code passes and all other automated tests continue to pass. This new test now becomes part of the suite of tests that must pass during continuous integration. If the functionality should happen to regress then the CI server will fail the build and the developers must resolve the issue before the defect makes it to the testers.

Adopting a new and different approach is another way to improve quality. The approach does not have to be entirely innovative; it only needs to be innovative for the team and the organization. For example, the practice of engineering analysis is well established, but some teams do not perform the basic analysis and design work before diving into coding. An indispensable step of engineering analysis is making sure the requirements are clearly and fully understood by the developer that has to implement the solution. Another important step is diagramming and describing the solution strategy so as to plan out the work involved. A further step is reviewing the design to make sure it is correct and appropriate. The practice of engineering analysis identifies gaps in requirements and weaknesses in design. In addition, it accelerates development since the proper solution is drawn out before coding starts. Once the plan-of-attack is reviewed and endorsed then the developer is able to work in a self-directed manner toward a quality solution.

Relationships

A ruthlessly helpful practice takes the current relationships and improves them. If individuals interacting are at the heart of software development then the condition of the relationships is a measure of the state of those interactions. Poor relationships lead to poor interactions and counterproductive behavior. Exceptionally good relationships lead to remarkably good interactions and incredibly productive behavior. There are team leaders who can build camaraderie within teams and excellent rapport between teams. These great relationships have everyone enthused and focused on project success. In contrast, for the teams with bad relationships, trust is all but gone and every topic and interaction is filled with misunderstandings and hot-button issues.

Coping with difficult relationships is not easy nor is it enjoyable. However, when individuals and teams are not interacting well, intervention is necessary if the situation is going to improve. A new and different practice ought to address the problem and produce a better outcome. For example, the relationship of the business analyst, developer, and tester is fundamental to creating great software. The practice of focusing on reaching a shared understanding of requirements is helpful: regardless of whatever other differences they might have, the features and functionality are the group's common ground. In this way, the practice moves them away from formal, structured documents and toward a dialog that gets them doing things like diagramming on a whiteboard. This more fluid process breaks down the formality and makes it harder to rigidly hold a position because the members of the group are vigorously confronting the problem, and not each other. A deeper understanding is reached and all sides can collaborate when everyone is better at communicating about the features and functionality.

There are ways to innovate when it comes to relationships. When the relationships are already good then the innovations work to make the relationships better. This is one of the key ideas behind Agile. Teams that have good interactions benefit from the short daily stand-up meetings. The information in these meetings is targeted at providing the minimal and essential status. The stand-up meetings strive to uncover obstacles and barriers to get to early problem solving. The rapid exchange of information and early identification of potential problems that Agile encourages is more efficient and productive. It is not hard to see that in team situations where problems are covered up and concerns are quickly dismissed, Agile is not beneficial. When the circumstances are wrong, the practice is not a helpful innovation. The daily scrum meeting is an innovation for teams that are comfortable talking openly about concerns, believe uncovering problems is a good thing, and feel free to ask for help and support.

Overall Improvement

Beyond any specific area of improvement, a ruthlessly helpful practice can bring overall improvement. A better practice can tie together many development areas. For example, more careful programming through unit testing reduces the system testing effort. Fewer bugs are found, written up, fixed, verified, and tracked. Other practices help strike the balance between spending too little or too much effort in a particular area of development. These practices help make sure that the necessary and sufficient time is spent while avoiding wasteful diversions and distractions.

Other ways that practices provide overall improvement is through renewal and sustainability. Positive improvements and outcomes revitalize the spirit of the team and the organization. The overall atmosphere is more optimistic and engaged. In addition, the result of better practices is a project that is more sustainable over time. Greater productivity and efficiency encourage higher levels of involvement and commitment. As individuals, each team member brings more creativity and energy to the project. These better practices actively improve and encourage sustainable achievement.

Balance

A ruthlessly helpful practice brings a balanced focus on improvement to multiple areas of software development. Inadequate focus on a development area implies that that area does not perform adequately, and the purposes of that area are not achieved. In the other extreme, excessive focus on an area means that too much time and effort are spent, and does not provide added benefit. The balanced approach recognizes the need to spend the proper amount of time and effort in that development area. This approach recognizes the risks associated with too little and the risks associated with too much. The important idea is to identify the purpose and rationale of the development area to ensure that an appropriate amount of time and effort is spent in that area. Furthermore, these benefits are seen as complementary across multiple development areas and the practices bring harmony and improvement to the overall development effort.

Five software development areas are listed in Table 1-2. Next to each area are examples of the consequences of too little focus in that area. On the other extreme are examples of what can happen when there is too much focus in that area. Between these two extremes are the benefits of a balanced approach. The best development practices help bring better results in multiple development areas. For example, the practice of unit testing is helpful to requirements, design, development, quality, and management. As the developer writes the unit tests, the requirements are reviewed, which can reveal incompleteness or confusion. This work prompts questions that are brought out and discussed with the analyst. Unit testing can also drive design improvements as new features are added. The development of tests ensures that the code-under-test is correct and thoroughly implemented. The quality improves since potential defects are identified early by the developer writing the code. Finally, unit testing raises awareness as to how the code is intended to be called by other parts of the system. Writing unit tests helps the developer plan, coordinate, and manage the work. The practice of unit testing clearly ties together many development areas and strengthens the overall process by balancing the focus across these multiple areas.

***Table 1-2.** Balancing Focus within Several Development Areas*

Area	Too Little	Balance	Too Much
Requirements	Incomplete, unclear, inconsistent, hasty decisions	Shared understanding, fitness of purpose, prioritization	Analysis paralysis, over-specification, over - demanding
Design	Insufficiency, inconsistency, confusion	Fundamental structure, integrity, clarity, proper consistency	Inflexibility, regulations, foolish consistency
Development	Inefficient, unproductive, carelessness	Productive, purposeful, thoroughness, correctness	Gold plating, perfectionism, postponement
Quality	Defects unnoticed, systemic problems overlooked	Defects identified, issues isolated, whole-system reliability	Hypercritical, focus on unimportant detail, formalities
Management	Thrashing, contention, out of control, overburdened	Planning, cooperation, coordination, objective oriented	Methodology, risk-anxiety, bureaucracy

Renewal

A ruthlessly helpful practice brings a sense of renewal to the team and the organization. For developers on teams that never improve, there is a spirit of hopelessness. The same problems resurface. There is no innovation. As individuals, each developer struggles with these problems and the day-to-day crisis. The team is overwhelmed and unable to implement the changes needed to affect positive change. Adopting new and different practices has the power to change the situation. Making even a modest change offers hope that the development environment is improving. This hope engages the team's optimism. With the implementation of one positive change comes talk of the next practice that is worth adopting. After that comes the next, and so on. Morale and productivity are greatly improved when better practices engage the spirit of renewal and hope.

Many developers are anxious to learn something new. While some are resistant to change, many like the idea of learning a new skill, tool set, or technology. The key is to find the right person to lead the effort to adopt a better practice. For example, automated deployments offer the opportunity to learn about deployment scripts and the associated deployment tools. The developer that has to iron out the problems with unreliable manual deployments is motivated to prevent these problems. That motivation can renew that person's desire to learn better practices. For another developer, a keen interest in doing something entirely new and different is the motivation. In either case, renewal comes in seeing that there is a better set of procedures, and that they are working. The end result is that the team has more reliable deployments, and the developer has a sense of accomplishment.

Adopting better practices makes projects more fun. Any practice that reduces headaches, raises productivity, or brings innovation is a source of enjoyment. Any time the team has more fun, the sense of renewal translates into higher levels of dedication and commitment.

Sustainability

A ruthlessly helpful practice brings sustainability to the team and the organization. In unsustainable situations the result is fatigue, mistakes, burnout, and failure. A poorly-planned project has too much work for too few people in too short a timeframe. The pressure and haste become the driving forces that influence everything the team does. The architecture is driven by haste, which means the high-level design is ill-considered and inadequate. The developers write code under schedule pressure and the result is carelessness, a lack of thoroughness, and poor judgment. For any significant project this constant diet of pressure and haste is unsustainable. When new and different practices focus on problem prevention and more effective issue resolution then the team is less overwhelmed by crisis. Adopting better practices improves planning, coordination, and productivity. Taken together, these improved approaches offer a more sustainable development environment.

For example, projects that are driven by haste often have integration problems that are deferred until late in the project. Some developers do not perform frequent check-ins or do not get the latest code since they do not want to be delayed by integration problems. Other developers push code that breaks the build for other developers. Often the team lead needs to straighten out the growing mess. This scenario is referred to as integration hell.[5] This situation becomes more unsustainable as the code base grows bigger and bigger. One way to address this issue is to change development practices. The team leader insists that all developers check in their code at the end of the day. Early the next day the team leader gets the latest code to a new folder and rebuilds everything. If the build breaks, then the problems get ironed out and the developers figure out whose code needs to change to fix the build. This daily integration prevents the unsustainable situation from continuing, but it also creates a compelling argument for continuous integration. The better practice is to set up a CI server to perform all the same steps that the team leader is performing. Also, this practice supports what many managers value: automation, monitoring, control, consequences, and accountability. The practice of continuous integration is even more compelling if it reveals the code push that broke the build within five minutes of the check-in.

Another way that better practices improve sustainability is in the careers of the developers. Learning better practices is an important part of career development and advancement. As an individual, adopting a better practice that increases productivity and effectiveness translates into better results. For example, purchasing development productivity tools that increase the speed and quality of the code you write helps you write better features faster. That greater rate of accomplishment makes you a more valuable member of the team. Consistently demonstrating positive outcomes for the team is a boost to

---

[5] A good description of integration hell is found at this link: `http://c2.com/xp/IntegrationHell.html`.

your reputation that has a long-term benefit to your career. As a team leader, the benefit of having every member of the team improve likewise improves your career.

Sustainability is about the long-term health of the individual, the team, and the organization. Better practices offer the prospect of reducing burnout and enhancing the overall effectiveness of everyone involved in the project.

Summary

In this chapter, you saw how selecting a new and different practice starts by understanding your current situation. A better practice has to be realistic and feasible within your situation. It is better if that practice is in common use and well documented. The practice ought to solve your current problems or provide innovations that improve delivery, quality, or relationships. A better practice is a model that others can follow with clear examples of how the practice is implemented.

Throughout this book, you will learn about many ruthlessly helpful practices. These practices have application for the individual, the team, and the organization. You can expect that the suggested practice is focused on improving your overall development environment and is targeted toward important areas of improvement. Carefully consider these practices without passion or bias. Do not hesitate to change, adapt, or discard the practice based on your circumstances. You should expect better results from better practices.

CHAPTER 2

.NET Practice Areas

This chapter is about identifying the sources of better .NET practices. The focus is on the areas of .NET development and general software development that provide an opportunity to discover or learn about better practices. Think of this chapter as providing a large-scale map that gives you the basic geography. Broadly speaking, the sources of better practices include:

- Understanding problems, issues, defects, or breakdowns
- Looking at the interconnected events and behaviors of development
- Finding sources of appropriate patterns, conventions, and guidance
- Applying tools and technologies
- New ideas, innovations, and research

There are .NET practice areas at the forefront of establishing new and widely-used tools and technologies for better practices. The list includes automated testing, continuous integration, and code analysis. These practice areas are so important that this book devotes a chapter to each topic:

- Automated testing is covered in Chapter 8.
- Continuous integration is covered in Chapter 10.
- Code analysis is covered in Chapter 12.

This chapter brings up .NET practice areas that are important and warrant further exploration. Hopefully, you get enough information to plan and prepare a deeper investigation into the .NET practice areas that are beyond the scope of this book. There are resources and references listed in Appendix A.

There is more to selecting, implementing, and monitoring practices than can be explained in one chapter. In subsequent chapters, the significance of focusing on results, quantifying value, and strategy is discussed, as follows:

- Delivering, accomplishing, and showing positive outcomes is covered in Chapter 3.
- Quantifying the value of adopting better practices is covered in Chapter 4.
- Appreciating the strategic implications of better practices is covered in Chapter 5.

The discussion of the areas covered in this chapter draws out ways to uncover better practices in these areas. In these cases, the recommended practice is highlighted and stated directly. All of the recommended practices in this chapter are summarized in Table 2-1. These are ruthlessly helpful practices that reveal new and different practices, which should uncover specific, realistic, practical, and helpful practices to you, your team, and your organization.

Table 2-1. Ruthlessly Helpful Practices to Reveal Better Practices

	Strategy
2-1	Monitor and Track Technical Debt to Uncover Inadvertent or Reckless Flaws
2-2	Review and Classify Defects in the Tracking System to Find Better Practices
2-3	Conduct Retrospective Analysis to Identify New and Different Practices
2-4	Perform Prospective Analysis to Foresee Potential Problems and Mitigate Them
2-5	Look for Systemic Problems and Ways to Improve the Application Lifecycle
2-6	Discover the Thinking Behind the .NET Framework in the Book *Framework Design Guidelines*
2-7	Learn from the Offerings of the Microsoft Patterns and Practice Group
2-8	Stay on Top of the Innovative Work of Microsoft Research
2-9	Investigate Automated Test Generation as an Emerging .NET Practice Area
2-10	Consider Code Contracts to Improve Testability and Software Verification
2-11	Appreciate Secure Application Development and the Microsoft Security Development Lifecycle

COMMENTARY

Many software development projects fail to deliver. When I join a project that has missed a major deadline or has other serious problems, one of the first things I do is review the issues in the defect tracking system. By simply reading the issues, sorting them into categories, and prioritizing them, many clear patterns emerge. There are often major pieces of functionality that none of the developers understand. There are modules that are error-prone and need to be redesigned. Generally speaking, there are many important practices that are not in place or are not being followed. The act of analyzing the defects, issues, and problems suggests better practices that are appropriate and help turn the project around.

In my earliest .NET projects, while working on class libraries, I struggled to figure out the right practices to follow. The practices I searched for related to things like naming conventions, proper usage of the .NET framework, and other development patterns. At some point I came across two things that both made a huge difference. The first is a book that is simply known as the *Framework Design Guidelines*[1], which is discussed later in this chapter. The second is a software tool called *FxCop*, which is presented in Chapter 11. I read *Framework Design Guidelines* from cover to cover and learned a whole lot about how the .NET Framework was built. That book revealed the thinking of the team that designed and built the .NET Framework and remains an essential source of important .NET practices. The FxCop tool complements the guidelines by giving you the ability to inspect .NET assemblies and drill into the details behind the rule sets it applies. I have learned and continue to learn a lot from FxCop. These two items, taken together, are a great source of many of the better .NET practices that I have adopted. I often recommend both as important learning material and sources for developers interested in finding better .NET practices.

Occasionally, I am asked to recommend the important .NET practice areas. Many developers are implicitly asking for a list of tools and technologies that they should learn. In those cases, I concentrate on tools and technologies within four topics: automated testing, continuous integration, code analysis, and automated deployments. In recent years, a lot of progress has been made in these areas. New products are coming out and exciting products are being improved quickly. These technologies have new and different practices built in as an inherent part of the tool set. For example, if you roll up your sleeves and dig into Team Foundation Server, you are going to learn a lot about these four .NET practice areas. My advice to those who are motivated by technology is to start taking a deep-dive into these products. Evaluate the products. Compare and contrast them. In this way, new and different .NET practice areas are going to present themselves.

Internal Sources

The problems, issues, defects, or breakdowns that your current team, project, or organization are experiencing are a gold mine of new and different practices. These internal sources are usually a lot more valuable than external sources because a suggested practice is

- *Undeniably relevant:* The practice is important; it is of interest

- *Well-timed:* The practice is urgently-needed because the issues are recent

- *Acceptable:* The practice is fitting or home-grown because it matches the situation

Better practices that derive from internal sources have less opposition and fewer debates because the need is backed-up by the value of the source itself. For example, if the source is a defect tracking system then the better practice is as important as reducing defects is to the organization. This significantly lowers the barriers to adoption. The discussion now focuses on the effectiveness of the new and different practice. After some time, the practice is measurable because the internal source ought to show the improvement that comes from the better practice. If the defect tracking system is the source then a better practice lowers the number of defects in some measurable way. Specific practices that relate to quantifying value with internal sources are presented and discussed in Chapter 4.

---

[1] Krzysztof Cwalina and Brad Abrams, *Framework Design Guidelines: Conventions, Idioms, and Patterns for Reusable .NET Libraries, 2nd Edition* (Upper Saddle River, NJ: Addison-Wesley Professional, 2008).

Technical Debt

The "technical debt" metaphor was created by Ward Cunningham as a way to understand and track the intentional and unintentional design and coding shortcomings of software.[2] We take on technical debt when we oversimplify a design or recklessly create a flawed design. We take on technical debt when we wisely or unwisely write code that does not work as well as it should. Taking this metaphor from the financial world, debt is one of the ways to finance an organization. It can provide the cash needed to make payroll. It provides the organization an opportunity to buy things like furniture and equipment. If the payments on interest and principal are well managed then the organization can properly handle the costs of financial debt. The same is true for technical debt. With technical debt, the "interest payments" are the added effort and frustration caused by the inadequacies of the current design and source code. In this metaphor, the "principal payments" are the effort needed to go back and remediate or improve the design and source code.

Some projects take on technical debt intelligently and deliberately. On these projects the technical debt often serves a useful purpose, and the consequence of the debt is understood and appreciated. On other projects the technical debt is recklessly accumulated, usually without regard to the consequences. Examining how your project accumulates and deals with technical debt is an excellent way to find new and different practices that improve the situation. In fact, the technical debt metaphor itself is a good way to get the team focused on following better practices.

Not all technical debt is created equal. There are minor design flaws that have little impact and there are major design flaws that require huge amounts of rework. For example, if localization is an ignored requirement, retrofitting tens of thousands of lines of code late in the project can be an expensive and error-prone effort.

It is useful to recognize that there are two distinct types of technical debt:

- *Design debt:* This can result from prudent decision-making, underappreciated requirements, inadequate architecture, or hurried development. Often the design limitations will eventually need to be addressed.

- *Code debt:* This can result from demanding circumstances, temporary simplification, imprudence, or hastiness that finds its way into the source code. Often the code should be reworked and improved.

Take some time to review the designs that you and your team create. Do the designs have flaws that need to be dealt with? What new and different practices should your team adopt to prevent or remediate these inadequate designs? Select better practices that ensure design debt is not accumulating without intention and that design debt is paid off before the consequences are disastrous.

Review the source code that you or your team is writing. Does the code need to be reworked or improved? What new and different practices should your team adopt to write better code? Select better practices that help the team to produce better code.

░ **Practice 2-1** Monitor and Track Technical Debt to Uncover Inadvertent or Reckless Flaws

---

[2] For more information see `http://c2.com/cgi/wiki?TechnicalDebt`.

A specific practice that helps deal with technical debt is to capture the technical debt as it accumulates. This raises awareness and goes a long way toward preventing inadvertent and reckless debt.[3] In addition, the team should use the information to make plans to pay down the technical debt as the project proceeds. With this information the team can take a principled stand against proceeding under a heavy burden of technical debt that is causing delay and jeopardizing the quality of the software. Monitoring and analyzing technical debt is an excellent way to find and adopt better ways of delivering software.

Defect Tracking System

In general, the defect tracking system provides feedback from testers and customers that indicates that there are problems. This is a rich source for improvements to the overall development process. By examining the defect tracking system there are a number of common problems that imply deficient practices:

- Requirements that are poorly defined or understood

- Designs that are inadequate or incomplete

- Modules that are error-prone and need to be redesigned or rewritten

- Source code that is difficult to understand and maintain

- Defect reports that are incomplete or unclear

- Customer issues that are hard to reproduce because of missing detail

---

≋ **Practice 2-2** Review and Classify Defects in the Tracking System to Find Better Practices

---

It is not uncommon to find clusters of defects in the tracking system that relate to the same feature, module, or code file. These defects are the result of something having been done properly. Ideas and support for new and different practices come from assembling those defects and making the case for a better practice. For example, if a large number of defects is caused by unclear or incomplete requirements then better requirements analysis and more design work are indicated. Improving the understanding and thoroughness of requirements goes a long way toward eliminating this source of defects.

In some cases the issues entered in the defect tracking system are the problem. They may lack steps to reproduce the issue. In other cases, the customer cannot provide adequate information and the developers are left guessing what caused the issue. Better practices, such as having the testers write complete and clear defect entries, improve the situation. Better system logging and debugging information is another way to improve the situation.

---

[3] Classify the nature of the technical debt. See
`http://martinfowler.com/bliki/TechnicalDebtQuadrant.html`.

Retrospective Analysis

A retrospective meeting is a discussion held at the end of an Agile sprint or project iteration. At the end of a project, a retrospective of the entire project is also held. The meeting often covers what worked well and what did not work well. A major goal of these meetings is to find out what could be improved and how to include those improvements in future iterations or projects. One technique for facilitating these meetings is the 4L's Technique.[4] This technique concentrates on four topics and the related questions:

- *Liked:* What did we like about this iteration?

- *Learned:* What did we learn during this iteration?

- *Lacked:* What did we not have or require during this iteration?

- *Longed for:* What did we wish we had during this iteration?

▦ **Practice 2-3** Conduct Retrospective Analysis to Identify New and Different Practices

---

Knowing what was liked and what was learned helps identify new and different practices that worked during the iteration. The things that the team liked are practices worth continuing. The things the team learned usually suggest better practices that the team implicitly or explicitly discovered. Sometimes what is learned is that some practices did not work. Be sure to discontinue those practices. Knowing what was lacking or longed for also suggests practices. The team should work with the retrospective discussion and analysis to define better practices that can apply to future iterations.

Prospective Analysis

Prospective analysis engages the team to imagine and discuss the potential for problems, errors, or failures. This work is done in advance of any significant requirements, design, or testing work. The goal is to think through the possible failure modes and the severity of their consequences. Prospective analysis includes activities such as the following:

- Evaluating requirements to minimize the likelihood of errors

- Recognizing design characteristics that contribute to defects

- Designing system tests that detect and isolate failures

- Identifying, tracking, and managing potential risks throughout development

---

▦ **Practice 2-4** Perform Prospective Analysis to Foresee Potential Problems and Mitigate Them

---

[4]The 4L's Technique: http://agilemaniac.com/tag/4ls/.

Risk identification and risk management are forms of prospective analysis commonly practiced by project managers. The same type of analysis is appropriate for technical development topics like requirements, design, and testing. This analysis engages the imagination and creative skills of the people involved. The better practices are suggested by anticipating problems and the effort to prevent problems from occurring.

Application Lifecycle Management

The traditional waterfall model of software development consists of distinct and separate phases. This approach has shown itself to be too rigid and too formal. Software applications have characteristics that make them more flexible and more powerful than a purpose-built hardware solution. If, instead of software, the team of engineers is building an airplane, then a waterfall approach is warranted. With hardware development, the extremely disruptive costs of late changes imply the need for the distinct, formal, and separate phases of the waterfall model. The virtue of software is that it is flexible and adaptable, and so, the waterfall model wrecks this responsiveness to change and detracts from software's primary virtue.

▓ **Note** The choice of life cycle, flexible or rigid, depends on the maturity and criticality of the application domain. Developing software to control a nuclear power plant should follow a waterfall methodology. The laws of physics are not going to change, and control software is a critical component. This domain has a strict set of physical circumstances and regulations that perfectly fits the waterfall methodology. The requirements of a social media site are difficult to formally specify because they are driven by a changing marketplace. An on-the-fly adaptation is needed, such as agile software development, to make sure the team delivers an application that serves the evolving social media landscape.

Let's consider the analogy of hiring a private jet flying from London to Miami. The passengers have an objective to fly to Miami safely, efficiently, and in comfort. Once hired, the charter company works with the passengers' representative to discuss cost, schedule, and expectations to book the charter. Once booked, the pilot and crew prepare the airplane by planning and performing activities like fueling the plane, filing a flight plan, and stocking the plane with blankets, beverages, and meals. Once in the air the pilot and crew make adjustments based on new information and changing realities. If the weather is bad, the airplane can fly around it or above it. If the passengers are tired and want to sleep, the cabin is made dark and quiet. The pilot and crew have some trouble abiding fussy and selective passengers, yet they make every effort to provide reasonable accommodations. With a different breed of erratic and demanding passengers, the pilot and crew are in for trouble. These are the high-maintenance passengers that demand the plane turn around to pick up something they forgot in the limousine but are unwilling to accept any delay. Worse yet, there are passengers that demand an in-flight change of destination from Miami to Rio de Janeiro. Very few charter airline companies are organized to satisfy the fickle demands of rock stars, world leaders, and eccentric billionaires. Similarly, software applications should be developed in a way that is responsive to relevant adjustments and adapts quickly to new information and changing realities. At the same time, the changes cannot be chaotic, impulsive, whimsical, and unrealistic.

The application lifecycle is a broad set of connected activities that happen throughout the software's lifetime. For the purposes of this discussion, the broadest phases of application lifecycle management (ALM) include:

- *Inception:* Form the vision, objectives, and core requirements.

- *Analysis:* Establish the core feature sets and desired behavior for the system.

- *Architecture:* Create the high-level design and system architecture.

- *Development:* Detail the functionality, low-level design, code, deploy, and test the system.

- *Operations:* Monitor the post-delivery system, discover issues, resolve issues, and address system improvements.

These five phases are illustrated in Figure 2-1.[5] Do not think of these phases as discrete and separate. This diagram is a conceptual model that shows how the application moves from an idea and vision, to common understanding and primary functionality, through strategy and approach, toward tactics and implementation, and finally into rollout and usage. The activities of each phase do adjust, inform, and change the conclusions and decisions of the previous phase, but they should not render the prior phases entirely pointless and irrelevant. A proper project Inception phase lays the groundwork for an effective Analysis phase. A proper Analysis phase lays the groundwork for an effective Architecture phase. The Development phase proceeds to develop and deploy an effective system that goes into operation. What was accomplished during the Development phase is on the whole a proper solution that is utilized during the Operations phase.

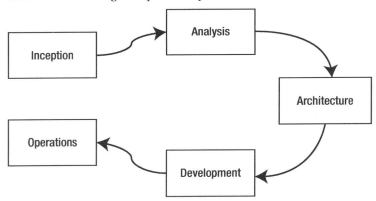

Figure 2-1. *The application lifecycle management phases*

A great many projects that turn into disasters have fundamental mistakes and misunderstandings rooted in the Inception, Analysis, and Architecture phases. These three phases are important areas to look for new and different practices for overall application development improvement. It is good to enhance the architecture during the Development phase, but there is something wrong when the entire

---

[5] Adapted from Grady Booch, *Object Solutions: Managing the Object-Oriented Project* (Menlo Park, CA: Addison-Wesley, 1996).

architecture is found to be wrong or inadequate. It is good to adapt to unforeseeable requirement changes during the Development phase, but there is something wrong when a vital, core feature set is overlooked or intentionally played down during the Analysis phase.

░ **Practice 2-5** Look for Systemic Problems and Ways to Improve the Application Lifecycle

---

Within the Development phase, the activities and disciplines cover many topics from change management to configuration management to release management. For many .NET developers, the important day-to-day activities are in the Development phase. When looking for new and different .NET practices, focus on key principles and the fundamentals of development. All the activities and disciplines connect to the following seven significant aspects of development:

- Requirements
- Design
- Coding
- Testing
- Deployment
- Maintenance
- Project Management

Consider Agile software development: the approach harmonizes and aligns these seven significant aspects of development. It promotes things like collaboration, adaptability, and teamwork across these seven aspects of the Development phase and throughout the application lifecycle.

The Visual Studio product team recognizes the importance of ALM, and Microsoft is doing more to develop tools that support integrating team members, development activities, and operations. In fact, the Microsoft Visual Studio roadmap is centered on the part of the application lifecycle management that focuses on the Development and Operation phases.[6] Microsoft calls its effort to bring better practices to the application lifecycle *Visual Studio vNext*. ALM is a .NET practice area that is important and is showing increasing relevance as teams and organizations continue to find ways to improve.

Patterns and Guidance

Today there are a lot of .NET developers who have excellent experience, good judgment, and common sense. Thankfully, they are writing books and posting to their blogs. Microsoft is clearly interested in having their best and brightest communicate through resources like the Microsoft Developer Network (MSDN). Microsoft has a patterns and practices group that is disseminating guidance, reusable components, and reference applications. There is a great number of sources of rich material available that points to better .NET practices.

---

[6] For more information see `http://www.microsoft.com/visualstudio/en-us/roadmap`.

The goal of this section is to raise your awareness of the places to look and topics to investigate, to round out your .NET practice areas. The section starts with general sources that offer guideline-oriented information, follows into important patterns, and provides tables with some specific tools.

Framework Design Guidelines

There is a single book that provides so much information on good and bad .NET development practices that it is a must-read book. That book is *Framework Design Guidelines: Conventions, Idioms, and Patterns for Reusable .NET Libraries (2nd Edition)* by Krzysztof Cwalina and Brad Abrams. The book strives to teach developers the best practices for designing reusable libraries for the Microsoft .NET Framework. However, this book is relevant to anyone developing applications that ought to comply with the .NET Framework best practices. It is very helpful to developers who are new to the .NET Framework and to those unfamiliar with the implications of designing and building frameworks.

⬚ **Practice 2-6** Discover the Thinking Behind the .NET Framework in the Book *Framework Design Guidelines*

The guidelines in *Framework Design Guidelines* present many recommendations, with uncomplicated designations, like the following:

- *Do:* Something you should always (with rare exceptions) do

- *Consider:* Something you should generally do, with some justifiable exceptions

- *Do not:* Something you should almost never do

- *Avoid:* Something that is generally not a good idea to do

Additionally, a great deal of what is described in *Framework Design Guidelines* is available online at MSDN, under the topic of "Design Guidelines for Developing Class Libraries." You will also find additional information on MSDN blog sites of the authors, Krzysztof Cwalina and Brad Abrams.[7]

Microsoft PnP Group

The Microsoft patterns and practices (PnP) group provides guidance, tools, code, and great information in many forms, including the following:

- *Guides:* Books that offer recommendations on how to design and develop applications using various Microsoft tools and technologies.

- *Enterprise library:* A reusable set of components and core functionality that help manage important crosscutting concerns, such as caching, encryption, exception handling, logging, and validation.

---

[7] Brad Abrams has left Microsoft, but his MSDN blog remains very helpful.

- *Videos, symposiums, and hands-on labs:* Many structured and unstructured ways to learn Microsoft technologies, guidance, and the Enterprise Library.

- *Reference applications:* The Enterprise Library download includes source code and sample applications that demonstrate proper usage.

Enterprise Library (EntLib) includes extremely thorough documentation and source code. It is a very valuable resource for learning better architectural, design, and coding practices.

≡ **Practice 2-7** Learn from the Offerings of the Microsoft Patterns and Practice Group

---

Presentation Layer Design Patterns

Whether you are building browser-hosted or Windows desktop applications, the presentation layer of the application is often a source of changing requirements and new features. The reason is that this is the surface of the application that the end-user sees and interacts with. It is the human-machine interface.

Developers have long struggled to implement systems that enable user interface changes to be made relatively quickly without negatively impacting other parts of the system. The goal of the Presentation Layer design pattern is to more loosely couple the system, in such a way that the domain model and business logic are not impacted by user interface changes. A great deal of important work has been done to bring better patterns to .NET user interface software. Investigating and adopting these design patterns offers an excellent opportunity to bring better .NET practices to your software development. Table 2-2 provides a list of presentation layer design patterns worth investigating further.

Table 2-2. Presentation Layer Design Patterns for .NET

Name	Description	More Information
Model-View-Presenter	MVP is very applicable for SharePoint applications. It separates presentation responsibilities. The View is responsible for the user interface. The Presenter is responsible for view and model interaction. The Model is responsible for business logic and persistence	msdn.microsoft.com/en-us/library/ff649571.aspx
Model-View-ViewModel	MVVM is very applicable for Windows Presentation Foundation (WPF) and Silverlight applications. The View is responsible for user interface. The ViewModel is for data binding between the View and the Model. The Model is responsible for business logic and persistence.	msdn.microsoft.com/en-us/magazine/dd419663.aspx

Name	Description	More Information
ASP.NET MVC	MVC separates presentation layer responsibilities. The View is responsible for user interface. The Controller is responsible for responding to view actions. The Model is responsible for business logic and persistence.	`www.asp.net/mvc`
Knockout.js	Knockout.js is a JavaScript library that uses observables and the MVVM design pattern to help keep the client-side user interface in sync with an underlying data model. This approach allows you to more easily create richer browser-hosted user interfaces with JavaScript and HTML.	`knockoutjs.com`

Object-to-Object Mapping

An object-to-object mapping framework is responsible for mapping data from one data object to another. For example, a Windows Communication Foundation (WCF) service might need to map from database entities to data contracts to retrieve data from the database. The traditional way of mapping between data objects is coding up converters that copy the data between the objects. For data-intensive applications, a lot of tedious time and effort is spent writing a lot of code to map to and from data objects. There are now a number of generic mapping frameworks available for .NET development that virtually eliminate this effort. Some of the features to look for include

- Simple property mapping
- Complex type mapping
- Bidirectional mapping
- Implicit and explicit mapping
- Recursive and collection mapping

There are many object-to-object mapping tools available. Table 2-3 provides a list of a few object-to-object mapping tools that are worth evaluating.

Table 2-3. *Object-to-Object Mapping Tools*

Name	Description	More Information
AutoMapper	A straightforward, convention-based object-to-object mapping framework. Ability to specify custom projecting rules for flattening.	`automapper.org`
EmitMapper	Performance-oriented object-to-object mapping framework. The tool uses a runtime code generation approach.	`emitmapper.codeplex.com`

Name	Description	More Information
ValueInjecter	Simple and very flexible object-to-object mapping framework. Also has support for flattening and unflattening.	valueinjecter.codeplex.com

Dependency Injection

The Factory Method pattern is an excellent way to move the logic needed to construct an object out of the class that uses the object. The class calls a factory method that encapsulates any complex processes, restricted resources, or details required to construct the object. What if the Factory pattern could be even easier? The class could define what it needs as arguments of a specific type in its constructor. Then the class would expect the code that is instantiating the object to pass in instances of classes that implement that interface. In other words, the class does not instantiate its external dependencies. The class expects any code that needs the class to instantiate and supply the external dependencies. This is the concept behind dependency injection (DI), specifically constructor injection. This is useful in unit testing, as it is easy to inject a fake implementation of an external dependency into the class-under-test.

Some of the benefits of DI include

- *Improved testability*: Providing fake implementations, stubs and mocks, for unit testing in isolation and interaction testing.

- *Configuration flexibility*: Providing alternative implementations through configuration.

- *Lifetime management*: Creating dependent objects is centralized and managed.

- *Dependencies revealed*: With constructor injection a class's dependencies are explicitly stated as arguments to the constructor.

░ **Note** Dependency injection does introduce abstraction and indirection that might be unnecessary or confusing to the uninitiated. Take the time to establish DI in a clear and appropriate way.

There are different forms of DI: constructor, setter, and interface injection. The concept of inversion of control (IoC) is closely associated to DI as this is a common way to implement tools that provide DI facilities. IoC commonly refers to frameworks, or "containers", while DI refers to the strategy. There are a great many IoC containers available for .NET development.[8] Table 2-4 provides a list of just a few that are worth evaluating.

---

[8] For more information see http://elegantcode.com/2009/01/07/ioc-libraries-compared/.

Table 2-4. Dependency Injection/Inversion of Control Containers for .NET

Name	Description	More Information
Autofac	Open-source, widely-used dependency injection container. Very straightforward and easy to use with support for constructor injection.	`code.google.com/p/autofac/`
StructureMap	Open-source, widely-used dependency injection container with support for setter and constructor injection.	`structuremap.net/structuremap/`
Unity Application Block	Unity is a lightweight extensible dependency injection container with support for constructor, setter, and method-call injection. Part of EntLib and supported by the MS PnP group.	`unity.codeplex.com`

Research and Development

Since 1991 Microsoft Research has performed ground-breaking research in computer science as well as in software and hardware development.[9] The Kinect product is a sensational example of the results of their work. There are many other projects with names like CHESS, Code Contracts, Cuzz, Doloto, Gadgeteer, Gargoyle, Pex, and Moles. Information on their work is available at the Microsoft Research and DevLabs websites.[10] Some of the research is targeted toward finding solutions to very specific problems while other work has broader applicability. Some of the results have not yet made it out of the lab while other work is now part of the .NET Framework. For the developer looking to apply new and innovative approaches to .NET development, this research work is a great source of information and new .NET practices.

░ **Practice 2-8** Stay on Top of the Innovative Work of Microsoft Research

---

In this section, the focus is on two specific .NET practice areas that have emerged from their research and development. There are many others and there will surely be more in the future. The purpose of this section is only to give you a taste of the kind of work and to show you how learning about research and development reveals new and different .NET practice areas.

---

[9] For more information see `http://research.microsoft.com`.

[10] For more information see `http://msdn.microsoft.com/en-us/devlabs/`.

Automated Test Generation

Writing test code is not easy, but it is very important. Chapter 8 of this book is dedicated to the topic of unit testing and writing effective test code. The challenges in writing test code come from the dilemmas that many projects face:

- There is a lot of untested code and little time to write test code.

- There are missing test cases and scenarios and few good ways to find them.

- There are developers that write thorough test code and some that do not.

- There is little time to spend on writing test code now and problems that could have been found through testing that waste time later.

One goal of automated test generation is to address these kinds of dilemmas by creating a tool set that automates the process of discovering, planning, and writing test code. Some of these tools take a template approach, where the tool examines the source code or assemblies and uses a template to generate the corresponding test code.[11] Another approach focuses on "exploring" the code and generating test code through this exploration.

░ **Practice 2-9** Investigate Automated Test Generation As an Emerging .NET Practice Area

---

A Microsoft Research project called Pex, which is short for parameterized exploration, takes an exploration approach to generating test code.[12] Pex interoperates with another tool known as Moles. It is beyond the scope of this book to delve into the details of Pex and Moles; however, Appendix A provides resources for further investigation. The important idea is that Pex and Moles provide two important capabilities:

- Generate automated test code

- Perform exploratory testing to uncover test cases that reveal improper or unexpected behavior

These two tools, Pex and Moles, are brought together as part of the Visual Studio Power Tools. MSDN subscribers can download Pex for commercial use. Pex works with Visual Studio 2008 or 2010 Professional or higher. The sample code is provided as a high-level look at the code that Pex and Moles produces and how these tools are a .NET practice area worth investigating.[13]

---

[11] I have used the *NUnit Test Generator* tool from Kellerman Software to generate literally hundreds of useful test method stubs to help write tests against legacy source code. For more information see http://www.kellermansoftware.com/p-30-nunit-test-generator.aspx.

[12] For more information see http://research.microsoft.com/en-us/projects/pex/downloads.aspx.

[13] Chapter 8 focuses on current automated testing practices while this section is about the emerging practice of automated test generation. An argument could be made that Pex and Moles belongs in Chapter 8. Think of this as a preview of one of the tools and technologies yet to come.

SAMPLE CODE: PEX AND MOLES

You may want to review the book's Introduction at this point to learn what is needed to run the sample code.

For these instructions, it is assumed that the code for this chapter is found in your *Samples\Ch02* folder. That folder is simply referred to with a dollar symbol ($).

1. To start, open the *Lender.Slos.sln* file in Visual Studio under the *$\2_PexAndMoles* folder.

2. In the `Lender.Slos.Financial` project there are two methods, `ComputeRatePerPeriod` and `ComputePaymentPerPeriod`, in the `Calculator` class. They perform very simplistic interest rate and loan payment computations.

3. In the corresponding test project, `Tests.Unit.Lender.Slos.Financial`, there is a set of test methods that achieve 100% code coverage.

Chapter 8 covers unit testing in-depth. The aim of this sample code is to focus on how Pex and Moles can add new insights to the test code that is already there. For many developers the goal of 100% code coverage is the ultimate metric that defines complete and comprehensive unit testing for them. With Pex and Moles, that illusion is broken.

Running Pex to generate the parameterized unit tests is a straightforward process; however, it is beyond the scope of this book. If you would like to learn how to use Pex to create the parameterized unit tests, start with the files under the *$\1_Start* folder and the Pex documentation.[14] The *Parameterized Unit Testing with Microsoft Pex* document is a detailed tutorial that covers parameterized unit testing and running Pex to perform exploratory testing.

Running Pex to create parameterized unit tests adds a new project named `Tests.Pex.Lender.Slos.Financial`, which contains the test code that Pex generated. Once generated, the next thing is to select Run Pex Exploration from the project's context menu.

The results of the Pex exploration include three failing test cases; the output is in the Pex Explorer window, as shown Figure 2-2. One of the test cases is failing because the `ComputePaymentPerPeriod` method is throwing a divide by zero exception. The other two are caused by an overflow exception in that method.

---

[14] For Pex documentation and tutorials see `http://research.microsoft.com/en-us/projects/pex/documentation.aspx`.

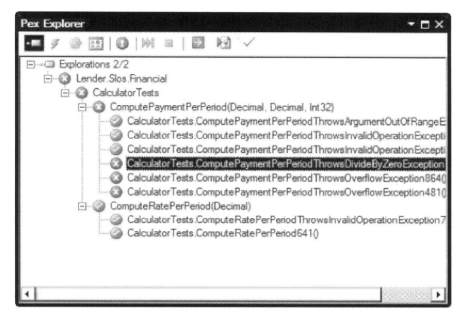

Figure 2-2. *Output shown in the Pex Explorer window*

These three test cases are failing because the method-under-test is throwing exceptions that are not expected. The code is almost certainly not working as intended, which is the case in this example. There is code missing from ComputePaymentPerPeriod and Pex has revealed it: the method argument ratePerPeriod is not guarded against invalid values with if-then-throw code.

By investigating, debugging, and analyzing the Pex tests, five new tests cases, as shown in Listing 2-1, are added to the test code in the Tests.Unit.Lender.Slos.Financial project. With this, the Pex test code has done its job and revealed the unit testing oversight. The Pex generated code might or might not remain a project of the solution, depending on your situation. As an individual developer you could use Pex and Moles to enhance your unit testing, or as a team leader, you could use Pex and Moles to review the test code of others. The new Pex project could remain a part of the solution and pushed to the code repository as a permanent set of automated tests.

In the end, the code in the method-under-test is improved with new if-then-throw statements so that all of these five test cases pass.

Listing 2-1. *Pex and Moles: Discovered Test Cases*

```
[TestCase(7499, 0.0, 113, 72.16)]
[TestCase(7499, 0.0173, 113, 72.16)]
[TestCase(7499, 0.7919, 113, 72.16)]
[TestCase(7499, -0.0173, 113, 72.16)]
[TestCase(7499, -0.7919, 113, 72.16)]
public void ComputePayment_WithInvalidRatePerPeriod_ExpectArgumentOutOfRangeException(
    decimal principal,
    decimal ratePerPeriod,
```

```
    int termInPeriods,
    decimal expectedPaymentPerPeriod)
{
    // Arrange

    // Act
    TestDelegate act = () => Calculator.ComputePaymentPerPeriod(
        principal,
        ratePerPeriod,
        termInPeriods);

    // Assert
    Assert.Throws<ArgumentOutOfRangeException>(act);
}
```

Through this example, it is very clear that Pex and Moles have the power to improve software. It revealed five test cases where invalid values of the argument `ratePerPeriod` were not being tested. The .NET practice area of automated test generation is emerging as a significant way to develop better test code. Microsoft Research has other projects that you can find within the general topic of Automated Test Generation.[15]

Code Contracts

Code Contracts is a spin-off from the Spec# project at Microsoft Research.[16] Code Contracts is available on DevLabs and is also a part of the .NET Framework in .NET 4.0, which is covered in Chapter 7. Code contracts are very relevant to code correctness and verification.[17] The work is related to the programming concept of design-by-contract that focuses on

- *Preconditions:* Conditions that the method's caller is required to make sure are true when calling the method

- *Postconditions:* Conditions that the method's implementer ensures are true at all normal exit points of the method

- *Object Invariants:* A set of conditions that must hold true for an object to be in a valid state

The `System.Diagnostics.CodeContract` class provides methods to state preconditions, postconditions, and invariants. Code Contracts is then supported by two tools: Static Checker and Rewriter, which turns the `CodeContracts` method calls into compile-time and runtime checks.

■ **Practice 2-10** Consider Code Contracts to Improve Testability and Software Verification

---

[15] For more information see `http://research.microsoft.com/en-us/projects/atg/`.

[16] For more information see `http://research.microsoft.com/en-us/projects/specsharp/`.

[17] For a very comprehensive treatment of Code Contracts, see this 14-part series of blog postings: `http://devjourney.com/blog/code-contracts-part-1-introduction/`.

The primary advantage of using Code Contracts is improved testability, a static checker that verifies contracts at compile-time, and the facility to generate runtime checking using the contracts. Code Contracts is a .NET practice area that is very powerful and should take off as the new features of .NET 4.0 are more widely employed.

Microsoft Security Development Lifecycle

The Microsoft Security Development Lifecycle (SDL) is a secure application development program developed and instituted at Microsoft. Their approach to developing secure applications has been made available to all developers. Microsoft makes the SDL information and tools available for free. It includes a lot of helpful information related to security practices, guidelines, and technologies. Everything is grouped into seven phases:

- Training
- Requirements
- Design
- Implementation
- Verification
- Release
- Response

Based on their internal software development, the SDL techniques embraced by Microsoft resulted in software that is more secure. When they followed the SDL for a product, the number of security defects was reduced by approximately 50 to 60 percent.[18]

※ **Practice 2-11** Appreciate Secure Application Development and the Microsoft Security Development Lifecycle

---

The Microsoft SDL process lists many practice areas. For example, within the Design phase the SDL practice of Threat Modeling is highlighted. Threat modeling is a structured approach to identifying, evaluating, and mitigating risks to system security. This .NET practice area offers sensible ways to anticipate attacks and reveal vulnerabilities. Threat modeling helps better integrate security into your development efforts.

The Verification phase points to the practice area of Fuzz Testing, commonly known as fuzzing. The idea behind fuzzing is straightforward:

- Create malformed or invalid input data.
- Force the application under test to use that data.
- See if the application crashes, hangs, leaks memory, or otherwise behaves badly.

---

[18] Source: Michael Howard, *A Look Inside the Security Development Lifecycle at Microsoft* available at http://msdn.microsoft.com/en-us/magazine/cc163705.aspx.

Fuzzing finds bugs and security vulnerabilities by trying to exploit problems that exist in the application.[19] If there are potential security issues in an application, bad guys will exploit them to impact you and your end-users through denial of service attacks or worse. Fuzzing is a .NET practice area that helps find and fix problems proactively.

It is important to know how to protect your applications from Cross Site Scripting (XSS), SQL Injection, and other attacks. A list of some of the key tools that the Microsoft SDL offers or is developing is presented in Table 2-5. These tools help in the development of more secure applications, which is an important .NET practice area.

Table 2-5. Microsoft SDL Tools

Name	Description	Benefits	More Information
Threat Modeling Tool	Proactive approach to application security that diagrams, identifies, addresses, and validates threats.	Helps to find and address security implications from the earliest design phases of a project. Moves development toward a "secure by design" attitude. Emphasizes threats based on component security and trust boundaries.	`www.microsoft.com/down load/en/details.aspx?d isplaylang=en&id=2955`
MiniFuzz	MiniFuzz is a very simple file fuzzing tool for use during development.	Fuzzing is very effective at finding bugs. Helps find denial of service and security vulnerabilities. Designed to ease adoption of fuzz testing by non-security people.	`www.microsoft.com/down load/en/details.aspx?d isplaylang=en&id=21769`
Code Analysis Tool .NET	CAT.NET v2.0 is a set of rules that integrate with VS 2010 and FxCop.	Helps find potential issues and vulnerabilities in the software, related to things like: dynamic SQL, cross site scripting, cookies, and viewstate encryption.	`blogs.msdn.com/b/secur itytools`
Windows Protection Library	WPL combines defenses related to Anti-Cross Site Scripting (Anti-XSS) and SQL Injection.	Helps prevent XSS attacks in ASP.NET applications. Uses a white-list of "known good characters". Adds protection across character sets in different languages.	`wpl.codeplex.com`
Web Application Configuration Analyzer	WACA scans an environment with respect to recommended .NET security practices.	Helps verify and validate the application configuration as a part of testing. Examines things like web configuration, IIS settings, SQL Server, and Windows permissions	`www.microsoft.com/down load/en/details.aspx?i d=573`

---

[19] For more information see `http://blogs.msdn.com/b/sdl/archive/2010/07/07/writing-fuzzable-code.aspx`.

Summary

In this chapter you learned about where you might find better .NET practices. Every day, new and different practices are being developed and adopted in areas like secure application development and Microsoft Research. The expertise and experience of the PnP group comes forth in guide books, the Enterprise Library, and the very thorough documentation and reference applications they offer.

Most importantly, you learned that your team and organization have internal sources of better .NET practices. The retrospectives, technical debt, and defect tracking system are rich sources of information that can be turned into better practices.

In the next chapter, you will learn the mantra of achieving desired results. Positive outcomes are the true aim of better practices and the yardstick with which they are measured.

CHAPTER 3

Achieving Desired Results

All throughout a project—and in the end—results matter. Good results can build trust and poor results can destroy trust. Results are how you and your team are evaluated. Consider a typical project situation: everything is aligned to produce the results you get. The way people interact or do not interact, the hardware, the software, the staffing, the planning or lack of planning; these and many more influences yield the results. When the situation improves, there are better results. But bringing about organizational change is very challenging and is likely outside the influence of the team and its members. The goal of this chapter is to raise your awareness of specific changes you can control or influence and provide pragmatic and helpful techniques to realize better outcomes.

This chapter is about being results oriented. As a developer or a team leader, positive outcomes come from taking practical approaches and concentrating on objectives. First, there is the planning that goes into making sure things start off right. You create the conditions for success by spending time listening and communicating about what the desired results are or should be. Achieving desired results is about making the effort to sort out the practical from the impractical, and about delivering, accomplishing, and showing positive outcomes. At the same time, a big part of achieving desired results is not allowing less important things or avoidable problems to divert or distract.

Since just about every project involves people trying to work together, it goes without saying that people skills play a big part in what is achieved or not achieved. The Agile Manifesto recognizes the importance of individuals interacting by listing this as the first value.[1] This chapter presents practical advice on how to get team members to collaborate with each other and work toward a common purpose.

The practices covered in this chapter are summarized in Table 3-1.

***Table 3-1.** Achieving Desired Results: Ruthlessly Helpful .NET Practices*

	Achieving Desired Results
3-1	Make Sure That Success Conditions Exist
3-2	Itemize All Things That Are out of Scope
3-3	Insist on Reaching a Common Understanding
3-4	Use Wireframes to Visually Unite Requirements, Structure, and Realism

---

[1] Available at http://agilemanifesto.org.

Achieving Desired Results	
3-5	Diagram, Document, and Communicate the System's Architecture
3-6	Create a Mockup for Every Report
3-7	Keep Asking for Detailed Examples
3-8	Establish an Archetype That Others Can Follow
3-9	Focus on Deliverables, Not on Activities
3-10	Compare Results to the Objectives, Metrics, and Focus Area
3-11	Visualize Trends to Understand and Appreciate Progress over Time

COMMENTARY

Many years back, I was on a large project building my employer's next generation of commercial financial software. As the project was getting off the ground it became clear that there were two significant differences of opinion. First was the question of whether the new application should be a port of the existing system or whether it should have a whole new set of features and functionality for new customers in a new market. Second was the question of whether the new application should be a stand-alone Windows desktop application or a browser-hosted, multi-tiered application. These are huge differences that generated a lot of conflict. Initially the decision was made to build the web application with all new functionality. Through planning and prototyping, it became clear that the budget and schedule were too small and the technical implications too big. Another round of planning and prototyping revealed that what would be delivered was not going to match the vision. Again and again, this project could never reconcile these differences. Executive management, vice presidents, product managers, developers, analysts, and testers each had their own opinions on these two topics. The project's success hinged on the team lining up behind a fundamental vision and direction, but it never came and the project was ultimately terminated. Without success conditions no project can achieve desired results.

On another project, I once sat in a requirements review meeting. The analyst who wrote the document guided the participants through each section, one section at a time. Every detail in the document was covered. As I sat there I became aware that the two people who needed to understand the requirements, the developer and the tester, were not engaged. These key individuals were not interacting with the analyst. I interrupted to ask the tester a question: "Is this what you think the users want?" The answer was an emphatic "no." She then spoke about how the current system works and how the users do their job and how the system is tested. Soon, the developer was at the whiteboard diagramming the process. The analyst was helping by pointing out new features and how the process needed to change. Soon, these folks were really communicating. They were engaged with one another. They were arriving at a common understanding of the desired results and how to achieve them.

Success Conditions

How a project starts often makes the difference between success and failure. If the conditions are right from the beginning, the project often maintains favorable conditions. The team keeps coming back together and regrouping when problems and challenges arise. When the wrong conditions exist from the outset, bad things, like conflict and confusion, remain. Soon, misunderstandings lead to more misunderstanding. Conflicts continue. Expectations are missed. Thrashing is never-ending.

There are projects that seem doomed to fail from the beginning, in which everyone knows that things are going to fail from the start and freely admits it. A different scenario is where everything starts off fine, and it is only in retrospect that the project seemed doomed. Sometime after the project fails to deliver or is cancelled, someone mentions that the project was hopeless and others join in and agree. It is as if everyone on the project knew that the project started out wrong and was prearranged to fail. If you were to interview the team and dig further you would find two things missing all along: awareness and acknowledgement. Either they were not aware that the project lacked the success conditions, or, if they were aware, they did not acknowledge the severity of the problems. Silently, the team members allowed the project to start off wrong and kept quiet as things continued to run badly. It was not until it was too late or in retrospect that failure seemed the likely outcome.

All project team members must take an active part in the project. Every individual must work hard to be aware of potential problems and raise their voice when success conditions are absent. The goal is not to eliminate problems but to raise awareness and get everyone to acknowledge problems, risks, issues, and concerns. On any given project, an individual can help everyone see the hidden flaws, point out undue optimism, and insist on a reasonable plan of approach.

▦ **Practice 3-1** Make Sure That Success Conditions Exist

Projects that have the right success conditions have few interruptions, intrusions, and interference; the project work is considered too important to disturb. In contrast, projects with a lot of stopping and starting, team members who join and leave, and external meddling and prying, are inevitably late, over budget, or fail. It is hard for individual team members to deal with all the task switching. Developers find it especially difficult owing to the nature of development work. Programming and debugging require a lot of concentration and a good short-term memory. A lot of task switching can destroy developer effectiveness. Developers need to work together to communicate and coordinate. This means they need to have a lot of available time to talk and work together, and to develop an understanding and a rapport. Everyone on the project must raise awareness and work to limit diversions, distractions, and disruptions that destroy project success.

▦ **Caution** There are many projects that have very ambitious and abstract success-conditions. This can be a good thing, as with NASA's Apollo program, but usually leaves the project feeling adrift. It is important to set smaller objectives that can be achieved in a limited amount of time. This is the concept behind agile sprints. Establish the short-term success conditions early and make sure they align to the overall success conditions. Compare and measure progress in the micro-scale sprint to that of the macro-scale project.

To this point the success conditions are defined by context and preconditions; it is hard to change or even influence the circumstances. You cannot avoid the types of problems that arise at this stage. You cannot stop their reoccurrences. These problems include things like team members' aptitude, long-standing grievances, and no training budget. The goal is to find coping strategies and ways to minimize the impact. Even as the project gets underway, however, there is one area that can improve: the capacity of the team members to deliver. This often comes in the form of on-the-job training and mentoring. In broader terms there are three areas to improve: knowledge, skill, and attitude. These areas of development are illustrated in Figure 3-1.

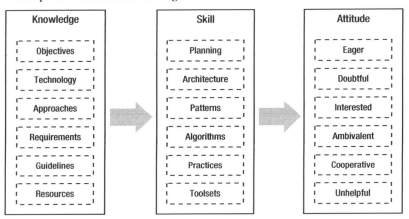

Figure 3-1. The conditions for success: knowledge, skill, and attitude

Knowledge is concerned with recognizing and understanding what to do. For team members, there is knowledge about many topics, such as project objectives, technology, reasonable plans-of-approach, features, coding standards, working with other teams, and many others. Clear, consistent, and complete communication is the way knowledge is transferred to and within the team.

Skill is about knowing how to do something. It is about experience and training and climbing the learning curve. Without the right skills, knowledge cannot be turned into action. A developer that lacks a crucial skill can appear stuck or unmotivated. Few want to draw attention to the fact that some competency is lacking, but without help there is no progress. Recognize the fact that without skill-development the results will suffer. Training, self-paced tutorials, demonstrations, and mentoring are all ways to develop skills within the team.

Attitude is about knowing why to do something and wanting to do it. It is about motivation and interest. Without the right attitude, even if the knowledge and skill are present, results lack efficiency and creativity. A developer without the right attitude can be blatantly uncooperative or quietly unproductive. There is an important sequence here, illustrated by the arrows in Figure 3-1. First, spend time to figure out if there is missing knowledge and discuss that. Then, spend time working on skills and proficiency to figure out if there is a problem in that area. Finally, if you are sure that a problem does not stem from lack of knowledge or skill, then focus on attitude. Spend time listening and diagnosing the problem. Once you fully understand the cause of the problem, solutions will present themselves.

For any project to be successful, the proper conditions must exist. As an individual team member you are able to gauge your own knowledge, skill, and attitude. Team leaders need to have a regular, open dialog with team members. Both one-on-one and in groups, ask team members to consider these questions:

- Do I know what to do?

- Do I know how to do it?

- Am I motivated to do it? If not, why not?

These questions apply to all aspects of the project, from requirements to technology to specific practices. These questions apply to all objectives and priorities. Table 3-2 lists a few possible priorities and examples of some of the knowledge, skills, and attitudes that might relate to that priority. For example, if correctness is a high project priority, then automated unit testing with the NUnit framework may be the way the team decides to address it. However, in this example, one team member does not know that automated testing is a serious priority, another does not have any experience with unit testing, and a third is skeptical of the benefits.

Table 3-2. *Examples of Priorities and How They Might Relate to Knowledge, Skill, and Attitude*

Priority	Knowledge	Skill	Attitude
Correctness	Automated Testing	NUnit	Unconvinced
Functionality	Loan Limits	Algorithms	Confused
Schedule	Plan	Estimation	Doubt
Testability	MVC Pattern	ASP.NET MVC	Excitement
Scalability	Analysis	Profiling	Overwhelmed

Knowledge is improved through communication and understanding. For example, in this case, keep repeating again and again that automated testing is important to you. Ask team members about the automated testing they are doing. Measure test coverage percentages and share the results.

▓ **Note** The advice here is to communicate what it is that you value. The emphasis in this example is on letting others know that you value automated testing. Since the ultimate goal is to have everyone self-supervise, refrain from strangling the process by being the "supervisor." Promote initiative, ownership, and results. Focus less on process and more on encouragement.

Skill is improved through training and experience. In this case, there ought to be hands-on examples of how to write proper unit tests. The test code needs to be reviewed. The focus is on learning and improving. Talk about project prerequisites, such as formal training. Add time to the schedule for mentoring and on-the-job training.

Attitude is a lot more complicated than knowledge and skills; however, it may be more important. There are no easy answers. Some negative concerns reflect real project dilemmas that ought to be addressed. The first priority is to become aware of the team member's honest attitudes, for better or for worse. Build off an acknowledgement that their rationale is important to get out on the table. Dialog is good even if there's no real solution. Perhaps the result is a statement of reluctant support: "I am not convinced automated testing is the right approach, but I will support it because I want to see the project succeed." An openly supportive skeptic is a lot better than a quietly unsupportive skeptic.

Project Inception

Every project starts with some initial period of time when things are just getting going. On some projects this is just an informal kickoff period when team members begin working together. On larger projects or with formal processes, there is a project inception phase. The team is forming, and everyone has a different idea of what the project is all about. As you would expect, there are differences. Some of the team members are excited to be using a new tool or technology. Some are expecting to have detailed requirements fully written up with use cases and scenarios. One is disappointed and angry that he is not the team lead. Others fear that the goals are unrealistic, the deadline unachievable, and expectations are way too high. Excitement, anticipation, anger, and fear; there is a lot of emotion before the project has really started.

First and foremost, project inception is a period of knowledge transfer. The project leaders must discuss and communicate with each other to ensure they are clear on what the project is all about. These leaders must then communicate to the team in consistent terms and expectations. The whole team must have an open dialog that completely covers topics and includes questions like the following:

- What is the business justification for the project?

- What is the project scope? What is definitely out of scope?

- What are the key features and objectives that drive the architecture?

- What are the candidate technologies and plans-of-approach?

- What are the identified risks? How will they be mitigated?

- What is the preliminary project schedule and budget?

Too often projects get started with a lot of lingering questions. Team members should not make assumptions. The tough questions need to be asked. Individuals must make and test assertions that press these issues.

During the inception period it is very important that everyone see the same big-picture concept. Everyone must know what deliverables are to be delivered. This is the time to both share the vision and have a meeting of the minds. As an individual team member, you must remain alert to any differences you are seeing and actively point them out.

Out of Scope

Perhaps more important than specifying the system's requirements is deciding what is definitely out of scope. People are reluctant to talk about what is not going to be done. Assumptions are made, which lead to future misunderstandings and unmet expectations. For example, developers must not automatically assume that globalization is out of scope. If you think globalization is out of scope then make that assertion and insist that the project manager record that it is not an objective.

▓ **Practice 3-2** Itemize All Things That Are Out of Scope

Take the time to list out all features and functionality that are out of scope. Be sure that the list is explicitly clear and completely detailed. The goal is to remove any assumptions, which lead to later misunderstandings.

Diversions and Distractions

Time is a resource you spend whether you want to or not. Any project can save money by not spending on servers, software, and training, but time marches forward. This is why diversions and distractions cause developers to fail to achieve desired results. Many interruptions and intrusions eat into precious development time.

One way to limit diversions is to cap the time spent on concerns that you can neither influence nor control. Use those criteria to estimate the value of spending time on a specific topic. For example, if you feel you have no influence on a decision, but getting to a decision is important, then put your time and effort into setting a deadline for the decision. Avoid spending time and energy on things you have no influence over.

Another way to limit diversions and distractions is by facilitating effective collaboration and communication that does not intrude and impose on the developer's time. Establish a set time to hold a very short meeting, such as the daily standup meeting favored by agile development. Prevent distractions, delays, and progress blockage by using collaboration tools like discussion boards instead of ad-hoc disruptions and the unreliable relaying of information from one developer to the next.

Almost by definition, something that distracts is not important to you or your team. It may be important to someone else, but their priorities are not your priorities. Take a moment to consider these questions:

- Is this issue or interruption important to me or the project?

- Where is the urgency of this issue or interruption coming from?

When an issue comes up, it may only be important to one person. A production crisis is important because users are impacted, but addressing a technical support question that the help desk ought to handle is unimportant. An executive's concerns are important because retaining that person's support is important to the project, but analyzing a favorite feature that is not in scope is unimportant. Someone intrudes on your time because it is important to them, but you are responsible for figuring out if it is important to you and your team. When unimportant issues are raised by important people, an effective strategy is to pivot the conversation from the specifics of the issue to a discussion of competing priorities for time and resources. It is amazing how quickly awareness and acknowledgement of your priorities changes things.

The Learning/Doing Balance

Developing a new skill can increase efficiency. Finding a better approach can dramatically improve a situation. Better practices do lead to better results. There is no doubt that you must spend some time learning to be more effective. To be more productive you must increase your capacity to produce. However, if you spend too much time learning then you cannot be productive. The learning/doing balance is about appreciating both sides of the equilibrium. Consider these questions:

- Will gaining new knowledge and understanding be more helpful than applying what I already know?

- Is the desired result to see developers gain greater competence, capacity, and efficiency, or is it to see them produce immediately?

- Will applying current know-how and practice be more useful than developing new understandings or better insights?

- Is there a belief that less effective, short-term results are more important than improved, long-term results?

Achieving desired results is about striking the right balance between increasing the capacity to accomplish and actually getting things done. There are many tasks that cannot be done properly without basic knowledge, yet there are some things that cannot be learned without doing. Most of what is taught in school and in training courses is the basic knowledge. Riding a bicycle, driving a car, and facilitating a meeting require experience to gain mastery. Know when to learn and when to apply what is already learned.

■ **Note** Schedule pressure is the enemy of learning new tools and technologies. If time constraints are an issue then you should not be considering unfamiliar tools and technology. Time pressure is very hard to manage while you are learning on the job. People usually jump directly into writing production code even though they are still learning the technology and only have a rudimentary or naïve understanding.

Common Understanding

Without a common understanding there is no agreement. Any differences in understanding are sure to cause problems. It could be a simple difference of fact: one person thought the decision was to put the control on the left-hand-side of the screen while another thought it was going on the right. It could be a difference in opinion: one thinks it is better on the left but another thinks it is better on the right. It could be a difference in priority: one thinks the users find it more usable on the left while another feels it is more obvious on the right. Reaching a common understanding of facts, opinions, and priorities is important. This practice is about working to gain that common understanding. At the high level, frequent misunderstandings center on project objectives, success criteria, and contending values. At the detail level, misunderstandings are about requirements, tools, technology, patterns, approaches, standards, and guidelines.

■ **Practice 3-3** Insist on Reaching a Common Understanding

Watch for the warning signs of misunderstandings: unclear objectives, vague success criteria, dubious value. Keep the individuals interacting until the specific differences are identified. Use clear diagrams and drawings to pull out facts from people's minds so that everyone can see them. As for opinions and values, decisions need to be made by the person or persons responsible for them. Discussion is a good way to reach consensus, but an authority decision may eventually be needed.

Wireframe Diagrams

Pictures are often a lot better than words. Many users cannot describe what it is they want, but they know it when they see it or when they like it. Why spend time discussing and describing what cannot be envisioned? Drawing at the whiteboard or creating a diagram helps everyone take their mental image and construct the same image.

User interface (UI) prototyping is often seen as an effective way to show what the results will look like. These UI prototypes tend to have two significant drawbacks:[2]

- There is some turn-around time from when the idea is discussed and the prototype is shown. The best UI prototyping tools still have a lag time that inhibits collaboration.

- A prototype can leave the wrong impression, with respect to completion. Many times it is only the developer who knows the extent to which a prototype is incomplete or fatally flawed. The primary design-drivers behind a prototype are haste, shortcuts, and illusion. This is a bad foundation for further development. Unlike a concept car or a model of a building, most users cannot distinguish between the software prototype and the expected result.

Avoid UI prototypes and favor wireframe mockups.

▧ **Practice 3-4** Use Wireframes to Visually Unite Requirements, Structure, and Realism

---

Wireframe diagrams offer an effective way to model and visualize. They strike a balance between collaboration and not leaving the wrong impression of completeness. With a wireframe mockup tool everyone can work together to fill in gaps and reconcile differences. Figure 3-2 shows an example of a wireframe mockup created with Balsamiq, a wireframing tool. In this illustration, the wireframe shows what information needs to go on the screen and what the user is able to do on the screen. Annotations explain specific rules and limitations. The purpose is focused squarely on arriving at a common understanding. This helpful activity pictures the screen and addresses topics such as

- Information to display

- Features and actions available

- Main purpose and areas of emphasis

---

[2] These statements are not true for proof-of-concept (PoC) prototypes. The PoC prototype is geared toward establishing and validating technical feasibility and design. The PoC prototype tells you what is flawed or what is hard to do at an early stage, which mitigates risk. The PoC prototype is a quick-and-dirty proving out of a solution strategy; therefore, you must explicitly prohibit developers from using PoC prototype code as the basis for production code.

- Rules, limitations, and options

- Use cases and scenarios

Time spent on wireframe mockups should focus on three topics: presentation of information, navigation within and between screens, and the layout and usability of a screen.

- Presentation of information is about what needs to go on the screen and how it can make things easy to read and understand.

- Navigation is about screen relationships, options to move around, and the workflow.

- Layout and usability are about the user interface design, which includes graphics, links, buttons, select-boxes, and other common UI elements.

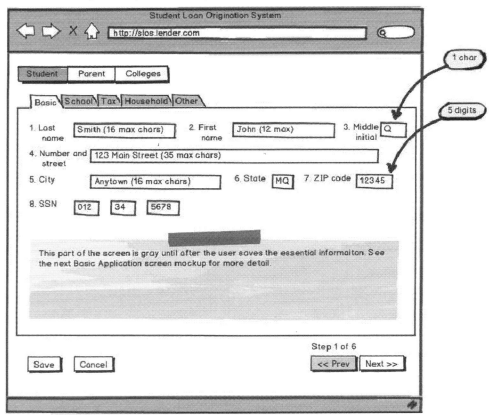

Figure 3-2. Example wireframe mockup using Balsamiq

Documented Architecture

The high-level design of the system brings order to development. With a good architecture, the detailed design and development aligns to the decisions and direction communicated between the project stakeholders and the development team. This alignment is important to establish a framework and an outline of the hardware, software components, interfaces, and interactions. The architecture is a common understanding of the solution strategy for the project.

░ **Practice 3-5** Diagram, Document, and Communicate the System's Architecture

---

The architecture must document, diagram, and communicate the high-level design of the system to include the following:

- Software components and their interaction
- Core technologies and toolsets
- Driving requirements and priorities
- Technical and non-technical constraints
- Important principles, guidelines, and standards

Report Mockups

Although not every system has separate reports, many do. The reports can represent a significant amount of work; they imply requirements for the database and are drivers of the design. For example, there are the requirements for how the reports display the data. There are requirements for the data that needs to be queried. Unfortunately, not enough attention is paid to reports early in the project lifecycle. This practice is about developing a common understanding of the reporting requirements of the project and providing the developer with enough detail to deliver proper reports.

Everyone ought to see the reports visually represented. Using a spreadsheet is an excellent way to mock reports. Real numbers with actual totals can be shown. The layout, fonts, and other visual elements can be shown. More importantly, a spreadsheet is something analysts can use to collaborate with users and keep the requirements up to date.

░ **Practice 3-6** Create a Mockup for Every Report

For each and every report use a spreadsheet, such as Excel, to create a mockup of the report. Include representative data and have every total and calculation accurately shown. The goal is a clear and complete understanding of everything that goes into making that report. Try not to short-circuit the process, otherwise important detail is going to be overlooked. As a developer, follow the data back to its source and resolve any inconsistencies or missing data in the database.

Detailed Examples

Too often the examples that are supplied to developers are too simplistic or incomplete. This is especially true for infrequent scenarios or exception cases. Initially, simple examples help to explain the concept and focus on the primary use cases. However, software systems are required to properly handle the more elaborate usage scenarios. As the requirements progress from the high level and get into the detail it is a lot more important to keep the detailed examples coming. A deeper common understanding comes from sweating the details.

Complicated algorithms and business rules require detailed examples. To write code that implements these algorithms and business rules, developers need to understand the details and verify that the code meets all of the requirements. Trivial examples lead to trivial code. Many complete and detailed examples help an effective developer unit test and correctly implement the code. Detailed examples also help with debugging and troubleshooting. The full intention of the code is better understood with examples.

▨ **Practice 3-7** Keep Asking for Detailed Examples

All through the project, from requirements to testing, keep asking analysts and testers to provide detailed examples of how the system is supposed to work. Ask that wireframes be filled in with sample data. Ask that report mockups show proper data. Ask that business rules be spelled out with examples and illustrations. Ask for data that reproduces defects and errors. Pressing for this information is important to properly develop, diagnose, and resolve many of the significant project issues.

Build an Archetype

Establishing an archetype is about creating a prime example that other developers should imitate and follow. An archetype is a prototype written in a specialized way; it ought to be imitated. This approach recognizes that many developers learn by example. If it is clear that there is an established archetype then their work can start by emulating a good model of the system. This practice is about creating models that others can and should follow. Other benefits of an archetype include

- Proving out the architecture

- Making abstract ideas real

- Allowing other developers to react to and improve the design

In addition to being a standard, the archetype helps to confirm and prove out the architecture. The high-level design started on a whiteboard or in the designers' heads. The ideas and approaches need to be proven. Build the archetype in such a way that it contains functionality that passes through all the layers of the architecture.

Many developers learn by example. Learning a new architecture involves either building something with it or referencing an existing model. A good archetype is like a tutorial that walks the developer through a modestly-sized, across-the-board application. When ASP.NET MVC first became available, one of the best ways to learn the concepts was to build the NerdDinner application.[3] The *NerdDinner application* is an archetype, serving to communicate "what to do" and "how to do it".

A good archetype is a lot clearer than many explanations. Many developers can react to and improve upon an archetype. Their suggestions are often very helpful. Many developers are "show me the code" oriented and are impatient with explanations and debate. They want to see a working example of the architecture and development style. In fact, the archetype is effective at solving the dilemmas associated with sorting out knowledge, skill, and attitude. For developers who have the proper attitude, the archetype is all they need to become productive. For developers who have genuine concerns, the archetype provides a way to discuss the specifics.

■ **Practice 3-8** Establish an Archetype That Others Can Follow

---

Create an archetype with enough detail to serve as a model for other developers to follow. Sometimes called a "vertical slice," the archetype is a top-to-bottom example of how the system is intended to work. It need not be a separate application. In fact, it is often better to work through a significant area of functionality. The important idea is to expect that other developers imitate the coding style, design patterns, and approaches. The archetype is the model you want others to follow, by and large.

Desired Results

The desired results of a project focus on the software that is delivered. There are many positive outcomes to achieve but without working software, most projects are judged to have fallen short. In general terms, the working software is the primary deliverable. Secondary deliverables, such as documentation, are important, but should not come at the expense of the primary deliverable.

In software projects, activities are not results. All activities must serve the purposes of obtaining results. On a day to day basis, programmers talk about writing code, but in the final analysis delivering quality features and functionality is how the programmer is evaluated. It is the positive outcomes from writing software that the project stakeholders are looking for. There is an expectation that all activity leads to positive outcomes.

Deliverables

Every deliverable represents some tangible or intangible thing. It could be an installation package or it could be the ability to save a loan application. In the first case, the installation package is a tangible file on the network somewhere. It is either there or it is not there. It either works or it does not work. In the second case, the user sits down to the system to enter a loan application. Assuming the user is entering the application properly, the system either lets the user save or it does not. Saving the application is the intangible deliverable of the user accomplishing their work.

In the final analysis, desired results are strongly tied to good deliverables. Measuring progress with interim results is important. Properly sized deliverables are either done or not done.

---

[3] See http://www.asp.net/mvc/tutorials/introducing-the-nerddinner-tutorial.

▩ **Practice 3-9** Focus on Deliverables, Not on Activities

A focus on deliverables should be results oriented. It can be described in objective terms, such as level of completeness, correctness, or consistency. Users see and experience deliverables. As a developer or team lead, focus on the deliverables and not the activities. Yes, the activities are important, but only insofar as they generate quality deliverables.

Positive Outcomes

One way to look at desired results is through the lens of satisfaction and quality. Customers and stakeholders are satisfied when the anticipated and expected features and functionality are delivered. Complete quality is when every requirement is met and the system serves every useful purpose. Consider a new car buyer. During the initial shopping period the customer focuses on the car's styling, bells and whistles, and various features. There's a lot of attention paid to a long wish list, but a car's indispensable purpose is to provide transportation. That can be taken for granted. The same is true for the structural quality. The customer implicitly expects the car to be well-engineered and reliable. While shopping, many car buyers are focused on what they want and not on what they expect. However, during the first year of ownership customers become keenly aware about whether the car is useful or not. After a few years of maintenance costs and reliability issues the structural quality becomes important.

Achieving long-term success depends on long-term satisfaction. For many projects the emphasis is always on features and functionality. In the earliest stages of the project the users and analysts focus on the wish list and what the current system cannot do. The minimum requirements and essential behavior are taken for granted. As the project continues, the quality assurance team focuses testing on the features and functionality of the system. This is referred to as "fitness of purpose" testing.

The system's end-users and customers are able to assess their satisfaction by comparing it to how pleased they are with what the software does or does not do. The testing team is able to gauge the quality of the system against the requirements. There is a favorable reception based on meeting the minimal, essential features and delivering wish-list items. Unfortunately, what results is a system that may be structurally unsound. The nonfunctional pieces are not in place and soon the initial happiness is replaced with dissatisfaction. Slow performance, bugs, scalability problems, and other nonfunctional deficiencies destroy trust.

Figure 3-3 divides satisfaction and quality into four quadrants. In quadrant 1 are the expected features and functionality that define basic quality. The outcomes in quadrant 2 are about building a robust system with reliable and performant code. In quadrant 3 outcomes are about the satisfaction that comes from getting more than was expected. In quadrant 4 the system is technically elegant, well written, and wonderfully designed.

For many projects the requirements are overly focused on the quadrant 3 outcomes: the wish list. As the project proceeds, completion is evaluated through testing that focuses on the outcomes in quadrant 1. For some projects these are the only two focus areas. It is during acceptance testing or after deployment that the quadrant 2 outcomes are put to the test. If the results are unsatisfactory then complaints about performance, reliability, and scalability start flooding in. A system that once looked good starts to look bad. As for quadrant 4, when the outcomes are not achieved the problems are usually internal to the system, but the implications of spaghetti code and restrictive designs are very real and show up in maintenance and enhancement costs.

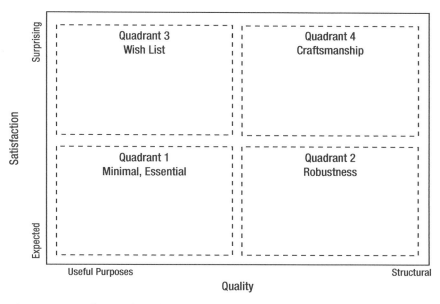

Figure 3-3. *Quadrants of satisfaction and quality*

To achieve positive outcomes that hold up in the long run there needs to be a logical sequencing of the project focus areas. Both quadrants 1 and 2 are foundational. It is necessary to perform much of the work that relates to these areas. This is especially true of requirements that relate to structural quality and performing structural testing. However, the overall system cannot neglect any of the four quadrants. The highest level of satisfaction comes from delivering in quadrants 3 and 4, but never to the exclusion of quadrants 1 and 2. Here is more detail on what is in each quadrant:

- *Minimal, Essential:* The basic features and functionality, which is the primary focus of the project. Working in outcomes in this quadrant is about delivering "the right things." Delivering results in this area is about both meeting the expected requirements and making sure the system does everything it needs to do. This is the expected. This is the system's capacity to serve its useful purpose.

- *Robustness:* The strength of the system is the secondary focus of the project. Working on outcomes in this quadrant is about delivering "in the right way." Delivering results in this area is about the structural soundness, performance, reliability, and dependability. These are the expected nonfunctional requirements.

- *Wish List:* The things that are desired or wished for is the third aspect to focus on. Working on outcomes in this quadrant is about delivering "the desirable items." Delivering results in this area is about adding functionality that users and customers are hoping for. These are beneficial features and functionality.

- *Craftsmanship:* Uncommon quality is the fourth aspect to focus on. Working on outcomes in this quadrant is about delivering with "superior experience and expertise." Delivering results in this area is about things like technique, insight, anticipation, and future-proofing. This produces surprising quality.

It is with these four quadrants in mind that the objectives, metrics, and expected value can be sorted out. Since all these aspects are important, objectives within each should be established. List all the objectives and how they relate to a focus area. Find ways to monitor or evaluate or otherwise measure each of them. Be sure to point out how too much focus on one quadrant reduces the focus on another. Short-term pressures will push out long-term value. Remember that the things customers or users value today are not what they value in the long term.

▓ **Practice 3-10** Compare Results to the Objectives, Metrics, and Focus Areas

---

This practice applies to either an individual or a team. Find a way to compare your results to the objectives. For example, a primary objective is to make sure the feature allows users to get their job done. Find a way to compare results with a metric or measure. For example, all of the project's minimal and recommended .NET framework guidelines are followed. Find a way to compare results to a focus area. For example, what has been completed so far needs to be tested under heavy use to be sure the system can scale properly. Positive outcomes are about more than immediate results; they are about achieving superior quality and exceeding expectations both in the short term and in the long term.

Trends

The desired results need to be viewed from more than just a single point in time. The trend over time is also very important. A graph that shows the trend communicates the rate of improvement. People have a difficult time appreciating the relationship between events that are disconnected in time. A trend graph can show how a better practice is slowly delivering the desired results. Conversely, it can show how the situation has deteriorated over time in the absence of an important practice. It is important to keep track of the results over time. It is important to know how the current situation relates to the past.

Trends help identify practices that work and those that do not work. Trends identify systemic problems, points of variation, and leading indicators. For example, if a graph that tracks the number of passing automated tests unexpectedly drops then it is an indicator that something noteworthy has changed. It might not be terrible, but it is important and worth investigating. If it is detrimental to the project then the change in trend sounded the alert. The burn down chart used in agile software development is an example of an important trending technique.[4] The burn down chart shows how completed work is being accomplished over the course of the sprint and compares the actual outcomes to sprint planning and expectations.

▓ **Practice 3-11** Visualize Trends to Understand and Appreciate Progress over Time

---

[4] For more information see `http://en.wikipedia.org/wiki/Burn_down_chart`.

Take some time to ensure that results data is collected at regular intervals. Use effective charts and graphs to visualize the trends. The goal is to understand how the situation is changing over time. It is important to create in your mind and the minds of others an appreciation for progress, abrupt change, or the need for improvement.

Summary

In this chapter you learned about achieving desired results. The first section discussed the success conditions and how all project participants need to take an active part in the project. The chapter also covered the importance of raising awareness and acknowledging gaps in knowledge, skill, and attitude.

You learned about the importance of common understanding. This chapter covered several specific techniques that foster agreement and draw out differences in understanding that might exist. These techniques included wireframe diagramming, documenting the architecture, creating report mockups, insisting on detailed examples, and building an archetype.

You learned about the importance of deliverables as opposed to activities. Special attention needs to be paid to both the short-term and the long-term positive outcomes of satisfaction and quality. In the final analysis, achieving desired results is measured against the objectives, key metrics and measures, and the overall value.

CHAPTER 4

Quantifying Value

Adopting better practices is about adding value to the development process. Common sense says that development is more effective when you follow sound principles, good practices, established guidelines, and known success paths. Similarly, development is more effective when you avoid erroneous ideas, bad practices, mistaken techniques, and failure paths. Unfortunately, common sense is not common practice. Switching to a new and different practice involves a change away from current habits and routines. To provide motivation, it is important and often necessary to quantify the value of a better practice.

This chapter presents the different stakeholder perspectives and how those perspectives influence the perceived benefits of changing a practice. The goal is to learn and understand what each individual or group values. Later, the sources of data are discussed. This includes quantitative and qualitative data, anecdotal evidence, and testimony. The emphasis is on how the data needs to be related back to the audience and their values.

As an individual developer, quantifying the value of adopting a new or different practice is important to justify or explain the change. For example, if you are adopting unit testing, quantifying the value in terms of a lower defect count could strengthen the perceived benefits. As a team leader, decisions you make to adopt a better practice should result in noticeable value for the time it takes to implement the change.

Although this chapter is written from the perspective of someone sitting on the outside of your situation, it is intended to be more than just consultative. However, without knowing your circumstances it is hard to connect in a way that is emotionally relevant to you. In practice, change that comes from inside the project and the organization is better received and longer lasting. The insider-champion helps break the emotional barriers and implements and sustains the change from within. You and your team members are the insiders. Hopefully, you receive this information as a renewed call to get concerned about and positively influence your projects. This chapter should get you fired up and emotionally involved in ways that serve to gain the support of others. This chapter describes specific practices to help with quantifying the value of adopting better development practices. The practices covered in this chapter are summarized in Table 4-1.

Table 4-1. Quantifying Value: Ruthlessly Helpful .NET Practices

	Quantifying Value
4-1	Learn and Understand What Different Stakeholders Value
4-2	Identify Financial Measures and Start Tracking Them
4-3	Connect Improved Practices to Improved Manageability

COMMENTARY

When I first started advocating best practices I made bold assertions, such as unit testing will yield higher quality. What I did not realize was that if my goal was 20% fewer defects, the project manager now expected zero defects. In time, my bold assertion was seen as just another big promise with small results. Even with the same expectations, does a 30% increase in developer time justify a 20% decrease in defects? Today, my advocacy is stated a lot more modestly: "Let's try unit testing and see if anything improves." I have learned to avoid bold assertions like "higher quality," "more affordable," "more maintainable," and "faster to build." I want to underpromise on the benefits and overdeliver on the results. I want the change process to be incremental and iterative. Even if the improvements are modest, the results are concrete and tangible. Bold assertions are abstract and imagined; everyone imagines and expects bold results.

Following a new practice, even if it is a better practice, requires a change from the current status quo to the new status quo. Introducing change is never easy. Everyone needs time to consider the impact of the new practice. People need to learn by experiencing the change before they agree that the change was for the better. The team needs to discuss the change and feel that they are involved before they commit. Get them involved in the discussions on potential changes. Seek agreement on a trial period that does not force the change down their throat. The important point is that a request to quantify the value is often really a diversion. What many people want is a sense of involvement before offering up their commitment.

Recently, I asked a team leader if his team was following a particular best practice. His reply was, basically, "We do not follow that practice. We feel like we wouldn't get significant value for the time it would take to implement." In one sense, he is right to feel that way. If he is not convinced the practice returns sufficient benefit for the time invested then he should not follow it. How do you convince him? One approach is to convince him that the value is more significant than he perceives. Another, convince him that the time to implement is lower than he perceives. If you are a team lead or project manager then a third option is to change the expected results of the team. Certain results, such as a daily NCover report, can only come from following a new practice.

Most people are looking for numbers and facts. Unfortunately, there is little hard data to support the rewards of adopting best practices. It would be nice to be able to point to reliable sources that show things like adopting a particular practice has a 23% return on investment. Sorry to say, these numbers are elusive and often unconvincing. I believe this is because implementing a new and different practice is incremental and iterative. Continuous improvement is about climbing the learning curve and gaining long-term effectiveness. For reluctant, skeptical, or cynical folks, the lack of hard data supports their stance. Since actions speak louder than words, it is important to start making positive changes in areas within your control and influence. Next, quantify the value of those changes. You will likely find that your results demonstrate how the improvements are bearing fruit and showing value.

Value

The term *value* means many things to many people; managers, developers, end-users, and customers. If a manager wants you to quantify the value of following a best practice then it is likely the manager wants an estimate of the financial reward. The manager is looking for a monetary cost-benefit analysis. They are also looking for better ways to manage and control development projects without risking the results they are already getting.

For many developers, the time and effort it takes to implement the practice is a driving cost. Developers want to know the benefits as they relate to getting their work done faster or easier or better. Customers and end-users often look at benefits in terms of more features and better quality. They fear that the practice comes at a cost to them or extends the delivery schedule. They need to know that you appreciate that a new or different practice is not a better practice if it does not fit within the current cost and schedule restraints. Spend the time to learn and understand the values that different stakeholders hold dear and the drawbacks they are concerned about.

■ **Practice 4-1** Learn and Understand What Different Stakeholders Value

---

In any development project there are many different stakeholders and each person may value different things. Let's put the focus on the following themes:

- Financial benefits

- Improving manageability

- Increasing quality attributes

- More effectiveness

Financial Benefits

In general, executive and senior managers are interested in hearing about financial rewards. These are important to discuss as potential benefits of a sustained, continuous improvement process. They come from long-term investment. Here is a list of some of the bottom-line and top-line financial rewards these managers want to hear about:

- Lower development costs

- Cheaper to maintain, support and enhance
- Additional products and services
- Attract and retain customers
- New markets and opportunities

On the other side of the coin is financial risk. This is usually the source of an unstated objection holding a manager back from approving a change. The implicit assumption is that the practice puts productivity and efficiency at risk. Do not ignore financial risk. Address it head on. Identify potential risks and explain how they are going to be mitigated. Whenever possible, advocate new and different practices that are either no cost or low cost, carry few potential risks, or offer powerful benefits.

Every organization is already tracking financial measures. The information may not be available to you, but you probably have indirect measures. The project manager or the accounting department tracks the total number of hours each person works on a project. Effort, measured in person-hours, is an indirect measure of cost. For example, attempt to find the total person-hours to find, report, fix, track, and verify a typical bug. You will be surprised at the total effort involved with a typical defect. As an individual developer, the fewer defects you create the more money you save the company. As a team lead, multiply that number by the size of your team. Is 20% fewer bugs worth an increase of 30% in development time? A compelling financial argument might be well within your reach.

■ **Practice 4-2** Identify Financial Measures and Start Tracking Them

---

For a small commercial software development company trying to grow, there may be many financial benefits that interest senior management. Table 4-2 lists a number of direct and indirect measures as they relate to potential financial benefits. Starting from the column on the right, identify the indirect measures that are relevant to your organization and start measuring them. New and better practices ought to improve these metrics. Over time, with better practices, the direct measures will probably improve. Test that hypothesis by asking about the direct measures your organization is tracking. If the results are showing up there, you can connect the dots—although it's not likely you will need to.

Table 4-2. Potential Financial Benefits As They Relate to Direct and Indirect Measures

Potential Benefit	Direct Measure	Indirect Measure
Lower cost of development	Wages, retention rate, contractor invoicing	Effort, defect count, initial support calls, morale
Lower cost of deployed system	Hardware costs, software licensing	Performance, scalability
Total cost of ownership	Total development lifecycle costs	Maintenance effort, support effort, enhancement effort
Revenue	Sales growth, renewal rates,	End-user happiness, positive

Potential Benefit	Direct Measure	Indirect Measure
	competitive advantage	reviews, new features
New customers	Sales to new customers, marketing response statistics	Better features, easier-to-use, improved accuracy
New markets	New product offerings, new countries, consumer sales	Delivering product, better design, globalization

Improving Manageability

Managers are under pressure to perform. This means that they are responsible for accomplishments through the efforts of others. If a change lowers their team's performance, they can expect to be held accountable for the consequences. This pressure puts the focus on managing and controlling in ways that favor the status quo. Ironically, many new and improved practices could actually help managers become better able to manage and control projects.

Project managers are usually the managers closest to the activities of developers. Functional managers, such as a Director of Development, are also concerned with the day-to-day work of developers. For these managers, important values spring from general management principles, and they seek improvements in the following areas:

- Visibility and reporting

- Control and correction

- Efficiency and speed

- Planning and predictability

- Customer satisfaction

░ **Practice 4-3** Connect Improved Practices to Improved Manageability

---

Table 4-3 illustrates the relationship between a new development practice and the expected improvement in project manageability. This table is not a comprehensive list of practices and the manageability they offer, but it should provide you with a place to start. The important point is that quantifying the value to many managers is about connecting the development practice to the principles they value. This is especially true if the practice gives them something that they do not already have; the capability to manage and control projects.

Table 4-3. Development Practices and Improved Manageability

Development Practice	Improved Manageability
Continuous integration	Visibility and reporting, control and correction
Automated testing	Control and correction, efficiency and speed
Automated deployment	Visibility and reporting, control and correction, efficiency and speed
Mockups	Planning and predictability, customer satisfaction
Code analysis	Control and correction, visibility and reporting

Increasing Quality Attributes

End-users and customers are generally interested in deliverables. When it comes to quantifying value they want to know how better practices produce better results for them. To articulate the benefits to end-users and customers, start by focusing on specific topics they value, such as

- More functionality
- Easier to use
- Fewer defects
- Faster performance
- Better support

The message to communicate is that by following better practices the team will produce a better product. That common sense message needs to be supported by enough detail to make it clear that customer satisfaction and quality are the team's goal.

▨ **Practice 4-4** By Definition, Better Practices Deliver Better Products

---

Table 4-4 shows a list of general quality attribute categories. Those in the left-most column are commonly referred to as FURPS: *functionality, usability, reliability, performance,* and *supportability.* There are certainly many more, such as localizability. (You can extend the list of categories as needed.) In the column just to the right of the FURPS are examples of specific components within each category. In the right-most column there is a list of development practices that relate to each FURPS category. By presenting specific details in a table, such as Table 4-4, you make it clear to end-users and customers how better development practices deliver better products.

Table 4-4. *General Quality Attributes Related to Development Practices*

FURPS	Specific Components	Development Practices
Functionality	Current feature set, new features, security, new capabilities	Wireframe mockups, report mockups, continuous integration, unit testing, security testing
Usability	Aesthetics, consistency, ease-of-use, tooltips	Wireframe mockups, report mockups
Reliability	Correctness, frequency of error, downtime	Code analysis, unit testing, stability testing, automated deployment
Performance	Speed, response time, throughput	Performance testing
Supportability	Lower effort/time to extend features, shorter turnaround time for bug fixes	Code analysis, unit testing, stability testing

More Effectiveness

Developers and team leads are generally interested in individual and team effectiveness. Quantifying the value of better practices to developers is a lot easier if the emphasis is on increasing effectiveness. The common sense argument is that by following better practices the team will be more effective. In the same way, by avoiding bad practices the team will be more effective. Developers are looking for things to run more smoothly. The list of benefits developers want to hear about includes the following:

- Personal productivity

- Reduced pressure

- Greater trust

- Fewer meetings and intrusions

- Less conflict and confusion

■ **Practice 4-5** Use Common Sense to Justify Improving Common Practice

---

Common sense reasoning is certainly not the whole story. Justification has another component. Changing to a new or different practice involves a change in habits. At this point it comes back to knowledge, skill, and attitude. For example, if writing unit tests is not an established habit then getting into the habit takes some time and patience. The need for patience is important. Also, developers ought to have some time to practice and develop skills. Developers need to experience the change before they accept the benefits. Quantify the value of new and different practices by using a combination of common sense arguments and learning by experience.

One very good metaphor that makes a lot of sense is the notion of technical debt (introduced in Chapter 2).[1] The principle behind technical debt is that many development decisions have implicit or hidden long-term negative consequences that exceed the short-term benefits. The short-term convenience pushes out long-term advantage. A shortcut causes long-term detriment. There is always future reckoning. The consequences of all the accumulated technical debt can be very severe. Technical debt is often taken on without intention. Often it builds up from a lack of awareness, unwillingness to acknowledge the deficit, or understating the potential impact. To be more effective the development team must accumulate technical debt judiciously. Table 4-5 presents one way to chart technical debt as it accumulates. Each development practice is carefully considered, one by one. There are five shown in Table 4-5.

Let's consider the first one, continuous integration, as an example. The development team considers the short-term reward of not practicing continuous integration. Since there is no CI server, there is no time spent setting up and configuring the CI server. Developers save time by deferring and ignoring any potential integration issues; no time is wasted contemplating integration. However, not following the continuous integration practice does have long-term risks. It is likely that there will be a much longer integration period. The team is probably going to spend time resolving issues or redesigning components. The amount of time and effort is both unavoidable and unpredictable. In the end, integration must occur and all integration issues will have to be resolved. It is quite clear that continuous integration offers significant value in areas like problem prevention, better design, and greater predictability.

Table 4-5. *Technical Debt Accumulation Chart*

Development Practice	Short-Term Reward	Long-Term Risk	Inevitability
Continuous integration	No CI server, no time spent integrating	Much longer integration period, time spent resolving issues	Must be paid in full
Wireframe mockup	Less dialog, shorter meetings	Missed expectations, finger pointing	Must be paid in full
Unit testing	No time spent writing test code, greater apparent productivity	Careless mistakes, integration issues, regressed functionality	Must be paid in full
Code analysis	No time spent analyzing	Violations of guidelines, poor maintainability, no problem prevention	Long-term debt
Automated deployment	No time spent automating	Configuration headaches, reoccurring mistakes, unpredictable deployments	Must be paid in full

---

[1]See http://www.martinfowler.com/bliki/TechnicalDebt.html.

Sources of Data

To quantify something you need data. This section is about identifying and tracking down that data. Let's focus on looking at the following three sources of data:

- Hard numbers

- Observations

- Anecdotes and testimony

Once the data is collected, it needs to be analyzed and understood. The goal is to find the meaning behind the data. Some things to consider:

- *Relevant*: Is the data related to one or more development practice?

- *Correlated*: If a practice is changed, is the data changing in an associated way?

- *Noticeable*: Is a change in a practice going to without a doubt change the data?

With the data and the analysis one or more conclusions are made and the results presented. It is the data that ultimately makes it possible to make and support conclusions that quantify the value of improving development practices.

Quantitative Data

In a broad sense, quantitative data involves numbers that can be measured. Many people feel that quantitative data is *hard* data because it is numeric and measurable. Since the numbers are collected and quantified, the data seems objective and rational. Quantitative data may be correct as a collection of measurements, but it is the interpretation that gives the data meaning. For example, a method that has a very high cyclomatic complexity (a code quality metric covered in Chapter 11) frequently indicates that the method is hard to maintain, but that is not always the case. If that method contains a very large `switch` statement then the cyclomatic complexity measure has a high numeric value, but a code review might decide that the method is reasonable and maintainable. The cyclomatic complexity measure prompting a code review is a good thing, but it should not always force a redesign or rewrite.

░ **Practice 4-6** Collect and Track Metrics and Numbers

Collecting and tracking quantitative data is valuable; facts are hard to argue with. Table 4-4 presents a list of the types of quantitative data to collect and some example measures. Remember, these numbers are facts. Collect and track this data with the intention of understanding the facts with analysis. They also support decisions, retrospectives, and learning. In Chapter 11 the discussion of static code analysis presents NDepend, which is a product that computes many quantitative measures.[2] Tracking these metrics can support manageability. For example, the measure of non-blank, non-commented lines of code (NCLOC) may seem unimportant for development; however, NCLOC correlates to the overall size

---

[2] Scott Hanselman provides a great overview of the NDepend metrics in a blog post at `www.hanselman.com/blog/EducatingProgrammersWithPlacematsNDependStaticAnalysisPoster.aspx`.

of the software system. In this way, tracking NCLOC helps to gauge overall progress. Using NCLOC, data can be normalized by calculating various relative-size ratios. It may be helpful to track the total number of unit tests divided by the NCLOC number for the code-under-test. Projects that write a lot of unit tests but only focus on the percentage coverage see a high initial test-count to NCLOC ratio if testing is thorough. If unit testing thoroughness drops dramatically then the ratio drops because unit tests that test boundary conditions and corner cases are being neglected.

Table 4-4. Types of Quantitative Data with Examples of Numeric Measures

Type of Data	Examples of Numeric Measures
Quantities	Test count, number of developers, builds-per-day, defects-reported-per-day, defects-fixed-per-day
Size	NCLOC, deliverablefile size, database size
Duration	Build time, deployment time, load time, project duration, time-to-code feature
Effort	Developer person-hours, tester person-hours, analyst person-hours, technical services person-hours, customer support person-hours, salesperson person-hours
Cost	CI server hardware, CI server software licenses, productivity tools, code analysis tools, code coverage tools, design analysis tools
Code quality metrics	Cyclomatic complexity, defects per NCLOC, percentage coverage, afferent and efferent coupling, depth of inheritance tree

Just as important is how the data is presented and interpreted. Draw careful conclusions. Make sure those conclusions are consistent with everything you know and believe about the circumstances. Shown in Table 4-5 are the counts of the number of classes under six namespaces. The counts are then broken down by ranges of maximum cyclomatic complexity (CCMax). In this example, the guideline is that classes with methods where CCMax is higher than 15 are generally harder to understand and maintain. Classes that have methods with a CCMax higher than 30 are particularly complex and should be split in smaller methods or redesigned. This example data is collected from NCover output reports. Unfortunately, the data in the table is tedious to collect and interpret. Figure 4-1 illustrates the same data in Table 4-5, but it is shown as a dashboard report.

Table 4-5. Example Data: Number of Classes and Maximum Cyclomatic Complexity

Namespace	No. of Classes	CCMax < =15	CCMax <= 30	CCMax > 30
Financial	29	15	11	3
Data Access Object	27	27	0	0
Model	15	13	2	0

Namespace	No. of Classes	CCMax < =15	CCMax <= 30	CCMax > 30
Web MVC Controllers	11	11	0	0
Data Access Layer	9	9	0	0
Common	10	0	5	5

The dashboard report in Figure 4-1 is generated and displayed with the continuous integration server. An MSBuild script reads the NCover XML, processes the data using XPath, and uses XSLT to generate the HTML report. This approach takes the quantitative data and provides an at-a-glance picture, which reveals the code complexity. With this information the team leader knows the classes within both the Financial and Common namespaces that warrant further code review. The project manager has visibility into these areas of complexity and appreciates the need to review the code.

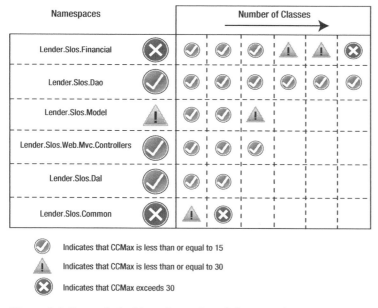

Figure 4-1. Example dashboard: number of classes and maximum cyclomatic complexity

Figure 4-2 illustrates how charting quantitative data helps coordinate between development objectives and management objectives. The solid line is the actual percentage coverage of the unit tests written to test the code developed during the Lender SLOS Upgrade project. The dashed line shows the trend. The developers are working to meet the following code coverage objectives:

- Greater than 60% coverage after 30 working days
- Greater than 75% coverage after 60 working days

• Greater than 85% coverage after 90 working days

Based on the data presented in the chart, there is now a clear retrospective story to relate. The first two objectives are met because of a surge in effort. Tracking the coverage percentage provides positive reinforcement to the developers. The project manager is looking for results and progress in this indicator of structural quality.

The trendline shows three stages of interest. The first is the early stage when developers are learning to write effective unit tests during the first 30 days. The second stage is the leveling off in the 30 to 60 day period. New code and new unit tests are added with continued practice and skill development occurring. The third stage represents a renewed effort based on new approaches and insight into how to write unit test code effectively. After 70 working days the symbol coverage percentage is at 92.9%. This is well ahead of plan.

The practice of code analysis, in this case measuring coverage percentage, is very useful and worthwhile. It is clear that the quantitative data helps explain the value of this practice.

Figure 4-2. Tracking percent coverage over time

Qualitative Data

Qualitative data deals with descriptions that can be observed but not measured. For example, when an end-user looks at a new web page design and describes its appearance, it is qualitative data. The observations are written down and compiled into a qualitative assessment. Qualitative data is subjective. Surveys are an effective way to take descriptions and observations and compile the results into charts and statistics. In effect, the qualitative data is projected into numeric measures. Unfortunately, a good survey is hard to design, conduct, and compile. It is unlikely to be helpful to start a lot of surveying to quantify the value of adopting better practices.

Since qualitative data is useful, a good strategy is to start collecting descriptions and observations. The principle to follow is to ask questions that evoke far-reaching answers. For example, ask the developers: is the source code elegant or is it ugly? Listen to the descriptions that come back in response. You might hear a lot of complaints, but you ought to dig in to gather specifics. Collect and track the descriptions and observations. The responses and discussions are likely to center on general qualitative topics, such as

- Appearance
- Usability
- Satisfaction
- Uncertainty
- Confidence
- Expectation

▓ **Practice 4-7** Collect and Track Descriptions and Observations

---

Table 4-6 provides examples of the kinds of evocative questions that get people relating qualitative descriptions and observations. The question is intended to provoke a response. Capture the response as feedback and qualitative data. Over time, if the better practices are adding value, the responses change. This is an informal survey of key individuals or a consensus opinion. It does not have to be scientific. It is intended to help show a trend in the subjective thinking. Over time, as people feel that they are being heard, the descriptions and observations get more specific and actionable. The important point is that you are tracking the improvements in terms that the respondent values.

Table 4-6. Evocative Questions and Qualitative Responses over Time

Evocative Question	Today	In 30 Days	In 60 Days	In 90 Days
Is the software elegant or is it ugly?	Ugly	Somewhat better	Much improved	Elegant
Is the software straightforward to use or is it cumbersome?	Cumbersome	A little easier	Much easier	Straightforward
Does talking about the software bring forth bliss or upset?	Upset	Less disappointing	Delighted	Bliss
Is the software being built with predictability or irregularity?	Irregularity	Some regularity	Mostly predictable	Predictability
Are the deployments providing confidence or doubt?	Doubt	Significant concerns	Few reservations	Confidence

Evocative Question	Today	In 30 Days	In 60 Days	In 90 Days
Is the software acceptable or insufficient?	Insufficient	Basic features	Many new features	Acceptable

Anecdotal Evidence

Anecdotal evidence helps when there is not enough other information available to quantify the value of a practice. An anecdote is a story that describes what happened under a particular set of circumstances. It is a one-sided story. To be evidence, the anecdote must be both true and verifiable. To be useful, the anecdote must provide information that helps the reader draw a meaningful conclusion.

There are two forms of anecdotal evidence that many find convincing: success stories and testimonials. The success story concentrates on the description of the experience, and the testimonial focuses on the credibility or the relevance of the source. Here are three examples of success stories that many managers find convincing:

- *Automated testing*: With automated testing, a very thorny bug was detected early in the development process and the problem was resolved by fewer people in a shorter amount of time. The bug was resolved before it made it to QA. The issue was resolved in 1.5 hours by the developer who introduced the problem. By most accounts it would have taken several people, both testers and developers, days to reproduce, diagnose, and resolve the issue if it had made it to QA.

- *Automated deployments*: The new automated deployments are much, much faster than the previous manual deployments. Deployment times have dropped from a range of 8 to 18 hours down to about 2 to 4 hours. The deployments are more reliable and more predictable. Because the maintenance window is shorter, deployments are less inconvenient to the end-user. Today, deployments are a great deal less stressful for the people involved.

- *Continuous integration*: With unit tests running in the continuous integration server there is now an acknowledgement that failing tests indicate an issue that needs to be addressed immediately. Developers are running all the unit tests proactively, before pushing code changes. They are fixing the code when they discover an unexpected issue. They are discussing the correct long-term solution to integration issues and recommending design changes to the team lead. The whole project team is actively engaged in improving quality, not just the QA testers.

Take the time to gather and compile the stories of success as new or different practices are adopted. Find ways to share the success stories in conversation, through a blog, or in an e-mail. The experiences of your own organization are naturally credible and relevant. Few people argue with success.

▓ **Practice 4-8** Gather and Share Stories of Success

A good testimonial needs a credible source and a relevant circumstance. If the testimonial is from an outside expert then that person's expertise and experience ought to be appreciated. If your organization is using Agile then the authors of *The Agile Manifesto* ought to be credible.[3] In Appendix A there is a list of books and articles by many well-respected authors and best practices advocates.

Testimonials from an end-user or customer are often a lot more credible and relevant than the opinion of an outside expert. These are stakeholders. If an end-user is happy with the results then that speaks very loudly. Happy customers are important because customers vote with their checkbook and managers never forget that fact.

⬛ **Practice 4-9** Pull Together Testimonials from Customers and Experts

---

Summary

Quantifying value is about knowing what others value and making arguments that make rational sense to them. For many, hard data is crucial. Since there is such variability from situation to situation, the only credible numbers are the ones your organization collects and tracks. It is a good practice to start collecting and tracking some of those numbers and relating them to the development practices that are showing improvements. Beyond the number, there are many observations and descriptions that support the new and different practices. It is time to start describing the success stories and collecting testimonials. Communicate how each improvement is showing results in many positive ways.

In this chapter, you learned about quantifying the benefits of new and different practices. You saw how senior managers, front-line managers, end-users, and developers often have different definitions for the value. Remember that what one group perceives as valuable, another might not value. You learned about the many sources of supporting data. You saw how indirect measures, qualitative data, and anecdotal evidence can blend together. You learned how to make the connections between the development practice, the conclusions from the data, and the values of others.

In the next chapter, you will learn about the importance of the many aspects of strategy. Too often developers are focused on tactical issues and implementing solutions. Strategy is about understanding problems, high-level planning, setting objectives, and gaining important insights. When you truly, fully understand the strategic situation then the better practices present themselves.

---

[3] See http://agilemanifesto.org/authors.html.

CHAPTER 5

Strategy

This chapter is about new and different practices that have strategic implications. The definition of strategy that this chapter's title refers to is "a plan, method, or series of maneuvers or stratagems for obtaining a specific goal or result: a strategy for getting ahead in the world.[1]" And so, ironically, this chapter provides you with *tactics* to help you focus on *strategy*.

In this chapter we focus on three strategic areas related to better development practices:

- *Awareness*: Make changes that improve perception and consciousness.

- *Personal process*: Make changes at the individual level.

- *Leverage*: Make changes that produce big results.

Even software projects that have every advantage can fail to deliver the desired results. The project can have the latest tools and technology. The team may be very well qualified. Everything might appear to be set up for success. However, the strategic questions are short-changed. In a rush to get the developers to the task of writing code, something important is missed. The developers do not know the strategy. Big questions remain in the developers' minds, such as

- What are the objectives we are trying to meet?

- Why are we trying to meet those objectives?

- Who wants us to meet those objectives?

- How can we best meeting those objectives?

The developers need to know the answers to these questions—clearly, correctly, and completely. Many projects dive quickly into the day-to-day, focus on technical minutiae, and waste time on other unimportant topics. Opportunities to focus on strategy are missed because they are pushed out by proximate, pressing issues. What is truly important, like answers to the strategic questions, is neglected. The practices listed in Table 5-1 are intended to move the focus back to strategy to the benefit of the whole project.

---

[1] Source: http://dictionary.reference.com/browse/strategy.

Table 5-1. Strategy: Ruthlessly Helpful .NET Practices

	Strategy
5-1	Use Brainstorming to Generate Ideas and Unleash Creativity
5-2	Planning Is Essential: Organize and Consider How to Best Meet Objectives
5-3	Add New and Better Ways to Monitor Conditions and Events
5-4	Communicate Repeatedly, Proactively, and Effectively
5-5	Plan the Effort to Build Capacity and Increase Ability
5-6	Establish Habits That Increase Teamwork and Release Creativity
5-7	Plan Tasks to Steadily Build Capacity and Increase Ability
5-8	Automate As Many Manual Steps As Possible
5-9	Develop Alert Systems to Help Make Adjustments

COMMENTARY

In my early days as a software developer, there was something I could never figure out. Why is it that two people can see exactly the same facts and come to different conclusions? To me there seemed to be no rational explanation. Why was this happening? In a design meeting I would argue, "Obviously, we need to do it my way, not your way. Look at the facts; mine is the better way." Then it dawned on me. Most of the disagreements were not about the facts. The conflict centered on differences of opinion and relative value. Each person had their opinions. One person valued one thing and another valued something else. Many developers are like this. The rationale I came to accept is that every developer arrives at a meeting with different experiences and knowledge. Underlying many of the strong opinions is a foundation of knowledge and expertise. Suddenly, my goals changed. I focused less on the facts and more on understanding the other developers' experience and know-how. I gained a new awareness and began to learn a lot from other developers.

While working for a commercial software company, I built a module for the mapping software. This was a core piece of functionality. I knew that if there was a defect in my work then it was going to be disruptive to other developers and hard to isolate. More importantly, QA would write bugs that would be hard to straighten out. My objective was to fully and completely test the module. I wrote a suite of tests that tested the module in every conceivable way. As I built the module, my manager seemed to think it was taking me too long. I planned. I wrote throwaway prototypes. I wrote a suite of tests as I wrote the code. I debugged the code. I built a suite of integration tests that ran every boundary condition I could imagine. In the end, I met the deadline and the system went to QA for system testing. In the following months there were only two bugs that were caused by a deficiency in that module. One was a small mistake, and the other was a corner-case I had not tested. Each took about 30 minutes to resolve and return to QA. During the team's daily meetings the other developers had long bug queues. I was self-assured and confident in my code. I was not under a lot of pressure and happily fixed bugs in other areas. My commitment to quality paid off; I was proud of my work. Soon after, I was assigned to another project to develop the next generation system.

Today, I have a somewhat regimented development style. These are habits that help me to be more effective. I write unit tests and step through every line of code in the debugger. Before I fix a bug I create a unit test that reproduces the bug. I run the entire application on my development box to make sure the code works as I intend it. Before pushing my changes, I get the latest code, merge changes, run a full rebuild, and make sure that all the unit tests pass. I do all this as part of a long-standing personal process. As I learn about new or better practices, I try them out and add them to my process, if the practice is helpful. When I find that something I am doing does not work, I improve my process. I assume that if I rush the process, I will make mistakes or problems will occur. I know that my personal process is not for everybody. That is fine. My personal process is my way of being careful and thorough. Not everyone appreciates it, but it keeps my defect rate low and my productivity consistent. More importantly, I have more fun writing software than trying to figure out why my code broke the build.

Awareness

The development cycle is full of opportunities to see important information as it emerges. Many of us miss this information, which could be a missed objective, an inadequate design, or a misunderstanding. This lack of awareness leads to future problems. Being able to see things clearly, especially when disconnected by distance or time, is strategically important. The strategy of raising awareness is about elevating the team's ability to perceive and be conscious of key aspects of development, such as

- *Patterns*: Things that repeat in some predictable way and present broad solutions to these common, reoccurring issues

- *Events*: Occurrences of some significance that are worth considering with regard to preventing problems, resolving issues, or improving a process

- *Conditions*: The state of things that point to instability, degradation, or a general need for improvement

- *Failure Paths*: Known causes of failure or processes that are likely to lead to failure

Perception is only one part of awareness. The other part is consciousness. You have to think about what it is that you see and hear. The thought process develops your reactions and choices. Information about code quality, for example, could be a warning sign that points to a real problem that is important to address immediately. On the other hand, the information could be unimportant. Both knowing there is an issue and knowing how to react to the issue are key elements of awareness.

There is individual awareness—that is, those things you are aware of or another person is aware of—and there is the group's awareness. Both are important. You may know there is an issue and believe it is significant. However, the rest of the team might not believe it is important. Generally speaking, communication is the way to handle differences in awareness. Through one-on-one and group dialog, knowledge and understanding improves for all. Perhaps each person perceives the situation differently because each has different experiences. You might see a pattern because you have read about the pattern. The important point is that effective communication is the strategic practice that raises the alertness of the whole team.

Brainstorming

There is something about the human brain that often makes it hard to do two things at one time. Talking and listening seems to be one of them. Understanding a significant, complex problem and solving that problem is another. For many tricky issues it is not until after you fully understand the problem that effective solutions present themselves. These problems have many variables, a lot of interrelated components, and hidden implications. To solve the problem, you must be aware of so many different things. Brainstorming opens the mind and engages the imagination. Ideas are spontaneously created and captured. Creativity takes over. The practice of brainstorming raises an awareness that allows people to see and hear new information.

▓ **Practice 5-1** Use Brainstorming to Generate Ideas and Unleash Creativity

---

No matter how intelligent or experienced a person is, everyone benefits from collaboration. It is one of the principles behind code reviews, pair programming, and the Coding Dojo.[2] Our ideas and thoughts are complemented or challenged by the ideas and thoughts of others. When you learn about the relevant experiences of others, the depth and quality of your thinking improves. Brainstorming is a way to facilitate this collaboration of ideas and experiences. Performed in a group setting, brainstorming techniques elicit new opinions and understandings that often help make the entire group more effective.

Many brainstorming techniques are useful for both an individual and a group setting. Table 5-2 contains a list of different ways to engage the imagination and generate new thoughts and opinions. On the Internet, there are many excellent sources of brainstorming techniques; take some time to try a few individually or in groups.[3]

Table 5-2. Brainstorming Techniques: Ways to Unleash Creativity and Openness

Name	Application	Getting Started	Rationale
Remove the Software	Business process, Workflow analysis	Ask how the business would accomplish its work without software or computers.	Focus on the business problem. Gain an understanding of the problem that is independent of the software solution.

---

[2] Developers sharpen their skills by performing a Code Kata (http://codekata.pragprog.com/) together.
[3] For a list of wide-ranging brainstorming techniques see http://celestinechua.com/blog/25-brainstorming-techniques/.

Name	Application	Getting Started	Rationale
Delphi Method	Exchange of opinions, decision making	Each group member submits written thoughts and opinions. A facilitator presents the ideas for the group to discuss and rank.	People improve their thoughts with the opinions and ideas of others. Anonymous opinion is more spontaneous and blunt.
Think About Yourself	Improve code quality, clearer to read, easier to maintain	Imagine that you just joined the project and now have to maintain the code. How specifically would you write the better code?	Generate some empathy today for the maintenance developers of tomorrow. Focus on reducing complexity and obfuscation.
Backward Pass	Positive outcomes, preparation, completeness	What needs to be ready before delivering or deploying? What ought to be rehearsed?	Identify things that need to be done that might otherwise be forgotten or rushed.
Planning Poker	Estimation, find differences	Use "voting cards" to reach a consensus on rough estimates and relative size of scope.	Focus less on topics of consensus. Outlier opinion and reasons explained to the group.

Planning

The process of planning is actually a series of activities, which organize thinking about reaching a goal or meeting objectives. By planning things out, the team considers the mandatory or preferred sequencing of development activities. Thought is given to estimates of effort and timelines. Obstacles and dependencies are more apparent. Assumptions and preconditions can also be explored. The process of planning raises awareness. Everyone has a chance to see the high-level plan. The team is conscious of what the project is about and what needs to be done.

A second element of planning is the plan-of-approach. For example, the architecture of the system is the technical plan-of-approach. It is developed through engineering analysis. The planning is about considering different options and making choices based on how best to meet the objectives. Take time to map out the approach at a high-level view of development topics, such as

- Tools and technologies
- Architecture and design patterns
- Components and modules
- Dynamics and interactions
- Deliverables and deployment

≋ **Practice 5-2** Planning Is Essential; Consider and Organize Around How to Best Meet Objectives

---

Sometimes overlooked, another part of planning is the idea of motivation. A project is done for someone or for some purpose. In the end, the project ought to serve an end-user or customer. During the planning process it is important to have an individual involved who can speak with the "customer voice." In Agile development, that person is the product owner. Perhaps the best reason to have the product owner involved in planning is that that person can speak to the priorities and objectives of the end-user or customer. The product owner helps guide the planning toward the project's goal. It is the product owner who keeps the team aware while planning.

Planning makes everyone aware of the proper sequencing and what was considered and selected. By having everyone on the same page, individuals make decisions that line up with the decisions within the team. Through planning, different teams make decisions that line up with other teams.

Monitoring

In software, things are monitored by knowing conditions or events. As events occur or conditions change, the software reacts or responds. Monitoring is the software's "awareness" of the state of the system. The same is true for the development process. With monitoring, the team is aware of conditions and events that improve development practices. For example, failing unit tests let the developer know that code is probably not working as intended.

▨ **Practice 5-3** Add New and Better Ways to Monitor Conditions and Events

---

Many of the development practices described in this book improve monitoring. The monitoring is intended to alert the team to a potential problem. However, not every condition or event is a problem. The idea is that the monitoring is alerting you to an issue. You perceive a *potential* problem. You are conscious of where the issue is and where to start investigating. For example, a failing unit test could mean there is a mistake in the source code, but it could also mean that the test code is wrong. The key benefit is that, whatever the cause, a change or correction is needed.

Over time monitoring becomes more and more valuable only if false alarms are rare. Each alarm ought to be meaningful. Initially, the automated tests that are written by the developers may generate false alarms. That does not mean you should stop running the tests. It means the tests need to be written more effectively. In Chapter 8 there are many specific practices that help improve test code.

Review the monitoring practices from time to time. Be sure that those practices can detect the proper conditions and events that alert the team to problems. Find ways to reduce the noise of false alarms.

Communication

Many development team leaders lament the fact that they spend so much time communicating. Ironically, under-communicating is usually the problem. In the beginning, the team lead does not send enough e-mails. The team lead does not keep an eye on whether the team is meeting objectives. Code reviews do not happen. Then, suddenly, the team lead is swamped by a tidal wave of communication that surrounds misunderstandings and missed expectations. As a team lead, if you do not feel like you are over-communicating then you are probably not communicating enough. You can find different approaches to keep it from being repetitive, but you must get the message out and confirm that it is received and understood correctly.

As a team member, there are many effective ways to ask for and get the communication you need. Ask the questions that need to be asked. You may be confused, so ask for an explanation. Another way is to send an e-mail to the team lead that both provides your status and indirectly asks an important question. For example, "I am almost done with the bug fixes for the Loan Payment Calculator screen. My bug queue is empty. Unless there is something you think I should be working on, this afternoon I will start helping Pat with the Quarterly Report." This message has the virtue of explaining your status and making a proposal. The e-mail provides the team lead with information to act upon and lets him know what you plan to do next.

■ **Practice 5-3** Communicate Repeatedly, Proactively, and Effectively

---

The whole topic of communication is quite vast. There are many things to learn and understand about how people communicate, and this section cannot cover it adequately. However, one insight to gain is that, through communication, the thoughts that are in your mind need to make it into another person's mind. To make matters worse, many fundamental assumptions are often not made explicit; what is in your mind is not at all what is in the other person's mind. For example, in a discussion on upgrading the object-relational mapping (ORM) package, the team leader is planning to switch from NHibernate 2.0 to Entity Framework 4.1, but the developers are thinking about upgrading to NHibernate 3.1. The task is always referred to as the "ORM upgrade." The team leader never explicitly said it was a switch to Entity Framework. Miscommunication is amusing when caught early. Caught late, it can be disastrous.

Good, effective communication is of strategic significance. It is something worth getting right. Poor communication leads to misunderstandings, hurt feelings, and inefficiencies. Communication is helped by drawing diagrams, asking questions, meeting face-to-face, listening carefully, and articulating concepts clearly. Much of this is common sense but not common practice. Combine many different techniques together and know not to short-change communication. Here are examples of how multiple practices combine:

- *Architecture*: Communicates with visuals and diagrams, at an appropriately high level, to give both an overview and multiple views of the system.

- *Convention over configuration*: Communicates by having the developers learn and follow conventions, so developers need only worry about exceptions.

- *Archetype*: Communicates a model of how the architecture works and provides software examples to emulate.

- Unit testing: Communicates detail design and how the code is intended to work in a way that can easily be run in the debugger.

There is such a thing as unhelpful communication. Inviting individuals or groups to meetings that they can skip is a typical example. Their attendance at the meeting is a waste of their time, or worse, the meeting could needlessly alarm or alienate them. Joel Spolskey offers a good description of the various forms of unhelpful communication.[4] To avoid unhelpful communication, sort out the boundaries for the communication by considering these questions:

---

[4] See http://www.inc.com/magazine/20100201/a-little-less-conversation.html.

- Who is the audience that needs to know this information?

- What is the audience expected to understand?

- How can the information be best conveyed?

- Why is the information useful or needed?

- When is the follow up going to happen?

These types of questions start the thought process regarding different communication options. For example, a blog post that explains a team convention is handy to have many weeks later when a new developer needs to know that same information. Instead of writing an e-mail, write the blog post and send an e-mail containing a link to the blog post. Examples of different ways to communicate are provided in Table 5-3. Try to combine multiple methods to provide a richer fabric of communication.

Table 5-3. *Communication Examples: Who Needs to Know What and Why*

Audience	Expectation	Method	Motivation	Follow Up
Developers	Keep this reference, learn this material, practice this, follow this convention	E-mail, stand up meeting, intranet site, blog post, wiki	To be helpful, establish convention	Walk around and check in, team meeting, follow up e-mail, nagging
Individual	Relate decision, urgent information, change this practice	Phone call, IM, e-mail, one-on-one and face-to-face	Get started, timely adjustment, correct behavior	Go over and check in, one-on-one encouragement
Project Manager	Here is the status	E-mail, stand up meeting, intranet site, tracking software	Show progress, report situation, avoid missed expectations	Ask for questions, dig up comments or concerns
Product Owner	Candid feedback	Team walkthrough, one-on-one	Improvement, recovery, correctness	Omissions, frankness, clarity, inconsistencies
QA Team	Features ready-to-test, defects fixed	E-mail, stand up meeting, defect tracking system	Report situation, avoid missed expectations	Ask for questions, dig up comments or concerns

Personal Process

As individuals we each have a personal process. What we do and how we do it can make us more effective or less effective. As part of an individual strategic practice, you should work to improve your personal process to see improved results. The results you can expect are in higher software quality, greater productivity, better communication, more enjoyment, and a more successful career. An improved personal process starts by making a commitment to excellence.

The practices presented in this book align to the principle of striving toward a more disciplined approach. This approach centers on learning, teaching, growing, and achievement. Consider carefully how to follow practices that deliver results for you and for others. For example, if you are more productive in the mornings then arrange your schedule to get up earlier and arrive at the office earlier. Eliminate distractions and propose later meeting times, whenever possible. Do this to maximize your productive time, which will show results for you and the team. Take a disciplined approach whenever you can.

The early effort you put into a project can pay huge dividends later. There are often slow periods before, between, or in the early stages of projects. Although tired from the last project, this is the time to put in the strategic effort to learn a new technology or development practice. By the same token, completing a successful project requires perseverance. Sticking with a difficult task may not seem worth the stress and strain, and in some projects it is not. However, for most projects the invaluable lessons come in the final push to get the project delivered. Remember that after the project is over, you get to keep the learning and experience. Hopefully you can apply them on your next project. What you gain from the effort and perseverance is of strategic benefit to you and the team.

Commitment to Excellence

There are many small ways to make a commitment to excellence. One way is to carefully double-check your code. Unit testing is a way to ensure that the code works the way you intended. Another is thoroughness. Take the time to consider every eventuality. Think through all the expected and unexpected ways your code could be called. Write unit tests to completely cover these conditions and scenarios. This carefulness and thoroughness has a huge benefit to you. It gives you confidence. You are certain that your code works the way you intend it to work. It is not false bravado; it is true confidence based on preparation and commitment to excellence.

An individual commitment to excellence can extend to the whole team or the entire project. As the developers deliver quality work it builds trust. It is a trust based upon seeing the desired results delivered. There will be defects, to be sure, but they will not be defects of carelessness. If the code does not work properly then it is because there is confusion over requirements or some other misunderstanding. The team's commitment to excellence allows the team to quickly acknowledge the defect and start working toward a solution.

▦ **Practice 5-5** Make a Commitment to Do Careful and Thorough Work

---

The relationship between teams also improves. Developers get more involved in trying to read and understand requirements. They want to do a better job, and so they ask questions, look for inconsistencies, and help uncover omissions. The requirements are clarified and explained. With greater involvement from all teams the overall commitment grows.

To many, all this talk of a commitment to excellence sounds overly optimistic and idealistic. In fact, it is optimistic, and it strives toward an ideal. Improved practices do not come from pessimistic thinking. New and different practices are not adopted by those who are resigned to the status quo. Optimism and a commitment to excellence are a strategic part of moving toward better practices.

Virtuous Discipline

This section is not about the harsh and severe discipline of punishment and control. Virtuous discipline is a valuable and beneficial discipline. It is the discipline of following conventions, improving, coordinating, and achieving. Notice how each of these is done best if done voluntarily. In individuals, this is the result of self-discipline, and for the team it is the result of leadership. In software development, there is a common negative reaction to the idea of team discipline. There is a fear that discipline limits creativity. Virtuous discipline should not limit creativity. Theatre companies and dance troupes have discipline, and they are creative. In fact, with many significant group activities, creativity is unleashed only once a fundamental discipline has been established. Teamwork, collaboration, and creativity are all enhanced once the standards and norms of the group are established. These are good development habits that are advantageous and promote project success.

▓ **Practice 5-6** Establish Habits That Increase Teamwork and Release Creativity

---

Listed in Table 5-4 are topic areas to examine for new and different disciplines and examples for each. The idea is to improve the way you and your team develops software. Develop new habits that have benefits to you and your team. Add more and more with each new project.

Table 5-4. Examples of Virtuous Discipline

Topic Areas	Examples
Learning and Practicing	Learn the habits and norms of role-model developers. Evaluate new tools and technologies. Learn and apply design patterns. Cross-train in quality assurance and project management.
Teaching and Growing	Present know-how within the team. Write tutorials for new developers. Present at a user group. Create checklists for junior developers.
Improving and Changing	Identify new practices. Stop bad practices. Adopt recommendations from retrospectives.

Effort and Perseverance

In difficult projects, the development team ends up exhausted, both mentally and physically. In the final stages, morale is low and mistakes are frequent. It is strategically important to balance the effort and exertion levels so you gradually build capacity and ability, but the work never destroys the developer. This is similar to how a marathon runner should train to run a marathon. The training is hard in the beginning, but once speed and endurance are built up the goal changes to remaining both injury-free and near peak ability. In software development, effort and exertion should increase as capacity and ability increase. Plan the effort curve around the goal of increasing the capacity to produce results.

Since the effort is so often greatest near the end of a project, it is ironic that the most significant and intellectually challenging work is often left to the end. The developers are tired and drained, yet the next major feature set is bigger than the last. It is demoralizing. This is the opposite of the way things should be. When people are fresh and energetic, that is the time to engage the intellect. Plan the effort so that projects start with the intellectual and complex challenges. Save the many straightforward and undemanding tasks for later. Having more time to think and develop the best approach to challenges is important. Also, the amount of work is often greater and the exertion level higher than planned. By tackling all the complicated work first, a more realistic estimate of the remaining effort can be made. What remains may be a lot of work, but it should be uncomplicated and predictable.

▓ **Practice 5-7** Plan Tasks to Steadily Build Capacity and Increase Ability

---

After the software is built and the project is over, many managers believe that all of the value is in the source code. Most of the value is actually in the minds of the developers. They retain all the learning and skill that was needed to build the software. Much of that learning and skill is in general programming, problem-solving, debugging, configuration, and technology. One way to know which developer learned the most is to ask: if you could write the software all over again, what would you do differently? The developer who answers that question thoroughly definitely learned a lot from the project.

In the end, successful projects deliver. What you deliver is an important part of long-term success. The experience of persevering until the software is delivered makes a huge difference to knowing what it takes to see the next project across the goal line. Perseverance pays off for you and your team when the positive outcomes are finally realized. Understandably, developers are often not willing or able to see the project to the end. Those developers often miss out on the rich rewards of seeing a project completed successfully. Coping with the discouragement, opposition, and near failure is an ugly, but important part of software development. Increasing perseverance is a practice well worth improving, but it only seems to come through trial and tribulation.

Leverage

The strategy of leverage is about making a small investment of time and effort to yield a high return in increased capacity to deliver results. The practices in this book are high-leverage practices. For example, a small investment in setting up a continuous integration (CI) server delivers automated builds that can find code integration issues soon after new source code is pushed to version control. (The CI server is discussed in more detail in Chapter 10.) The automated build detects these problems shortly after the issue is first introduced, without anyone having to manually get the latest code and rebuild.

In addition to the specific practices presented in this book, you and your team should be looking for new and different high-leverage practices that may be unique and helpful to your project. Some ideas build upon or improve existing practices, while others use special tools and scripts purpose-built for your project. The CI server affords the team the ability to run build scripts, unit tests, code analysis, and automated deployments. Most CI servers can be configured to run many automated tasks, and include database scripts, UI tests, and notification e-mails. The idea is to leverage automation as much as possible.

With the CI server running code analysis, a lot of data about the quality of the software is generated. If no one regularly reads and thinks about this data, these reports are not very useful. To gain the full value from code analysis there needs to be an early warning system that processes the data and sends out an alert when important thresholds are exceeded. Building alert systems is a high-leverage practice. Look for issues, such as slowing progress or recurring problems, and think of ways to incorporate an early warning into the alert system. Search for the data and indicators that might help detect future issues and incorporate them into the alert system.

Ironically, after a major issue has been resolved, that is when you read or learn about another project that had the exact same issue. It would be nice to never make the same mistake twice. By learning about the experiences of others, you can prevent issues before they happen. Seek out the advice and expertise of other developers. Use their experience as a high-leverage way to avoid difficult, time-consuming problems.

Automation

As a general practice, convert manual processes to automated processes. For example, if after deployment the integration server needs to be manually configured, have the CI server make the configuration changes after an automated deployment. This prevents misconfigurations and eliminates the need to perform the manual steps. Look at every manual step and consider how that step could be automated.

For individual developers, there are many steps that you might not have automated. For example, many developers create a local development database. With a simple batch file and MSBuild script, the database is created and the database scripts are run in the proper order. The sample code in Chapter 8 provides an example of how this is accomplished. In larger projects, many developers manually create the database and manually run scripts to create or alter the database. Developing automated approaches does take time. However, when multiplied by the number of times the manual method is run and the cost of fixing the manual errors, automating the steps is usually worth it.

■ **Practice 5-8** Automate As Many Manual Steps as Possible

For the team leader, automation offers a lot of consistency and saves heartache. Often it is the team leader or a more senior developer who needs to resolve problems created by manual processes. If the server is misconfigured or a developer's database is incorrect then the more experienced team member has to stop and resolve the problem. This reduces the team's overall effectiveness. Instead, provide the team members with simple ways to automate their repetitive tasks. One idea is to have a command file that rebuilds, runs all the unit tests, and performs all the code analysis on the developer's workstation. In this way, the developer is expected to verify that the build will not break before they push their code. The team leader is able to enforce a convention that limits the amount of time wasted by other team members dealing with broken builds and failing unit tests.

Beyond automating the manual steps, there are other ways to automate. One of those ways is through code generation. Entity Framework makes heavy use of code generation.[5] Microsoft is using a code generation strategy and T4 text templates increasingly within Visual Studio and other applications. More and more, the trends are to use metadata gathered through a rich user interface and turn that metadata into source code. If you think about it, that is the same evolution that took us from punch cards in the early mainframes, to console applications in DOS, to graphical user interfaces in Windows. Each is, in effect, using the computer's increasing ability to automate the input/output to change the entire experience and level of productivity. Developers need to look at new and different practices the same way and find uses for automation in more of the day-to-day development work.

---

[5] The EDMX file is used to generate the code. See http://msdn.microsoft.com/en-us/library/cc982042.aspx.

Alert System

The project's alert system provides an early warning for issues, problems, and the need for correction. The continuous integration (CI) server is a foundation upon which you can build an alert system. The CI server collects a lot of data from the build configurations. There are also code quality reports and metrics that the CI server generates. This information can be used to determine key indicators of potential problems. For example, if the number of passing tests drops from 1400 to below 1330 over a two-week period, more than a 5% drop, that drop could be a significant sign. Perhaps one developer is commenting out unit tests rather than fixing them. Code coverage cannot reveal if the logic is properly tested, but it does point to where new code is recently added without any unit tests. The alert system is often most useful to the team lead and the project manager.

The alert system can also help the individual developer. When the CI server gets the latest source code and fails to rebuild, the developer is warned not to get the latest source code until after the build is fixed. Similarly, developers who run the entire suite of unit tests can find issues before pushing their code. This is the alert system identifying a potential problem early enough to prevent disruption and inconvenience to others. For the developer, the various alert systems also include code analysis, quality metrics, and test code coverage.

▓ **Practice 5-9** Develop Alert Systems to Help Make Adjustments

---

Like a compass or navigation system, the alert systems help the team to stay on course by making the proper adjustments. Minor issues are dealt with near to when they first occur. The alert system can keep new problems from creeping into the software and help prevent problems from compounding and perpetuating. Also, the alert system helps the team establish a regular practice of following up on issues. By addressing integration issues and failing unit tests early, the monitoring and notification of an alert system improves the entire development process.

It is important that the alert system does not generate a lot of false alarms. It is important to not ignore a failed build or failing unit test. It is much better to resolve the build or failing test than risk ignoring the alarm. Also, when it comes to code analysis metrics, the values that trigger alerts need to change over time. Often, as the team gets better the thresholds are set higher and higher. The alert system is a strategic part of making sure practices stay improved and continue to improve into the future.

Experience and Expertise

Experiential learning is the kind of understanding that comes from encountering and working through the material. Many things can only be understood through experience. New knowledge is gained through involvement in or exposure to a software technology. Skill is gained through practice with the technology. What is described in writing is enhanced and reinforced by the experience. This is an important part of any person's process. Individual team members need time to incorporate what they have learned into their development practices. An effective strategy for any project is to allow time for new tools and technologies to be practiced.

It is interesting to note that people's attitude improves with experience. Initially, a new practice may seem awkward and unproductive. The same is true for a new software tool set. However, with practice and skill development the attitude starts to change. This is because most people do not like the feeling of incompetence they experience before gaining a comfortable level proficiency. During that early period it is common for people to complain and resist. That resistance does not mean the new or different practice is not a better practice. It means that the person is still learning. Provide enough time and space to allow people to try it, learn it, and develop a level of mastery. If the new practice is a better practice then the skeptic will likely become the advocate.

Developers with expertise have acquired a level of technique and skill. Working with these developers affords you the opportunity to learn from their expertise. Look for ways to tap into that expertise to elevate and improve development practices. As a team leader, look for experts who can consult with and train team members. Propose and promote ways to bring that expertise in to work with the team, either through direct mentoring or training. Many projects adopt better practices once a credible expert takes time to share their experience and know-how. Valuing and benefiting from the judgment and wisdom of experts improves and informs development practices.

Summary

In this chapter you learned about better practices focused on strategy. You learned about the importance of brainstorming as a way to engage the power of imagination and new ideas. You learned how planning prevents significant problems and aligns teams with objectives. In addition, you learned about the strategic importance of building capacity and increasing ability, leveraging automation, and developing early warning systems.

In the next chapter you will learn about important .NET Framework guidelines and conventions. These include widely-accepted standards for .NET applications, and guidelines that encourage developer productivity and consistency.

CHAPTER 6

.NET Rules and Regulations

For some developers, the statement that there are .NET rules and regulations goes too far. But this chapter does not lay down the law in a series of commandments. Development is about creativity, imagination, passion, and inventiveness; it is not about rejecting all convention in favor of individual expression. There are accepted standards and guidelines that are appropriate for you, your team, and your organization. There are generalized statements, principles, and procedures that describe what is true and good in nearly all cases. It is important to sort out those practices that best serve as rules and regulations, as a way to establish norms and to govern behavior, which supports innovative development.

As a developer, following the .NET rules and regulations helps you to remain aligned with good practices and avoid bad practices. As a team leader, the rules and regulations help the members of the team to be consistent and to align with one another. As an organization, the alignment across teams helps achieve compliance with accepted standards, effective development principles, and good practices.

A foolish consistency is not the goal. The goal is a prudent and intentional consistency that helps build upon the experiences and expertise of many .NET developers. The goal is to avoid bad practices, known failure paths, and systemic problems. The goal is to achieve positive outcomes by avoiding the painful and costly mistakes of other developers. By following the advice that underlies the rules and regulations, you benefit from the collective wisdom of expert developers. These are ruthlessly helpful .NET practices for you, your team, and your organization (see Table 6-1).

Table 6-1. *Ruthlessly Helpful .NET Rules and Regulations*

	Practice
6-1	Examine the .NET Coding Standards and Guidelines Others Have Written
6-2	Do Not Catch General Exception Types
6-3	Rethrow to Preserve Stack Details
6-4	Instantiate Argument Exceptions Correctly
6-5	Types That Own Native Resources or Disposable Fields Should Be Disposable
6-6	Dispose an Object Before the Object Loses Scope

	Practice
6-7	Do Not Dispose Objects Multiple Times
6-8	A Constructor Should Not Call Virtual Methods
6-9	Consider Explicitly Defining the Zero-Value Element of an Enumeration
6-10	Prefer Returning an Empty Instance Over Null
6-11	Avoid a Publicly Visible Constant Field
6-12	Sort Out Comments That Do Not Add Value or That Complicate the Code

COMMENTARY

When I sat down to write this chapter I wavered and hesitated on the idea of establishing .NET rules and regulations. First, a complete set of rules and regulations that covers the entire .NET Framework would take an entire book. Second, there cannot be a single set of .NET rules and regulations because many project situations call for variances and exemptions. I came up a few thoughts that I believe are important for you to understand this chapter. The .NET rules and regulations that this chapter focuses on are based on my development experiences. They describe bad practices that caused problems on projects I have worked on. They describe good practices that have keep me and other developers away from trouble. I mention them specifically because I believe they deserve special commendation. The various sources this chapter provides allow you to select and adopt many more based on what you, your team, or your organization needs.

There really are many excellent sources of .NET coding standards and guidelines available today. In the early days of .NET development there was a lot of confusion and uncertainty. Those of us who were C++ developers brought our own set of opinions. Those developers who wrote VB code brought another set of opinions. It was hard work ironing out agreement and establishing the norms. Today things are different. A lot is settled, although areas of disagreement remain. Microsoft provides a lot of direct and indirect guidance through articles, books, MSDN, and other sources. There is a lot of .NET thought leadership and a great deal of .NET community development. As the tools and technologies evolve the challenge will remain to digest and distill this information into a practical field manual of .NET rules and regulations that you can apply today and into the future.

Coding Standards and Guidelines

The Microsoft All-In-One Code Framework (AIOCF) team has established and documented the .NET coding standards and guidelines that that team follows. That document is broad; it covers C++, C#, and VB.NET. The *IDesign C# Coding Standards* document is specific to C#, but covers .NET Framework–specific guidelines that include topics like ASP.NET and web services, data access, and security. The IDesign and AIOCF documents are different in many ways, yet similar in many others. Your team or organization could benefit from adopting one or the other or synergizing them together, or perhaps neither document suits the people and circumstances.

This section has two purposes. First, to provide you with sources and material to develop .NET rules and regulations. Second, to provide specific examples of .NET rules and regulations that—in this author's opinion—are widely-accepted and especially helpful practices. With this information you can assemble and establish the .NET rules and regulations appropriate to your circumstances.

Sources

There are many sources of .NET rules and regulations (see Table 6-2 for a list). Other teams have written coding standards documents and made them widely available. Other organizations have written and published coding standards documents, as well. Some of these sources are short and to the point. Others are very comprehensive with detailed justification and code examples. The most important thing to appreciate is that other experienced developers have put a great deal of thought and discussion into defining these coding standards and guidelines.

■ **Practice 6-1** Examine the .NET Coding Standards and Guidelines Others Have Written

---

The primary virtue of building upon the .NET coding standards and guidelines that others have written is that your rules and regulations can focus on making a statement. Your rules and regulations use emphatic phrases (such as, "Do," "Do Not," "Never," "Avoid," and "Always") and let the source material support the assertions. Remember, the rules and regulations are a lot more likely to be accepted if they are succinct, plain-spoken, and backed up by credible coding standards and guidelines.

It is important to highlight that Microsoft has established the "minimum recommended" rule set that focuses on what they deem the most critical coding problems. These include potential security holes, application crashes, and other important logic and design errors. You should review the Microsoft Minimum Recommended Rules rule set[1] and strive to include these rules in the .NET rules and regulation you create for your projects.

Table 6-2. Sources of .NET Rules and Regulations

Name	Description	More Information
AIOCF .NET Coding Standards	The Microsoft All-In-One Code Framework[2] (AIOCF) project provides excellent documentation on the .NET coding standards and guidelines that the team follows.	1code.codeplex.com
C# Coding Guidelines	A set of coding guidelines for C# that covers development principles and rules.	csharpguidelines.codeplex.com
CAT.NET Rules	CAT.NET is a Microsoft Security tool that helps identify security vulnerabilities.	www.microsoft.com/security/sdl/adopt/tools.aspx

---

1 For more information see http://msdn.microsoft.com/en-us/library/dd264893.aspx.
2 The All-In-One Code Framework is also known as CodeFx.

Name	Description	More Information
Encodo C# Handbook— Conventions, Style, and Best Practices	Covers many aspects of writing C# code, including many widely-adopted conventions and practices.	`http://archive.msdn.micr osoft.com/encodocsharpha ndbook`
FxCop Rules	FxCop is a Microsoft Windows SDK tool that performs static code analysis of .NET assemblies and provides many dozens of rules.	Discussed more in this chapter and in Chapter 13
Gendarme Rules	Gendarme is a Mono-project tool that performs static code analysis of .NET assemblies and provides many dozens of rules.	`www.mono-project.com/Gendarme`
IDesign C# Coding Standards	A concise and direct document that focuses on the essential standards to help enforce best practices, avoid pitfalls, and disseminate knowledge.	`www.idesign.net`
Design Guidelines for Developing Class Libraries	Microsoft guidelines intended to help designers and developers create good class libraries. These guidelines are a resource for many standards documents and are referenced throughout this book.	`msdn.microsoft.com/en-us/library/ms229042.aspx`
ReSharper Code Inspections	ReSharper can apply many hundreds of code inspections to provide continuous code quality analysis that detects issues while writing code.	`www.jetbrains.com/reshar per/features/code_analys is.html`

■ **Note** Much of the .NET rule and regulation verification can be automated using tools associated with some of these sources. Chapter 11 describes practices to automate code analysis using FxCop.

Exceptions

Throwing exceptions is the primary .NET mechanism for reporting errors. Every .NET method, property, event, or other member ought to throw an exception if it cannot successfully fulfill its purpose. In other words, an exception should be thrown if the code execution failed or could not complete through a normal exit path. Also, when there is an error, throw exceptions and do not return error codes.

It is important to know when and how to appropriately set up a try-catch block. In general, only catch the specific exceptions that the code needs and knows how to handle. For example, catch a specific exception if necessity dictates that the code must check for a condition that is likely to occur and handling the exception is appropriate. This can be enforced by Code Analysis rule CA1031, which is part of the Microsoft Basic Design Guideline Rules rule set.

∭ **Practice 6-2** Do Not Catch General Exception Types

Do not swallow errors by writing a catch block that catches all exceptions or catches exceptions as a non-specific exception type, such as System.Exception. Catch only specific exceptions that the code knows how to handle. Do not catch all exceptions and rethrow the exception. Examples of code that violates this practice are illustrated in Listing 6-1.

Listing 6-1. Swallowing Exceptions: Bad Practice

```
// Do not swallow all exceptions
try
{
    return Calculator.ThrowsExceptions(
        principal,
        ratePerPeriod,
        termInPeriods);
}
catch
{
    // Unhelpful message
    Log.WriteError(
        "Generic message: try block did not work");
}

// Do not catch exceptions that the code does not know how to handle
try
{
    return Calculator.ThrowsExceptions(
        principal,
        ratePerPeriod,
        termInPeriods);
}
catch (SystemException exception)
{
    // Misleading message
    Log.WriteError(
        "The principal amount is invalid: '{0}'",
        exception.Message);
}

// Do not catch all exceptions and rethrow them
try
{
    return Calculator.ThrowsExceptions(
        principal,
        ratePerPeriod,
        termInPeriods);
}
```

```
catch
{
    // try-catch block serves no useful purpose
    throw;
}
```

For all exception types that the code expects and knows how to handle write a catch block for those specific exception types. If a general exception type is required to be caught, rethrow the exception as the last statement in the catch block. An example of properly catching general exceptions is illustrated in Listing 6-2.

Listing 6-2. Catching Exceptions: Good Practice

```
// Assumption: the code is required to catch and log all exceptions.
try
{
    return Calculator.ThisMethodThrowsExceptions(
        principal,
        ratePerPeriod,
        termInPeriods);
}
catch (ArgumentException exception)
{
    Log.WriteError(
        "The parameter '{0}' is invalid: {1}",
        exception.ParamName,
        exception.Message);
    throw;
}
catch (InvalidCastException exception)
{
    Log.WriteError(
        "Could not cast properly: {0}",
        exception.Message);
    throw;
}
catch (Exception exception)
{
    Log.WriteError(
        "Unexpected exception: {0}", exception.Message);
    throw;
}
```

■ **Note** Although there are rare cases when swallowing exceptions is acceptable, such cases ought to be cautiously scrutinized and approved by the project's technical leaders.

Depending on the way .NET code rethrows exceptions, important stack information can be preserved or lost. It is important to understand the difference between the throw and throw exception statements.

⬛ **Practice 6-3** Rethrow to Preserve Stack Details

An example of code that catches an exception and incorrectly specifies it when rethrowing the exception is shown in Listing 6-3. This improper rethrow causes the stack trace to point to the throw exception statement, which is not where the error occurred. This can be enforced by Code Analysis rule CA2200, which is part of the Microsoft Minimum Recommended Rules rule set.

Listing 6-3. Rethrowing Exceptions: Bad Practice

```
try
{
    return Calculator.ThrowsExceptions(
        principal,
        ratePerPeriod,
        termInPeriods);
}
catch (ArgumentException exception)
{
    Log.WriteError(
        "The parameter '{0}' is invalid: {1}",
        exception.ParamName,
        exception.Message);

    // Original stack trace is lost
    throw exception;
}
```

Write an empty throw statement when catching and rethrowing an exception. This is the established way to preserve the call stack. The empty throw statement makes sure the stack trace points to the method where the exception originated to help with debugging an error. An example of properly rethrowing an exception is illustrated in Listing 6-4.

Listing 6-4. Rethrowing an Exception: Good Practice

```
try
{
    return Calculator.ThrowsExceptions(
        principal,
        ratePerPeriod,
        termInPeriods);
}
catch (ArgumentException exception)
{
    Log.WriteError(
```

```
                    "The parameter '{0}' is invalid: {1}",
                    exception.ParamName,
                    exception.Message);

            throw;
}
```

It is important to guard a method against invalid arguments passed in from code that calls the method. When writing if-then-throw blocks that validate arguments, the code should throw the most specific exception that is sensible and appropriate.

■ **Practice 6-4** Instantiate Argument Exceptions Correctly

For example, do not throw the base type `ArgumentException` if a null argument is passed. Also, it is a bad practice not to provide the name of the parameter to the exception constructor. Both of these bad practices are shown in Listing 6-5. This can be enforced by Code Analysis rule CA2208, which is part of the Microsoft Basic Design Guideline Rules rule set.

Listing 6-5. Argument Exceptions: Bad Practice

```
if (principal == null)
{
    throw new ArgumentException();
}

decimal principalAmount;
if (!decimal.TryParse(principal, out principalAmount))
{
    throw new ArgumentException();
}
```

If null is passed for the `principal` argument then throw `ArgumentNullException`. Instead of calling the default argument exception constructor, call one of the overloads with the parameter name. Whenever it would be helpful, provide a message to the argument exception constructor that means something to the developer that calls the method. Examples of properly instantiating argument exceptions are shown in Listing 6-6.

Listing 6-6. Argument Exceptions: Good Practice

```
if (principal == null)
{
    throw new ArgumentNullException("principal");
}
```

```
decimal principalAmount;
if (!decimal.TryParse(principal, out principalAmount))
{
    throw new ArgumentOutOfRangeException(
        "principal",
        string.Format("Cannot convert to decimal: '{0}'", principal));
}
```

Disposable Pattern

Using the disposable pattern is the primary .NET mechanism for releasing native and unmanaged resources. The disposable pattern is implemented by implementing the System.IDisposable interface. It is common to declare a separate Dispose(bool) method that encapsulates all the resource cleanup logic so that the logic can be reused for both the System.IDisposable.Dispose method and a finalizer method, if applicable.

░ **Practice 6-5** Types That Own Native Resources or Disposable Fields Should Be Disposable

---

If a class owns native resources or fields that are IDisposable types then the class should implement the IDisposable interface. If the class is not IDisposable then the native resource and fields are not disposed of efficiently. To free up resources, disposable types ought to be disposed of as soon as the class no longer uses them. Listing 6-7 shows the bad practice of declaring a class that owns fields that are IDisposable types, yet the class does not implement IDisposable. This can be enforced by Code Analysis rule CA1049, which is part of the Microsoft Minimum Recommended Rules rule set.

Listing 6-7. Type That Owns Disposable Fields: Bad Practice

```
public class OwnsDisposableFields
{
    private DisposableResource disposableResourceOne;
    private DisposableResource disposableResourceTwo;
    // Other fields continue to be declared here.

    public void OperationThatAllocatesResources()
    {
        disposableResourceOne = new DisposableResource();
        disposableResourceTwo = new DisposableResource();
    }

    ...

}
```

When a .NET type owns native resources or disposable fields, that type should implement IDisposable. To release the unmanaged resources properly, call each of the field's Dispose method from within the implementation of the Dispose method. This is illustrated in Listing 6-8.

Listing 6-8. *Type That Owns Disposable Fields Implements IDisposable: Good Practice*

```
public class OwnsDisposableFields : IDisposable
{
    private DisposableResource disposableResourceOne;
    private DisposableResource disposableResourceTwo;
    // Other fields continue to be declared here.

    private bool disposed;

    ~OwnsDisposableFields()
    {
        Dispose(false);
    }

    public void OperationThatAllocatesResources()
    {
        disposableResourceOne = new DisposableResource();
        disposableResourceTwo = new DisposableResource();
    }

    // The System.IDisposable.Dispose method.
    public void Dispose()
    {
        Dispose(true);

        // Use SupressFinalize in case a subclass of this one
        // implements a finalizer.
        GC.SuppressFinalize(this);
    }

    protected virtual void Dispose(bool disposing)
    {
        // If you need thread safety, use a lock around these
        // operations, as well as in your methods that use the resource.

        // Protect from being called multiple times.
        if (disposed)
        {
            return;
        }

        if (disposing)
        {
            // Clean up all managed resources
            if (this.disposableResourceOne != null)
            {
                // Release managed resources
                this.disposableResourceOne.Dispose();

                // Free the unmanaged resource
```

```
            this.disposableResourceOne = null;
        }

        if (this.disposableResourceTwo != null)
        {
            // Release managed resources
            this.disposableResourceTwo.Dispose();

            // Free the unmanaged resource
            this.disposableResourceTwo = null;
        }
    }

    disposed = true;
    }
}
```

■ **Practice 6-6** Dispose an Object Before the Object Loses Scope

---

It is a bad practice to instantiate a local object of an IDisposable type but not write code to ensure that it is disposed before the object is out of scope. Code that does not dispose an IDisposable object before the object loses scope is shown in Listing 6-9. Whenever possible the object should be explicitly disposed before the object loses scope. This issue can be identified by Code Analysis rule CA2000, which is part of the Microsoft Minimum Recommended Rules rule set.

Listing 6-9. Code That Does Not Dispose an Object Before the Object Loses Scope: Bad Practice

```
var tempFilename = Path.GetTempFileName();

var filestream = File.OpenWrite(tempFilename);

var letters = Encoding.ASCII.GetBytes("Text to write.");
foreach (var letter in letters)
{
    filestream.WriteByte(letter);
}

return tempFilename;
```

The using statement allows the code to declare when objects that implement IDisposable should be properly disposed. The using block wraps the object's scope so as to automatically call the Dispose method after the close of the block to ensure that the object is disposed once it loses scope. This is illustrated in Listing 6-10.

Listing 6-10. The Using Block Ensures That the Object Is Disposed Once It Loses Scope: Good Practice

```
var tempFilename = Path.GetTempFileName();
```

```
using (var filestream = File.OpenWrite(tempFilename))
{
    var letters = Encoding.ASCII.GetBytes("Text to write.");
    foreach (var letter in letters)
    {
        filestream.WriteByte(letter);
    }
}

return tempFilename;
```

■ **Practice 6-7** Do Not Dispose Objects Multiple Times

Nested using statements can cause the Dispose method of an object to be called multiple times. An improperly implemented Dispose method may not expect to be called multiple times, and so, the Dispose method responds by throwing an exception or by behaving badly.

In the example code shown in Listing 6-11, the inner variable declared in the nested using statement has a field that contains a reference to the specializedResource object from the outer using statement. When the nested block completes, the Dispose method of inner then calls the Dispose method of the specializedResource object. Next, the outer using block completes and attempts to dispose specializedResource; this calls the object's Dispose method for a second time. Multiple calls to the Dispose method are not always handled properly and should be avoided. This issue can be identified by Code Analysis rule CA2202, which is part of the Microsoft Minimum Recommended Rules rule set.

Listing 6-11. Code That Calls the Dispose Method Twice: Bad Practice

```
using (var specializedResource = new SpecializedResource())
{
    specializedResource.Initialize();

    using (var inner = new OperatesOnSpecializedResource(specializedResource))
    {
        inner.DoSomething();
    }
}
```

To prevent the Dispose method from being called twice, write code that uses a try-finally block instead of the outer using statement, as shown in Listing 6-12. Once the inner variable is declared, the specializedResource variable is set to null to ensure that the Dispose method is not called on that variable. The finally block contains a guard that makes sure the specializedResource variable is not null before the code calls the Dispose method. This ensures that the Dispose method is called if an exception occurs before inner can take responsibility for the specializedResource object's disposal.

Listing 6-12. Code That Prevents Dispose from Being Called Twice: Good Practice

```
SpecializedResource specializedResource = null;
try
{
    specializedResource = new SpecializedResource();

    specializedResource.Initialize();

    using (var inner = new OperatesOnSpecializedResource(specializedResource))
    {
        // OperatesOnSpecializedResource takes responsibility
        // for SpecializedResource disposal.
        specializedResource = null;

        inner.DoSomething();
    }
}
finally
{
    if (specializedResource != null)
    {
        specializedResource.Dispose();
    }
}
```

Miscellaneous

There are many more practices covering more topics than the ones already covered. This section brings together a miscellaneous set of practices covering a range of topics.

Calling Virtual Methods in Constructors

If an abstract or virtual method is called in the constructor of a base class then the overridden method, which is implemented in the derived class, is called before the derived class's constructor is run. This may be unexpected and improper behavior that can be very difficult to debug. An example of calling a virtual method in the constructor is shown in Listing 6-13. This issue can be identified by Code Analysis rule CA2214, which is part of the Microsoft Minimum Recommended Rules rule set.

Listing 6-13. Constructor Calling a Virtual Method: Bad Practice

```
public class BaseClass
{
    public DateTime CurrentTime { get; protected set; }

    protected BaseClass()
    {
        this.InitializationSteps();
    }
```

```
    protected virtual void InitializationSteps()
    {
        // Base initialization code
    }
}

public class DerivedClass : BaseClass
{
    public DerivedClass()
    {
        this.CurrentTime = DateTime.Now;
    }

    protected override void InitializationSteps()
    {
        // Relies on CurrentTime having been set,
        // but the DerivedClass constructor is not called
        // until after the BaseClass constructor is done.
    }
}
```

▪ **Practice 6-8** A Constructor Should Not Call `Virtual` Methods

A better implementation moves the call to the virtual method out of the base class constructor and into a separate `Initialize` method in the base class. This is shown in Listing 6-14.

Listing 6-14. Move Virtual Method Calls out of the Base Class Constructor: Good Practice

```
public class BaseClass
{
    public DateTime CurrentTime { get; protected set; }

    public bool Initialized { get; private set; }

    protected BaseClass()
    {
    }

    public void Initialize()
    {
        this.InitializationSteps();
        this.Initialized = true;
    }

    protected virtual void InitializationSteps()
    {
        // Base initialization code
```

```
    }
}

public class DerivedClass : BaseClass
{
    public DerivedClass()
    {
        this.CurrentTime = DateTime.Now;
    }

    protected override void InitializationSteps()
    {
        // The CurrentTime has been set
        // before the Initialize method is called.
    }
}
```

Defining a Zero-Value enum Element

The default value of an uninitialized enumeration is zero. Often the code logic is assuming that the enumeration value was explicitly set when it is actually an uninitialized value. For example, the caller of a class did not set the enumeration value of a property, but the method's code cannot make that determination because the zero-value in the enumeration is valid. In the enumeration declaration shown in Listing 6-15 the Beginning enumeration element has an implicit value of zero, which is the same as an uninitialized enumeration, and this coincidence may cause unexpected or erroneous behavior.

Listing 6-15. First Enumeration Element Is Inadvertently Set to Zero: Bad Practice

```
public enum WorkflowStep
{
    Beginning,
    Middle,
    End,
}
```

■ **Practice 6-9** Consider Explicitly Defining the Zero-Value Element of an Enumeration

---

A better practice explicitly defines the zero-value enumeration element, whenever appropriate. This allows methods to write code to guard against uninitialized enumeration values. It also makes it easier to understand the value when debugging the code. This approach is shown in Listing 6-16.

Listing 6-16. Enumeration Zero-Value Is Explicitly Set to 'Unknown': Good Practice

```
public enum WorkflowStep
{
    Unknown = 0,
    Beginning,
    Middle,
    End,
}
```

Returning an Empty Instance

Often the caller of a method or property does not perform a null check on the object that is returned. If your code returns a string or enumeration then it is likely the caller will not check for null before using the object.

■ **Practice 6-10** Prefer Returning an Empty Instance over Null

---

The better practice is to return an empty instance, such as `string.Empty`, whenever the empty instance is semantically equivalent to returning null. This is a good defensive-programming measure when there is a high likelihood that the caller will not perform a check for null before using the return value. This practice is also appropriate for methods and properties that return arrays, collections and many other enumerable types, where an empty instance is appropriate.

Publicly Visible static readonly Fields

In .NET the constant field is designed to be used for values that are never intended to change. Public constant field values ought to be invariable numbers, like the number of days in a week. The const keyword is for permanent, unchanging, and fixed values. Because of their permanence and for the sake of efficiency, when a client assembly uses these const fields the value is copied into the other assembly. As a result, a change to the const field's value requires all assemblies that use the field to be recompiled to receive the updated value. Take a look at the code in Listing 6-17. The const field MaximumLoanAmount is the maximum loan amount for the Calculator class. If another assembly references the value of 17,500 then that value, not a reference to the field, is provided to the client assembly. And so, if the MaximumLoanAmount is changed to 18,000 then the client assembly still has the value of 17,500 until the client assembly's source code is recompiled.

Listing 6-17. Publicly Visible Constant Fields That Are Changeable: Bad Practice

```
public static class Calculator
{
    public const int MaximumLoanAmount = 17500;
```

```
...

}
```

■ **Practice 6-11** Avoid a Publicly Visible Constant Field

A better practice is to define a publicly visible field as static readonly. Declaring the field in this way allows the value to change without requiring client assemblies to recompile to receive the updated value. This makes sense for the MaximumLoanAmount value because that amount is changeable. This better approach is shown in Listing 6-18.

Listing 6-18. Changeable Constant Values Declared As Static Readonly Fields: Good Practice

```
public static class Calculator
{
    public static readonly int MaximumLoanAmount = 17500;

...

}
```

Code Smells

While reviewing source code, there are times when you sense something is not quite right. Perhaps the code is not clear. Perhaps the design seems overly complicated. You are not certain, but you have a distinct feeling that the code is suspect. Kent Beck coined the term *code smell* to describe when source code is gives you the inkling that there is a problem that can and should be improved.[3] The idea is to use that awareness to investigate further, understand the design, and suggest improvements, if appropriate.

Table 6-3. Sources That Describe Code Smells

Name	Description
97 Things Every Programmer Should Know	Although this book does not explicitly list code smells, many of the essays point to common problems and pain-points that lead to code smells.
Clean Code: A Handbook of Agile Software Craftsmanship	A widely-regarded book on writing good code that covers transforming bad code into good code. The examples are in Java, but the principles of writing clean code apply to .NET development.

---

[3] Source: http://en.wikipedia.org/wiki/Code_smell.

Name	Description
Code Complete: A Practical Handbook of Software Construction	Considered a must-read for professional software developers, this book provides practical information that is well researched and well considered.
Refactoring: Improving the Design of Existing Code	This book devotes an entire chapter to identifying and addressing bad smells in code. The discipline of refactoring is key to removing bad smells and improving code.
Ward Cunningham's wiki (http://c2.com/cgi/wiki)	The Code Smell page (http://c2.com/cgi/wiki?CodeSmell) provides a long list of hints, clues, and symptoms that tell you something might be wrong.

Comments

Comments should only be written to explain or clarify the source code. There are good reasons to write comments. The comments might provide background information. The comments state important underpinnings, rationales and limitations. However, too often comments are written to counteract the odor of poorly written code. When the source code is well written, redundant comments are unnecessary because the source code is clear and easy to understand. In extreme cases, comments complicate the code because the comments are no longer true or are misleading. Comments that do not add value, misrepresent the code, or are superfluous need to be removed from the source code.

■ **Practice 6-12** Sort Out Comments That Do Not Add Value or Complicate the Code

An all too common code smell occurs when comments are written as a substitute for helpful variable names. These comments are usually seen near the variable declaration. The variable is declared with a vague or cryptic name and there's a comment that describes the variable, as shown in Listing 6-19.

Listing 6-19. Comments Substituting for Helpful Variable Names: Bad Practice

```
string p; // principal as string
decimal r; // rate per month
int t; // term in months
```

A variable's name should speak for itself. The variable name must indicate what the variable stands for. The variable name must be clear, correct, and consistent. For example, if the variable is a string representation of a principal amount then the fact that it is not a decimal ought to be clear from the variable name. Better variable names are shown in Listing 6-20.

Listing 6-20. Clear Variable Names Instead of Comments: Good Practice

```
string principalAsString;
decimal ratePerMonth;
int termInMonths;
```

A dilemma occurs when comments are wrong or misleading. Believe the code or believe the comment. An experienced developer who maintains source code with untrustworthy comments learns to ignore the misleading or wrong comments. Other developers perform double duty by maintaining both the code and the comments. The source code becomes littered with comments that are unhelpful or only serve to complicate things. In Listing 6-21 the comments directly contradict the code, which leaves a bad smell for future developers.

Listing 6-21. The Comments Are Wrong or Misleading: Bad Practice

```
// Round the rate per month to 4 significant digits
// by rounding toward the nearest even number
return Math.Round(ratePerMonth, 6, MidpointRounding.AwayFromZero);
```

Comments can be important reminders or messages to other developers. They ought to speak to intention and justification. Let the code speak for itself. Better comments clarify an important principle or rationale that endures over time, as shown in Listing 6-22.

Listing 6-22. Comment to Clarify Rationale or Justification: Good Practice

```
// The rate needs to be properly rounded
return Math.Round(ratePerMonth, 6, MidpointRounding.AwayFromZero);
```

Sometimes comments are added to describe an entire block of code within a method. The developer feels that it is important to explain the significance of this section of code. In fact, the comments are describing the need to extract the code into a new method or use an existing method. In Listing 6-23 the comment clearly describes where an algorithm begins and ends; however, this code really belongs in a separate method.

Listing 6-23. Comments That Describe a Missing Method: Bad Practice

```
...
    // Begin: compute the rate per month from the APR
    decimal ratePerMonth;

    if (annualPercentageRate < 0.01m ||
        annualPercentageRate >= 20.0m)
    {
        throw new InvalidOperationException(string.Format(
            "AnnualPercentageRate {0}% is not valid",
            annualPercentageRate));
    }

    ratePerMonth = (annualPercentageRate / 100m) / MonthsPerYear;
```

```
    ratePerMonth = Math.Round(ratePerMonth, 6, MidpointRounding.AwayFromZero);
    // End
...
```

Comments that are really clues to missing methods are examples of where the code is not speaking for itself. By extracting the code into a separate method the complexity of the code is reduced. In Listing 6-24 the commented section of code is extracted to the new ComputeRatePerMonth method. With a properly named method the comments are unnecessary.

Listing 6-24. *Extract a Method to Uncomplicate Code: Good Practice*

```
...
    ratePerMonth = ComputeRatePerMonth(annualPercentageRate);
...

private static decimal ComputeRatePerMonth(
    decimal annualPercentageRate)
{
    if (annualPercentageRate < 0.01m ||
        annualPercentageRate >= 20.0m)
    {
        throw new InvalidOperationException(string.Format(
            "AnnualPercentageRate {0}% is not valid",
            annualPercentageRate));
    }

    var ratePerMonth = (annualPercentageRate / 100m) / MonthsPerYear;

    // The rate needs to be properly rounded
    return Math.Round(ratePerMonth, 6, MidpointRounding.AwayFromZero);
}
```

There is one last point to make about comments. A lot of source code files end up with lines and sections of commented-out code. In extreme cases, entire classes or methods that are no longer needed are commented out. It seems that many of us have a hard time letting go of the code we write. However, leaving code commented out does a real disservice to the developers that follow. The best practice is to delete the unused code and let the version control system track the changes. Some developers like a two-phase approach. First, comment out the code and check in the changes. Second, delete the commented-out code and check in the removal as a separate change set. Whatever the approach, the end result ought to be that source code files do not have a lot of commented-out code.

Way Too Complicated

It is all too common for source code to become overly complex and downright complicated. Rarely is it helpful to go back and figure out why the code turned out the way it did. A much more useful endeavor is to regularly and consistently reduce the complexity and improve the situation. The discipline of refactoring is a method for improving the design of existing source code. A comprehensive discussion of refactoring includes both the proper diagnoses and an effective prescription. This section focuses on symptoms of code that is way too complicated and would probably benefit from refactoring.

Some common symptoms of overly complicated source code include the following:

- *Long Method:* A method that is hard to read and understand because it is too long.

- *Long Parameter List:* A method that has so many parameters that it is too complicated.

- *Conditional Complexity:* A method that has so much conditional branching and logic that it is difficult to follow.

- *Large Class:* A class that is hard to read and understand because it is so large.

- *Speculative Generality:* Code that is hard to read and understand because it has functionality based on imagined requirements or a perceived need for future extensibility.

From these and many other symptoms comes the motivation to improve the code's readability and maintainability. The art and practice of refactoring encompasses an entire book unto itself. Under Appendix A you will find resources for the effective application of refactoring. The important point here is that source code must not become overly complex. Establish rules and regulations appropriate to you, your team, and your organization to prevent code from becoming way too complicated.

Unused, Unreachable, and Dead Code

Enhancing or extending software that contains many lines of unused, unreachable, or dead code can get tricky. Sometimes the code defines private methods that are never called. Code is written within conditional branches that can never be reached. Other times there are intermediate values that are calculated but are never used. How does this unnecessary code get in there? The developer who writes the code may not even realize that the code is not used. Also, during maintenance a change in requirements can cause the code to become superfluous.

The problem with unused, unreachable, and dead code is that the code is a diversion and a distraction. At some point, a developer reads the code to understand the purpose and rationale only to conclude that it is unimportant. That wastes time and mental energy. Developers might lose their train of thought or get confused by the unnecessary code. This reduces their productivity. Whether it is a 10% or 1% effect, the effect is still there. Establish rules and regulations to find and eliminate the unneeded code to keep the source code clean and clear.

Summary

In this chapter you learned about the sources of .NET standards and guidelines and how to integrate them to establish .NET rules and regulations that are right for your situation. You also learned about the importance of code smells and how better .NET practices are established to avoid bad code smells.

In the next chapter, you will learn practices that relate to the C# language and its power.

CHAPTER 7

Powerful C# Constructs

The .NET Framework has remained very vibrant since the introduction of .NET 1.0 in early 2002. Over the years, along with the major releases of .NET, Microsoft has added new languages, features, and technology sets. It is very clear that a lot of planning and consideration has gone into the .NET Framework. The same thoughtfulness is apparent in the evolution of the C# language. With each release, the C# language has added new and powerful constructs that have improved the language and the way developers write code in C#.

With C# 2.0, the language designers introduced new features, such as

- Generic types and methods

- Nullable types

- Simplified delegates and anonymous methods

- Iterators and the yield statement

- Partial classes

With C# 3.0, the following new features were added:

- Implicitly typed local variables

- Anonymous types

- Extension methods

- Lambda expressions

- Query syntax and LINQ

With C# 4.0, the language brought more features:

- Optional parameters and named arguments

- Dynamic binding and the Dynamic Language Runtime (DLR)

- Covariance and contravariance

This chapter will review some of the powerful C# constructs, as they relate to following best practices. The most important concept is that effective C# development is a key part of following .NET practices. Take the time to dive into the C# language to learn how to take full advantage of the language. Table 7-1 lists the ruthlessly helpful practices that take advantage of some of the powerful C# constructs.

Table 7-1. Powerful C# Constructs: Ruthlessly Helpful Practices

	Practice
7-1	Use Extension Methods to Add Behavior to Types That Are Closed to Modification
7-2	Use the var Keyword to Loosely Couple Local Variables from Their Implicit Type
7-3	Use Nullable Types to Designate Variables, Parameters, and Properties That Are Nullable
7-4	Use the Null-Coalescing Operator (??)To Efficiently Apply Null-Value Assignment Logic
7-5	Define a Method with Optional Parameters to Replace Overloaded Methods
7-6	Use Generics to Help the Compiler Enforce Type Checking at Compile Time
7-7	Develop Class Libraries That Use Generics for Type Safety and to Enforce Proper Usage
7-8	Use LINQ to Perform Querying in a Way That Is Incorporated into the C# Language
7-9	Attain Proficiency in Both the LINQ Query Syntax and Method Syntax
7-10	Understand Deferred Query Execution to Use the Full Power of LINQ

Extension Methods

Extension methods are a special kind of static method. They allow you to write methods as if they were instance methods on an existing type. This approach does not involve creating a derived type, nor does it involve recompiling or modifying the original type. The extension method is called as if it is a method on the type it extends and appears (even through Visual Studio IntelliSense) as if it is actually defined as a method of the type.

Let's take a look at the power of extension methods by way of an example. In the example system there is different logic that is driven by the current day of the week. There is a frequent need to know if today's date is a weekday or a weekend. By using the DayOfWeek property of System.DateTime it is simple to properly branch the logic. Listing 7-1 shows a typical section of code with logic that repeats throughout the codebase.

Listing 7-1. Repeating Code That Acts on a DateTime

```
DateTime importantDate = new DateTime(2011, 5, 7);

switch (importantDate.DayOfWeek)
{
    case DayOfWeek.Saturday:
    case DayOfWeek.Sunday:
        WeekendProcessing();
        break;
    default:
```

```
        WeekdayProcessing();
        break;
}
```

For this example, the team wants to reduce the amount of repeating code. To accomplish this the team employs the Library pattern and writes a DateTimeHelper class.[1] Notice the uses of the static keyword. This is a static class with a static method named IsWeekend, which is shown in Listing 7-2.

Listing 7-2. Library Pattern Introduces the IsWeekend Helper Method

```
public static class DateTimeHelper
{
    using System;

    public static bool IsWeekend(DateTime dateTime)
    {
        switch (dateTime.DayOfWeek)
        {
            case DayOfWeek.Saturday:
            case DayOfWeek.Sunday:
                return true;
            default:
                return false;
        }
    }
}
```

The helper method approach does achieve reuse. The code in Listing 7-3 performs exactly the same as the original code in Listing 7-1 in a lot fewer lines of code. The code in Listing 7-3 achieves all the desired results. It promotes reuse, and the resulting code is straightforward and readable, although the semantics of calling a method on a helper class is a bit awkward.

Listing 7-3. Helper Method Approach to Calling IsWeekend

```
DateTime importantDate = new DateTime(2011, 5, 7);

if (DateTimeHelper.IsWeekend(importantDate))
    WeekendProcessing();
else
    WeekdayProcessing();
```

This reuse is helpful, but it would be nice if System.DateTime actually had the IsWeekend method. That way any developer on the team wouldn't need to know which methods are part of DateTime and which methods are in the helper class. By using an extension method, the IsWeekend method can effectively extend DateTime, appearing to be one of the DateTime methods.

Writing the IsWeekend method as an extension method is shown in Listing 7-4. The only real difference between the helper method in Listing 7-2 and the extension method in List 7-4 is that the method parameter starts with the this keyword. The static keyword is applied in the same way and the logic is identical.

---

[1] The Library pattern is described in Kent Beck, *Implementation Patterns* (Upper Saddle River, NJ: Addison-Wesley Professional, 2008).

Listing 7-4. Declaring the IsWeekend Extension Method

```
namespace Lender.Slos.Extensions
{
    using System;

    public static class DateTimeExtensions
    {
        public static bool IsWeekend(this DateTime dateTime)
        {
            switch (dateTime.DayOfWeek)
            {
                case DayOfWeek.Saturday:
                case DayOfWeek.Sunday:
                    return true;
                default:
                    return false;
            }
        }
    }
}
```

▨ **Note** The naming convention for a class that contains extension methods is usually {Type Name}Extensions. For the namespace name there's no clear convention. A common practice is to create a separate project and put all extension methods under one namespace, such as, Lender.Slos.Extensions.

Extension methods must be defined as static methods in a static class and are identified by placing the this keyword in front of the first parameter in the method signature. The method extends the behavior of an object of the type of the first parameter. There are a few other restrictions, but they are rarely an issue.[2]

In Listing 7-5, the IsWeekend extension method appears, for all intents and purposes, to be a method of System.DateTime. There is no reference to the DateTimeExtensions class; the compiler knows how to find the extension method without needing to specify the class.

Listing 7-5. Extension Method Approach to Calling IsWeekend

```
DateTime importantDate = new DateTime(2011, 5, 7);

if (importantDate.IsWeekend())
    WeekendProcessing();
else
    WeekdayProcessing();
```

---

[2] Extension methods cannot extend a static class. Also, if there is already an existing method in a type with the same signature as an extension method then the extension method is never called.

In many ways this is remarkable. From the code listing and through Visual Studio IntelliSense, the IsWeekend method appears to be defined within System.DateTime, a .NET type that is defined in another assembly. The extension method approach has the following benefits:

- Code reuse through a helper method

- Straightforward and readable code

- Visual Studio IntelliSense support

- Code semantics are clear and convenient

To continue this example, other application-specific methods could be defined as extension methods, such as, IsHoliday or IsWorkingDay. These extension methods can be found in the sample code within the *Samples\Ch07\1_ExtensionMethods\Lender.Slos\DateTimeExtensions.cs* file.

In general, extension methods are an effective way to add new behavior and functionality to a type that is closed to modification.

■ **Practice 7-1** Use Extension Methods to Add Behavior to Types That Are Closed to Modification

---

Implicitly Typed Local Variables

Should you use the var keyword to declare a local variable in C#? This question seems to come up a lot. Ever since implicitly typed local variables were introduced in C# there have been frequent discussions about whether and when it is a good idea to use implicit typing. As with so many things, there are uses for and misuse of implicitly typed local variables.[3] This section focuses on the usefulness of declaring local variables using the var keyword.

Before discussing the usefulness of implicitly typed local variables, it is important to dispel any misconceptions. Some common fallacies are laid out in Table 7-2.

---

[3] For more information see http://blogs.msdn.com/b/ericlippert/archive/2011/04/20/uses-and-misuses-of-implicit-typing.aspx.

Table 7-2. The var Keyword: Dispelling the Fallacies

Fallacy	Fact
There is an erroneous belief that when a local variable is declared using the var keyword that then the variable is a variant type, similar to a variant in COM or VB6.	An implicitly typed local variable is not a variant. The variable type must be unambiguously inferred by the compiler and the type can never change. The confusion might be because the terms *var* and *variant* sound similar.
Another misconception is that the var keyword makes C# a weakly typed programming language.	C# is still a strongly typed language. The difference is that every local variable no longer needs to be explicitly typed if the compiler can unambiguously infer the type.
Yet another fallacy is that variables declared with the var keyword are dynamically typed at runtime.	An implicitly typed local variable is statically typed. If the variable's type cannot be unambiguously inferred by the compiler, the code will not compile.

There are situations where the var keyword is required. For anonymous types to work, implicitly typed local variables are required. Since the type is anonymous, the developer cannot explicitly type the variable. The compiler handles all the implicit typing of anonymous types. In this code snippet, the compiler creates a strongly typed album variable based on the specification implicit in the anonymous type declaration. The compiler performs type checking of the album variable's usage. IntelliSense lists the Artist and Title properties just like any other type.

```
var album = new { Artist = "U2", Title = "Rattle And Hum" };

Console.WriteLine("\"{0}\", by {1}", album.Title, album.Artist);
```

Beyond anonymous types and the essential need for the var keyword, implicit typing serves other useful purposes. An obvious reason is that by using the var keyword the code is made more readable by eliminating redundant type declarations. Compare the following two code fragments. Clearly, there is no value in writing out the explicit type when declaring the artists and albums local variables. The type of both artists and albums is self-evident in the Process2 method. There is no disadvantage to using the var keyword in this circumstance.

```
private void Process1()
{
    List<Artist> artists = new List<Artist>();
    Dictionary<Artist, Album> albums = new Dictionary<Artist, Album>();
...

private void Process2()
{
    var artists = new List<Artist>();
    var albums = new Dictionary<Artist, Album>();
...
```

Perhaps the best argument for the implicit typing of local variables relates to code refactoring. For example, the code in Listing 7-6 explicitly types the results variable as ApplicationCollection. However, the code only uses the results variable's IEnumerable<Application> interface to loop through the collection. In other words, the code is tightly coupled to the ApplicationCollection class for no good reason.

Listing 7-6. Sample Code That Uses Explicit Typing

```
ApplicationRepository repository
    = new ApplicationRepository();

string lastNameCriteria = "P";

Controller controller = new Controller(repository);

ApplicationCollection results = controller.Search(lastNameCriteria);

foreach (var result in results)
{
    Console.WriteLine("{0}, {1}",
        result.LastName,
        result.FirstName);
}
```

This is the signature of the Search method that is called by the code in Listing 7-6. The call to the Search method is explicitly typed to ApplicationCollection, not because the code requires that type, but because it is the return type of the method.

```
public ApplicationCollection Search(string lastNameCriteria)
```

Listing 7-7 shows this example rewritten using implicitly typed local variables. The results variable is declared with the var keyword to loosely couple the variable from the Search method's return type. As long as the results can be iterated over in the foreach loop then the code works as intended. More importantly, the compiler enforces the minimum essential requirements of the results variable.

Listing 7-7. Sample Code That Uses Implicit Typing

```
var repository = new ApplicationRepository();

var lastNameCriteria = "P";

var controller = new Controller(repository);

var results = controller.Search(lastNameCriteria);

foreach (var result in results)
{
    Console.WriteLine("{0}, {1}",
        result.LastName,
        result.FirstName);
}
```

At some future date, the signature of the Search method could change to return the
IEnumerable<Application> type, as follows:

```
public IEnumerable<Application> Search(string lastNameCriteria)
```

This change has no impact on the code in Listing 7-7 because the compiler has implicitly typed the
results variable. However, this change causes the code in Listing 7-6 to generate a compiler error
something like the following:

```
Error   Cannot implicitly convert type 'IEnumerable< Application>' to
'ApplicationCollection'.
```

There are advantages to using implicit typing whenever the compiler permits. This is especially true
for unit test code where implicitly typed local variables help to keep the test code loosely coupled to the
code under test. This point is made again in Chapter 8 when better practices for automated testing are
presented. Using implicit typing whenever the compiler permits is a more aggressive stance that
recognizes that the compiler knows what type the variable must be without you having to explicitly type
it out. If it is not implicitly clear then there will be a compiler error.

■ **Practice 7-2** Use the var Keyword to Loosely Couple Local Variables from Their Implicit Type

---

In general, refactoring is made easier with implicit typing. Between compiler checking and
automated testing, there is virtually no semantic reason not to implicitly type local variables. There are
other reasons to explicitly type variables. These reasons are often based on opinion, a team preference,
or better readability. Considering your specific situation

- If it is important that someone reading the code knows the type of the variable at a
  glance, use explicit typing.

- Experiment writing the code both ways and adopt the style you consider more
  readable.

Nullable Types

In the C# language, variables of reference types (classes, interfaces, and delegates) can be assigned the
null value. Value types (enumerations, numeric types, Booleans, and user-defined structs) cannot be
assigned the null value. Nullable types, introduced in .NET 2.0, are used to assign the null value to a
variable that represents an underlying value type. These nullable types are instances of the
System.Nullable<T> struct, where the type parameter T is a value type. More common is the syntax T?,
which is a shorthand for System.Nullable<T>, where T is a value type.

Let's take a look at an example of how nullable types are used. The code in Listing 7-8 defines the
Application class. The Id property is defined with the value type of System.Guid. The logic in the Save
method assumes that if the Id property is the default value of Guid.Empty then the proper action is to
create the entity, otherwise the Save method updates the entity. This logic works; however, it can be
made more explicit if the Id property is defined as a nullable type.

Listing 7-8. The Application Class Not Using a Nullable Id Property

```
public class Application
{
...

    public Guid Id { get; private set; }

...

    public void Save()
    {
        Validate();

        var entity = CreateEntity();

        if (Id == Guid.Empty)
        {
            entity.Id = _applicationRepo.Create(entity);
        }
        else
        {
            entity.Id = Id;
            _applicationRepo.Update(entity);
        }

        Syncronize(entity);
    }

...
}
```

In Listing 7-9, the Application class is rewritten with the Id property defined as a nullable Guid. Now, the logic in the Save method is written with clear semantics. If the Id property does not have a value then the entity is created. Otherwise, the entity's Id property is assigned the Id value and the record is updated.

Listing 7-9. The Application Class with Id Defined As a Nullable Type

```
public class Application
{
...

    public Guid? Id { get; private set; }

...

    public void Save()
    {
        Validate();

        var entity = CreateEntity();
```

```
        if (!Id.HasValue)
        {
            entity.Id = _applicationRepo.Create(entity);
        }
        else
        {
            entity.Id = Id.Value;
            _applicationRepo.Update(entity);
        }

        Syncronize(entity);
    }

    ...
}
```

Any variables, parameters, or properties that are defined using a nullable type make it clear that null is a legitimate and anticipated value. Alternately, defining a variable, parameter, or property with a value type makes it clear that an explicit value assignment is expected. This helps make the method and class usage clearer to the consumer.

■ **Practice 7-3** Use Nullable Types to Designate Variables, Parameters, and Properties That Are Nullable.

The Null-Coalescing Operator

The null-coalescing operator (??) is used to define a default value for both nullable types and reference types. In the expression count ?? -1, the null-coalescing operator returns the left-hand operand (the value of count) if it is not null; otherwise it returns the right operand (-1).

Listing 7-10 shows examples of how the null-coalescing operator provides a succinct way to handle null values. For this example class, if the DateOfApplication property of the class is null then the DateOfApplication property of the returned entity is DateTime.Today. This logic is handled in one line, which is shown in bold in Listing 7-10, by using the null-coalescing operator. In this listing, there are other properties that are coalesced so as to return the proper default value. This includes the two strings properties, MiddleInitial and Suffix, and the three numeric values.

Listing 7-10. Handling null Value Assignment with the Null-Coalescing Operator

```
private ApplicationEntity CreateEntity()
{
    return new ApplicationEntity
        {
            LastName = LastName,
            FirstName = FirstName,
            MiddleInitial = MiddleInitial ?? string.Empty,
            Suffix = Suffix ?? string.Empty,
            DateOfBirth = DateOfBirth,
            DateOnApplication = DateOnApplication ?? DateTime.Today,
```

```
        Principal = Principal ?? MaximumLoanAmount,
        AnnualPercentageRate = AnnualPercentageRate ?? DefaultAnnualPercentageRate,
        TotalPayments = TotalPayments ?? DefaultTotalPayments,
    };
}
```

▪ **Practice 7-4** Use the Null-Coalescing Operator (??) to Efficiently Apply Null-Value Assignment Logic

---

Optional Parameters

VB.NET has had optional parameters for quite a while. In C# 4.0, optional parameters were introduced as a new language feature. When you specify that a method parameter is optional, no argument has to be supplied for that parameter when the method is called. Optional parameters are indicated by assigning the parameter a value in the method definition. For instance, the middleInitial parameter of a method written as string middleInitial = null defines it as an optional parameter. The primary restriction is that all optional parameters must come after required parameters of a method[4].

The code shown in Listing 7-11 defines a method that instantiates an Application class based on the parameter values provided. Only the first three parameters, lastName, firstName, and dateOfBirth, are considered required parameters.

Listing 7-11. The CreateApplication Method with All Parameters

```
public Application CreateApplication(
    string lastName,
    string firstName,
    DateTime dateOfBirth,
    string middleInitial,
    string suffix,
    DateTime dateOnApplication,
    decimal principal,
    decimal annualPercentageRate,
    int totalPayments)
{
    if (string.IsNullOrWhiteSpace(lastName))
    {
        throw new ArgumentNullException("lastName");
    }

    if (string.IsNullOrWhiteSpace(firstName))
    {
        throw new ArgumentNullException("firstName");
    }
```

---

[4] There are other restrictions described at http://codebetter.com/2011/01/11/c-in-depth-optional-parameters-and-named-arguments-2.

```
    if (dateOfBirth < Application.MinimumDateOfBirth)
    {
        throw new ArgumentOutOfRangeException("dateOfBirth");
    }

    return new Application(null)
    {
        LastName = lastName,
        FirstName = firstName,
        MiddleInitial = middleInitial ?? string.Empty,
        Suffix = suffix ?? string.Empty,
        DateOfBirth = dateOfBirth,
        DateOnApplication = dateOnApplication,
        Principal = principal,
        AnnualPercentageRate = annualPercentageRate,
        TotalPayments = totalPayments,
    };
}
```

Before optional parameters were introduced into C#, method overloading was the general way to provide method callers different calling signatures. The code in Listing 7-12 illustrates how the one method in Listing 7-11 is overloaded with a method that requires only the mandatory parameters.

Listing 7-12. Method Overloads of CreateApplication with Various Parameters

```
public Application CreateApplication(
    string lastName,
    string firstName,
    DateTime dateOfBirth)
{
    return CreateApplication(
        lastName,
        firstName,
        dateOfBirth,
        string.Empty,
        string.Empty,
        DateTime.Today,
        Application.MaximumLoanAmount,
        Application.DefaultAnnualPercentageRate,
        Application.DefaultTotalPayments);
}
```

The method overloading concept in Listing 7-12 can be further extended to many more methods that simply add in the optional parameters, such as the following:

```
public Application CreateApplication(
    string lastName,
    string firstName,
    DateTime dateOfBirth,
    string middleInitial)
{
    ...
}
```

```
public Application CreateApplication(
    string lastName,
    string firstName,
    DateTime dateOfBirth,
    string middleInitial,
    string suffix)
{
    ...
}
```

With .NET 4.0 optional parameters finally came to the C# language. Instead of writing a series of method overloads, it is now possible to define one method that has optional parameters. In Listing 7-13, the CreateApplication is rewritten using optional parameters. This one method replaces the method in Listing 7-11 and the six overloaded methods that might have been written.

Listing 7-13. The CreateApplication Method with Optional Parameters

```
public Application CreateApplication(
    string lastName,
    string firstName,
    DateTime dateOfBirth,
    string middleInitial = null,
    string suffix = null,
    DateTime? dateOnApplication = null,
    decimal? principal = null,
    decimal? annualPercentageRate = null,
    int? totalPayments = null)
{
    if (string.IsNullOrWhiteSpace(lastName))
    {
        throw new ArgumentNullException("lastName");
    }

    if (string.IsNullOrWhiteSpace(firstName))
    {
        throw new ArgumentNullException("firstName");
    }

    if (dateOfBirth < Application.MinimumDateOfBirth)
    {
        throw new ArgumentOutOfRangeException("dateOfBirth");
    }

    return new Application(null)
    {
        LastName = lastName,
        FirstName = firstName,
        MiddleInitial = middleInitial ?? string.Empty,
        Suffix = suffix ?? string.Empty,
        DateOfBirth = dateOfBirth,
        DateOnApplication = dateOnApplication ?? DateTime.Today,
        Principal = principal ?? Application.MaximumLoanAmount,
```

```
        AnnualPercentageRate =
            annualPercentageRate ?? Application.DefaultAnnualPercentageRate,
        TotalPayments = totalPayments ?? Application.DefaultTotalPayments,
    };
}
```

Instead of writing many method overloads to handle the various method signatures, one method with optional parameters can help make the code easier to maintain.

■ **Practice 7-5** Define a Method with Optional Parameters to Replace Overloaded Methods

---

There is an important cautionary note that relates to constant value assignment when declaring an optional parameter. It is probably better to describe the potential problem with an example. In the following code snippet, the optional loanAmount parameter is provided a constant value of 17500, if the parameter is not provided.

```
public class LoanValidator
{
    public static readonly int LoanLimit = 17500;

    public int LoanCeiling(int loanAmount = 17500)
    {
        return loanAmount;
    }
}
```

When the code calls the LoanCeiling method without the optional parameter, the compiler references the value and copies it directly into the calling code. The implications are that if you change the default value, such as 18000, all the code that calls the method must be recompiled to get the new value. The following output demonstrates the results from a test assembly that is not recompiled after the value changes from 17500 to 18000. The method call to the test assembly still uses the original value and the test fails.

```
Errors and Failures:
1) Test Failure :
Tests.Unit.Lender.Slos.OptionalParameters.OptionalParametersTests.LoanCeiling_WithNoParamete
r_ExpectProperValue
  Expected: 18000
  But was:  17500
```

The better practice is to use a nullable type when defining an optional parameter. In this way the null-coalescing operator is used to encapsulate how the code ought to properly handle the case when the parameter is not explicitly provided by the calling code. This is shown in the following code sample:

```
public class LoanValidator
{
    public static readonly int LoanLimit = 17500;
```

```
    public int LoanCeiling(int? loanAmount = null)
    {
        return loanAmount ?? LoanLimit;
    }
}
```

Generics

Since .NET 2.0, there are two forms of generics in the C# language:

- *Generic Types*: A class, structure, interface, or delegate defined with one or more type parameter

- *Generic Methods*: A method defined with one or more type parameter

Before .NET 2.0, the ArrayList class was in common use. This collection type can contain a list of any object type. Since every type is derived from the object type, the list could contain any type. There was no type safety and improper usages might not be found until runtime. For example, the following code sample has a simple mistake. The value in the names array is improperly cast into the dateOfBirth variable.

```
var names = new ArrayList();
var datesOfBirth = new ArrayList();

names.Add("Public, John Q.");
datesOfBirth.Add(new DateTime(1993, 11, 13));

for (int index = 0; index < names.Count; index++)
{
    DateTime dateOfBirth = (DateTime)names[index];

    Console.WriteLine("{0}, DOB: {1}",
        names[index],
        dateOfBirth.ToShortDateString());
}
```

This mistake is not found by the compiler. When the code is run the result is the following runtime error:

```
InvalidCastException: Specified cast is not valid.
```

In .NET 2.0 and beyond, the code can easily be rewritten to use generic lists. The explicit cast to DateTime is no longer necessary. Without the cast it is clear that the dateOfBirth variable should not be assigned from the names list.

```
var names = new List<string>();
var datesOfBirth = new List<DateTime>();

names.Add("Public, John Q.");
datesOfBirth.Add(new DateTime(1993, 11, 13));
```

```
for (int index = 0; index < names.Count; index++)
{
    DateTime dateOfBirth = names[index];

    Console.WriteLine("{0}, DOB: {1}",
        names[index],
        dateOfBirth.ToShortDateString());
}
```

The compiler finds the DateTime conversion error and the code will not compile. Even if dateOfBirth is defined as an implicitly typed local variable, this mistake is found by the compiler and the code will not compile, reporting this error:

```
'string' does not contain a definition for 'ToShortDateString' and no extension method
'ToShortDateString' accepting a first argument of type 'string' could be found (press F4 to
add a using directive or assembly reference)
```

≡ **Practice 7-6** Use Generics to Help the Compiler Enforce Type Checking at Compile Time

Since .NET 2.0 introduced them, the generic collection types are now widely used. These generic classes have gone a long way to prevent improper usage, such as calling instance methods with improper arguments. The compiler catches the error if the Add method is called passing the wrong type. This same type safety and compiler enforcement of the generic types and generic methods written by you and your team is very useful.

≡ **Practice 7-7** Develop Class Libraries That Use Generics for Type-Safety and to Enforce Proper Usage

LINQ

LINQ is an acronym for language-integrated query. It is a powerful .NET technology that brings querying capabilities directly into the C# language (and other .NET languages). With the introduction of LINQ in .NET 3.0, querying was brought to C# as a major language construct, as fundamental as foreach loops, delegates, and extension methods. It is hard to overstate the impact that LINQ has had on developing .NET applications that perform a lot of queries and the developers who write them.

LINQ is a large topic. There are many relevant language features vital to LINQ, including extension methods, lambda expressions, anonymous data types, and partial methods. There are many keywords and many query constructs. Entire books are devoted to LINQ.[5] For this reason, this section discusses the

---

[5] An excellent book on LINQ is Joseph Rattz and Adam Freeman, *Pro LINQ, Language Integrated Query in C# 2010* (New York: Apress, 2010).

importance of LINQ and why it is a powerful C# construct, and provides advice to encourage new and different practices.

There are two basic ways to write LINQ queries:

- *Query Syntax:* A declarative syntax introduced in C# 3.0, which is translated at compile time to method calls understood by the .NET common language runtime (CLR).

- *Method Syntax:* The standard query methods understood by the .NET CLR, called directly instead of using the query syntax.

There is no semantic difference between query syntax and method syntax. Query syntax is often considered to be simpler and more readable. It is certainly analogous to the structured query language (SQL), which is the de facto standard way to query in database products like Microsoft SQL Server. The following C# statement (using the LINQ to SQL provider) queries a database in the LINQ query syntax:

```
var results = from a in Albums
        where a.Artist.Name.StartsWith("B")
        select a;
```

The statement reads like a reshuffled SQL query. In fact, it is equivalent to the following SQL statement:

```
SELECT [t0].*
FROM [Album] AS [t0]
    INNER JOIN [Artist] AS [t1]
    ON [t1].[ArtistId] = [t0].[ArtistId]
WHERE [t1].[Name] LIKE 'B%'
```

The power of LINQ comes from the way the query syntax is directly supported by the C# language. For example, the LINQ provider presents the inner join relationship between Artist and Albums as a property of the class. In addition, the Name property is strongly typed as a string. These relationships and types are checked and enforced by the compiler. With LINQ, querying is incorporated into the C# language in a fundamental and robust manner.

▪ **Practice 7-8** Use LINQ to Perform Querying in a Way That Is Incorporated into the C# Language

---

The .NET common language runtime (CLR) does not directly use the query syntax. The compiler transparently translates the query syntax into the method syntax. The query syntax statement above is equivalent to the following statement written in the method syntax:

```
var results = Albums
    .Where(x => x.Artist.Name.StartsWith("B"));
```

Many C# developers who are more familiar with fluent interfaces and lambda syntax prefer writing LINQ expressions in method syntax. It seems logical that if the team prefers one convention over another then the team should stick to that convention. With a little practice, it should not be hard for developers to adapt from one convention to the other.

Even if you prefer the query syntax, it is important to learn the method syntax:

- Some queries can only be expressed as method calls.

- The MSDN reference documentation of the System.Linq namespace uses method syntax.

Even if you prefer the method syntax, it is important to learn the query syntax:

- The query syntax supports a local *range variable*, which represents each element in the source sequence. This can make complex queries a lot more readable.

- The query syntax supports the use of a *let* clause, which is useful to store the result of a sub-expression. The let clause helps make complex queries more readable.

Some developers seem to draw the battle lines with either LINQ query syntax or method syntax. A better approach is to see the need for *both* LINQ query syntax *and* method syntax. The project or the organization may have a preference and establish a convention, and that can be the final form written for the production code. However, you and your team will certainly benefit from gaining proficiency and fluency in both syntaxes, which will make your development more effective.

■ **Practice 7-9** Attain Proficiency in Both the LINQ Query Syntax and Method Syntax

---

For years, developers have been using the Microsoft SQL Server Management Studio to develop SQL queries. The SQL query development is effective and supported by features, such as the query analyzer and IntelliSense.

When developing LINQ queries against databases it is important to find a similar way to quickly develop query expressions. One very effective tool for developing LINQ queries is a product called LINQPad.[6] LINQPad is not open source, but the standard edition is free to download and use. The auto-completion feature and the professional edition cost extra.[7]

Figure 7-1 shows the main interface to LINQPad. This screenshot shows how the MvcMusicStore database is queried using the LINQ query syntax. In a manner similar to SQL Enterprise, LINQPad lets you interactively query databases, in either the LINQ query syntax or method syntax.

---

[6] For more information see www.linqpad.net.
[7] For those addicted to IntelliSense, LINQPad auto-completion is worth the additional cost.

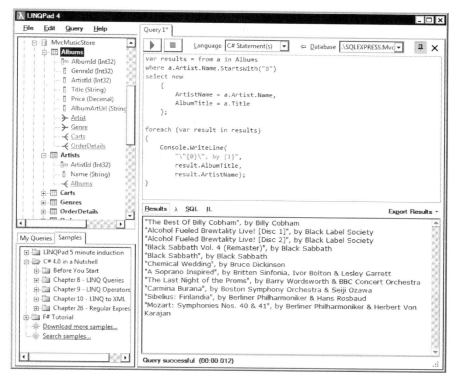

Figure 7-1. *Developing queries with LINQPad 4*

With the introduction of LINQ, the concept of a *deferred query* became important to understand and appreciate. Deferred query execution is often misunderstood.[8] This can lead to unanticipated performance problems. It is important to recognize how you can make deferred queries work for you. Listing 7-14 shows a series of LINQ statements that query the MvcMusicStore database. Although there are two LINQ query statements, the query does not execute until the line with the foreach statement.

Listing 7-14. *Deferred Query Execution in LINQ*

```
var albums = Albums
        .Where (x => x.Price < 9.00m);

var results = albums
        .Where (n => n.Artist.Name.StartsWith("B"))
        .Select (n =>
        new
```

---

[8] For more information see http://blogs.msdn.com/b/charlie/archive/2007/12/09/deferred-execution.aspx.

```
        {
                AlbumTitle = n.Title,
                ArtistName = n.Artist.Name
        });
```

foreach (var result in results)
```
{
        Console.WriteLine(
                "\"{0}\", by {1}",
                result.AlbumTitle,
                result.ArtistName);
}
```

Since the query execution is deferred, the LINQ provider (LINQ to SQL) combines the queries that underlie the two LINQ statements and executes only one query. In effect, the query combination is equivalent to this single SQL query, which returns 11 rows:

```
SELECT [t0].[Title] AS [AlbumTitle], [t1].[Name] AS [ArtistName]
FROM [Album] AS [t0]
    INNER JOIN [Artist] AS [t1]
    ON [t1].[ArtistId] = [t0].[ArtistId]
WHERE ([t1].[Name] LIKE 'B%')
    AND ([t0].[Price] < 9.00)
```

Unfortunately, developers who do not appreciate deferred query execution might write the same logic, but in a way that breaks the deferred query execution, as shown in Listing 7-15. The database query now executes on the line with the ToList method call.

Listing 7-15. LINQ Statements That Break Deferred Query Execution

```
var albums = Albums
        .Where (x => x.Price < 9.00m)
        .ToList();

var results = albums
        .Where (n => n.Artist.Name.StartsWith("B"))
        .Select (n =>
        new
        {
                AlbumTitle = n.Title,
                ArtistName = n.Artist.Name
        });

foreach (var result in results)
{
        Console.WriteLine(
                "\"{0}\", by {1}",
                result.AlbumTitle,
                result.ArtistName);
}
```

The query execution is no longer deferred. With the call to the ToList method, the LINQ provider queries the database with a SQL query similar to the following, which returns 246 rows:

```
SELECT [t0].*
FROM [Album] AS [t0]
WHERE [t0].[Price] < 9.00
```

The remaining query logic acts upon the objects that are retrieved into memory for this first query. It is easy to see how by not appreciating deferred query execution code can result in database queries that are very inefficient. In this simple example, the database query brought back hundreds of rows, but less than a dozen rows met the combined criteria. There are examples of how improperly written LINQ statements returned tens of thousands of unnecessary rows from the database, which destroyed performance[9].

■ **Practice 7-10** Understand Deferred Query Execution to Use the Full Power of LINQ

Database LINQ providers, including Entity Framework, NHibernate, and LINQ to SQL, support deferred execution. These providers do a lot of work before executing a query to create an optimized SQL statement to send an efficient query to the database. It is important to write LINQ queries with a full appreciation for how deferred query execution optimizes these queries.

The power of LINQ is also found when working with Reactive Extensions in .NET 4.0, more commonly abbreviated as *Rx*. Rx is an innovation from Microsoft researcher Erik Meijer, who is cited by many as the father of LINQ. Rx brings a new "push model" to .NET for event-subscription programming, such as user interface and network events.[10] The principal Rx types are the IObservable<T> and IObserver<T> interfaces, which allows the provider of data to "push" to subscribers, who react to the newly available data. In the *pull* model you enumerate available data. In the *push* model you subscribe to *observable* data events. LINQ is designed to be applicable for this *inverse* model. Basically, LINQ to Rx is written to use LINQ constructs that give you the ability to query Rx providers and use LINQ in reactive programming applications. At Microsoft Research, DryadLINQ is further demonstrating the power of LINQ and how it is applicable to distributed computing on thousands of servers for large-scale data parallel applications.[11]

Summary

In this chapter you learned about many powerful C# language constructs. These language features have added new and better ways to write better software. In many ways the code is easier to write, easier to read, and more maintainable.

In the next chapter you will learn about automated testing and many related better practices.

---

[9] Scott Hanselman describes a curious case of performance problems when the query execution was not deferred:
www.hanselman.com/blog/TheWeeklySourceCode52YouKeepUsingThatLINQIDunnaThinkItMeansWhatYouThinkItMeans.aspx

[10] For a nice introduction to LINQ to Rx see section 12.5 of Jon Skeet, *C# in Depth (2nd Edition)* (Greenwich, CT: Manning, 2011).

[11] For more information see http://research.microsoft.com/en-us/projects/dryadlinq/.

CHAPTER 8

Automated Testing

This chapter is *not* about automated testing in the Quality Assurance (QA) sense. This chapter is about the automated testing that developers perform. Throughout this book, when you see the word *testing* it refers to a developer performing *intention checking*. In this sense, test code checks that the code-under-test works and continues to work as a developer deliberately planned it to work.

The topics of test-driven development (TDD) and the red-green-refactor development methodology are covered well in many books, blog postings, and websites. (Appendix A provides a list of resources that cover TDD and how-to write tests.) This chapter is not going to describe how to write your first unit test. It provides practices that focus on the following objectives:

- *Readability:* Writing test code that is easy to understand and communicates well

- *Maintainability:* Writing tests that are robust and hold up well over time

- *Automation:* Writing tests that require little setup and configuration (preferably none)

As discussed in Chapter 4, quantifying the value of automated testing is very important. These practices produce benefits that relate to early detection of problems, reducing the risk of future changes, identifying how two separate components and sections of code need to work together, and making sure code is written correctly.

Automated testing covers more topics than unit testing. It covers different forms of test code and automated test suites. The topics include forms of testing that developers find helpful and that can be automated:

- Unit testing

- Surface testing

- Automated integration testing

    - Smoke testing

    - Stability testing

    - Performance testing

- Database testing

Surface testing is a specialized form of testing that is introduced later in this chapter. Some testing is beyond the scope of this book. There are simply too many effective applications of automated testing to cover them all; if you learn the principles behind them, you can apply them broadly. This chapter describes many specific practices to improve automated testing, consistent with those principles. The practices covered are summarized in Table 8-1.

Table 8-1. Automated Testing: Ruthlessly Helpful .NET Practices

	Automated Testing Practice
8-1	Focus on Writing Maintainable Test Code
8-2	Adopt an Effective Naming Convention
8-3	Use the Arrange-Act-Assert (3-As) Pattern
8-4	Prefer Many Short Tests over Few Long Tests
8-5	Avoid More Than One Line of Action
8-6	Avoid More Than One Primary Assertion
8-7	Avoid Explicit Typing Variables in Test Code; Use the Var Keyword
8-8	Use a TestsContext Class to Reduce Repetition and Manage Complexity
8-9	Build TestHelper Classes to Promote Reuse
8-10	Data-Drive Test Methods for Multiple Test Cases
8-11	Perform Boundary Analysis to Cover All Scenarios
8-12	Use Stubs to Test in Isolation
8-13	Use Only One Mock when Testing Interaction

COMMENTARY

I believe the word *testing* in "unit testing" is an unfortunate choice. A programmer is not a tester, and programmers rarely consider themselves testers. A primary role of QA is to *independently* verify and validate the system. Many in QA are unsettled by the idea that the person writing the code is testing the code. Unit tests are programmer tests, and unit testing is not independent verification and validation. The principle behind unit testing is that the developer confirms that the code works as intended. Instead of using the word *testing* a more accurate phrase might be *intention checking*. However, since unit testing is so widely used it is now entrenched.

This book owes a debt to the many books and websites that describe and explain important conventions, standards, principles, and practices. The code samples for this chapter use NUnit, Moq, and NDbUnit, which are free and open source. Without this groundbreaking work, many projects would either continue to roll their own frameworks or not use automated testing. The experience and expertise of these authors and the developers of the testing frameworks provides an excellent foundation for all developers to build well-tested software upon.

Metaphorically, test code is like the clothing and equipment of firefighters. If an oxygen tank, respirator, and protective clothing are too heavy, unwieldy, and unreliable, the firefighter is not helped. A firefighter might not want to wear the equipment because it is actually an impediment to fighting a fire. This is safety equipment and a firefighter should want to wear it and should rely on it for protection; these are life-saving devices that no reasonable firefighter should be without. In the same way, developers rely on test code and should see it as a help and not a hindrance. If it is unreliable and burdensome, then over time the tests will be commented out, ignored, or abandoned.

There are a lot of examples of test code available on the Internet. Much of this test code is written to illustrate how to write unit tests. The problem comes when the examples do not focus on writing maintainable test code (although, since that is not that writer's intent, not focusing on maintainability is understandable). Such examples present basic methodology; the code explicitly types variables and adds verbose comments throughout. There are long arrangement steps and several assertions demonstrating a framework's versatility and the code sample spells out everything. Sadly, this sows the seeds of a maintenance burden that can cause test code to be abandoned. It can also detract from the goal of singularly focusing on checking just one intention.

Another type of testing that must not be overlooked is security testing. This is a sizeable category that can be automated, yet it is often performed manually. Consider security requirements as part of the system requirements and do not overlook them.

Model-based testing (MBT) is an emerging discipline for testing complex software systems. Visual Studio has a model checker called SpecExplorer that can be used to generate test cases for model-based testing.

Microsoft's Pex and Moles are a set of important tools and technology worth investigating, but they are just a little beyond the scope of this chapter. Working together, Pex and Moles can automatically generate test cases by performing automatic code exploration.

Appendix A provides resources for further learning and research.

Case Study

Imagine you are a software developer working at Lender Inc., a fictional bank that originates student loans using their internally-developed Student Loan Origination System (SLOS) software. The technical lead has assigned you the task of guiding an effort to improve testability as part of the next release cycle. You will be writing automated tests and incorporating automated testing into the development process.

STUDENT LOAN ORIGINATION SYSTEM

When a student needs a loan to pay for their education, Lender Inc. uses their in-house SLOS system to enter and process the student loan application, originate the loan, and make disbursements to the college or university. The system has been in use for many years and is critical to Lender's student loan department. The system is thoroughly tested by QA before every release and is generally reliable and performs the calculations correctly. There are, however, several key functional and non-functional improvements planned for the next release. Development intends to use automated testing to reduce the number of defects found by QA during regression and system testing.

There is a new business validation to be added to the system. For legal reasons, the student must be no less than 16 years of age and no more than 26 years old.

An important enhancement is to add an Estimated Monthly Payment Calculator to allow monthly payment amounts to be computed during the application process. Currently, the amount is only available during the loan approval workflow. Customers frequently request an estimate of their monthly payment when applying, which is now done using a spreadsheet. SLOS needs to be enhanced to use the same loan calculator that is in the loan approval process, during application. The payment calculator computes a ballpark estimate given a principal amount, a percentage rate, and payment terms. QA will independently verify and validate that the monthly payment estimate shown is correct and matches the monthly payment calculated during loan approval.

On the non-functional side, the system's data access layer (DAL) needs to be upgraded. The DAL performs create, retrieve, update, and delete (CRUD) operations using ADO.NET calling stored procedures. The goal is to switch to using an object-relational mapping (ORM) package. The ORM package selected is NHibernate. Today, each of the database tables requires at least four stored procedures, one for each CRUD operation. Maintaining the DAL is expensive and a frequent source of defects discovered by QA during regression and system test. To limit scope and mitigate risk the non-CRUD operations will not be impacted during the project. The non-CRUD querying of the database, which includes various ad hoc queries and any query that retrieves multiple records, continues to go through the DAL. The existing DAL and the ORM need to work side by side.

As part of the release cycle the QA testing team performs a full and complete regression test of SLOS. Any defects found during regression test are expensive: in addition to the effort to fix the issue and verify the fix, there is the effort to report and track the issue. The expectation has been set that Development will make effective use of automated testing to ensure that these enhancements work as intended and that all existing functionality continues to work properly in the next release.

You plan to use automated testing to do the following:

- Ensure that the new business-logic validations work as intended.

- Check that the monthly payment amount calculated for an application is exactly the same as the monthly payment amount calculated for a loan with identical terms. Both amounts must compute properly.

- Verify that when the same CRUD operations are performed using the ORM package instead of the DAL, the database operation is done correctly and is completely consistent with the DAL.

- Verify that data retrieved from and stored in the database for any CRUD operation is performed properly using either the DAL or the ORM.

- Prove that any code modules that depend on the DAL continue to interact through the same interface without requiring code changes.

■ **Caution** All of the financial formulas and sample code are presented for the purpose of illustrating the practices. They are too simplistic to use in *any* financial application.

Brownfield Applications

To understand the term *brownfield*, imagine an industrial site that needs repair and rehabilitation.[1] It still serves a useful purpose, but a lot of work needs to be done to bring everything up to par. The site might be running, but it has the capacity to produce more. There is a waste mound and a lot of old, outdated equipment. The site needs more than a spring cleaning; it needs an overhaul.

Similarly, a brownfield software application does not deserve to be abandoned, but it will take a lot of work to improve the situation. The code base is deemed to be worth the investment. This is in contrast to legacy code. By definition, a legacy application is considered not worth the cost of enhancing or redesigning. A legacy system is usually patched up, retired, or replaced.

Figure 8-1 shows the architecture of the SLOS system. On the left-hand side of the diagram is the system's architecture as it currently stands. On the right-hand side is the architecture after the planned system overhaul and redesign. In this case SLOS is a brownfield application; Lender Inc. clearly wants to enhance the functionality. Also, the DAL replacement requires an investment.

---

[1] The origin of the term *brownfield* is described in Baley and Belcham, *Brownfield Application Development in .NET* (Greenwich, CT: Manning, 2010).

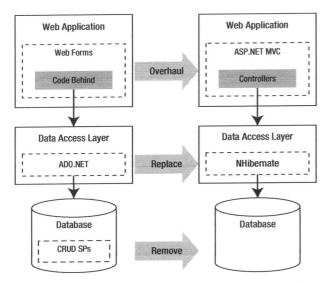

Figure 8-1. *A brownfield application example*

Within the scope of the case study is the work to change the DAL from using ADO.NET to using NHibernate. Once NHibernate is fully implemented, the plan is to remove the CRUD stored procedures. In a future project the Web application is planned to be overhauled.

There is risk when changing a brownfield application. First, the payment calculator must continue to calculate the payment amounts correctly. Second, replacing the DAL stored procedures with an ORM might generate many bugs. If these changes are not done properly, the project will not improve SLOS; it will make the system worse. To mitigate risk and increase effectiveness in an upgrade or enhancement project, use automated testing to your advantage. Automated testing provides continuous feedback as to whether the system is holding its integrity and continues to work as intended.

Let's take a look at refactoring the payment calculator. The automated testing and development strategy is to perform unit testing, as follows:

1. Write unit tests around the ComputePayment method in the Loan class.

2. Make sure the tests cover all possible test cases.

3. Have all the automated unit tests run on the continuous integration (CI) server after every build is made.

4. Refactor the code into a financial calculator class; the payment calculation method is separated from the Loan class.

5. Verify the Loan class continues to compute the payment amount correctly using the Calculator class.

6. Clone these LoanTests methods to the ApplicationTests class and repurpose them for the enhancement of the Application class.

7. Add the `ComputePayment` method functionality the `Application` class, checking to sure everything works properly by running the unit tests.

8. Verify that the both the `Application` and the `Loan` classes compute payment amounts correctly.

The DAL replacement effort involves replacing an entire subsystem, and so the automated testing strategy is *not* unit testing. The strategy is built upon a specialized automated integration testing approach called surface testing. Since it is a much bigger undertaking, let's postpone the detailed discussion of the DAL replacement. Surface testing is discussed in detail in its own section later in this chapter. For now, it is sufficient to say the DAL replacement starts with automated testing using the DAL interface as the "surface" to write tests against.

■ **Caution** In my experience, writing a lot of unit-specific tests against a brownfield application can be counterproductive during system overhaul and redesign. I prefer automated integration tests. Also, existing unit test suites can become very unhelpful. Unit tests are written at the unit level, but the planned work focuses on significantly changing the code. Code units might be relocated, combined, or dramatically altered. Since unit tests verify that the unit continues to work as written, the unit tests start failing as improvements are made; maintaining the many outmoded and failing unit tests is now burdensome and counterproductive.

Greenfield Applications

The word *greenfield* conjures up images of a site ready to receive a brand new factory. Everything will be shiny, innovative, and modern. Everyone mentally creates the factory of their dreams without being constrained by physical realities. The architect draws designs that are not limited by budget or structural engineering. Because project realities are not immediate, the vision does not conflict with reality. However, the planning and design phases gradually bring vision in line with reality. Designs must conform to the laws of physics. Schedule and cost control begin to tame the vision. People give up their passionate dreams and live within budgets and deadlines.

Greenfield software projects ought to be in a similar situation, but often they are not. Instead, an elaborate planning phase is bypassed.[2] The developers jump right into writing code. At the project's inception everyone still has their own vision of what the system will be, unconstrained by reality. At this stage the customer, analyst, or developer probably does not feel pressure to compromise their vision because they suspect everyone is agreeing to their mental creation. There is no common understanding, no meeting of the minds.

Automated testing provides a way out. The developer must be clear on what the code is intended to do in order to plan the tests. Conflicting requirements have to be resolved. Requirements must be complete enough to both write the test code and the code-under-test. In writing the tests, as each new scenario is explored, many questions arise:

---

[2] An elaborate planning phase is not necessarily good; it can get stuck in analysis paralysis. The important thing is to come to a common understanding of the scope and the objectives of the project.

- What is the code required to do under each test case?

- How should the code react when unanticipated situations arise?

- Why does some new piece of code break an existing test?

The accumulating set of tests must all continue to pass, and so, gradually, a shared understanding between analyst and developer evolves and is defined: complete, clear, and consistent.

By working to understand and verify that the code-under-test works as intended, the developer forces a meeting of the minds. For efficiency's sake, it would be ideal if the meeting of the minds happened before coding but, to the extent that a common understanding is not there, the writing of tests reveals gaps. Automated testing provides continuous feedback as to whether the system holds its integrity during development. All code written to that point has to continue to hold up under the scrutiny of rigorous intention checking.

In the case of SLOS, the system is *not* a greenfield application. The business-logic validation is new development work. As tests are written for that enhancement, key questions arise that require the developer to go back to the analyst for clarification.

Automated Testing Groundwork

Automated testing is the generally-accepted way to check that code is and continues to work as intended. Automated tests meet very specific criteria:

- Every developer must be able to run the combined collection of all the developer's tests.

- The CI server must be able to run the entire suite of tests without manual intervention.

- The outcome of the tests must be unambiguous and repeatable. Usually, the standard is that if one test fails the entire test run fails.

The automated tests allow any developer to verify that their current changes do not break existing code-under-test. Any developer needs to be able to run the entire automated test suite with little to no setup or configuration. The exception to this rule is long-running automated integration tests. The CI server should run these tests as part of the full and thorough build cycle, but the developers should not because they are time and resource intensive. Also, automated tests allow the CI server to fulfill a key role of efficiently verifying that the system works properly.

Test Code Maintainability

Perhaps the most underrated objective for test code is readability. The second most underrated objective is maintainability. A lot of test code is abandoned because it is too hard to understand or it breaks too often. For projects that invest time and money in writing test code only to find it abandoned, a deep cynicism grows about the value of writing test code.

Hard-to-maintain test code is one of the reasons test code falls out of use or is simply abandoned. It is important to realize that test code needs to be written with maintainability in mind. Testing a single method can require a half dozen or more test cases to fully and completely test all of the functionality. The implication, even if the code-under-test is well written, is that if the test code is difficult to maintain, it soon becomes a chore. The value of the test code becomes lost and the effort wasted. This section focuses on what you can do to make your test code maintainable.

▓ **Practice 8-1** Focus on Writing Maintainable Test Code

Here is a list of ways to make sure test code is maintainable:

- Adopt an effective naming convention for test namespaces, classes, and methods.
- Use a pattern for the test method body.
- Keep test methods short; strive for fewer than ten lines of code.
- Limit the test actions to one or two lines of code.
- Make one and only one primary assertion in the test method.
- Use the var keyword whenever it is allowed.
- Create a context class to encapsulate repeating arrangement code.
- Write helper classes to hold code that is common to tests across the suite.
- Pass data as arguments into the test method to data-drive the testing.

▓ **Note** Open the Visual Solution file *Lender.Slos.Express.sln*, which is found within the *Samples\Ch08\6_DAL_NH* folder, to see the completed sample code. The sample code serves as a model of how to follow the practices that are described in this chapter. When code in the text shows what *not* to do, it won't be in the sample code.

Naming Convention

There are different naming conventions for test code in common use. Each has its advocates and some have critics. This book takes the pragmatic approach of selecting one, explaining the rationale of each element, and staying consistent.[3] You may want to read up on alternate naming standards and select the one that's right for you and your team. The most important thing is to pick a convention and stay consistent.

Test code should *not* be written according to the same naming convention as production code. It serves a very different purpose and is run under different circumstance. Test code is never supposed to make it into production. A clear and effective naming convention should be used to meet the unique goals of making the test code easier to maintain and to help identify why a test is failing.

---

[3] This naming convention comes from Roy Osherove, *The Art of Unit Testing* (Greenwich, CT: Manning, 2009).

■ **Practice 8-2** Adopt an Effective Naming Convention

The naming convention presented in this book is helpful in these ways:

- The test namespace identifies both the category of the test and the assembly being tested.

- The test class name identifies the class-under-test, which is the class that the tests are testing.

- The test method name describes three key aspects of the test:

    - Method-under-test

    - Conditions of the test

    - Expected results of the test

■ **Tip** Because test code is run from within a test runner, it is important to choose an effective naming convention. There are command-line runners, CI server runners, Visual Studio plug-in runners, and stand-alone GUI runners. Each runner may present results grouped alphabetically by project, namespace, tests class name, or test method name. This naming convention aligns well with common sorting and grouping options.

An example of test code that illustrates the naming convention is shown in Listing 8-1. The namespace of Tests.Unit.Lender.Slos.Model indicates that the tests class contains a set of unit tests and that the class-under-test is declared under the Lender.Slos.Model namespace. A tests class name of LoanTests makes it clear that Loan is the class-under-test.

A test method name of ComputePayment_WithProvidedLoanData_ExpectProperPaymentAmount spells out three things:

1. The method-under-test is ComputePayment.

2. It is called with loan data provided.

3. It is expected to compute the proper payment amount.

Listing 8-1. Example Using the Test Code Naming Convention

```
namespace Tests.Unit.Lender.Slos.Model
{
    using global::Lender.Slos.Model;

    using NUnit.Framework;

    public class LoanTests
```

```
{
    [Test]
    public void ComputePayment_WithProvidedLoanData_ExpectProperPaymentAmount()
    {
        // Arrange
        Loan loan =
            new Loan
            {
                Principal = 12000m,
                AnnualPercentageRate = 12m,
            };

        // Act
        decimal actual = loan.ComputePayment(300);

        // Assert
        Assert.AreEqual(126.39m, actual);
    }
...
```

In Listing 8-2 the output from a failing test is shown. From the listing it is clear which test method failed and why. The output from a failed test is your first clue to finding and resolving the issue. For a large code base there will be many hundreds of test methods, so it is helpful to have a naming convention that points to the failing test. In this case, the ComputePayment method is not working.

Also, the stack trace has breadcrumbs for you to track down the problem. Your choices include both investigating the test code and the method-under-test. Contacting the developer directly may be an option if you know who is working on that class.

Listing 8-2. Output from a Failed Test

```
LoanTests.ComputePayment_WithProvidedLoanData_ExpectProperPaymentAmount : Failed
    Expected: 126.39m
    But was:  126.32m

at
Tests.Unit.Lender.Slos.Model.LoanTests.ComputePayment_WithProvidedLoanData_ExpectProperPayme
ntAmount() in LoanTests.cs: line 24
```

Let's take a look at each aspect of the naming convention one by one.

Namespaces

The naming convention starts by using the same namespace as the class-under-test and adds a prefix. The prefix has two terms; the word Tests and a category for the tests. Both terms are separated by a period. Categories that you might use include names like Unit, Surface, or Stability. An example of the name of an assembly with integration tests is Tests.Integration.Lender.Slos.Dal.dll.

Adding the word Tests to the beginning of every namespace may seem redundant; however, it is important for several key reasons. Test assemblies that begin with Tests.* ...

- Are clearly understood as being for testing use only.

- Can easily be sorted from production assemblies, allowing you to prevent test assemblies from going into production.

- Can be discovered by convention in build scripts and other CI techniques.

- Can be excluded, through the use of wildcarding, from code coverage tools and other program analysis.

The category name is also important because various testing categories have different setup and configuration requirements. The namespace lets everyone know what to expect:

- `Tests.Unit.*` require absolutely no setup or configuration and must execute quickly. Unit tests must always run as automated tests.

- `Tests.Integration.*` require significant setup and configuration. These tests should be run manually.

- `Tests.Surface.*` are specialized automated integration tests, called surface tests. These require a one-time setup and configuration, but can be run by developers as automated integration tests.

- `Tests.Stability.*` require setup and configuration and are normally performed after deployment on an integration server. These tests should run automatically by the CI server.

Choose a test project and assembly name to be consistent with these namespaces to reap the benefits of this convention.

Tests Classes

The naming convention uses a `<ClassUnderTest>+Tests` format to name the class that contains the test methods. If the class-under-test is named `StudentDal` then the test class name is `StudentDalTests`. The test class name is distinct from the class-under-test's name and is both short and clear. It follows the alphabetization rules of the class-under-test, which makes it easy to find the class-under-test using Visual Studio's class or solution explorers.

▓ **Note** In the phrase *tests class* the word *tests* is intentionally plural. It refers to the class that contains the tests, which is also known as the *test fixture class*.

Test Methods

First and foremost the method name must communicate the intention of the test. Three important facts need to be clear from the test method's name:

- Method-under-test

- Conditions under which the test is performed

- Expected result needed to pass the test

The test method naming convention fits a readability pattern and clearly communicates the intention of the test. Also, it is not unnecessarily wordy. The convention is MethodUnderTest_WithSpecifiedCondition_ExpectThisResult. The following are examples of test methods that follow the naming convention:

- ComputePayment_WithProvidedLoanData_ExpectProperAmount

- ApproveLoan_WhenLoanDataIsValid_ExpectLoanSaveCalledExactlyOnce

- ComputeBalance_ForNegativeBalanceScenarios_ExpectOutOfRangeException

This short-and-sweet test method naming convention is used by the code samples and throughout the book. The important principle is to establish a naming convention that clearly states how the method-under-test is expected to behave under the conditions provided by the test.

The Test Method Body

The test method body also needs to follow a convention. All developers on the project should be able to find the test code and understand it right away. If all test code follows the same convention then this happens quickly. Going one step further, if all test code within the organization follows the same convention, it is easier for developers to join projects or get new projects off on a good footing.

Arrange-Act-Assert

There are certainly other ways to organize test methods, but the Arrange-Act-Assert (or 3-As) pattern is an effective standard[4]. The 3-As pattern is a widely-used and helpful convention. The *Arrange* section of a test method contains the steps that establish preconditions, define dependencies, create the class-under-test, and assign needed values. The *Act* section contains the steps the test code executes to perform the test. The *Assert* section contains the steps needed to verify and validate the test and forces it to fail if expectations are not met.

▓ **Practice 8-3** Use the Arrange-Act-Assert (3-As) Pattern

Referring back to Listing 8-1, that test method followed the 3-As pattern. It is customary to include the comments Arrange, Act, and Assert in your code to clearly show the start of each section.

```
[Test]
public void ComputePayment_WithProvidedLoanData_ExpectProperPaymentAmount()
{
    // Arrange
    Loan loan =
        new Loan
        {
```

---

[4] The Ward Cunningham wiki describes the 3-As pattern at http://c2.com/cgi/wiki?ArrangeActAssert.

```
        Principal = 12000m,
        AnnualPercentageRate = 12m,
    };

    // Act
    decimal actual = loan.ComputePayment(300);

    // Assert
    Assert.AreEqual(126.39m, actual);
}
```

Keep Tests Short

A lengthy test method is hard to read and understand. The code within the test method needs to be kept short to manage the test's complexity. Dealing with a short method is especially helpful when trying to resolve another developer's failing test. One of your code changes might fail another developer's test for a variety of reasons: a new requirement, inconsistent behavior, or a just-made-obsolete test case. Each test method describes the code-under-test and how it is intended to work.

▨ **Practice 8-4** Prefer Many Short Tests over Few Long Tests

---

Keep tests short to help focus on checking the smallest single intention. By following a *one test method is testing one intention* approach you allow the test code to have a much longer useful life. It also allows any developer to quickly address a failing test, instead of ignoring it. Because the test code is short and uncomplicated, the developer is more likely to deal with the situation.

Limit Test Actions

Before looking at the Arrange section let's look at the Act section. If a test performs more than one action, it is probably testing too much. The test likely has a lot of arrangement code to establish the preconditions needed for the many actions. To keep the test method short, make every effort to keep the Act section to just one line of straightforward code. A big reason to avoid more than one line of action is that, when a test method fails, multiple action steps require investigation to sort out the line that is failing the test. With one action step it is clear what test code is involved.

▨ **Practice 8-5** Avoid More Than One Line of Action

In Listing 8-3 there are five lines of code within the Act section. If there is an error in the Get method it is not immediately clear if it is caused by the first or the second call to the Get method. If the whole test fails, which of the many action lines caused the problem?

Listing 8-3. Too Many Action Steps

```
[Test(Description = "Too many action steps")]
public void Save_WhenPrincipalIsChanged_ExpectNewPrincipalValueInDatabase()
{
    // Arrange
    Application classUnderTest = new Application();
    classUnderTest.Principal = 999.91m;
    classUnderTest.Save();
    int id = classUnderTest.Id;

    // Act
    classUnderTest.Get(id);
    classUnderTest.Principal = 1009.81m;
    classUnderTest.Save();
    classUnderTest.Get(id);
    decimal actual = classUnderTest.Principal;

    // Assert
    Assert.AreEqual(1009.81m, actual);
}
```

In Listing 8-4 the test method has only one line of code in the Act section. From the test method name, calling the Save method is the action step of this test. There is more arrangement code, but let's address that detail later in the chapter.

Listing 8-4. One Action Step

```
[TestCase(Description = "One action step")]
public void Save_WhenPrincipalIsChanged_ExpectNewPrincipalValueInDatabase()
{
    // Arrange
    var expectedPrincipal = 1009.81m;

    ApplicationTestsContext.SetupTestDatabase("ApplicationDalTests_Scenario01.xml");

    var classUnderTest = ApplicationTestsContext.CreateInstance();
    classUnderTest.Id = 97;
    classUnderTest.Principal = expectedPrincipal;

    // Act
    classUnderTest.Save();

    // Assert
    var actual = ApplicationTestsContext.Retrieve<decimal>(
        "Principal",
        "Application",
        string.Format("[Id] = {0}", 97));
    Assert.AreEqual(expectedPrincipal, actual);
}
```

To make sure test code is readable, avoid writing test methods with more than one line of code in the Act section. Also, did you notice that the number 97 is hard-coded in two places? Later, you will see how values like this one are passed in as an argument.

Primary Assertion

Tests should have a narrow focus. One of the best ways to keep the focus sharp is to limit the test method to one primary assertion. Assertions verify and validate that the test works as intended. The *primary assertion* lines up with the expectation stated in the test method's name and needs to match with it.

▨ **Practice 8-6** Avoid More Than One Primary Assertion

For example, if the expectation in a test method name is `ExpectCorrectPaymentAmount` then the primary assertion statement ought to be:

```
// Assert
var expectedPaymentAmount = 126.39m;
Assert.AreEqual(expectedPaymentAmount, actual);
```

It is unambiguous; the proper payment amount must be $126.39. If the code-under-test returns a value that is not that amount then the test fails.

There are a number of ways assertions can be made. They include

- *Comparison:* Compare expected value to actual value and verify that the values are one of the following: equal, not equal, one less than the other, one greater than the other, etc.

- *Expected Interaction:* Verify a required dependency is one of the following: called a specific number of times, passed specific arguments, not called with invalid arguments, etc.

- *Throws:* Verify an expected exception of the specific type is thrown.

- *Collection:* Validate that an element exists in a collection.

- *Object Instance:* Verify the actual instance is one of the following: null, not null, an instance of a specific type, etc.

- *Boolean:* Verify that an expression is true or false.

- *Constraint-Based:* Verify that an instance meets a constraint.

▨ **Tip** The constraint-based syntax—called using the `Assert.That` method in NUnit —is very powerful. In the NUnit framework many assert methods implement their behavior by wrapping a call to `Assert.That`. The constraint-based syntax also allows you to implement your own custom constraints.

The term *primary assertion* prompts the question: is there such a thing as a secondary assertion? Yes, a *secondary assertion* is any useful but less important assertion that helps explain why a test fails. In Listing 8-5 the statement in bold is the primary assertion; it is a good primary assertion. The Arrange and Assert sections each contain non-primary assertions. Another good practice to mention: assert only one condition at a time. Avoid combining multiple conditional tests in a single call with `Assert.True`. This only makes it harder later when trying to understand and debug a failing test.

Listing 8-5. Guard and Secondary Assertions

```
// Arrange
var application = Application.GetById(73);
var classUnderTest = application.Student;

Assert.NotNull(classUnderTest);

// Act
School highSchool = classUnderTest.HighSchool;

// Assert
Assert.NotNull(highSchool);
Assert.AreEqual(expectedState, highSchool.State);
```

What happens if the `highSchool` variable returned by the `classUnderTest.HighSchool` is null? If the secondary assertion of `Assert.NotNull(highSchool)` is not there, the test method fails because the method-under-test throws a `NullReferenceException`. Here is sample output:

```
StudentTests.HighSchool_WithValidSchoolInfo_ExpectProperState : Failed
    System.NullReferenceException : Object reference not set to an instance of an object.

at
Tests.Unit.Lender.Slos.Model.StudentTests.HighSchool_WithValidSchoolInfo_ExpectProperState()
in StudentTests.cs: line 28
```

The secondary assertion makes the issue more apparent by verifying that `highSchool` is not null before the primary assertion is made. If `highSchool` is null the secondary assertion fails and the test output looks like this:

```
StudentTests.HighSchool_WithValidSchoolInfo_ExpectProperState : Failed
    Expected: not null
    But was:  null

at
Tests.Unit.Lender.Slos.Model.StudentTests.HighSchool_WithValidSchoolInfo_ExpectProperState()
in StudentTests.cs: line 28
```

It is clear from this output why the test failed. The purpose of a secondary assertion is to turn any important, implicit assumptions into direct assertions. Secondary assertions are often made at the beginning of the Assert section.

In addition to secondary assertions in the Assert section there are *guard assertions* in the Arrange section. The only practical difference is that guard assertions are made before entering the Act section. In Listing 8-5, notice that there is a Assert.NotNull(classUnderTest.Student) statement at the end of the Arrange section. If the Student property returns null before the test method enters the Act section then the test output makes it obvious. The Arrange section adds these guard assertions to make explicit any vital assumptions that are a condition of the class-under-test performing properly.

■ **Caution** Avoid over-specifying the test method's expectations. Be sure that any guard and secondary assertions play only a supporting role.

Any guard assertions need to support getting the test method to the *Act* section. Any secondary assertions need to help get the test method to the primary assertion. If you find yourself adding secondary assertions after the primary assertion then they are probably not needed. The trap to avoid is over-specifying the expectations, which leads to unnecessary code to maintain.

Listing 8-6 shows an example of a test method that has over-specified the expectations.

Listing 8-6. Over-Specified Expectations

```
[Test(Description = "Over-specified expectations")]
public void ComputePayment_WhenInvalidTermInMonthsIsZero_ExpectArgumentOutOfRangeException()
{
    // Arrange
    Loan loan =
        new Loan
        {
            Principal = 7499,
            AnnualPercentageRate = 1.79m,
        };

    Assert.NotNull(loan);

    // Act
    TestDelegate act = () => loan.ComputePayment(0);

    // Assert
    ArgumentOutOfRangeException exception =
        Assert.Throws<ArgumentOutOfRangeException>(act);
    Assert.AreEqual("termInPeriods", exception.ParamName);
    Assert.AreEqual(
        "Specified argument was out of the range of valid values.\r\n" +
        "Parameter name: termInPeriods",
        exception.Message);
}
```

At the end of the Arrange section there is a guard assertion that asserts that loan is not null. There really is no reason to do that because .NET takes care of constructing the new Loan; the test code is in effect testing that the C# compiler works.

Now take another look at Listing 8-6; there are two secondary assertions that come after the primary assertion. The order here is not important. What is important is that both assertions over-specify the requirements of the code-under-test. Is there really a requirement that the ComputePayment method's parameter is named termInPeriods? Also, the message in the exception must be exactly right or the test fails. By looking at the test method's name, a better implementation is suggested as follows:

```
[Test]
public void ComputePayment_WhenInvalidTermInMonthsIsZero_ExpectArgumentOutOfRangeException ()
{
    // Arrange
    Loan loan =
        new Loan
        {
            Principal = 7499,
            AnnualPercentageRate = 1.79m,
        };

    // Act
    TestDelegate act = () => loan.ComputePayment(0);

    // Assert
    Assert.Throws<ArgumentOutOfRangeException>(act);
}
```

So far this chapter has focused on ways to make test code clear and concise. The next sections build on readability with some additional practices for writing more maintainable test code.

The var Keyword

Since the var keyword was introduced in C# 3.0, frequent debates have arisen as to whether or not to use implicit typing. Let's dispel any fear, confusion, and misconception regarding the var keyword:

- It is not a variant type from COM or VB6.

- It does not make C# weakly typed.

- It is statically typed; the variable's type is unambiguously inferred by the compiler.

The C# compiler knows the type without you having to explicitly enter it. Stated another way, if it is not entirely clear to the compiler, a compilation error occurs. There are definitely recommendations on when and why to use the var keyword in production code.[5] However, in test code the explicit type of the variable is usually not important; it is normally clear from the context. It is best to use implicit typing in test code to concentrate on the higher-level goal of maintainability. There are no practical drawbacks; with IntelliSense you can easily discover the variable's type.

▨ **Practice 8-7** Avoid Explicit Typing Variables in Test Code; Use the var Keyword

---

[5] Recommendations for implicit typing in production code are provided in Jon Skeet, *C# in Depth* (Greenwich, CT: Manning, 2008).

There are definite benefits to using implicit typing in test code. If a type in the code-under-test changes, then the test code does not change as long as it has no material impact on any test. The compiler makes sure of that. A corollary benefit is that if the type change does matter, then test code directly impacted by the change breaks. The compiler highlights the test code that needs to be examined.

Test Context Classes

Following the practices to this point, the Act section is one line and the Assert section is limited to a primary assertion. Test code will become more elaborate as more complicated scenarios are tested. Any reason the test method is long must be found in the Arrange section. The amount of repeating arrangement code becomes obvious. In addition, a lot of test methods basically repeat. At some point refactoring the test code is needed.

▪ **Practice 8-8** Use a Tests Context Class to Reduce Repetition and Manage Complexity

---

A solution to the repeating arrangement problem is to write a `TestsContext` class. This uses the Library Class pattern.[6] The approach is to create a class and add static methods to hold a small library of repeating arrangement code specific to a tests class.

In Listing 8-7 the Arrange section is too long. Also, parts of the arrangement are used in other test methods within the same test class. It is helpful to extract the repeating code from all the test methods in this class and place them in an `ApplicationTestsContext` class. Note the bold lines in the listing, where the `classUnderTest` is created. This code repeats in other test methods in the tests class.

Listing 8-7. Arrange Section Too Long

```
namespace Tests.Unit.Lender.Slos.Model
{
    public class ApplicationTests
    {
        [Test]
        public void Save_WithValidNewApplication_ExpectApplicationRepoCreateCalledOnce()
        {
            // Arrange
            var mockApplicationRepo =
                new Mock<IRepository<ApplicationEntity>>(MockBehavior.Strict);
            mockApplicationRepo
                .Setup(e => e.Create(It.IsAny<ApplicationEntity>()))
                .Returns(73)
                .Verifiable();

            var stubIndividualRepo =
                new Mock<IRepository<IndividualEntity>>(MockBehavior.Loose);
```

---

[6] The Library Pattern is described in Kent Beck, *Implementation Patterns* (Upper Saddle River, NJ: Addison-Wesley Professional, 2008).

```
var stubStudentRepo =
    new Mock<IRepository<StudentEntity>>(MockBehavior.Loose);

var classUnderTest =
    new Application(
        stubIndividualRepo.Object,
        stubStudentRepo.Object,
        mockApplicationRepo.Object)
        {
            Student =
                {
                    LastName = "Smith",
                    FirstName = "John",
                    DateOfBirth = new DateTime(1993, 5, 7),
                    HighSchool =
                        {
                            Name = "Our Town High School",
                            City = "Anytown",
                            State = "OO"
                        }
                },
            Principal = 7499,
            AnnualPercentageRate = 1.79m,
            TotalPayments = 113
        };

// Act
classUnderTest.Save();

// Assert
mockApplicationRepo
    .Verify(e => e.Create(It.IsAny<ApplicationEntity>()), Times.Once());
}
...
```

▪ **Caution** For those considering using class inheritance to achieve code reuse in test code, it has more drawbacks than benefits. Tests class inheritance couples tests and negatively impacts maintainability. The one exception is using a tests base class for shared testing infrastructure, such as surface testing.

In Listing 8-8 a new internal static class named ApplicationTestsContext is shown. Note that the naming convention is <Tests Class Name>+Context. We add to that class a CreateInstance method, which returns a valid Application instance. It is useful to bring the declaring of the stubs into the CreateInstance method. By using default parameters, the method instantiates stubs whenever a dependency override is not provided. For now, let's leave the discussion of stubs and mocks for a later section.

■ **Caution** Make sure to keep the tests context class for the exclusive use of the tests class. This prevents one set of tests from becoming coupled to another set of tests. The naming convention helps make things obvious.

Listing 8-8. The Tests Context Class

```
namespace Tests.Unit.Lender.Slos.Model
{
    internal static class ApplicationTestsContext
    {
        // Creates an instance of a new valid Application for use by ApplicationTests
        public static Application CreateInstance(
            IRepository<IndividualEntity> individualRepo = null,
            IRepository<StudentEntity> studentRepo = null,
            IRepository<ApplicationEntity> applicationRepo = null)
        {
            var stubIndividualRepo =
                new Mock<IRepository<IndividualEntity>>(MockBehavior.Loose);
            var stubStudentRepo =
                new Mock<IRepository<StudentEntity>>(MockBehavior.Loose);
            var stubApplicationRepo =
                new Mock<IRepository<ApplicationEntity>>(MockBehavior.Loose);

            return new Application(
                individualRepo ?? stubIndividualRepo.Object,
                studentRepo ?? stubStudentRepo.Object,
                applicationRepo ?? stubApplicationRepo.Object)
            {
                Student =
                {
                    LastName = "Smith",
                    FirstName = "John",
                    DateOfBirth = new DateTime(1993, 5, 7),
                    HighSchool =
                    {
                        Name = "Our Town High School",
                        City = "Anytown",
                        State = "QQ"
                    }
                },
                Principal = 7499,
                AnnualPercentageRate = 1.79m,
                TotalPayments = 113
            };
        }
    }
...
```

In Listing 8-9 the test method has a shorter Arrange section: only three lines of code. The first two handle the mock object and the third uses the context class to make an instance of a valid Application.

Listing 8-9. Now Using the Tests Context Class

```
namespace Tests.Unit.Lender.Slos.Model
{
    public class ApplicationTests
    {
        [Test]
        public void Save_WithValidNewApplication_ExpectApplicationRepoCreateCalledOnce()
        {
            // Arrange
            var mockApplicationRepo =
                new Mock<IRepository<ApplicationEntity>>(MockBehavior.Strict);
            mockApplicationRepo
                .Setup(e => e.Create(It.IsAny<ApplicationEntity>()))
                .Returns(73)
                .Verifiable();

            var classUnderTest = ApplicationTestsContext
                .CreateInstance(
                    null,
                    null,
                    mockApplicationRepo.Object);

            // Act
            classUnderTest.Save();

            // Assert
            mockApplicationRepo
                .Verify(e => e.Create(It.IsAny<ApplicationEntity>()), Times.Once());
        }
...
```

Test Helpers

Another way to achieve reuse is to build up helper classes. Like the TestsContext class, this technique uses the Library Pattern. The idea here is to put common code found across many tests classes into a shared location. It is important that this code relate to a common aspect or concern across many test methods in the tests assembly.

▓ **Practice 8-9** Build Test Helper Classes to Promote Reuse

---

In Listing 8-10 the BuildNameString method generates a random string that is of random length. When a street, city, or last name is needed, this helper method can generate one. By using optional parameters this method can have functionality added over time, such as multiple-word names. Other applications of test helper methods include randomly generating a date, amount, or a percentage rate, each falling within a range of valid values.

Listing 8-10. Helper Method to Build a Random Name

```
namespace Tests.Unit.Lender.Slos.Model.Helpers
{
    internal static class TestDataHelper
    {

...

        public static string BuildNameString(
            int? length = null)
        {
            var randomizer = new Random();
            var generatedLength = length ?? randomizer.Next(1, DefaultMaxStringLength);

            Assert.Greater(generatedLength, 0);

            var stringBuilder = new StringBuilder(generatedLength);
            stringBuilder.Append(
                UpperCaseLetters[randomizer.Next(0, UpperCaseLetters.Length - 1)]);
            for (var index = 1; index < generatedLength; index++)
            {
                stringBuilder.Append(
                    LowerCaseLetters[randomizer.Next(0, LowerCaseLetters.Length - 1)]);
            }

            return stringBuilder.ToString();
        }

...
```

░ **Caution** Do *not* put any logic that is specific to the code-under-test in these helpers. Test helpers should remain generalized.

Avoid making test helper methods that are specific to the application's domain. For example, a method that calculates a loan payment amount to save to the database might be used by a series of test methods in the Arrange section. If the helper method changes for one test class, say LoanTests, then a lot of other arrangement code may need to change. Avoid writing test helper methods that inappropriately couple the tests classes.

Data Scenarios

As the tests are written, it becomes apparent that many of the test methods are exactly the same code, only using different values in the Arrange section. Several testing frameworks offer ways to call the same test method with different input data. For example, with NUnit the TestCase attribute does this. MbUnit has the RowTest attribute and xUnit.net has the Theory attribute. Features of testing frameworks are covered in detail in Chapter 12.

■ **Practice 8-10** Data-Drive Test Methods for Multiple Test Cases

In the SLOS system the payment calculator guards against an invalid termInMonths argument. There are many invalid argument scenarios to test. In Listing 8-11 these many scenarios are combined into one test method using the TestCase attribute. Instead of seven test methods to maintain for each scenario, there is one method with seven TestCase attributes.

Listing 8-11. Data-Driven Test Cases

```
[TestCase(7499, 1.79, 0, 72.16)]
[TestCase(7499, 1.79, -1, 72.16)]
[TestCase(7499, 1.79, -73, 72.16)]
[TestCase(7499, 1.79, int.MinValue, 72.16)]
[TestCase(7499, 1.79, 361, 72.16)]
[TestCase(7499, 1.79, 2039, 72.16)]
[TestCase(7499, 1.79, int.MaxValue, 72.16)]
public void ComputePayment_WithInvalidTermInMonths_ExpectArgumentOutOfRangeException(
    decimal principal,
    decimal annualPercentageRate,
    int termInMonths,
    decimal expectedPaymentPerPeriod)
{
    // Arrange
    var loan =
        new Loan
        {
            Principal = principal,
            AnnualPercentageRate = annualPercentageRate,
        };

    // Act
    TestDelegate act = () => loan.ComputePayment(termInMonths);

    // Assert
    Assert.Throws<ArgumentOutOfRangeException>(act);
}
```

The important point is that without using the TestCase attribute, a lot more test methods would be needed to completely test that one ComputePayment method. Writing maintainable test code needs to focus on ways to reduce the ratio of test code to code-under-test. By using data to drive a single test method these many cases are tested with minimal code. This achieves a significant reduction in the amount of test code to maintain.

■ **Tip** Use prime numbers to help avoid coincidental arithmetic issues and help make debugging easier. Also, avoid using hardcoded strings. Use `Guid.NewGuid.ToString()` or use a test helper method like `TestHelper.BuidString()` to ensure uniqueness and variability.

Notice how the test cases use prime numbers. A common coincidental arithmetic problem occurs when a test uses the number 2. These three expressions: `2 + 2, 2 * 2`, and `System.Math.Pow(2, 2)` all equal to four. When using the number 2 as a test value, there are many ways the test falsely passes. Arithmetic errors are less likely to yield an improper result when the test values are different prime numbers. Consider a loan that has a principal of $12,000.00, a term of 360 payments, an annual interest rate of 12%, and, of course, remember there are 12 months in a year. Because there is a coincidental factor of 12 in all these numbers, that data scenario is a very poor choice as a test case.

Unit Testing

A sample of test code that puts together all practices covered to this point is shown in Listing 8-12. The test code

- Follows the naming convention
- Follows the 3-As pattern
- Keeps the arrangement code short
- Performs only one action
- Makes only one assertion
- Is a single test method driven by data to cover multiple scenarios
- Uses prime numbers to avoid coincidental arithmetic issues and to make debugging easier

Listing 8-12. Example Unit Test Code

```
namespace Tests.Unit.Lender.Slos.Model
{
    public class LoanTests
    {
        [TestCase(7499, 1.79, 113, 72.16)]
        [TestCase(8753, 6.53, 139, 89.92)]
        [TestCase(61331, 7.09, 367, 409.5)]
        public void ComputePayment_WithProvidedLoanData_ExpectProperMonthlyPayment(
            decimal principal,
            decimal annualPercentageRate,
            int termInMonths,
            decimal expectedPaymentPerPeriod)
        {
            // Arrange
            var loan =
```

```
            new Loan
            {
                Principal = principal,
                AnnualPercentageRate = annualPercentageRate,
            };

        // Act
        var actual = loan.ComputePayment(termInMonths);

        // Assert
        Assert.AreEqual(expectedPaymentPerPeriod, actual);
    }
...
```

At this point, it seems that the method-under-test is fully tested. It is not. Although this test method is readable and maintainable, it does not fully test the method-under-test. For example, the test code should test how the ComputePayment method reacts when called on a Loan object that has a negative Principal amount.

SAMPLE CODE: OVERVIEW

You may want to review the book's Introduction at this point to learn what is needed to run the sample code.

For these instructions, it is assumed that the same code for this chapter is found in your *Samples\Ch08* folder. That folder is simply referred to with a dollar symbol ($).

There are six subfolders. Each contains the code for the steps covered in this chapter:

- *Deploy:* The database scripts used to create the database
- *Start:* The sample code at the beginning of the SLOS upgrade project
- *Validate:* After the validation requirements and test code are complete
- *Calculator:* After the payment calculation code is refactored to a common library
- *DAL SP:* The automated test code written against the stored-procedure DAL
- *DAL NH:* The automated testing of the NHibernate DAL

Before compiling and running the code, a Microsoft SQL Server database needs to be created. Since all sample connection strings assume the server instance is *(local)\SQLExpress* you may need to modify your connection strings with a different instance name. A database with the name Lender.Slos needs to be created. To create this database go to the *$\1_Deploy\Database\Scripts* folder and run the batch file named *DbCreate.SqlExpress.Lender.Slos.bat*. If you prefer to create the database manually, make sure it has the name Lender.Slos.

For the sake of simplicity there are two types of batch files that use MSBuild: one type runs database scripts and the other builds and runs the tests. These batch files assume you defined the following environment variables:

- *MSBuildRoot:* The path to *MSBuild.exe*
  For example, *C:\Windows\Microsoft.NET\Framework64\v4.0.30319*

- *SqlToolsRoot:* The path to *sqlcmd.exe*
  For example, *C:\Program Files\Microsoft SQL Server\100\Tools\Binn*

- *NunitRoot:* The path to *nunit-console.exe*
  For example, *C:\Tools\NUnit\v2.5.10.11092\bin\net-2.0*

With the database created and the environment variables set, run the *Lender.Slos.CreateScripts.bat* batch to execute all the SQL create scripts in the correct order. If you prefer to run the scripts manually then you will find them in the *$\1_Deploy\Database\Scripts\Create* folder. The *script_run_order.txt* file lists the proper order to run the scripts. If all the scripts run properly there will be three tables (Individual, Student, and Application) and twelve stored procedures (a set of four CRUD stored procedures for each of the tables) in the database.

The automated tests use the MSBuild script file named *runner.msbuild*. Listings of output from running the *runner.msbuild* script from within Visual Studio are presented throughout this chapter. Instructions on how to set up and use the Visual Studio External Tools feature to run the tests are described in Chapter 12.

For your convenience, a *runner.bat* file is provided to execute the MSBuild script. The script performs a rebuild of the solution and then runs all the tests. This approach allows any developer to perform all the automated steps in a way that is identical to how a CI server executes the script.

SAMPLE CODE: UNIT TESTING

The goal of this sample code is not to teach you how to write unit tests. The goal is to demonstrate test code that is readable and easy to maintain. All of the tests are automated, in the sense that any developer is able to run them with zero setup and configuration and the CI server is able to run all of them with MSBuild, using the *runner.msbuild* script

In the *$\2_Start* folder is the code at the beginning of the SLOS project.

The code in the *$\3_Validate* folder is the result of developing unit tests as part of developing the Validate method for the Student class. There is the new Tests.Unit.Lender.Model project, which has two unit tests classes, StudentTests and LoanTests. The tests in LoanTests cover the ComputePayment method in the Loan class.

In the *$\4_Calculator* folder is the code that results from refactoring the ComputePayment method out of Loan and into a separate Calculator class. In the Tests.Unit.Lender.Model project, there are new unit tests classes to test the *Estimated Monthly Payment Calculator* enhancement to the Application class. There are two new projects, Lender.Slos.Financial and Tests.Unit.Lender.Slos.Financial. These contain the new Calculator and CalculatorTests classes, respectively.

Boundary Analysis

For every method-under-test there is a set of valid preconditions and arguments. It is the domain of all possible values that allows the method to work properly. That domain defines the method's boundaries. Boundary testing requires analysis to determine the valid preconditions and the valid arguments. Once these are established, you can develop tests to verify that the method guards against invalid preconditions and arguments.

▨ **Practice 8-11** Perform Boundary Analysis to Cover All Scenarios

---

Boundary analysis is about finding the limits of acceptable values, which includes looking at the following:

- All invalid values
- Maximum values
- Minimum values
- Values just on a boundary
- Values just within a boundary
- Values just outside a boundary
- Values that behave uniquely, such as zero or one

All of the .NET Framework primitive data types have important limits. Boundary values for commonly-used .NET data types are shown in Table 8-2.

Table 8-2. Boundaries for Some Common .NET Types

Type	Maximum	Minimum	Default	Special	Edge Cases
String	(variable)	string.Empty	null	--	special chars
Int32	MaxValue	MinValue	0	--	-1, 0, 1
Decimal	MaxValue	MinValue	Zero	MinusOne	(situational)
Double	MaxValue, PositiveInfinity	MinValue, NegativeInfinity	0d	NaN	(situational)
DateTime	MaxValue	MinValue	"zero date"	Now, Today	(situational)
Guid	--	--	Empty	--	--

An example of a situational case for dates is a deadline or time window. You could imagine that for SLOS, a loan disbursement must occur no earlier than 30 days before or no later than 60 days after the first day of the semester. Another situational case might be a restriction on age, dollar amount, or interest rate. There are also rounding-behavior limits, like two-digits for dollar amounts and six-digits for interest rates. There are also physical limits to things like weight and height and age. Both zero and one behave uniquely in certain mathematical expressions. Time zone, language and culture, and other test conditions could be relevant. Analyzing all these limits helps to identify boundaries used in test code.

▓ **Note** Dealing with date arithmetic can be tricky. Boundary analysis and good test code makes sure that the date and time logic is correct. In this example, there is a risk of confusion when validating the upper age limit because the age boundary is described using the number 26 in the requirements, but an age of 27 is exactly on the boundary.

Invalid Arguments

When the test code calls a method-under-test with an invalid argument, the method should throw an argument exception. This is the intended behavior, but to verify it requires a negative test. A *negative test* is test code that *passes* if the method-under-test responds negatively; in this case, throwing an argument exception.

The test code shown in Listing 8-13 fails the test because ComputePayment is provided an invalid termInMonths of zero. The result of the failing test is shown in Listing 8-14.

Listing 8-13. Test Code Is Not Expecting an Exception

```
[TestCase(7499, 1.79, 0, 72.16)]
public void ComputePayment_WithProvidedLoanData_ExpectProperMonthlyPayment(
    decimal principal,
    decimal annualPercentageRate,
    int termInMonths,
    decimal expectedPaymentPerPeriod)
{
    // Arrange
    var loan =
        new Loan
        {
            Principal = principal,
            AnnualPercentageRate = annualPercentageRate,
        };

    // Act
    var actual = loan.ComputePayment(termInMonths);
```

```
    // Assert
    Assert.AreEqual(expectedPaymentPerPeriod, actual);
}
...
```

Listing 8-14. Output from Unexpected Exception

```
LoanTests.ComputePayment_WithProvidedLoanData_ExpectInvalidArgumentException : Failed
System.ArgumentOutOfRangeException : Specified argument was out of the range of valid
values.
Parameter name: termInPeriods

at
Tests.Unit.Lender.Slos.Model.LoanTests.ComputePayment_WithProvidedLoanData_ExpectInvalidArgu
mentException(Decimal principal, Decimal annualPercentageRate, Int32 termInMonths, Decimal
expectedPaymentPerPeriod) in LoanTests.cs: line 25
```

The challenge is to *pass* the test when the exception is thrown. Also, the test code should verify that the exception type is InvalidArgumentException. This requires the method to somehow catch the exception, evaluate it, and determine if the exception is expected.

In NUnit this can be accomplished using either an attribute or a test delegate. In the case of a test delegate, the test method can use a lambda expression to define the action step to perform. The lambda is assigned to a TestDelegate variable within the Act section. In the Assert section, an assertion statement verifies that the proper exception is thrown when the test delegate is invoked.

The invalid values for the termInMonths argument are found by inspecting the ComputePayment method's code, reviewing the requirements, and performing boundary analysis. The following invalid values are discovered:

- A term of zero months

- Any negative term in months

- Any term greater than 360 months (30 years)

In Listing 8-15 the new test is written to verify that the ComputePayment method throws an ArgumentOutOfRangeException whenever an invalid term is passed as an argument to the method.

Listing 8-15. Negative Test; Expected Exception

```
[TestCase(7499, 1.79, 0, 72.16)]
[TestCase(7499, 1.79, -1, 72.16)]
[TestCase(7499, 1.79, -2, 72.16)]
[TestCase(7499, 1.79, int.MinValue, 72.16)]
[TestCase(7499, 1.79, 361, 72.16)]
[TestCase(7499, 1.79, int.MaxValue, 72.16)]
public void ComputePayment_WithInvalidTermInMonths_ExpectArgumentOutOfRangeException(
    decimal principal,
    decimal annualPercentageRate,
    int termInMonths,
    decimal expectedPaymentPerPeriod)
```

```
{
    // Arrange
    var loan =
        new Loan
            {
                Principal = principal,
                AnnualPercentageRate = annualPercentageRate,
            };

    // Act
    TestDelegate act = () => loan.ComputePayment(termInMonths);

    // Assert
    Assert.Throws<ArgumentOutOfRangeException>(act);
}
...
```

Invalid Preconditions

Every .NET object is in some arranged state at the time a method of that object is invoked. The state may be valid or it may be invalid. Whether explicit or implicit, all methods have expected preconditions. Since the method's preconditions are not spelled out, one goal of good test code is to test those assumptions as a way of revealing the implicit expectations and turning them into explicit preconditions.

For example, before calculating a payment amount, let's say the principal must be at least $1,000 and less than $185,000. Without knowing the code, these limits are hidden preconditions of the ComputePayment method. The following test code makes them explicit by arranging the classUnderTest with unacceptable values and calling the ComputePayment method. The test code asserts that an expected exception is thrown when the method's preconditions are violated. If the exception is not thrown, the test fails.

Listing 8-16. Testing Invalid Preconditions

```
[TestCase(0, 1.79, 360, 72.16)]
[TestCase(997, 1.79, 360, 72.16)]
[TestCase(999.99, 1.79, 360, 72.16)]
[TestCase(185000, 1.79, 360, 72.16)]
[TestCase(185021, 1.79, 360, 72.16)]
public void ComputePayment_WithInvalidPrincipal_ExpectInvalidOperationException(
    decimal principal,
    decimal annualPercentageRate,
    int termInMonths,
    decimal expectedPaymentPerPeriod)
{
    // Arrange
    var classUnderTest =
        new Application(null, null, null)
            {
                Principal = principal,
                AnnualPercentageRate = annualPercentageRate,
            };
```

```
    // Act
    TestDelegate act = () => classUnderTest.ComputePayment(termInMonths);

    // Assert
    Assert.Throws<InvalidOperationException>(act);
}
```

Implicit preconditions should be tested and defined by a combination of exploratory testing and inspection of the code-under-test, whenever possible. Test the boundaries by arranging the class-under-test in improbable scenarios, such as negative principal amounts or interest rates.

■ **Tip** Testing preconditions and invalid arguments prompts a lot of questions. What is the principal limit? Is it $18,500 or $185,000? Does it change from year to year? Maintain an open IM window or send a daily e-mail with questions for the analyst.

Microsoft's CodeContracts are part of .NET 4 and are discussed in Chapter 2. Code contracts are very relevant to code correctness and verification. Unit tests ought to test that these contracts are in place, and that they enforce and verify at runtime that pre- and post-conditions are proper.

Fakes, Stubs, and Mocks

The term *fake* is a general term for an object that stands in for another object; both *stubs* and *mocks* are types of fakes.[7] The purpose of a fake is to create an object that allows the method-under-test to be tested in isolation from its dependencies, meeting one of two objectives:

- *Stub:* Prevent the dependency from obstructing the method-under-test and to respond in a way that helps it proceed through its logical steps.

- *Mock:* Allow the test code to verify that the code-under-test's interaction with the dependency is proper, valid, and expected.

Since a fake is any object that stands in for the dependency, it is how the fake is used that determines if it is a stub or mock. Mocks are used only for interaction testing. If the expectation of the test method is *not* about verifying interaction with the fake then the fake must be a stub.

---

[7] These terms are explained very well in *The Art of Unit Testing* by Roy Osherove.

Table 8-3. Stub vs. Mock

Type	Description	Objective
Stub	Stands in for an object instance that the method-under-test depends upon or fails without it.	To allow the test code to continue to work isolated from its dependencies. The stub performs the minimum/essential behavior needed to allow the code-under-test to work. For clarity, in test code prefix stub-object variables with *stub*.
Mock	Provides the ability to verify the interactions that the method-under-test has with the object instances it works with.	To verify and validate that the test method properly interacts with dependencies. Any expected or unexpected interaction can be defined and later verified. For clarity, in test code prefix mock-object variables with *mock*.
		Note: there should never be more than one mock declared within a test method.

Isolating Code-Under-Test

The code-under-test may not have any dependencies; this just means the code is isolated. However, many classes and methods collaborate with and are dependent on other objects. When writing test code, those dependencies and interactions can often make it difficult to test in isolation.

The idea behind a stub is to prevent a dependency from keeping the test from accomplishing its task of testing the code. The stub has both default behavior and the facility to set up behavior to get the code-under-test to work.

▩ **Practice 8-12** Use Stubs to Test in Isolation

For the sake of readability, when a stub is declared in test code use a variable name prefixed with *stub*. In Listing 8-17 two stubs are declared as stubIndividualRepo and stubStudentRepo to stand in for the two repositories. This is done by using the Moq framework. Since the test's primary assertion has nothing to do with verifying the interaction with these repositories, these fakes are not mocks. The stubs only need to simulate the dependencies just enough to get the method to throw the exception. This enables the test code to evaluate the primary assertion under these conditions.

Listing 8-17. Isolating Test Code with Stubs

```
[Test]
public void Save_WithAnExistingStudentImproperlyCreated_ExpectInvalidOperationException()
{
    // Arrange
    var today = new DateTime(2003, 5, 17);

    const int ExpectedStudentId = 897931;
```

```
var stubIndividualRepo = new Mock<IRepository<IndividualEntity>>();
stubIndividualRepo
    .Setup(e => e.Update(It.IsAny<IndividualEntity>()));

var stubStudentRepo = new Mock<IRepository<StudentEntity>>();
stubStudentRepo
    .Setup(e => e.Retrieve(ExpectedStudentId))
    .Returns(default(StudentEntity));
stubStudentRepo
    .Setup(e => e.Create(It.IsAny<StudentEntity>()))
    .Returns(23);

var classUnderTest =
    new Student(stubIndividualRepo.Object, stubStudentRepo.Object)
    {
        Id = ExpectedStudentId,
        Today = today,
        DateOfBirth = today.AddYears(-19),
    };

// Act
TestDelegate act = () => classUnderTest.Save();

// Assert
Assert.Throws<InvalidOperationException>(act);
}
```

▪ **Caution** It is not a good idea to declare a stub for a dependency when the method-under-test does not use the dependency. Set it to null or some invalid value, which forces the method to fail if the code-under-test interacts with the dependency. In Listing 8-16 the Application class is constructed with null for all dependencies because the ComputePayment method is never supposed to interact with the repositories.

Testing Dependency Interaction

When the code-under-test interacts with an object that it depends on, that interaction may be proper or improper. The goal of testing dependency interaction is to verify that interaction is happening correctly. The expected interaction with a dependency includes interactions such as the following:

- A specific method of the dependency is called a specific number of times.

- A specific method of the dependency is not called.

- When a method of the dependency is called it is passed the correct arguments.

- The property-getter of the dependency is accessed a specific number of times.

- A property of the dependency is set with an expected value.

There are more, to be sure. The idea is that test code is testing an expectation concerning the proper interaction behavior. The mock is used to verify the *primary* assertion, which relates to an expected interaction within the code-under-test. Since there is one primary assertion, there should only be one mock object.

▪ **Practice 8-13** Use Only One Mock Object for Interaction Testing

---

The essential steps in testing interaction are to declare the mock, establish the expected interaction as a mock-setup expression, and use the mock to verify that the interaction happened correctly. In Listing 8-18 there are two parts to working with the mock. This mocking functionality is provided by using the Moq framework. In the Arrange section, the mock is created and Setup declares the expectation that the Create method will be called. Later in the test method, within the Assert section, the mock verifies that the Create method was called exactly one time. If the Create method was not called or was called more than once then the mock throws an exception.

Listing 8-18. Interaction Testing with a Mock

```
[Test]
public void Save_WhenStudentIsValid_ExpectIndividualDalCreateIsCalledOnce()
{
    // Arrange
    var today = new DateTime(2003, 5, 17);

    const int ExpectedStudentId = 897931;
    var studentEntity = new StudentEntity { Id = ExpectedStudentId, };

    var stubStudentRepo = new Mock<IRepository<StudentEntity>>();
    stubStudentRepo
        .Setup(e => e.Retrieve(ExpectedStudentId))
        .Returns(studentEntity);

    var mockIndividualRepo = new Mock<IRepository<IndividualEntity>>();
    mockIndividualRepo
        .Setup(e => e.Create(It.IsAny<IndividualEntity>()))
        .Returns(ExpectedStudentId);

    var classUnderTest =
        new Student(mockIndividualRepo.Object, stubStudentRepo.Object)
        {
            Today = today,
            DateOfBirth = today.AddYears(-19),
        };

    // Act
    classUnderTest.Save();
```

```
    // Assert
    Assert.AreEqual(ExpectedStudentId, classUnderTest.Id);
    mockIndividualRepo
        .Verify(e => e.Create(It.IsAny<IndividualEntity>()), Times.Once());
}
```

In Chapter 12 more detail is provided on mocking frameworks and the interaction testing facilities they provide. At this point, the key concept is to use a mock to test expected interaction and to limit a test method to testing one dependency-interaction at a time.

Surface Testing

The concept behind testing a surface is to identify a set of interfaces or API of a subsystem or module.[8] That programming interface is the surface. Build a suite of automated integration tests against the identified surface. These tests verify and validate the subsystem works as an integrated whole.

In general, a system surface is any part of the system where interaction or coupling occurs. It might be an API or user-interface. What is important is that the surface is stable. There are important reasons why a surface is not currently changing that might include

- An internal interface accessible to another module or system layer; the SLOS DAL is an example.

- An external interface accessible to an another system; for example, a web service or an API.

- A database table, view or stored procedure accessible to reporting services, a data warehouse, or a legacy system.

- User-accessible functionality, such as a user interface, web page, or report.

In Figure 8-2 the diagram shows the layers of the SLOS system. There are three logical layers to this brownfield application: Web Application, Data Access Layer, and Database. The end-user accesses the functionality and accomplishes their work using a browser-hosted interface. The web pages are delivered to the browser through a combination of the *aspx* files in the Web Forms and the C# code in the Code Behind. The Code Behind uses the Data Access Layer to access data in the Database layer.

For the SLOS project, the Data Access Layer (DAL) is being overhauled. The calls to the CRUD stored procedures are to be replaced with the equivalent NHibernate implementation. However, the DAL must continue to provide the same interface to the Code Behind layer.

For SLOS, the surface is identified as the IRepository interface to the DAL used by the Code Behind layer. During the DAL overhaul project this interface must not change. Ideally, no code changes are needed in the Code Behind.

Figure 8-2 shows the two conceptual steps involved with surface testing the DAL:

1. *Data Setup:* Create a database with a known initial state.

2. *Run Tests:* Execute the suite of automated tests.

---

[8] The term *surface* comes from its usage in API surface analysis as it relates to system coupling.

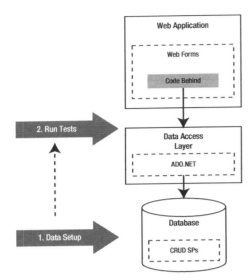

Figure 8-2. Surface testing

This diagram is conceptually accurate, but this model is not practicable. The obstacles include

- Each test method likely requires a different initial data setup.

- Tests need to return the database to the initial state so each test is isolated.

- Any test that inserts records in a table with an identity column must reset the identity column.

A lot of setup and tear-down logic is needed to return the database to the proper initial state. Fortunately, there are test frameworks to help perform the database setup. The database test framework used in the sample code is NDbUnit. This database test framework is used to put the database into a defined state before each test is run. With this framework, the following surface testing steps are straightforward to achieve:

1. *Initial Database Setup:* Create the database and run scripts to create the tables, views, stored procedures, or other database resources.

2. *Test Fixture Setup:* Use the testing framework to connect to the database.

3. *Test Setup:* Perform any data cleanup or initialization common to all test methods in the tests class. A script removes data from all tables and resets identity columns.

4. *Test Arrangement:* In the Arrange section, use the database testing framework to load up the database with data specific to the test case.

5. *Execute Test:* Proceed through the remaining arrangement, perform the test action steps, and make the necessary assertions.

In the sample code, NDbUnit connects to the database and uses a DataSet that describes the database schema. Each test fixture setup runs a script to initialize the database. The test method provides the name of an xml data file that NDbUnit uses to put the correct data into each table. This sets up each test with a defined initial state. More detailed discussion of NDbUnit is found in Chapter 12.

SAMPLE CODE: SURFACE TESTING

The Surface testing sample code is in two parts. First, under the $\Ch08\5_DAL_SP folder is the Tests.Surface.Lender.Slos.Dal project. It has all the surface tests written against the DAL calls stored procedures. Second, under the $\Ch08\6_DAL_NH folder is the data access layer re-implemented to use NHibernate instead of calling stored procedures.

The SurfaceTestingBase<TContext> class implements the methods that the tests classes and test methods in the Tests.Surface.Lender.Slos.Dal project use for database initialization and data setup. This surface testing base class uses NDbUnit to put the Lender.Slos database in a well-defined initial state before each test is run.

In the $\Ch08\6_DAL_NH\Lender.Slos.Dal folder there are both a new and an original version of classes that implement the data access layer. If you want to switch implementations of the ApplicationDal, remove the ApplicationDal.new.cs file from the project and then add ApplicationDal.orig.cs to the project. Rebuild and re-run all the tests. All tests should pass.

Shown in Listing 8-19 is a test method that tests ApplicationDal.Retrieve. There is one line in the Arrange section, a call to TestFixtureContext.SetupTestDatabase, which sets up the database using the provided xmlDataFilename filename. To support multiple test cases, different XML filenames are passed to the test method using the TestCase attribute. One test method is able to support many test cases having different data scenarios.

Listing 8-19. Surface Testing: Application DAL Retrieve

```
namespace Tests.Surface.Lender.Slos.Dal
{
    public class ApplicationDalTests
        : SurfaceTestingBase<ApplicationDalTestsContext>
    {
        [TestFixtureSetUp]
        public void FixtureSetUp()
        {
            this.SetUpTestFixture();
        }

        [TestFixtureTearDown]
        public void FixtureTearDown()
        {
            Dispose();
        }
```

...

```
[TestCase("ApplicationDalTests_Scenario01.xml", 5)]
public void Retrieve_WhenEntityWithIdStoredInDatabase_ExpectEntityHavingIdIsRetrieved(
    string xmlDataFilename,
    int id)
{
    // Arrange
    TestFixtureContext.SetupTestDatabase(xmlDataFilename);

    var classUnderTest = TestFixtureContext.CreateInstance();

    // Act
    var actual = classUnderTest.Retrieve(id);

    // Assert
    Assert.NotNull(actual);
    Assert.AreEqual(id, actual.Id);
}
```

...

The `ApplicationDalTests` class is dependent upon the Surface Testing framework to keep the test methods readable and maintainable. In order to access this testing framework `ApplicationDalTests` is derived from the `SurfaceTestingBase<ApplicationDalTestsContext>` class.

Automated Integration Testing

Many integration tests are performed manually. There is often some setup and configuration required to perform the tests. However, the same integration tests, if automated, would be very helpful to all developers. In the last section you learned about the power of surface testing as a specialized automated integration testing technique. When properly applied to replacing a subsystem or redesigning the system, surface testing is very useful. Other forms of automated integration testing are listed in Table 8-3.

Table 8-3. Automated Integration Testing Approaches

Name	Description
Smoke Testing	This approach involves an automated deployment followed by automated tests that exercise a small set of minimal, essential functionality to verify that the system does not blow up.
Stability Testing	This approach involves an automated deployment followed by automated tests that verify that the system is behaving well.
Performance Testing	This approach involves an automated deployment followed by automated tests that verify important non-functional requirements.

Smoke testing starts with an automated deployment of the system to an integration environment, one that the CI server can control. For example, the CI server could deploy to a virtual machine on a server after a nightly build. By using the techniques described for surface testing, the database is then set up and placed in a known initial condition. The CI server then initiates the running of the smoke tests. These tests use a narrowly focused set of automated UI tests that make sure the software does not blow up. These tests include simple tasks like a user logging in and viewing the main screen or a web page. The goal is to make sure the deployment was successful and the system carries out a set of minimal and essential functionality. To test through the user interface, a testing framework such as *Selenium RC* is used. Some available options for UI testing frameworks are described in Chapter 12. The CI server evaluates the results of the tests and determines if the tests passed or failed.

Stability testing answers the question: Is the build stable enough to release to QA for system or regression testing? In other words, if the system is failing the stability tests then it would be madness to ask QA to test it. Stability tests are automated tests run by the CI server. The mechanics are nearly identical to smoke testing. The goal, however, is expanded to perform a broader set of testing of features and functionality. Since the build must create a system suited for its intended purpose, stability tests confirm it. Pick a set of features and functionality that expresses the indispensable purpose of the system. For example, with the SLOS system, the stability testing focuses on the lifecycle of a student loan, from the application, through loan approval, to cutting checks, and going into repayment.

Performance testing focuses on the non-functional requirements of the system. Does a page load fast enough? Is a calculation or query too slow? Beyond the time-oriented performance tests, they might include scalability, resources, logging, security, audit trails, and any number of non-functional requirements. Some non-functional requirements are specified in the requirements, while others are only defined after there is an issue. The important point is to add new automated performance tests for each significant non-functional requirement that is discovered. If a performance problem develops, then these tests reveal it before it makes it to QA. The mechanics of running automated performance tests are the same as smoke and stability tests.

■ **Tip** Building up all these automated integration tests can be a daunting task. Start by building the Smoke Testing suite. Focus on automating just one smoke test. Get that one test to pass by incorporating smoke testing in a CI server configuration. Build upon that work as your foundation.

Database Considerations

A database contains elements of the system such that, if the database does not work as intended, then the system does not work. The goal of automated testing is to ensure the system continues to work as intended, and so it is often necessary to write automated tests against the database. This form of automated testing focuses on the following aspects:

- Tables, columns, defaults, views, referential integrity, and indices

- Stored procedures

- Triggers

- Concurrency conflict and control

For the code to work properly, the database must have all the required tables and views. The columns need to be properly named with the proper SQL type. If the ORM offers an effective way to validate the schema mapping then build a Surface Testing suite that verifies the mappings. Many databases have a programming interface for data management; for example, there is SQL Server Management Objects (SMO). Surface tests could use SMO to verify and validate the database. As an alternative, call a stored procedure that returns the tables and columns found in the system tables. Be careful to test whether a column has the correct type and default value. Similar approaches apply to testing views, referential integrity, and indices. Test to ensure the database system objects and schema catalog are correct for the latest build.

When stored procedures contain a lot of query and data manipulation logic it is important that the stored procedure (SP) works correctly. For example, write surface tests that put the database in a known initial state and execute a stored procedure. Verify and validate it performs properly. Analyze the boundaries of the SP parameters. Inspect the SP and look for exceptions and verify that errors are raised under the appropriate conditions.

In some applications, triggers provide a feature or functionality of the system. One example might be auditing. Write surface tests that set up the data scenario and then update the table in a way that should fire the trigger. Verify that the audit table now contains the expected entry.

Concurrency conflict and control is important in many systems. As a non-functional requirement, it may be overlooked or underspecified. Whether it is an optimistic or pessimistic strategy, at the very least, the user should experience the impact of concurrency contention the way the system's designers had intended. Write tests that put the database in a known initial state. In the test arrangement retrieve a record using the proper data access method. Use a test helper method to modify the data directly. In the Act section, perform the steps to update the record in the database through the system. In the Assert section, verify that the concurrency problem is detected or otherwise controlled. Make sure the proper exception is thrown.

Since many systems depend on a database, the database must work as expected for the code to behave properly. Use surface testing to develop a suite of tests to verify and validate the database; address issues before they are found in QA testing or production.

Summary

In this chapter you learned about automated testing practices that developers use to effectively check the intention of their code and the system as a whole. This chapter presented practices focusing on three key areas:

- Readability
- Maintainability
- Automation

You learned many practices that help to develop and apply effective automated testing to projects. You learned about the different forms of automated test suites, including

- Unit Testing
- Surface Testing
- Automated Integration Testing
  - Smoke Testing
  - Stability Testing
  - Performance Testing

- Database Testing

In the next chapter you will learn how to use MSBuild to remove error-prone steps, establish repeatability and consistency, and strive to improve the build and deployment processes.

CHAPTER 9

Build Automation

In the early days of software development the phrase *build automation* referred to automating the steps necessary to compile and link a program to create an application. Today, that phrase encompasses so much more. Creating an automated build refers to things that include build integration, unit testing, code analysis, and deployment. This book distinguishes between build automation and continuous integration (CI). By way of analogy, think of the build tools as musical instruments and build automation as the playing of those instruments. In this analogy, the practice of continuous integration is the orchestration, which is discussed in Chapter 10.

This chapter covers build tools in their traditional role of compiling and integrating the application. In addition, this chapter delves into common build tasks and how the build tools serve as general scripting tools that can create folders, copy files, archive files, execute programs, and perform all manner of other tasks.

This chapter also covers the next logical step in the build process: automated deployment. There are two distinct activities within automated deployment. They are

- *Packaging*: Creating a build package that contains all the application files, database scripts, or anything else needed for deployment.

- *Deploying*: The act of setting up the target environment. This includes installing files, setting the configuration, stopping and starting services, upgrading the database, converting the data in the database, or other tasks that put the target environment into a ready-for-use state.

The key concept here is *automated*. Ideally, once the script starts, all the tasks should run without manual intervention. It should not require that the build output be manually copied to a server. There should not be any post-deployment configuration. Having said this, there are often obstacles between the vision of automation and the reality of the situation and circumstances. The goal is to use build automation to remove error-prone steps, establish repeatability and consistency, and strive to improve the build and deployment processes over time. Table 9-1 lists ruthlessly helpful build automation practices.

Table 9-1. Build Automation: Ruthlessly Helpful Practices

	Practice
9-1	Learn the Fundamentals of Build Automation Scripting with MSBuild
9-2	Use a Logger to Record Information That Helps Diagnose Build Script Issues

	Practice
9-3	Use Parameters to Provide Script Values and Control Logic and Actions
9-4	Extend the Power of Build Automation by Using Task Libraries
9-5	Import Common Scripts to Promote Reuse
9-6	Define Custom Task Logic as Inline Code to Perform Simple Tasks
9-7	Make Effective Use of the Date, Time, and Duration Functions Within a Script
9-8	Have the Script Tie the Assembly Version Back to the Build and Revision Number
9-9	Read and Write XML Data from Within the Build Script
9-10	Learn How to Create Zip File Archives from Within the Build Script
9-11	Deploy the Same Build to Multiple Target Environments to Confirm Readiness
9-12	Define the Packaging Approach That Works for Both the Customer and the Team
9-13	Use a Tool That Makes Deployments Automated, Robust, and Reliable

Build Tools

Build tools are software programs and platforms that automate the software build processes. Generally speaking, build tools run a script that defines how that build process is to be carried out. Because of the widely-used *make* utility, an important scripting form is the makefile format.[1] As MSBuild and NAnt have become popular build tools for .NET developers, the prevalent form of scripting uses XML to describe the build process and its dependencies. Whatever the format, the script is what the developer creates. The script defines the build steps and the dependencies of those steps. The script defines any actions to perform within each step and the order of those actions.

It is hard to advocate for one build tool over another. Your organization may have a number of developers very familiar and proficient with NAnt. Since MSBuild is a part of the .NET Framework, more and more developers are learning how to write MSBuild scripts. Other build tools offer important features that make them well suited for key tasks. Table 9-2 offers a list of build tools worth evaluating.

---

[1] For more information see http://en.wikipedia.org/wiki/Makefile.

Table 9-2. *Build Tools*

Name	Description	More Information
MSBuild	This Microsoft build tool comes as part of the .NET Framework. It is used within Visual Studio and Team Foundation Server for many build automation tasks. A lot of information is available through books, MSDN, and the web postings.	msdn.microsoft.com/en-us/library/0k6kkbsd.aspx
NAnt	A free and open-source build tool that is based on the Java build tool known as Ant. NAnt is popular with .NET developers for scripting the continuous integration process. Since NAnt is widely used, there is a lot of good information available on how to use NAnt for build automation.	nant.sourceforge.net
PowerShell	This Microsoft shell tool supports scripting and automating many administrative tasks on Windows Server and most Microsoft server applications.	technet.microsoft.com/en-us/library/bb978526.aspx
Rake	A Ruby build program with capabilities similar to make (rake = ruby + make). It is popular with teams familiar with Ruby and accustomed to using one of the make-oriented build tools.	rake.rubyforge.org

MSBuild has been part of the .NET Framework since version 2.0. It is heavily used within Visual Studio and Team Foundation Server. Today, many .NET developers are turning to MSBuild as the build automation tool of choice. However, it is not uncommon for continuous integration servers to use MSBuild only to compile the source code and to use NAnt, PowerShell, or Rake scripts to perform other steps. There are many good reasons to use various build tools in your development organization, and those reasons make tool selection important. Select the build tools appropriate to you.

Since MSBuild is a part of the .NET Framework, and this book is targeted toward the .NET developer, all the samples are MSBuild scripts. This approach also eliminates the need for you to get a third-party build tool to run the samples. Many of the concepts presented are generally applicable to other build tools and scripting languages.

MSBuild Fundamentals

Some developers are surprised to learn that MSBuild is part of the .NET Framework and that Visual Studio uses MSBuild to perform many build steps. In fact, Visual Studio project files are MSBuild scripts. In addition, Microsoft Team Foundation Server relies very heavily on MSBuild to perform many build automation steps. Increasingly, knowing the fundamentals of MSBuild is important to understanding how .NET applications are built with the Microsoft tool set.

■ **Practice 9-1** Learn the Fundamentals of Build Automation Scripting with MSBuild

This section is *not* going to teach you everything you need to know about MSBuild and how to write sophisticated MSBuild scripts. For tutorials and MSBuild in depth, take a look at the resources available in Appendix A. This chapter touches upon many of the key concepts and illustrates how to perform common build tasks using MSBuild.

Tasks and Targets

MSBuild uses a task to execute an action during the build process. The tasks are grouped under one or more targets. To execute an MSBuild script one or more targets are invoked. Perhaps an example would be helpful right now.

The MSBuild script in the *Samples\Ch09\0_General\HelloWorld\runner.msbuild* file is shown in Listing 9-1. This is an ordinary XML file. The outermost element is the Project element. This script has a single Target element within the Project element. This is an MSBuild target. The target has a Name attribute, which is assigned a value of Hello. Within the Target element is a single Message element, which is an MSBuild task. This task takes two parameters, which are passed through the Text and Importance attributes.

Listing 9-1. The Message Task Called Within the Hello Target

```xml
<?xml version="1.0" encoding="utf-8"?>
<Project DefaultTargets="Hello"
         xmlns="http://schemas.microsoft.com/developer/msbuild/2003"
         ToolsVersion="4.0"
         >
  <Target Name="Hello">
    <Message Text="Hello world!"
             Importance="high"
             />
  </Target>
</Project>
```

The output from running the *Samples\Ch09\0_General\HelloWorld\runner.msbuild* script file is shown in Listing 9-2. The script is executed from the command line as follows:[2]

```
%MSBuildRoot%\msbuild.exe "runner.msbuild"
```

The output tells you when the build started and the name of the project file that MSBuild is running. The MSBuild engine then writes to the output log that Target Hello is executed. This target has the one task to execute, which is to write the message to the output. There it is. The text Hello world! is written to the log.

---

[2] The msbuild.exe is located in the .NET Framework 4.0 installation folder, which is customarily *C:\Windows\Microsoft.NET\Framework\v4.0.30319*. Create the environment variable *MSBuildRoot* to reference the proper folder for your environment.

Listing 9-2. The Output from Running the HelloWorld Sample Script

```
Build started 9/25/2011 3:32:45 PM.

Project "C:\Samples\Ch09\0_General\HelloWorld\runner.msbuild" (default targets):

Target Hello:
    Hello world!

Build succeeded.
    0 Warning(s)
    0 Error(s)

Time Elapsed 00:00:00.13
```

The next example is more involved, but the concept is pretty much the same. There is a target and the target has a task. The MSBuild script in the *Samples\Ch09\0_General\Build\runner.msbuild* file is shown in Listing 9-3. This script has a single `Target` element with a `Name` attribute of `BuildAll`. The task is the `MSBuild` task, which is the task to execute another script. In this case, the two scripts that are executed are both Visual Studio project files, which are defined as `ProjectToBuild` elements under the `ItemGroup` element. And so, when the target in this script is invoked it will invoke the `Build` target in two other scripts, both of which are Visual Studio projects. In this way, the *runner.msbuild* script is automating the build for these two projects.

Listing 9-3. The MSBuild Task Called Within a Target Element

```xml
<?xml version="1.0" encoding="utf-8"?>
<Project DefaultTargets="BuildAll"
         xmlns="http://schemas.microsoft.com/developer/msbuild/2003"
         ToolsVersion="4.0">

  <ItemGroup>
    <ProjectToBuild Include=".\Lender.Slos.Financial\Lender.Slos.Financial.csproj" />
    <ProjectToBuild ↵
Include=".\Tests.Unit.Lender.Slos.Financial\Tests.Unit.Lender.Slos.Financial.csproj" />
  </ItemGroup>

  <Target Name="BuildAll">
    <MSBuild Projects="@(ProjectToBuild)"
             Targets="Build"
             Properties="Configuration=DEBUG"
             />
  </Target>
</Project>
```

This is the basic idea of MSBuild scripts: invoke targets which execute tasks. A task can even invoke targets in another script. There is a lot more to tasks and targets—rather than delve into the details, let's stay at the high level to look at other major features of an MSBuild script.

PropertyGroup and ItemGroup

Properties are used in MSBuild scripts to store values and pass values to tasks. Properties are declared in the script file as child elements of a PropertyGroup element. The name of the child element is the name of the property. The content within the child element is the value of the property.

The MSBuild script in the *Samples\Ch09\0_General\Properties\runner.msbuild* file is shown in Listing 9-4. Near the top of the script a PropertyGroup element is defined. The child element of GlobalProperty is a property with the value of DEBUG. The Target with the name First writes the value of the GlobalProperty to the log by referencing the value using the $(GlobalProperty) notation. Within this same target the value of LocalProperty is also written to the log. It is important to know that although the LocalProperty is not yet defined, MSBuild does not raise an error when the property is referenced.

Within the Target section named Second, there is a PropertyGroup element that defines the LocalProperty and assigns the value of Lender.Slos to that property. The values of both the GlobalProperty and LocalProperty properties are written to the log. Within the Target named Third, there are no properties defined. In this target section, the values of both the GlobalProperty and LocalProperty properties are written to the log.

Listing 9-4. Properties Declared Outside and Within a Target Section

```xml
<?xml version="1.0" encoding="utf-8"?>
<Project DefaultTargets="First;Second;Third"
         xmlns="http://schemas.microsoft.com/developer/msbuild/2003"
         ToolsVersion="4.0"
         >
  <PropertyGroup>
    <GlobalProperty>DEBUG</GlobalProperty>
  </PropertyGroup>

  <Target Name="First">
    <Message Text="In the First target the global property is: '$(GlobalProperty)'"
             Importance="high"
             />
    <Message Text="In the First target the local property is: '$(LocalProperty)'"
             Importance="high"
             />
  </Target>

  <Target Name="Second">
    <PropertyGroup>
      <LocalProperty>Lender.Slos</LocalProperty>
    </PropertyGroup>

    <Message Text="In the Second target the global property is: '$(GlobalProperty)'"
             Importance="high"
             />
    <Message Text="In the Second target the local property is: '$(LocalProperty)'"
             Importance="high"
             />
  </Target>
```

```
<Target Name="Third">
  <Message Text="In the Third target the global property is: '$(GlobalProperty)'"
           Importance="high"
           />
  <Message Text="In the Third target the local property is: '$(LocalProperty)'"
           Importance="high"
           />
</Target>
</Project>
```

The output from running the *Samples\Ch09\0_General\Properties\runner.msbuild* script file is shown in Listing 9-5. The output from the First target displays the expected GlobalProperty value of DEBUG. The yet-to-be-declared LocalProperty value is an empty string. The output from the Second target displays the expected GlobalProperty and LocalProperty values. The output from the Third target displays the expected GlobalProperty value. The output from the LocalProperty value is not an empty string; it is Lender.Slos. It is helpful to know that even when a property is declared within a target, once the target is called and the property value is set, that is the property's value which is set for the remainder of the script's execution.

Listing 9-5. The Output from Running the Properties Sample Script

```
Build started 9/25/2011 3:32:45 PM.
_____
Project "C:\Samples\Ch09\0_General\Properties\runner.msbuild" (default targets):

Target First:
    In the First target the global property is: 'DEBUG'
    In the First target the local property is: ''
Target Second:
    In the Second target the global property is: 'DEBUG'
    In the Second target the local property is: 'Lender.Slos'
Target Third:
    In the Third target the global property is: 'DEBUG'
    In the Third target the local property is: 'Lender.Slos'

Build succeeded.
    0 Warning(s)
    0 Error(s)

Time Elapsed 00:00:00.19
```

Next, let's take a look at the concept of the MSBuild Item. Items are declared in the script file as child elements of an ItemGroup element. The name of the child element defines the Item type. Item types are essentially named lists of items. Items are usually passed as parameters to tasks.

The MSBuild script in the *Samples\Ch09\0_General\Items\runner.msbuild* file is shown in Listing 9-6. Near the top of this script, there are two ItemGroup elements. The first ItemGroup element contains two ContentToInclude elements. The first ContentToInclude element defines the items to include in that list by assigning the Include attribute a value, which is $(SourcePath)***.ico. This tells MSBuild to generate the item list by recursively looking for files under the $(SourcePath) folder, where the filename has an extension of *ico*. The second ContentToInclude element adds all the filenames with an extension of *bmp* to the item list with the same name.

The second ItemGroup element contains two ContentToExclude elements. The first ContentToExclude element defines the items to include in that list by assigning the Include attribute a value, which is $(SourcePath)***.gif. This tells MSBuild to generate the item list by recursively looking for files under the $(SourcePath) folder, where the filename has an extension of *gif.* The second ContentToExclude element adds all the filenames that match the wildcard of *Webcontrol*.bmp.*

In Listing 9-6, near the bottom of the script, there is a target named CopyToOutput. Within the target is an ItemGroup that contains the ContentFiles element. The way these attributes are assigned tells MSBuild to generate the item list by including the items from the ContentToInclude item list and to exclude the items from the ContentToExclude item list. The ContentFiles item list is then used in the parameters to the Copy task.

The Copy task has two attributes that act as parameters for this task. The first is the SourceFiles attribute that has the @(ContentFiles) item list assigned to it. The second is the DestinationFiles attribute that has this expression assigned to it:

@(ContentFiles->'$(OutputPath)\%(RecursiveDir)%(Filename)%(Extension)')

This expression has special meaning. It uses the MSBuild item metadata to transform the ContentFiles items into a new list of items.[3] The new items have the same relative path, filename, and extension of the ContentFiles items, but they have the base folder defined in the OutputPath property. The Copy task receives a transformed file as the destination file for each of the source files.

Listing 9-6. Item Lists as Parameters to the Copy Task

```
<?xml version="1.0" encoding="utf-8"?>
<Project DefaultTargets="CopyToOutput"
        xmlns="http://schemas.microsoft.com/developer/msbuild/2003"
        ToolsVersion="4.0"
        >
  <PropertyGroup>
    <SourcePath>.\Content</SourcePath>
    <OutputPath>.\Output</OutputPath>
    <DefineConstants>DEBUG;TRACE</DefineConstants>
  </PropertyGroup>

  <ItemGroup>
    <ContentToInclude Include="$(SourcePath)\**\*.ico" />
    <ContentToInclude Include="$(SourcePath)\**\*.bmp" />
  </ItemGroup>

  <ItemGroup>
    <ContentToExclude Include="$(SourcePath)\**\*.gif" />
    <ContentToExclude Include="$(SourcePath)\**\Webcontrol*.bmp" />
  </ItemGroup>

  <Target Name="First">
    <Message Text="In the DefineConstants property is: '$(DefineConstants)'"
            Importance="high"
            />
```

---

[3] For more information on the MSBuild Well-known Item Metadata see http://msdn.microsoft.com/en-us/library/ms164313(v=VS.100).aspx.

```
    </Target>

    <Target Name="Second">
      <Message Text="In the ContentToInclude is: '@(ContentToInclude)'"
               Importance="high"
               />
    </Target>

    <Target Name="Third">
      <Message Text="In the ContentToExclude is: '@(ContentToExclude)'"
               Importance="high"
               />
    </Target>

    <Target Name="CopyToOutput"
            DependsOnTargets="First;Second;Third;Clean"
            >
      <ItemGroup>
        <ContentFiles Include="@(ContentToInclude)"
                      Exclude="@(ContentToExclude)"
                      />
      </ItemGroup>

      <Message Text="In the ContentFiles is: '@(ContentFiles)'"
               Importance="high"
               />

      <Copy SourceFiles="@(ContentFiles)"
            DestinationFiles="@(ContentFiles->↵
 '$(OutputPath)\%(RecursiveDir)%(Filename)%(Extension)')"
            />
    </Target>

    <Target Name="Clean" >
      <RemoveDir Condition="Exists('$(OutputPath)')"
                 Directories="$(OutputPath)"
                 />
    </Target>
</Project>
```

The output from running the *Samples\Ch09\0_General\Items\runner.msbuild* script file is shown in Listing 9-7. Notice that the contents of the ContentFiles item list is a semicolon-separated list of files that includes all the files in the ContentToInclude item list but excludes the files in the ContentToExclude item list. The Copy task logs a message indicating the source file path and destination file path, which results from the transformation expression, for each file that is copied.

Listing 9-7. The Output from Running the Items Script

```
Build started 9/25/2011 3:32:45 PM.
```

```
Project "C:\Samples\Ch09\0_General\Items\runner.msbuild" (default targets):
```

```
Target First:
    In the DefineConstants property is: 'DEBUG;TRACE'
Target Second:
    In the ContentToInclude is:   ↵
'.\Content\icons\install.ico;.\Content\icons\search.ico;.\Content\icons\search4people.ico;.\Co
ntent\icons\share.ico;.\Content\images\Webcontrol_Pagecatalogpart.bmp;.\Content\images\Webcont
rol_Sqldatasrc.bmp;.\Content\images\window.bmp'
Target Third:
    In the ContentToExclude is:   ↵
'.\Content\animations\download_FTP_00.gif;.\Content\animations\status_anim.gif;.\Content\image
s\Webcontrol_Pagecatalogpart.bmp;.\Content\images\Webcontrol_Sqldatasrc.bmp'
Target Clean:
    Removing directory ".\Output".
Target CopyToOutput:
    In the ContentFiles is:   ↵
'.\Content\icons\install.ico;.\Content\icons\search.ico;.\Content\icons\search4people.ico;.\Co
ntent\icons\share.ico;.\Content\images\window.bmp'
    Creating directory ".\Output\icons".
    Copying file from ".\Content\icons\install.ico" to ".\Output\icons\install.ico".
    Copying file from ".\Content\icons\search.ico" to ".\Output\icons\search.ico".
    Copying file from ".\Content\icons\search4people.ico" to  ↵
".\Output\icons\search4people.ico".
    Copying file from ".\Content\icons\share.ico" to ".\Output\icons\share.ico".
    Creating directory ".\Output\images".
    Copying file from ".\Content\images\window.bmp" to ".\Output\images\window.bmp".

Build succeeded.
    0 Warning(s)
    0 Error(s)

Time Elapsed 00:00:00.24
```

Basic Tasks

Many tasks are included with MSBuild. The samples use a number of the MSBuild tasks throughout. These tasks provide for the basic functionality that MSBuild offers. As you will learn, a lot of the power of MSBuild comes through the third-party tasks provided in task libraries.

Some of the commonly used basic MSBuild tasks include

- *Message*: Writes a message to the log

- *Warning*: Writes a warning to the log based on an evaluated condition

- *Error*: Stops the build based on an evaluated condition and writes an error to the log

- *Exec*: Runs a program or command with the specified arguments

- *CallTarget*: Invokes a target in the project file

- *MSBuild*: Invokes targets in another project file

- *Copy*: Copies files from a source to a destination

- *Move:* Moves files to a new location
- *Delete:* Deletes files
- *MakeDir:* Creates a directory
- *RemoveDir:* Removes a directory and all of its files and subdirectories
- *ReadLinesFromFile:* Reads from a text file

Logging

There usually comes a time when the build script does not perform the build actions as expected. In order to diagnose and correct the problem a logging facility can be used to review the progress and state of the build script. With MSBuild the default output uses ConsoleLogger to write to the console window. To capture the log output to a file MSBuild provides the FileLogger facility, and the parameters for the logger can be passed to MSBuild using the command-line option */logger* (or */l* for short). It is also possible to write your own logger by implementing the ILogger interface directly or deriving from the Logger base class.[4] The MSBuild log records build events, messages, warnings, and errors. Within the scripts that you create, writing messages to the log can help diagnose any build script issues when the script is being developed or running remotely on the build server.

■ **Practice 9-2** Use a Logger to Record Information That Helps Diagnose Build Script Issues

---

Within the MSBuild script the Error task is used to report an error to the log. If the Condition attribute of the Error element evaluates to true, the value of the Text attribute is logged and the build stops. Similarly, the Warning task is used to report a warning message based on a conditional statement, but the build continues. Within the MSBuild script the primary way to write an informational message to the log is with the Message task. The Message task has an Importance attribute that the logger interprets to determine if the message should be written to the log, based on the verbosity level. The Importance attribute can be set to high, normal, or low. In Listing 9-8 the sample *runner.msbuild* script file is shown. It has three Message tasks, each having the Importance attribute set to a different value.

Listing 9-8. Writing Messages to the Log

```
<?xml version="1.0" encoding="utf-8"?>
<Project DefaultTargets="Default"
        xmlns="http://schemas.microsoft.com/developer/msbuild/2003"
        ToolsVersion="4.0">

  <Target Name="Default">
    <Message Text="This message is 'high' importance"
            Importance="high"
            />
    <Message Text="This message is 'normal' importance"
```

---

[4] For more information see http://msdn.microsoft.com/en-us/library/ms171471.aspx.

```
                Importance="normal"
                />
    <Message Text="This message is 'low' importance"
                Importance="low"
                />
  </Target>
</Project>
```

When the *Samples\Ch09\0_General\Logging\runner.msbuild* file is run through MSBuild from the command line, as shown in Listing 9-9, the logging option (*/l*) is used to provide the parameters for logging. In this example, the FileLogger,Microsoft.Build.Engine part indicates that the built-in file logger is the logger to use. The logfile=logs\normal.log part provides the relative path to the log filename.

Listing 9-9. Running MSBuild with the File Logging Option

```
%MSBuildRoot%\msbuild.exe "runner.msbuild" ↵
/l:FileLogger,Microsoft.Build.Engine;logfile=logs\normal.log
```

When the script is run, MSBuild creates or overwrites the log file. The optional *append* parameter can be used to append the log file if it already exists. Since the optional *verbosity* parameter is not provided, the global verbosity setting is used for the file logger. After the command line is run the output is logged to the *normal.log* file. The output in this file is shown in Listing 9-10.

Listing 9-10. Output in the normal.log File

```
Build started 9/25/2011 3:32:45 PM.
_____
Project "C:\Samples\Ch09\0_General\Logging\runner.msbuild" (default targets):

Target Default:
    This message is 'high' importance
    This message is 'normal' importance

Build succeeded.
    0 Warning(s)
    0 Error(s)

Time Elapsed 00:00:00.10
```

To provide more detailed output in the log file, include the optional verbosity parameter and assign it the *detailed* value. Two separate command lines that set the verbosity are shown in Listing 9-11. The first command line includes that /v=detailed option, which sets the global verbosity level for all loggers. The second command line adds the verbosity level option to override the global verbosity setting for only that file logger.

Listing 9-11. Running MSBuild with the Detailed Logging Options

```
%MSBuildRoot%\msbuild.exe "runner.msbuild" /v=detailed ↵
/l:FileLogger,Microsoft.Build.Engine;logfile=logs\detailed.log

%MSBuildRoot%\msbuild.exe "runner.msbuild" ↵
/l:FileLogger,Microsoft.Build.Engine;logfile=logs\detailed.log;verbosity=detailed
```

When the *runner.msbuild* script file is run with the verbosity level set to *detailed,* a lot more information is written in the log file, as shown in Listing 9-12. Notice that the low importance message is now written to the log file. In addition, there is now a line that indicates that a task starts executing and that a task is done, for each task that is executed. At the beginning of the script, there is more information that includes the build tool version and the `Message` task used in the script.

Listing 9-12. Output in the detailed.log *File*

```
Build started 9/25/2011 3:32:45 PM.

Project "C:\Samples\Ch09\0_General\Logging\runner.msbuild" (default targets):

Building with tools version "4.0".
Target Default:
  Using "Message" task from assembly "Microsoft.Build.Tasks.v4.0, ↵
Version=4.0.0.0, Culture=neutral, PublicKeyToken=b03f5f7f11d50a3a".
  Task "Message"
    This message is 'high' importance
  Done executing task "Message".
  Task "Message"
    This message is 'normal' importance
  Done executing task "Message".
  Task "Message"
    This message is 'low' importance
  Done executing task "Message".

Done building project "runner.msbuild".

Build succeeded.
    0 Warning(s)
    0 Error(s)

Time Elapsed 00:00:00.08
```

Having the ability to control the global verbosity level independently of the verbosity level of the logger is very helpful. The valid values for the verbosity option include

- quiet

- minimal

- normal

- detailed

- diagnostic

The important point is that while writing scripts you should include many Message tasks. These informational messages serve to describe and record how the script is behaving as it runs. By including messages that have the Importance attribute set to low, the script can provide detailed output to the log file during development. Later, when the script is running on the build server the normal output will not include this verbose information unless or until the verbosity level is raised.

Parameters and Variables

Since the goal is to write a single build script that can perform a variety of tasks under various conditions, it is important to be able to provide the build script with parameters and variables. Each build tool has different mechanisms for passing in these parameter values. The key concept is to use these variables to write a single script that can perform a range of tasks under different circumstances and conditions.

■ **Practice 9-3** Use Parameters to Provide Script Values and Control Logic and Actions

---

When running MSBuild from the command line, parameters can be passed to the build script using the parameter option (*/p*). Usage of the parameter option is illustrated in Listing 9-13. The first parameter is named ParamOne and has the value of 42. The second parameter is separated from the first parameter with a semicolon. The second parameter is named ParamTwo and has the value of First;Second;Third. Notice how the second parameter value is enclosed in quotation marks so that the value can include semicolons. The third parameter is named ParamThree and has the value of C:\My Documents\. This third parameter uses the double backslash notation as an escape character to indicate that the trailing backslash is part of the ParamThree value.

Listing 9-13. Passing MSBuild Parameters Through the Command Line

```
%MSBuildRoot%\msbuild.exe "runner.msbuild" ↵
/p:ParamOne=42;ParamTwo="First;Second;Third";ParamThree="C:\My Documents\\"
```

In Listing 9-14, the three Message tasks show how to insert the parameter values as part of the Text that is written to the log. The $(ParamOne) notation indicates that the value stored in the ParamOne property is written into the Parameter 1: '42' output line. At the bottom of Listing 9-14, the output from each of the three parameters is shown. These parameter values can be used in a wide variety of ways, which are shown over the course of this chapter.

Listing 9-14. The Script Logging the Values from the Parameters

```
...

    <Message Text="Parameter 1: '$(ParamOne)'"
             Importance="low"
             />
```

```
<Message Text="Parameter 2: '$(ParamTwo)'"
         Importance="low"
         />
<Message Text="Parameter 3: '$(ParamThree)'"
         Importance="low"
         />
```
...

Parameter 1: '42'
```
Parameter 2: 'First;Second;Third'
Parameter 3: 'C:\My Documents\'
```

Providing a long list of parameters and dealing with special character escaping on the command line is not the only way to pass values in to an MSBuild script. Another way to pass values into the script is through the use of environment variables. This is a helpful technique to use when the same build script runs on a variety of machines with different configurations. For example, if a build script is written to run FxCop then an *FxCopRoot* environment variable can be created on each of the machines where the script will run. The *FxCopRoot* environment variable contains the path to the FxCopCmd.exe program that is specific to that machine. In Listing 9-15, the build script inspects the FxCopRoot property, which MSBuild generates and sets according to the corresponding environment variable. The logical condition is examined in the Condition attribute of the Error task. If the value is empty, the script throws an error explaining that the *FxCopRoot* environment variable is required. If the property value is not empty, the error condition is not met and the script proceeds to write out the FxCop installation folder as part of the message to the log.

Listing 9-15. Script Property Values from an Environment Variable

...

```
<Error Condition="'$(FxCopRoot)'==''"
       Text="Environment variable 'FxCopRoot' must be set."
       />
<Message Text="FxCop Installation Root: '$(FxCopRoot)'"
         Importance="low"
         />
```
...

A third way that an MSBuild script can set a property value from an external source is from the Windows registry. In Listing 9-16, there are two property values that are assigned values from the registry. The first is the Username property, which is set to the username of the currently logged on user. The second is the DotNetFxRoot property, which is set to the .NET Framework installation folder. Property values from the command line, environment variable, and the registry are all powerful ways to write one build script that performs a variety of tasks under many different circumstances.

Listing 9-16. Script Properties Read from the Registry

...

```
<PropertyGroup>
  <Username>$(Registry:HKEY_CURRENT_USER\Volatile Environment@USERNAME)</Username>
```

```
    <DotNetFxRoot>$(Registry:HKEY_LOCAL_MACHINE\SOFTWARE\Microsoft\↵
.NETFramework@InstallRoot)</DotNetFxRoot>
    </PropertyGroup>

    <Message Text="Current user's login id: '$(Username)'"
             Importance="low"
             />
    <Message Text=".NET Framework Installation Root: '$(DotNetFxRoot)'"
             Importance="low"
             />
...
```

Libraries and Extensions

Every build tool provides a base set of features that form the foundation of the tool's build automation functionality. However, there are also many common build tasks that are not included in the many build tools. For additional capabilities most build tools provide facilities to extend the functionality.

For MSBuild there are libraries available that provide a broad range of additional functionality. Two of the commonly used libraries are

- MSBuild Extension Pack

- MSBuild Community Tasks

Both of these libraries are free and open source. Information on how to obtain these libraries is provided in Appendix A. Both the Extension Pack and the Community Tasks include help documentation that is very thorough and includes many examples of how to use the tasks provided within the library. Both libraries are widely used to extend MSBuild scripts and there are many examples available in books and on the Internet that explain how to use these libraries to accomplish common tasks.

■ **Practice 9-4** Extend the Power of Build Automation by Using Task Libraries

---

In addition to using an MSBuild library that others have developed, you can create your own MSBuild custom tasks library. This is a straightforward process, but it is a little beyond the scope of this book. In Chapter 11, there is sample code that calls StyleCop from an MSBuild script by using a custom build task. The resources in Appendix A include books and articles on MSBuild that delve into writing custom MSBuild tasks.

Import and Include

Over time the build scripts that you write may get quite long and repeat sections and tasks across many build scripts. Most build tools provide a way to import and include partial scripts to promote reuse. Using this approach, the reused sections of the script are placed in a common script that is included within the main build script.

■ **Practice 9-5** Import Common Scripts to Promote Reuse

In MSBuild the Import task is used to include one script within another build script. The Import element uses the Project attribute to reference the file within the calling script. For all intents and purposes, the Import task inserts the contents of the imported file's Project section within the main script at the Import line, when the script begins to execute. In this way, the main script references targets and properties as if they are defined in the main script. Any MSBuild files that are intended to be imported are, by convention, named with the *Targets* file extension.

In Listing 9-17, the entire contents of the main MSBuild script file are shown. The Import task provides the relative path to the *Common.Targets* file. The Default target references a Preconditions target defined in the *Common.Targets* file. Also, the property BinariesOutputPath can be referenced because it is defined in the *Common.Targets* file.

Listing 9-17. Script that Imports Common.Targets *File*

```
<?xml version="1.0" encoding="utf-8"?>
<Project DefaultTargets="Default"
         xmlns="http://schemas.microsoft.com/developer/msbuild/2003"
         ToolsVersion="4.0">

  <Import Project=".\Build\ImportTargets\Common.Targets"/>

  <Target Name="Default"
          DependsOnTargets="Preconditions">
    <Message Condition="Exists('$(BinariesOutputPath)')"
             Text="Yes, the '$(BinariesOutputPath)' folder exists."
             Importance="low"
             />
    <Error Condition="!Exists('$(BinariesOutputPath)')"
           Text="No, the '$(BinariesOutputPath)' folder does NOT exist."
           />
  </Target>
</Project>
```

Let's take a look at the contents of the *Common.Targets* file, which is shown in Listing 9-18. There is a PropertyGroup section that defines two properties, ArtifactsPath and BinariesOutputPath. The values in these properties are accessible to any script that imports this file. Notice the Condition attribute on the ArtifactsPath property. This property will not be set if that property is already set in the script that imports this file. This technique allows you to override a property value defined in an imported targets file by defining it in the main script before the Import target statement.

The *Common.Targets* file also defines a Target element with the name Preconditions. This target uses properties that are assumed to already be defined before this script is imported. It also uses the ArtifactsPath and BinariesOutputPath properties that are defined earlier in this file.

Listing 9-18. Script Within the Common.Targets *File*

```
<?xml version="1.0" encoding="utf-8" ?>
<Project xmlns="http://schemas.microsoft.com/developer/msbuild/2003"
```

```
            ToolsVersion="4.0"
        >
  <PropertyGroup>
    <ArtifactsPath Condition="'$(ArtifactsPath)'==''">↵
.\Artifacts</ArtifactsPath>
    <BinariesOutputPath Condition="'$(BinariesOutputPath)'==''">↵
$(ArtifactsPath)\Binaries</BinariesOutputPath>
  </PropertyGroup>

  <Target Name="Preconditions" >
    <Error Condition="'$(FxCopRoot)'==''"
          Text="Environment variable 'FxCopRoot' must be set."
          />
    <Message Text="FxCop root: '$(FxCopRoot)'"
          Importance="low"
          />
    <MakeDir Condition="!Exists('$(ArtifactsPath)')"
          Directories="$(ArtifactsPath)"
          />
    <MakeDir Condition="!Exists('$(BinariesOutputPath)')"
          Directories="$(BinariesOutputPath)"
          />
  </Target>
</Project>
```

Inline Tasks

Some build tools provide the facility to define custom task logic as inline code within the build script. In general, because these inline-code tasks are often reused, they are commonly written in a script file that is imported. The purpose of these inline tasks is not to replace custom task libraries but to provide a way to write a short function without resorting to writing a full-blown custom task.

■ **Practice 9-6** Define Custom Task Logic as Inline Code to Perform Simple Tasks

---

Version 4.0 of MSBuild adds the facility to write custom tasks inline in the project file, which is called Inline Tasks.[5] The inline code can be written in C#, VB.NET, or JavaScript. Listing 9-19 shows the relevant section of the runner.msbuild sample script file. The Example1 target calls the ExecuteSum task, which is defined as the inline task, shown in Listing 9-19. The caller provides the values from the Values property by assigning this property's value to the Input attribute. The output from the ExecuteSum task is returned and stored in a property named SumFromTask.

---

[5] For more information see http://msdn.microsoft.com/en-us/library/dd722601.aspx.

Listing 9-19. Script That Calls the ExecuteSum Inline Task

```
...

  <PropertyGroup>
    <Values>16.37|11.13|1129.7057|2.417|6569.1</Values>
  </PropertyGroup>

...

  <Target Name="Example1">
    <ExecuteSum Input="$(Values)">
      <Output PropertyName="SumFromTask" TaskParameter="TaskMessage"/>
    </ExecuteSum>

    <Message Text="Sum from 'ExecuteSum' task: $(SumFromTask)"
             Importance="high"
             />
  </Target>
...
```

In Listing 9-20, the build script that defines the ExecuteSum inline task is shown. Some important features to note include the use of input and output parameters. The Input property is defined as a parameter of an element within the ParameterGroup. Also, the TaskMessage parameter is defined as an output parameter that is a decimal type. Within the Code element the inline C# code is defined. The Input parameter is accessed just like a property of a class. Similarly, the TaskMessage parameter is set as if it is a property of a class.

Listing 9-20. Script That Defines the ExecuteSum Inline Task

```
...

  <UsingTask TaskName="ExecuteSum"
             TaskFactory="CodeTaskFactory"
             AssemblyFile="$(MSBuildToolsPath)\Microsoft.Build.Tasks.v4.0.dll" >
    <ParameterGroup>
      <Input Required="true"/>
      <TaskMessage ParameterType="System.Decimal" Output="true"/>
    </ParameterGroup>

    <Task>
      <Code Type="Fragment" Language="cs">
        const string Separators = ",;|";
        var sum = decimal.Zero;

        if (!string.IsNullOrWhiteSpace(Input))
        {
          foreach (var value in Input.Split(Separators.ToCharArray()))
          {
            decimal decimalValue;
```

```
            if (decimal.TryParse(value, out decimalValue))
            {
              sum += decimalValue;
            }
          }
        }
      }

      TaskMessage = sum;
    </Code>
  </Task>
</UsingTask>
...
```

Common Tasks

There are common build automation tasks that come up time and time again. Many of these are made easier by the custom tasks available in extension libraries. It is important to review the tasks in several libraries to remove the need to rediscover the challenges and reimplement the solutions associated with these custom tasks. This section covers a handful of samples that illustrate how to perform these common tasks within MSBuild, using the MSBuild Extensions Pack or with the MSBuild Community Tasks. The larger message of this section is that it is very helpful for you to develop small, focused build scripts that use these libraries to accomplish tasks that are common in your situation. In practice, these targeted scripts isolate the techniques involved and help refine the approach before bringing them to the main build script. In addition, any effort to track down or isolate problems in getting the small script to work is a lot easier to debug.

Date and Time

Very common tasks involve determining today's date, the current time, and event durations. Perhaps the script needs to write an informational message to log when the build begins. Other applications include creating folder names that include the date and time as part of the string. Whatever the need, it is helpful to learn how to effectively determine the date, time, or duration for use in the build script.

■ **Practice 9-7** Make Effective Use of the Date, Time, and Duration Functions Within a Script

---

Within an MSBuild script there are a few ways to determine the current date and time. The MSBuild Extension Pack provides the MSBuild.ExtensionPack.Framework.DateAndTime task to help perform a number of time-related operations. This task allows you to easily determine the current date and time and calculate elapsed time. The *Samples\Ch09\1_DateAndTime\runner.msbuild* script file provides several examples of how to use this Extensions Pack to work with time-related values.

One of the simplest ways to determine the current date and time from within an MSBuild script is by using property functions. This technique is illustrated in the fragment of the build script in Listing 9-21. The TodaysDate property is assigned today's date based on the property function $([System.DateTime]::Today.ToString("dddd, MMMM dd, yyyy")). This approach uses the syntax that MSBuild defines to get a value from a static class property: the Today property of the .NET System.DateTime class. The call to the ToString method uses the conventional .NET format string to assign the value to the TodaysDate property. A similar approach assigns the current time to the CurrentTime property.

Listing 9-21. Script That Assigns the Current Date and Time to Properties

```
...

    <Message Text="Use the MSBuild property functions to get the current date and time"
            Importance="low"
            />
    <PropertyGroup>
      <TodaysDate>$([System.DateTime]::Today.ToString("dddd, MMMM dd, yyyy"))</TodaysDate>
      <CurrentTime>$([System.DateTime]::Now.ToString("h:mm:ss tt"))</CurrentTime>
    </PropertyGroup>

    <Message Text="     Today's date is: $(TodaysDate)"
            Importance="high"
            />
    <Message Text="     Current time is: $(CurrentTime)"
            Importance="high"
            />
...
```

When the *Samples\Ch09\1_DateAndTime\runner.msbuild* script file is executed the messages that are written out display today's date and the current time, which is illustrated in Listing 9-22.

Listing 9-22. Output That Displays the Current Date and Time

```
...

Using the MSBuild property functions to get the current date and time
      Today's date is: Sunday, September 25, 2011
      Current time is: 3:32:45 PM
...
```

Assembly Info

The assemblies that are created during the build process contain properties that can help the .NET Framework to properly identify and reference the correct assemblies. Among these assembly properties is the Assembly Version property. It is very helpful to have the build server track and provide the proper build number to the build script to establish the correct Assembly Version property value. From the build server's perspective, this is a "build number" that is defined, incremented, and passed to the build script when it is run. For example, it is common for a build server to maintain a build number in a specified format (such as, {major version}.{minor version}.{build counter}.{vcs revision number}) and pass the value in to the script as a "build number" property value. The trick is to write the build script in a way to properly receive the build number and assign it to the assemblies as their version number. Having a version numbering system that ties the assembly back to the build and revision number is very helpful when debugging and diagnosing problems.

▓ **Practice 9-8** Have the Script Tie the Assembly Version Back to the Build and Revision Number

---

There is an MSBuild Extension Pack task that helps deal with the assembly information for .NET Framework projects. The MSBuild.ExtensionPack.Framework.AssemblyInfo task is able to properly assign assembly information from within a build script. In Listing 9-23, this extension task is used to assign four assembly information values to each of the *AssemblyInfo.cs* files under the source folder. The ItemGroup element uses wildcarding to provide a recursive list of all the assembly information files. Later, this list of files is passed to the MSBuild.ExtensionPack.Framework.AssemblyInfo task using the AssemblyInfoFiles attribute. This task applies each of the property values to the assembly information files. The property values include the correct company name, copyright notice, assembly version, and file version. The result is consistent and correct assembly information assignment across the entire set of source files.

Listing 9-23. Script That Updates the AssemblyInfo.cs Files

```
...
<Target Name="AssemblyInformation" >
  <ItemGroup>
    <AssemblyInfoFiles Include="$(SourceFolder)\**\AssemblyInfo.cs" />
  </ItemGroup>

  <Time Format="yyyy">
    <Output TaskParameter="FormattedTime" PropertyName="CurrentYear" />
  </Time>

  <PropertyGroup>
    <AssemblyCompany>Lender Inc.</AssemblyCompany>
    <AssemblyCopyright>Copyright © $(CurrentYear) $(AssemblyCompany)</AssemblyCopyright>
    <AssemblyVersion>$(BUILD_NUMBER)</AssemblyVersion>
    <AssemblyFileVersion>$(BUILD_NUMBER)</AssemblyFileVersion>
  </PropertyGroup>

  <MSBuild.ExtensionPack.Framework.AssemblyInfo
    AssemblyInfoFiles="@(AssemblyInfoFiles)"
    AssemblyCompany="$(AssemblyCompany)"
    AssemblyCopyright="$(AssemblyCopyright)"
    AssemblyVersion="$(AssemblyVersion)"
    AssemblyFileVersion="$(AssemblyFileVersion)"
    />
</Target>
...
```

XML Peek and Poke

There are many XML files associated with a build. Some are configuration files that are part of the source. Others are output files and reports generated during the build. In both cases, it is helpful to have the build script be able to read or write to an XML file. For example, after running *FxCopCmd.exe* the build script can read the XML report to determine the number of errors that were written to the report. If the number of errors and warnings that are in the report exceed defined threshold limits, the build script can fail the build. The *Samples\Ch09\3_XmlPeekAndPoke\runner.msbuild* script file demonstrates how to stop the build if an FxCop report contains errors or warnings that exceed the thresholds.

▨ **Practice 9-9** Read and Write XML Data from Within the Build Script

---

There are custom task libraries that read or write to an XML file for use in MSBuild scripts. In Listing 9-24, the MSBuild Community Tasks library is used to update the *Web.config* file's connection string. This listing is an excerpt from the *Samples\Ch09\3_XmlPeekAndPoke\runner.msbuild* script file. The ConnectionString property contains the properly formatted connection string based on the externally defined parameters for the server name, database name, user id, and password. The XmlUpdate task uses the XPath attribute value to update the *Web.config* file's connection string with the proper value.

Listing 9-24. Script That Updates the ConnectionString Element in a config File

...

```
<Target Name="UpdateConnectionStrings">
  <PropertyGroup>
    <ConfigFile>.\bin\Web.config</ConfigFile>
    <ConnectionKey>Lender.Slos.Database</ConnectionKey>
    <ConnectionString>Data Source=$(ServerName);Initial Catalog=$(DatabaseName); ↵
User Id=$(UserId);Password=$(Password);Trusted_Connection=False;</ConnectionString>
  </PropertyGroup>

  <Error Condition="!Exists('$(ConfigFile)')"
         Text="Config file not found '$(ConfigFile)'"
         />
  <XmlUpdate ContinueOnError="False"
             XPath="/configuration/connectionStrings/↵
add[@name='$(ConnectionKey)']/@connectionString"
             XmlFileName="$(ConfigFile)"
             Value="$(ConnectionString)"
             />
  <Message Text="Connection string updated successfully in '$(ConfigFile)'"
           Importance="low"
           />
</Target>
```
...

Zip Archive

Many build scripts are written to package the deliverables for later deployment. Ahead, the section on automated deployment describes several options that are applicable under different deployment situations. This section focuses on the common task of creating a zip archive file to store build artifacts or otherwise organize the build output. Some common applications of this task include packaging database scripts, content files, binaries, and build reports. There are so many good reasons to compress, archive, and store files during the build process that this is a common task.

▪ **Practice 9-10** Learn How to Create Zip File Archives from Within the Build Script

---

Using the MSBuild Community Tasks library to create a zip archive file is a widely-used technique. Let's look at a piece of the *Samples\Ch09\4_Zip\runner.msbuild* build script file shown in Listing 9-25. Starting at the bottom of the listing, there is a Target element with the name Package. This target calls the Zip task, which is part of the Community Tasks library. The Zip task takes all the files defined within the FilesToZip item array and adds them to the archive file defined in the ZipFileName attribute. Notice that the ZipFileName attribute is formatted based on the project name and build number to create a unique zip filename.

The earlier Target section named CopyToPreserve is responsible for copying the correct source files to the proper destination folder, using the Copy task. Therefore, the CopyToPreserve target needs to be called first. Once it copies the files, the Package target is called to create the zip archive file and add those files to the archive. At some later stage in the build script another target could copy all the archive files to a file server for storage and future use.

Listing 9-25. Script That Creates a Zip File Archive

```
...

  <Target Name="CopyToPreserve" >
    <PropertyGroup>
      <SourceFolder>.\Lender.Slos.Financial\bin\$(Configuration)</SourceFolder>
    </PropertyGroup>

    <ItemGroup>
      <ContentExclude Include="$(SourceFolder)\**\*.pdb" />
      <ContentExclude Include="$(SourceFolder)\**\*.gif" />
      <ContentExclude Include="$(SourceFolder)\**\Webcontrol_*.bmp" />
    </ItemGroup>

    <ItemGroup>
      <ContentFiles Include="$(SourceFolder)\**"
                    Exclude="@(ContentExclude)"
                    />
    </ItemGroup>

    <Copy SourceFiles="@(ContentFiles)"
          DestinationFiles=↵
"@(ContentFiles->'$(PreservePath)\%(RecursiveDir)%(Filename)%(Extension)')"
          />
  </Target>
```

```
<Target Name="Package">
  <ItemGroup>
    <FilesToZip Include="$(PreservePath)\**\*.*"
                Exclude="$(ArtifactsPath)\**\*.zip"
                />
  </ItemGroup>

  <Zip Files="@(FilesToZip)"
       WorkingDirectory="$(ArtifactsPath)"
       ZipFileName="$(ArtifactsPath)\$(ProjectName).$(Configuration).v$(BUILD_NUMBER).zip"
       ZipLevel="9"
       />
</Target>
...
```

Automated Deployment

Manual deployments are tedious, tiresome, and time consuming. Many times steps are missed; other times the steps are done improperly. People make mistakes. The bigger problem is that manual deployments often become an error-prone part of the project that hurts the reputation of those who deploy the application. Many developers feel that they are saddled with the task of deploying the application and that breeds apathy and carelessness. Repeatedly performing any set of tedious and unwelcome tasks is a recipe for problems.

Automated deployment offers a way out of the morass of manual deployments. Consider the tasks associated with a typical web application deployment:

- Take the target web site offline

- Copy files and folders

- Update the database schema

- Set read/write permissions on folders

- Assign the proper configuration settings

- Bring the site back online

Many of these steps can be replaced by an automated script using straightforward techniques. You and your team can improve the reliability of deployments by automating just a few of these steps. By automating the entire deployment you can expect dramatic results in shorter deployment times, fewer and less frequent errors, and greater confidence that the deployment is complete and correct.

Build Once, Deploy Many

Ideally, the build creates a set of artifacts that can be deployed to a target environment. The purpose of the deployment is to make the application available for evaluation and use. For example, if the build-artifacts are deployed to a test environment, the quality assurance (QA) testers are then able to independently verify and validate that specific build. The trick is to be able to deploy the same build-artifacts to all the environments. The confidence in the build increases as the same build moves from integration, to testing, to staging, and into production. Being able to track and confirm the stability, completeness, correctness, and reliability of the same build across target environments is a valuable practice.

▧ **Practice 9-11** Deploy the Same Build to Multiple Target Environments to Confirm Readiness

---

The practice of "build once, deploy many" is founded on the idea that the automated deployment is loosely coupled to the automated build. The automated deployment script ought to be able to take a build number or some other parameters that the script uses to select the proper build artifacts. This idea is sometimes referred to as artifact build dependency. Some common artifact dependencies include

- *Latest Successful Build*: Used to deploy the latest software. This is often used for continuous deployment and stability testing.

- *Latest Tagged Build*: Used to deploy the software based on a provisional designation. Designating this build is sometimes called tagging or pinning. This is useful for QA to select a build for deployment to system test or staging.

- *Specific Build Number*: Used to deploy the software based on a fixed designation. This is useful for establishing a consistent deployment and redeployment of the same build to system test, staging, and production environments.

To make the "build once, deploy many" strategy work well, the automated deployment script should be able to deploy to any of the target environments. Stated another way, the deployment script should be written so that it takes in parameters that control its logic and actions so as to deploy properly to all target environments.

An outline of an automated deployment script's parameters could include

- *Artifact Dependency*: A parameter that controls how the script obtains the artifacts for the deployment.

- *Target Environment Server*: A parameter that controls which server the script deploys the artifacts to.

- *Target Database Connection*: A parameter that controls which database the script configures as the database for the target environment.

- *Target Configuration Settings*: A parameter that controls how the deployment script establishes the proper configuration settings.

With these parameters the automated deployment script retrieves the proper artifacts, properly sets the *Web.config* file or other configuration settings, and deploys to the correct server.

Packaging Tools

Packaging is often unappreciated until the time comes to hand the responsibility of deployment over to the internal IT department, the customer's IT department, or some other person responsible for installing the application. In far too many cases there is a last minute rush to assemble the artifacts and write up instructions for others to follow. It would be so much easier to have thought through the final delivery beforehand. Today, many customers and IT departments simply will not accept a cobbled-together deliverable. It is important to take the time early in the development process to consider how the application needs to be packaged. Find out what is preferred and what is acceptable to the consumer of the package. Figure out what the development team can reasonably put together. Determine if there is a significant gap. Perhaps the customer expects an MSI but the developers are publishing the web application from Visual Studio or Team Foundation Server. Asking the right questions and developing the appropriate strategy for packaging the deliverables is important. It sets the stage for a smooth rollout and delivery, which makes everyone's life a whole lot easier.

▧ **Practice 9-12** Define the Packaging Approach That Works for Both the Customer and the Team

---

There are many packaging tools that offer benefits for different circumstances. Table 9-3 provides a list of packaging options worth considering. At Microsoft, the IIS team and the ASP.NET team worked hard to put together the latest Web Deployment Tool (Web Deploy 2.0). Although it is often used within Visual Studio to publish a web application directly, with Web Deploy you can create a deployment package. The package this tool creates is literally one zip archive file. It can easily be deployed on a remote server using the IIS Admin Tool or from the command-line. If you are deploying a web application to IIS then you will benefit from all the experience and expertise in Web Deploy 2.0. There are several resources in Appendix A that can help you get proficient at making Web Deploy packages.

Table 9-3. *Packaging Options*

Name	Description	More Information
MSI Packages	Create a Windows Installer package (MSI) for the application. Windows Installer is a base service of the operating system that provides a consistent and reliable way to customize installations, upgrade applications, and resolve installation problems. The Visual Studio Setup projects and the Windows Installer XML (WiX) Toolset are definitely worth evaluating. As the requirements grow, creating MSI packages becomes much more involved, so consider commercial products that help make creating MSI packages easier.	msdn.microsoft.com/en-us/library/ee721500.aspx and wix.sourceforge.net
Web Deploy 2.0	Create a Web Deploy package, which allows you to package all the configuration and content of the Web application and database. This tool is for use with IIS Web servers, web applications and web sites. The Web Deploy packaging process can occur by running the command line from the build script.	www.iis.net/download/web deploy
Zip Archive	Create a compressed file archive from the build script using an extension library. This is a straightforward approach to simple application deployment needs. Also, there are many free and commercial products to assist in creating file archives.	en.wikipedia.org/wiki/Co mparison_of_file_archive rs

Deployment Tools

Packaging and deployment go hand in hand. Often the selected packaging approach implies a deployment strategy. For example, using Web Deploy to create a deployment package means you will want to use Web Deploy to deploy to the target environment. Perhaps the most important thing to consider and work out is how to automate the deployment with a scripting tool. Combine the effectiveness of the deployment tool and the build tool in complementary ways to eliminate as many manual steps as possible to create an automated, flexible, reliable, and repeatable deployment process.

■ **Practice 9-13** Use a Tool That Makes Deployments Automated, Robust, and Reliable

The deployment options in Table 9-4 complement the packaging options presented in Table 9-3. Each of these can be automated with a build tool or through the command line.

Table 9-4. Deployment Options

Name	Description	More Information
Msiexec.exe	This is the command-line tool that installs MSI packages. This is a standard Windows method for installing an application and its components on a user's computer or Windows server.	msdn.microsoft.com/en-us/library/aa367449(v=VS.85).aspx
Web Deploy 2.0	Web application deployment tool for IIS that has significant advantages over directory or file replication approaches.	www.iis.net/download/web deploy
Robocopy	The Robust File Copy (Robocopy) tool is a command-line directory replication command that supersedes the *xcopy* deployment approach.	technet.microsoft.com/en-us/library/cc733145(WS.10).aspx

Summary

In this chapter you learned about build tools. More specifically, you learned practices related to using build tools to perform common build automation tasks. You also learned about better practices related to the logical next steps of packaging and deploying the build. For you, your team and your organization it is important to develop proficiency and mastery of build automation in order to reduce-to-practice the many tedious and inglorious activities of building, packaging, and deploying the application.

In the next chapter all the build automation you learned in this chapter is orchestrated through the practices of continuous integration. Chapter 10 introduces the continuous integration lifecycle, which employs and is underpinned by build automation. In Chapter 11 you will learn about code analysis and see examples of how to automate analysis tools, like StyleCop and FxCop, with build automation. In addition, build automation provides the means to automate the unit testing frameworks and test runners you will learn about in Chapter 12.

CHAPTER 10

Continuous Integration

The practice of *continuous integration* (CI) has the ability to transform software development from a set of manual processes to a logical series of reproducible, automated processes. At the heart of continuous integration is the CI server, which is the fundamental tool and technology that initiates, performs, coordinates, and reports on the CI phases. This chapter introduces you to CI server alternatives and describes their basic product offerings.

In this chapter you will learn about the CI lifecycle. This lifecycle is a conceptual model that describes the series of development processes that establish an effective, automated progression from source code to accepted deliverable. The CI lifecycle consists of the following major processes:

- *Rebuilding:* Source code is integrated and compiled into binaries.

- *Unit Testing:* Automated testing is performed to check the integrity of the build.

- *Analysis:* Code analysis and monitoring is carried out to confirm code quality.

- *Packaging:* Build artifacts are assembled and delivered as an installation package.

- *Deployment:* The installation package is deployed to a target environment.

- *Stability Testing:* Automated testing verifies the stability of the deployment.

Each of these processes is described in detail with a description of the steps involved within each process. Along the way many specific practices for continuous integration are described, summarized in Table 10-1. By using these CI practices, you can expect to save time, improve team effectiveness, and move the focus toward early detection of problems and prevention.

Table 10-1. Continuous Integration: Ruthlessly Helpful .NET Practices

	Continuous Integration Practice
10-1	Trigger a Rebuild After Every Code Push
10-2	Start Rebuilding with a Clean Working Folder
10-3	Organize Build Artifacts into a Single Archive File
10-4	Run Unit Tests to Confirm That the Latest Build Works as Intended
10-5	Perform Monitoring Analysis and Report Failure if Violations Occur

	Continuous Integration Practice
10-6	Generate Complete Analysis Reports for Ongoing Review
10-7	Package the Components and Content into One Deliverable
10-8	Create One Script That Deploys to All Target Environments
10-9	Smoke Test the Deployment to Find Configuration Problems
10-10	Run Stability Tests to Verify the Deployment Is Ready for QA
10-11	Generate Reports That Demonstrate Progress and Delivery

COMMENTARY

There is sometimes a little bit of confusion and debate regarding the word *continuous* in *continuous integration*. For developers the important idea is to have the processing happen quickly and in rapid succession. This makes sense. Developers need timely feedback on whether the build broke, unit tests failed, or code quality standards were violated. A developer's progress depends on knowing if the latest code push is causing an issue. This fast-paced timeline is not appropriate for the QA team, for whom testing seeks to verify and validate a stable progression of builds. Each build improves and expands upon the capabilities of the last. The testing team tries to avoid builds that have lost functionality.

Many people in software development have heard the construction metaphor that compares the predictability of scope, cost, and schedule of new-home construction to software development. But few non-developers understand how the equivalent of a house's plumbing, for example, could have been completed one day and vanished the next. Yet in software development such dramatic changes happen intermittently. Developers do not seem to worry because they know that tomorrow all the plumbing will be back, that it was not stolen or lost to carelessness, and its disappearance was the unintended consequence of some action taken by, say, the master electrician. To the QA lead or the project manager, however, this sudden reversal of progress is shocking and troublesome. They rarely expect it and often imagine the worse.

Continuous integration is actually about managing expectations. Developers expect problems and need to know as soon as one occurs so that priorities can shift to address the issue. The expectation is that the CI server is relentlessly keeping an eye on the build, the unit tests, and the source code quality. Even when all developers are careful and thorough, the CI server finds integration problems that are too subtle for any one developer to foresee. For the rest of the team the expectations are different. The QA team seeks stability and reliability. The QA lead is looking for CI to assure them that deployments are done properly and that basic stability is assured. The project manager wants insight into the development process. The PM needs to know that progress is not stalled and activities are producing deliverables.

Case Study

You are the lead software developer working at Lender Inc., a fictional bank that originates student loans using their internally-developed Student Loan Origination System (SLOS) software. As the technical lead, you are assigned the task of improving the software development processes. Based on the retrospectives from past projects, you will bring about changes and improvements that address the pain points of previous projects.

SLOS PROCESS IMPROVEMENT

In the past, the SLOS development projects have experienced problems. Management and the project team hope to avoid these problems on the next project. For the developers, the problems included difficulty bringing together and aligning code changes, many failing unit tests, and poor code quality. A project might start off well, but the problems gradually worsened. For the QA team, the deployments to the system testing environment were erratic and lacked reliability. When the deployment was good, the testers were productive, but when the deployment was bad, basic functionality was compromised. The QA team's progress was often delayed and their trust in the developers was often low. The project manager did not see smooth progress being made. The unpredictable delivery made it difficult to report status and forecast milestones and schedule.

The code changes that each developer made were not always compatible with the changes made by other developers; from time to time, the lead developer had to take down the latest code and deal with these incompatibilities. Resolving these integration problems was challenging and frustrating. The lead developer often needed to spend time with the various developers sorting out how each change should integrate with another. One developer's changes were causing another developer's unit tests to fail, but this was ignored. A lot of thrashing took place as the interrelated code was aligned. The lead developer worked hard to make sure all the unit tests passed and to ensure everything worked as intended. However, it was not until the long-delayed code review that the lead developer found that code quality had been suffering.

The QA team found many problems with each deployment to the system testing environment, including recurring configuration issues. Entire configuration sections were missing, connection strings were not properly set, and there were incompatible or missing components. Even after the basic configuration problems were ironed out and the system testing environment was ready, the testers found additional problems. On several occasions critical functionality and important features did not work. Some of the system capabilities that had worked now no longer worked. There were deployments that were completely unusable. The QA team lost many hours of testing time waiting for a new deployment, and the testing delays impacted the project schedule.

Today, the SLOS project manager is looking for a way to better coordinate the entire project team. The developers need to integrate the source code early and often. The lead developer must know when unit tests are failing and resolve them quickly, and must monitor the code quality and address problems straightaway. The QA team needs to have more control over the deployments to the system test environment. Only after the QA lead is confident that a new build is ready to be tested should it be deployed to the system test environment. Throughout this entire process the project manager needs to see less thrashing and have more visibility into how the teams are progressing.

You are clearly aware that SLOS process improvements are needed and you plan to work with individual developers to improve their development practices. It is the systemic problems you plan to address with continuous integration. You intend to take the following actions to improve the situation:

- Set up a CI server.

- Configure the CI server to monitor the version control system for changes.

- After each code push, have the CI server get the latest code and rebuild the solution.

- Run all automated tests from the CI server.

- Have the CI server monitor the quality of the code by running code analysis tools.

- Perform automated deployments, which are complete, consistent, and correct, to the system test environment.

- Use the CI server's reporting capabilities to communicate progress and status to the entire project team.

The CI Server

At the heart of continuous integration is the tool and technology of the continuous integration server. The CI server is an application, usually running in the background as a service application, which initiates, executes, and reports on all the processes of the continuous integration lifecycle. The CI server provides key capabilities such as

- Integrating with and monitoring the version control system

- Triggering events, such as on source code commits, on a schedule or in sequence

- Running build automation and deployment scripts

- Running tests

- Performing analysis

- Providing notification, status messages, and build logs

- Storing artifacts and related output

There are many CI servers available. Table 10-2 provides a list of some widely-used CI servers, which are worth evaluating.

Table 10-2. Continuous Integration Servers

Product	Terms	More Info
CruiseControl.NET	Free, open source	ccnet.thoughtworks.com
Jenkins[1]	Free, open source	jenkins-ci.org
TeamCity	Commercial, Professional Server is free	www.jetbrains.com/teamcity
Team Foundation Server	Microsoft Visual Studio and MSDN licensing	msdn.microsoft.com/en-us/vstudio/ff637362

In the sections that follow, each of these four CI servers is summarized. The goal is to provide you with enough information to begin an evaluation of the CI server that is right for your project and organization.

CruiseControl.NET

CruiseControl.NET is the.NET version of the CruiseControl continuous integration software package. It is commonly abbreviated as CCNet. The primary component is the CCNet Server, which is the automated integration server. The CCNet Server runs as either a console application or a Windows service. In general, running the service is preferable so that the CCNet Server runs in the background and requires no user intervention.

Another significant component of CCNet is the Web Dashboard application, which provides project status and reporting information. The Web Dashboard provides build progress, drill-down detail, and history on the CCNet projects. It is an effective way to communicate build information to all project stakeholders.

A third component of CCNet is the CCTray utility. This is a client system tray application that provides feedback on build status and progress. This utility is especially useful to developers as build notifications are received through a tray application instead of by e-mail. It notifies on events such as whether the most recent build was successful or failed.

There are many reasons to choose CCNet. There is a lot of information available in Internet postings that provide tutorials and detailed examples. Some other reasons to choose CCNet include

- Free and open source

- .NET-based

- Widely-used and well documented

- Integration with a wide variety of tools and technologies

---

[1] Jenkins was previously the Hudson CI server. After Oracle's acquisition of Sun, the source code was forked and Oracle continues development under the Hudson name.

CCNet does have drawbacks. Perhaps the biggest drawback is that the CCNet Server is controlled through XML configuration files. For those familiar with CruiseControl for Java or Ruby this might be an advantage because the configuration blocks follow a similar model. There is a lot of documentation on the configuration blocks; however, the learning curve can take some time to climb.

Jenkins

Jenkins is a Java-based continuous integration server package. It is commonly used for Java projects but is suited for .NET projects because Jenkins can work with many common .NET version control systems, can run MSBuild scripts, and has a very active plug-in development community; much of what any CI server does is not .NET specific. The primary component of Jenkins is the server, which runs within a Java servlet container, such as Apache Tomcat. Jenkins is easy to install and use; the fact that it is Java-based should not represent an impediment to .NET development shops. Jenkins provides an impressive browser-hosted project management dashboard. For those familiar with using Jenkins for Java development, the advantage is in using a familiar technology. Some of the reasons to evaluate and choose Jenkins include

- Free and open source

- Widely-used and well documented

- Integration with a wide variety of tools and technologies

- Vibrant user community

TeamCity

TeamCity is a Java-based continuous integration server package. The TeamCity installation and configuration is quick and easy. The fact that it is Java-based should not be an impediment to .NET development shops. The TeamCity server is a main component, but the browser-hosted interface serves as the primary way to administer TeamCity users, agents, projects, and build configurations.

The TeamCity browser-hosted dashboard is superb. It provides project status and reporting information suitable for a broad range of users and project stakeholders. It provides build progress, drill-down detail, and history information on the projects and configurations.

With TeamCity there is a system tray utility to provide feedback on build status and progress. The tray utility is useful so build notifications are received in the tray instead of by e-mail. The TC tray application notifies on events such as whether the most recent build was successful or failed.

There are a lot of good reasons to choose TeamCity. The product is very well documented and there are a lot of examples and tutorials available. Out on the Internet there are many postings ranging from setting up basic CI with TeamCity to advanced topics such as using TeamCity's built-in NUnit test runner. Some other reasons to choose TeamCity include

- Professional Server is free for up to 20 build configurations. You can run as many instances of Professional Edition Server as needed. Larger organizations may require the purchase of the Enterprise Server version.

- Easy to set up, easy to use, and easy to configure

- Widely-used and well documented

- Integration with a wide variety of tools and technologies

In this chapter, TeamCity is the CI server used to illustrate the key concepts in the continuous integration lifecycle.

Team Foundation Server

The primary benefit of Team Foundation Server (TFS) is that it is an integrated CI environment with strong Visual Studio integration. It is supported by Microsoft. TFS is integrated with Visual Studio in a way that is geared toward developing software within the entire "enterprise" using an Application Lifecycle Management approach. This is an integrated-whole solution, not a best-of-breed solution. Some of the reasons to choose TFS include:

- Strong IDE integration with Visual Studio

- Metrics tracking, check-in policy enforcement, and Windows authentication

- Widely-used and well documented

TFS is a significant investment in budget and configuration management resources. Team Foundation Server is a good choice when the development team is large, the TFS/Visual Studio integration is important, and the Application Lifecycle Management approach is attractive.

CI Lifecycle

The continuous integration lifecycle (shown in Figure 10-1) is a model for how the CI server manages and moves through the phases. It starts with the latest code push and ends with a report on the stability of the deployment. All along the way, each phase provides a report on the actions performed during and the results from each phase. Once the CI server has successfully performed the packaging, a new deliverable joins the steady stream of deliverables that flows from the lifecycle. As each phase continues successfully, it confirms that the source code is sound and that development is progressing.

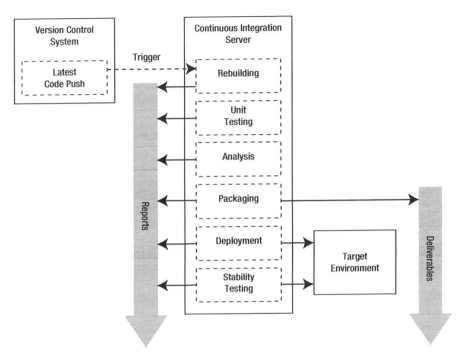

***Figure 10-1.** The continuous integration lifecycle*

Within TeamCity the CI lifecycle is implemented through project configurations. Figure 10-2 illustrates the TeamCity project administration interface with all six of these configurations created. Each configuration defines how the process is triggered, the steps taken, and how the results are handled. When each configuration is run, TeamCity maintains a log of activities and reports either the success or failure of the run.

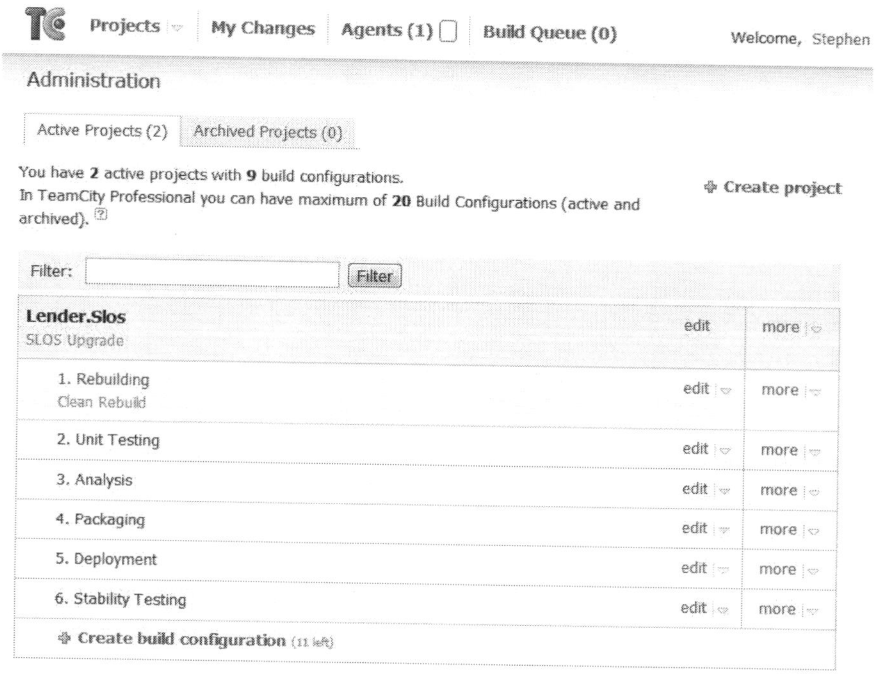

Figure 10-2. The SLOS project in TeamCity

Rebuilding

The first phase in the continuous integration lifecycle is the Rebuilding phase. The aim of this phase is to carry out the build automation steps. Figure 10-3 illustrates the Rebuilding phase of the CI lifecycle. The goal of this phase is to provide timely feedback to all of the developers about the health of the build. In other word, the team is trying to avoid Integration Hell.[2] The phase starts with a clean directory, gets all the latest source code, and rebuilds the solution from the source code. If, for many possible reasons, the build breaks, then the team is notified that there is an integration issue that requires urgent attention. Speed is very important. Ideally, the Rebuilding phase on the CI server should have a goal of less than 5 minutes. Note: For large software development projects the goal of 5 minutes is not realistic. Builds can take 30 minutes or more. This is especially true when the Rebuilding phase starts with a clean folder, as described in Practice 10-2. These are ideals that actually present a dilemma that is often resolved by a compromise between getting timely builds and having "clean" build conditions. Over time, strive to use faster CI server hardware and incremental builds to move toward the goal of very fast builds.

The rebuilding begins with a triggering event; typically, the CI server detects that a source code change was pushed to the version control system (VCS). A working directory is created or cleaned; this establishes a reproducible and known initial condition. The CI server then gets all the latest source code, content, and other input necessary to compile the source code.

---

[2] Ward Cunningham describes Integration Hell in his wiki: http://c2.com/cgi/wiki?IntegrationHell.

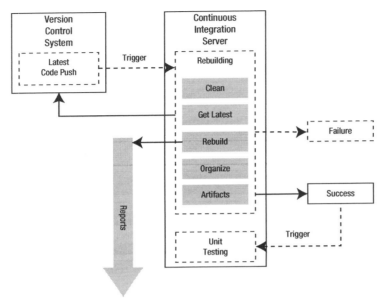

Figure 10-3. *The Rebuilding phase in the CI lifecycle*

With a clean working folder and the latest code from VCS, all the prerequisites are in place. The CI server now runs the build automation script. The build automation script performs a complete rebuild. The rebuild is usually the automated method of performing the same build steps to generate the target output manually through Visual Studio. After a successful rebuild, the binaries and other output may be scattered under various project output directories. The next step copies and organizes these binaries, content, and target output into a coherent arrangement of files and folders. The CI server makes this output available as build artifacts.

At any time during the Rebuilding phase, any of the steps might result in a failure. Usually, a build failure is the result of a compilation error; however, it could be the result of a configuration or build script error. Whatever the reason, the CI server reports the failure and sends out notifications. Since the CI server maintains a log of all output from each of the build steps, the build log is the primary way to understand why a build failed.

When the Rebuilding phase results in success, the CI server sends notification of a successful build. There are two key results from a successful build.

- First, the CI server publishes the build artifacts and makes them available as the input for many of the subsequent phases.

- Second, the CI server triggers the next phase in the lifecycle, which is the Unit Testing phase.

Rebuilding Trigger

The rebuild ought to be triggered after every code push to the version control system. This provides timely feedback to the developer who pushed the change set, and it catches integration problems at the earliest point in time. The CI server vigilantly monitors the VCS and initiates the Rebuilding phase immediately after code is pushed.

▪ **Practice 10-1** Trigger a Rebuild After Every Code Push

The choice of the word *immediately* describes the ideal. In real-world scenarios, use a VCS setting delay or a schedule-based trigger to allow a window of opportunity for multistep commit operations. Frequent integration is the top priority and the key principle behind this practice. It makes it very clear that a code change broke the build. To avoid confusion, the development team must immediately stop all other code pushes when the build fails. Fixing the build is the team's first priority. As long as the build is broken, the only code change that should happen is a change that directly relates to fixing the build.

In order to make sure VCS triggering is effective, the entire Rebuilding phase must run quickly by following these guidelines:

- Use a fast-performing CI server

- Make sure the rebuild step runs quickly

- Cut back the artifacts to the minimum and essential

- Encourage code pushes that balance frequency and substance

The TeamCity build triggering configuration is illustrated in Figure 10-4. This configuration is set to trigger a rebuild after a VCS change is detected. Any CI server ought to support a VCS trigger that uses the project's version control settings to monitor and respond to check-in activity.

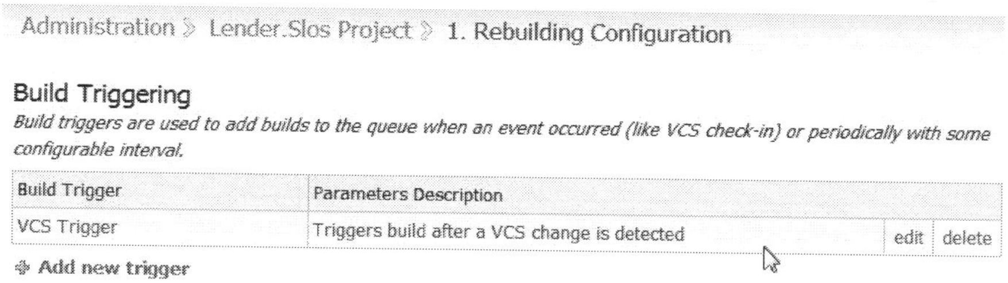

Figure 10-4. The TeamCity VCS trigger

In some large projects there are many developers pushing code changes frequently. In those situations it is sometimes argued that making a switch from a VCS-driven build trigger to an infrequent schedule-driven trigger is warranted. The thinking is that the CI lifecycle is incessantly driven by the frequent code pushes. Similarly, when the build phase takes a long time, a switch to a schedule-driven process is sought. It is better to focus the effort on speeding up the build or changing the developer practices. Avoid dropping the VCS trigger because other triggers postpone the feedback and increase the likelihood of integration problems.

The arrangement for VCS triggering is adjusted depending on the type of build. For very large software products the complete, end-to-end build can take a very long time, sometimes hours. Consider dividing up the build types based on concepts, such as

- *Development*: VCS triggering with an incremental build, not with a clean working folder; since build speed is an issue the goal is to provide efficient feedback.

- *Nightly Integration*: Schedule triggering with a complete build, starting with a new working folder and followed by full stability and integration test suites.

Clean Working Directory

The ability to reproduce the build is an essential characteristic of the Rebuilding phase. Given identical conditions, each build should be 100% reproducible. The reason this is important is that it eliminates the unknown variables and the sources of confusion. It verifies that the build script is able to compile the binaries and generate the output using only the source code in VCS. For this reason the CI server needs to start with an empty working folder.

■ **Practice 10-2** Start Rebuilding with a Clean Working Folder

---

A CI server usually offers the option of either creating a new working folder for each build or cleaning all the files from the working folder before the build. The advantage of a new working folder is that folders from prior builds are available, if the need should arise. In this case, old directories will eventually need to be deleted to save disk space. The alternate approach reuses the working folder, but the CI server cleans up before the build begins. This second approach assumes that the working folders from prior builds are no longer needed, which is often the case; either the build failed or, if it was successful, then the artifacts are already saved.

In some large projects the source control repository is very large or the version control system is slow. Either starting with a new working folder or cleaning the working folder adds an unacceptably long delay to the build. In this case, perform an incremental build using the existing working folder, since build speed is important to provide timely feedback. Another approach adds a "clean up" step within the build script to remove all intermediate files and output folders. This "clean up" step is shown later on as the first step in Figure 10-6. In general, it is helpful to start with the cleanest conditions possible and keep the build times reasonably short.

Get Latest Source Code

In the next step of this phase, the CI server creates a local working copy of the files using the VCS settings. For TeamCity this is accomplished by configuring a VCS Root for the project, which is illustrated in Figure 10-5. Using the VCS settings, the CI server performs a "check-out" of the latest revision of the source code. Now the working folder contains the source code from the check-in that triggered the Rebuilding phase.

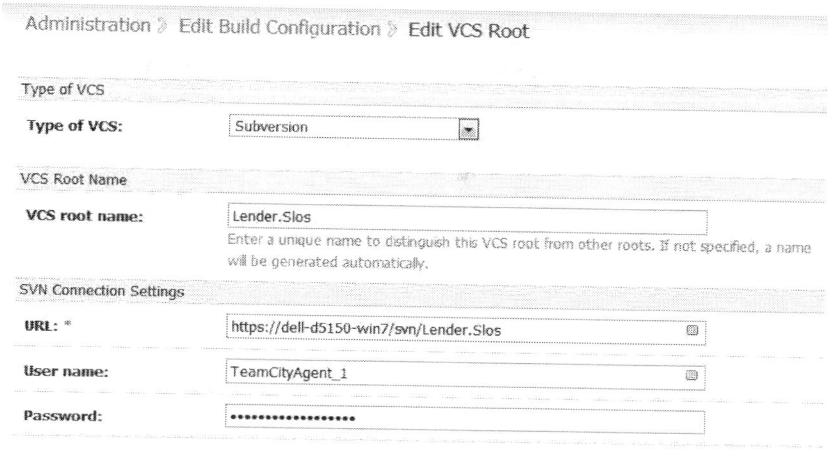

Figure 10-5. The TeamCity VCS Root

Rebuild the Solution

Once the CI server retrieves the latest source code from version control, the next stage is to rebuild the entire solution. Since Visual Studio works together with MSBuild, this is easily accomplished using an MSBuild script. Most build scripting tools make it easy to rebuild given a Visual Studio solution file name as input. The goal is to have the CI server be able to run a script or command-line tool to rebuild the necessary Visual Studio project or solution files.

TeamCity supports more than one build step within a configuration. Figure 10-6 illustrates three steps in the Build phase. In this example, the second step performs the solution rebuild. It uses MSBuild to run the *runner.msbuild* script with a target name of Rebuild.

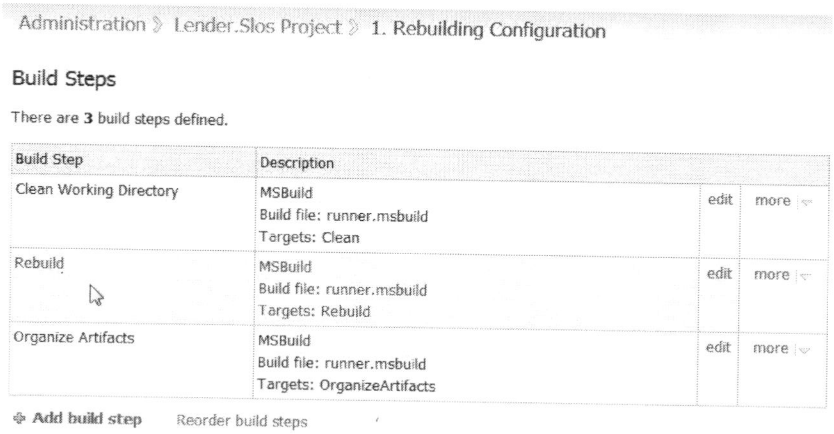

Figure 10-6. The TeamCity build steps

213

In some large projects it is helpful to have multiple build steps that build the solution by calling various scripts or performing various actions. Either the multiple build steps are configured, as shown in Figure 10-6, or a primary build script encapsulates all the steps to happen in the proper sequence, calling secondary scripts as needed. Whatever the choice, this stage of the Rebuilding phase fully and completely rebuilds the entire solution from the bottom up.

In TeamCity each MSBuild step has a number of configuration options. In Figure 10-7 the MSBuild step calling the Rebuild target is illustrated. Each step is configured to call an MSBuild script file, which in this case is named *runner.msbuild*. In TeamCity, the MSBuild configuration supports earlier versions of .NET as well as the 32-bit and 64-bit platforms. Two more important configuration settings are the targets and the command-line arguments. The targets allow you to specify one or more MSBuild targets that allow you to execute multiple targets in one step. Also, the command-line parameters to MSBuild.exe can be specified, which gives you full control of MSBuild execution.

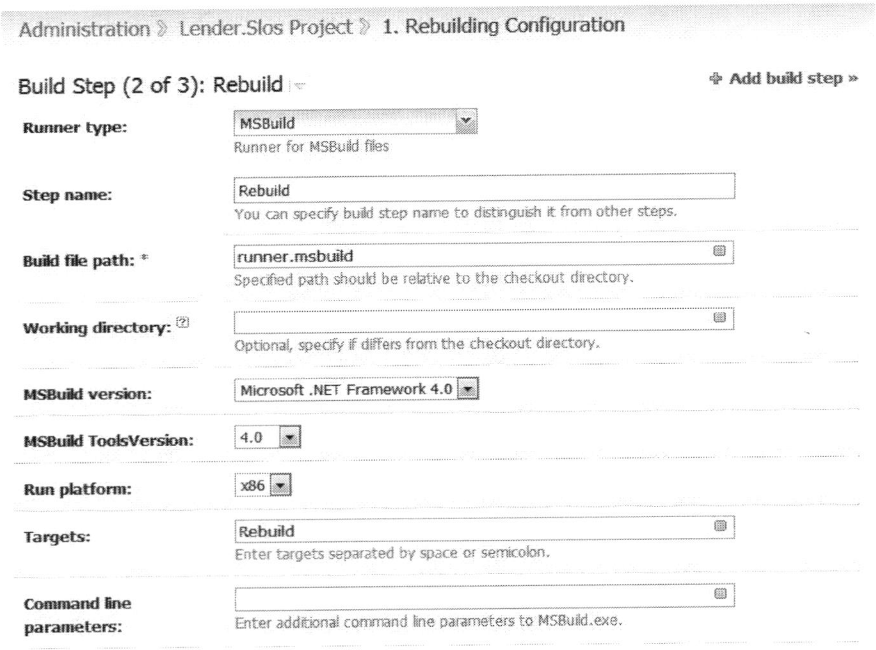

Figure 10-7. Defining the MSBuild configuration for a TeamCity build step

Organize Artifacts

In general, the artifacts are any files you want to save as the results of running a build configuration. In this step, files are copied from the output folders to organize the artifacts into a coherent and consistent layout. The goal is to arrange the files in a way that is best suited for the subsequent steps in the CI lifecycle. Strive to copy just the minimum files but also include all the essential files needed for any subsequent phases. To save space, it is often best to compress everything into one archive file.

■ **Practice 10-3** Organize Build Artifacts into a Single Archive File

---

An effective way to accomplish this task is with a build script. The third step shown in Figure 10-6 performs this task. The OrganizeArtifacts target of the build script copies all the relevant files from the build output folders into a folder structure that supports the upcoming Unit Testing, Analysis, and Packaging phases.

Unit Testing

The next phase in the CI lifecycle is commonly referred to as the Unit Testing phase. The basic steps in the Unit Testing phase are shown in Figure 10-8. Customarily, this phase involves running unit tests and all automated tests that meet all of the following criteria:

- Fast running tests, with no single test running longer than 10 seconds

- Tests focused on checking that the system continues to work as intended

- Automated tests that can run in isolation on the CI server

Unit tests, by definition, must meet these criteria. However, other automated integration testing, specifically the surface tests (discussed in Chapter 8) are designed to meet all the criteria. The important goal is to provide immediate feedback, by reporting a failure if the system is no longer working the way the developers had intended it to work.

The Unit Testing phase begins with a triggering event; usually, the CI server starts this phase right after a successful build completes. A working directory is created and the files are copied in from the latest successful build's artifacts. With the files in place the automated testing begins.

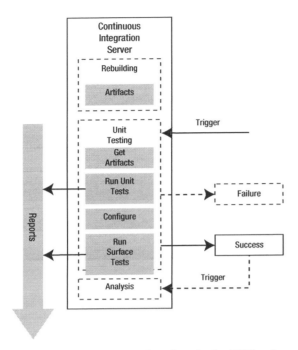

Figure 10-8. The Unit Testing phase in the CI lifecycle

At any time during the testing, one or more tests might fail. Any failing test results in a failure of the current run. The CI server sends out failure notification. The primary way to understand why a test failed is to look at the test-results report. When the testing completes without any failed tests, the CI server sends notification of a successful run.

Just like in the Rebuilding phase, speed is very important. The Unit Testing phase on the CI server should not take longer than 10 minutes and the ideal is well under 5 minutes. The purpose of this phase is to provide timely feedback to developers when the recent code push has created an issue. It is important that the developers address the failed tests as their top priority. Invariably, the cause of the failed test is found in the code that was just pushed; however, a failed test can have several causes and remedies:

- The code-under-test is not working as intended; fix the code.

- The test is incorrect or incomplete; fix the test code.

- The test is not isolated, stable, or otherwise reliable; fix the test code.

- The test is obsolete; remove the test code.

The CI server publishes a report of the results from the testing. This report provides important measures of progress and visibility into the project. The CI server can then trigger the next phase in the lifecycle, which is the Analysis phase.

Testing Trigger

The Unit Testing phase ought to be triggered to begin right after a successful Rebuilding phase completes. This sequencing provides the team with feedback that is correlated between the recent code change set and the failing tests.

The TeamCity build triggering for the Unit Testing phase is illustrated in Figure 10-9. This trigger is set to begin this phase as soon as the last build step successfully completes in the Rebuilding phase. The CI server ought to support a successful-build trigger, which helps to properly sequence the phases.

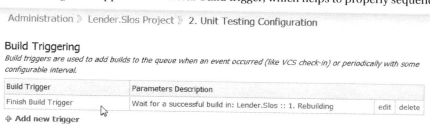

Figure 10-9. The TeamCity Finish Build Trigger event

Get Artifacts

At the end of the last successful rebuild the artifacts were organized and saved. The Unit Testing phase begins by retrieving the artifacts it needs to run the tests. The artifacts files are copied to this configuration's current working directory.

Run Unit Tests

With all the necessary artifact files in the proper place the CI server is ready to run the suite of unit tests. Most CI servers support the common testing frameworks. In cases where the CI server does not directly support the testing framework, the other options include running the tests using a command-line runner, which is described in Chapter 12, or with a build script.

■**Practice 10-4** Run Unit Tests to Confirm That the Latest Build Works as Intended

---

Unit tests are the essence of test-driven development. They are the fundamental way that developers know that the system is working as intended. The CI server needs to run all the unit tests and report the failure of any unit test. If a unit test fails then the system is not working as the developers had intended and all development should stop unit the failing test is resolved.

Configure Surface Tests

Any automated integration tests that run on the CI server might require a minimal amount of configuration. As an example, in order to run the Surface tests described in Chapter 8, the CI server needs a change to the configuration file to set the proper database connection string. In this step, the required configuration changes are made so that the CI server can properly run the automated integration tests.

Run Surface Tests

In a manner similar to running the unit tests, the CI server runs the surface tests. This is an optional suite of automated integration tests that are very useful in brownfield application development. The tests check that an entire integrated subsystem or module continues to work properly. Surface tests are important during major redesign, refactoring, or restructuring projects.

Analysis

The Analysis phase involves running code analysis to achieve two important purposes. One purpose is to monitor the system. The other purpose is to generate reports that are used for later code analysis. The subject of Code Analysis is presented in depth in Chapter 11. What is important to know, as it relates to the CI lifecycle, is that during this phase the monitoring and report generation is carried out by the CI server.

The Analysis phase begins with a triggering event. A working directory is created and the files are copied in from the latest successful build's artifacts. With the files in place the analysis begins (see Figure 10-10).

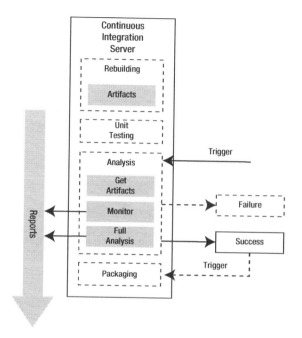

Figure 10-10. The Analysis phase in the CI lifecycle

In Figure 10-10 the Monitor and Full Analyses are shown as two distinct steps. The monitoring analysis is performed with a specific goal in mind; fail the build if any quality standards or other analysis thresholds are not met. For example, a build failure might be reported if any of the mandatory FxCop rules are violated. The full analysis is performed with the goal of generating reports. The reports should be reviewed later as part of the effort to evaluate and improve the code. These two steps are conceptually distinct; however, in practice they may occur together or as several separate steps in reverse order.

If the analysis results in a failure then the CI server sends out notification and the analysis reports are used to resolve the failure. When the analysis successfully completes, the CI server can then trigger the next phase in the lifecycle, which is the Packaging phase.

Analysis Trigger

To this point, the trigger events have focused on putting together a sequence of build events. The rebuilding is triggered by a code push and the automated testing is triggered by a successful rebuild. For the Analysis phase, the triggering choices depend on the answers to a number of questions:

- How quickly is the analysis performed?

- How often are the reports from the analysis reviewed?

- Are the monitoring analysis and full analysis performed together or separately?

An effective solution is to create two separate analysis configurations. One configuration is focused on performing the fastest-running analysis with the goal of providing developers timely feedback on things like violations of coding standards, FxCop rules, or code quality metrics. This configuration is triggered by the last successful run of unit testing. The second configuration is focused on generating complete and thorough analysis reports that take a long time to run. If these full reports are reviewed once daily then that helps determine a schedule trigger of running once a day during off-hours. A TeamCity schedule trigger event, running daily at 4 AM, is illustrated in Figure 10-11.

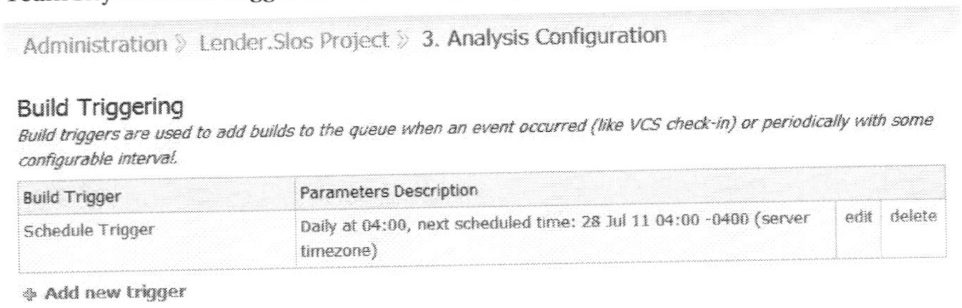

Administration ❯ Lender.Slos Project ❯ 3. Analysis Configuration

Build Triggering

Build triggers are used to add builds to the queue when an event occurred (like VCS check-in) or periodically with some configurable interval.

Build Trigger	Parameters Description		
Schedule Trigger	Daily at 04:00, next scheduled time: 28 Jul 11 04:00 -0400 (server timezone)	edit	delete

✛ Add new trigger

Figure 10-11. The TeamCity schedule trigger event

Monitoring Analysis

The monitoring analysis is theoretically a separate step in the Analysis phase. The monitoring can come before, after, or as a part of full analysis. The idea of monitoring is to perform analysis for the purpose of keeping an eye on the system. It is used to verify that established thresholds continue to be met as the system is developed and enhanced. Examples of specific monitoring analysis steps would include

- Running FxCop with an enforced rule set; fail the build if there are violations.

- Running StyleCop using mandatory coding standards; fail the build if violations are reported.

- Running tests under code coverage; fail the build if the percentage coverage is below a lower limit.

- Running code quality metrics; fail the build if maximum cyclomatic complexity is above a defined threshold.

Within a build script, for example, perform one or more automated analysis steps. Evaluate the results and compare them to expected results. If there are violations or the results are outside an acceptable range, then the CI server reports a failure. The team uses this notification to take timely and appropriate action to keep the system under control.

▪**Practice 10-5** Perform Monitoring Analysis and Report Failure if Violations Occur

---

In Chapter 11 the many code analysis tools, technologies, and approaches are discussed in depth. Ongoing monitoring with these tools and approaches is performed by the CI server in this step of the Analysis phase.

Full Analysis

As part of the ongoing effort to understand and improve the software system, a complete set of full analysis is performed. The output of this analysis is reviewed from time to time to find opportunities to improve the system. These analysis reports help the team notice trends or new circumstances that warrant time and attention.

▦ **Practice 10-6** Generate Complete Analysis Reports for Ongoing Review

---

Much of this analysis presents important information the team needs to know, but the pressures of the project schedule often keep the review from becoming a priority. As is discussed in Chapter 11, the full analysis is about problem detection and prevention and ongoing code improvement. For projects that value these analysis reports, the CI server provides a way to generate the reports on a recurring schedule starting early in the project.

Packaging

To this point, the CI lifecycle has followed from code push, to rebuilding, to unit testing and through analysis. Assuming a sequence of continuous, successful phases is complete, confidence that the artifacts are healthy will be high. This phase assembles the healthy artifacts into one or more installation packages and readies them for the Deployment phase.

For commercial software applications, the Packaging phase can get somewhat involved. There might be installation packages for different products, target platforms, databases, and languages. In other situations, these artifacts might need to be combined with the latest documentation, release notes, or other redistributable packages. On other projects, the packaging is more about removing test assemblies and other files, with the goal of creating a pristine subset of the same artifacts.

The installation packages are the project deliverables. Early in the project these deliverables are often called nightly builds and, as the release approaches, they are seen as release candidates. The important point is that after the packaging successfully completes, the deliverable is made available to QA or other project stakeholders. This step might be as simple as creating a properly-named folder on a file server and copying the packages to that folder. In another case, the packages are delivered through an elaborate release management system.

Once the packaging is successfully completed and the result is made available, the CI server reports and notifies that a new deliverable is available. The Packaging phase is shown in Figure 10-12.

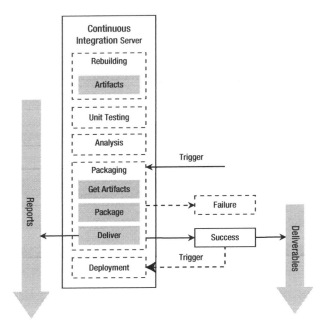

Figure 10-12. The Packaging phase in the CI lifecycle

Packaging Trigger

The Packaging phase can be trigged by the successful completion of the previous phase. Generally, this is not the case. In projects where developers are frequently pushing code changes, a succession of triggered events will generate a lot of deliverables. There are many intermediate deliverables that are not used and take up space on the server. Also, it is confusing and difficult to sort out which deliverable has what functionality and fixes.

For most projects, the Packaging phase is triggered by a nightly scheduling event. This establishes a daily rhythm of deliverables. The nightly deliverable has the functionality and fixes added from the previous day's work. For the QA team and other project stakeholders the nightly delivery occurs at a manageable and predictable pace.

Package Deliverable

For large software applications, the packaging phase can be somewhat involved. There could be installation packages for different product lines, different target platforms, different databases, and multiple languages. In other situations, the binary artifacts might need to be combined with the latest documentation, release notes, and redistributable software packages. In contrast, for some projects the packaging simply removes test assemblies and non-redistributable components, creating a pristine subset of the artifacts.

■**Practice 10-7** Package the Components and Content into One Deliverable

---

No matter how simple or complex the gathering and assembling is, the packaging of the deliverable takes place during this step. The goal is to package everything into one deliverable file. At this point, it is important to explicitly mention build versioning. The CI server ought to have a mechanism that helps assign the appropriate version number to the deliverables based on your versioning scheme. Also, for each "formal" build, if the source code in the source control system is tagged with that build version number it helps make debugging and diagnosing issues a lot more effective. A good versioning scheme ties each deliverable back to all the coding changes that comprise and impact the deliverable.

Some of the most common approaches to package project deliverables include creating a zipped archive or building a Microsoft Windows Installer (MSI) file.

Make Deliverable Available

All of the individual deliverable files, in their totality, represent the intermediate deliverables of the project as it proceeds through the development lifecycle. It is important to keep these intermediate deliverables in case it is necessary to go back and install a prior version of the application. It is also visible evidence of ongoing progress.

After the packaging is done, the CI server makes the deliverable available. This step can be as simple as creating a named folder on a file server and copying the packages to that folder. Figure 10-13 illustrates how the deliverables are made available within folders on a shared network resource. The CI server runs a build script that creates the proper folder and copies the deliverable file under each folder.

In another project situation, the packages are delivered through a more elaborate process. For example, the CI server might need to update a database, copy files to a website, or interface with a release management system.

Figure 10-13. Using directory folders to distribute the packaged deliverables

Deployment

The Deployment phase takes the deliverable and automates the deployment to a target environment. The target environment might include

- Integration testing

- System testing

- User acceptance testing

- Staging

- Production

The Deployment phase is not just one configuration. In fact, there should be a separate configuration for each target environment. The steps to deploy to each environment may be the same, but the parameters for each configuration are very different.

This phase is concerned with retrieving the appropriate deliverable and performing all the automated deployment steps. Figure 10-14 illustrates the basic steps within the Deployment phase.

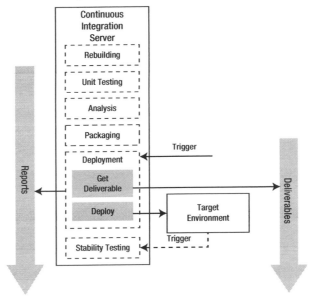

Figure 10-14. *The Deployment phase in the CI lifecycle*

Deployment Trigger

Triggering a deployment to a target environment varies widely depending on the target environment. For the integration environment, the deployment ought to be triggered to begin right after a successful Packaging phase completes. In contrast, the deployment to the production environment needs to be carefully controlled and should not occur until everyone has signed off on the deployment. How each trigger might vary depending on the target environment is presented in Table 10-3.

Table 10-3. Deployment Trigger by Target Environment

Target Environment	Trigger	Rationale
Integration Testing	After successful packaging	Provide timely feedback
System Testing	Manual trigger by QA lead	Limit testing team disruption
User Acceptance Testing	Manual trigger upon authorization	UAT must perform a complete test cycle
Staging	Manual trigger after certification	Release candidate must be chosen
Production	Controlled release upon approval	End-user expectations and production outage must be managed

Get the Deliverable

In the Packaging phase, the deliverable is made available. The CI server retrieves the deliverable that is appropriate for the target environment. For the integration testing environment, the latest deliverable is used. For the system testing environment, the QA lead can request a specific deliverable version.

Deploy to Target Environment

The next step is the automated deployment to the target environment. This step usually involves running an automated deployment script. This script can perform actions such as stopping the web server, deleting files, running database scripts, changing configuration settings, and restarting the web server.

For the sake of consistency it is helpful to have one script deploy to all the target environments. This goes a long way toward verifying and validating the deployment script. Parameters to the build script are used to set target environment–specific variables.

■ **Practice 10-8** Create One Script that Deploys to All Target Environments

---

With TeamCity, each configuration can have its own parameters. This is very useful for deployment configurations. As illustrated in Figure 10-15, a deployment script can use the `DeploymentServerName` parameter to target that specific server for the deployment. In this way, multiple configurations are created with each targeting a different server for the deployment.

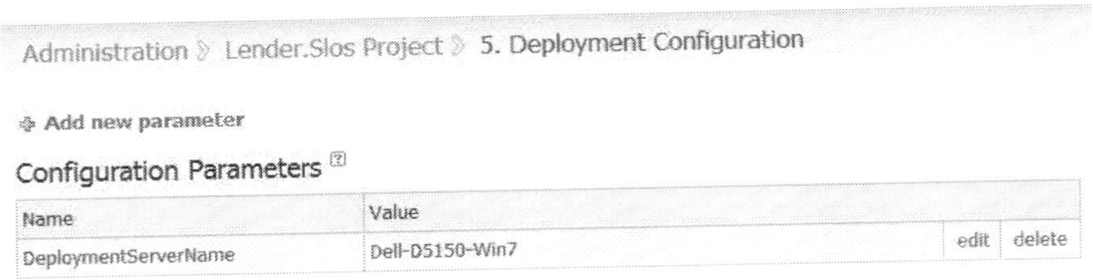

Administration 〉 Lender.Slos Project 〉 5. Deployment Configuration

✦ Add new parameter

Configuration Parameters ⑦

Name	Value		
DeploymentServerName	Dell-D5150-Win7	edit	delete

Figure 10-15. The TeamCity configuration parameter

Stability Testing

The CI lifecycle progression started with the code change and built the solution. The subsequent processes tested, analyzed, packaged, and deployed the deliverable to the target environment. What is established so far is that a new deliverable is deployed and ready for independent verification and validation. Before anyone begins expending time and effort evaluating this new release, the CI server ought to make sure the deployment is ready and stable. The Stability Testing phase runs automated integration tests to find out if the deployment is healthy and all set for further evaluation.

The Stability Testing phase is focused on two forms of automated integration testing:

- *Smoke Testing:* Exercises a small set of minimal, essential functionality to verify that the system does not blow up

- *Stability Testing:* Performs a broader set of tests of the features and functionality that characterize the entire system as well-behaved

The Stability Testing process is illustrated in Figure 10-16. It begins with a triggering event, usually a successful deployment to the target environment. First, the suite of smoke tests is run against the target environment. The results from the smoke testing are reported. If the smoke testing is successful, then the suite of stability tests is run against the target environment. Again, the results are reported. As with any of the prior phases, if the tests fail then a failure of the Stability Testing phase is reported by the CI server.

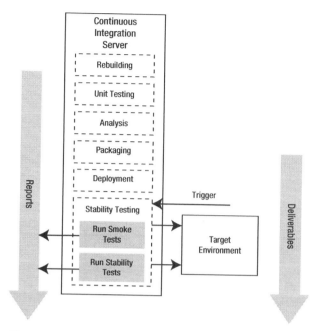

Figure 10-16. *The Stability Testing phase in the CI lifecycle*

The rationale behind the Stability Testing phase is to hold on to and raise the confidence level of the team that receives the deployment. For example, the QA team does not want to start system testing a deployment that is broken or has severely regressed. System stability is an important factor when QA decides to start testing a new release. With continuous integration, the QA team knows that if the system is failing the Stability Testing phase then it is senseless to begin system testing that deployment.

Stability Testing Trigger

The Stability Testing phase ought to be triggered after a successful Deployment phase completes. By running the smoke and stability tests, the CI server verifies that the latest deployment is healthy and stable. Even in the largest project, this is important. When the stability tests take a long time to completely finish, the Packaging or Deployment phases are best set to a nightly schedule. The goal is to trigger this phase and have all the stability tests run successfully against the latest deployment before the next workday begins.

Run Smoke Tests

There is a reason that there are two different sets of tests. Smoke tests find missing or improper configurations, systemic runtime issues, and failure-to-launch errors. The goal is to make sure the deployment was successful and the system carries out a set of indispensable functionality. Smoke tests reveal problems that are at the foundation of the software and its deployment.

■ **Practice 10-9** Smoke Test the Deployment to Find Configuration Problems

---

In the early stages of new software development, before the system is stable, start defining and running the smoke tests. Continue to build up the smoke tests to detect problems early and to validate that the deployment script is working properly.

As development proceeds, the smoke tests represent a great opportunity to do multiplatform integration testing. For example, in web applications build and run your integration tests using a tool like Selenium to cover as many browsers and platforms as are required. The smoke tests should run for all "formal" builds including nightly integration, QA testing, and targeted deployments.

Run Stability Tests

As the software development team makes progress, the system begins to achieve stability. There is now a broader set of features and functionality and the system is getting bigger and more capable. Stability testing is the way to evaluate the new deliverable to ensure it has not regressed dramatically. These tests make sure that the indispensable features, functionality, and capabilities of the system work as expected for this newly deployed deliverable. Knowing that a deliverable is stable is important to the QA team.

■ **Practice 10-10** Run Stability Tests to Verify the Deployment Is Ready for QA

The QA team should help guide the stability testing. Sitting down with the QA lead and identifying the most important and basic functionality establishes the baseline. As more features and functionality are added, the QA team should help create new stability tests.

Generate Reports

Each phase in the CI lifecycle generates a report. For the rebuilding, it is a build log. For unit testing and analysis, there are specific results reports. For stability testing, a detailed HTML report might list all the features and functionality that passed stability testing.

The project manager and all the project stakeholders benefit from having visibility into the activities and progress underway. There is no clearer indication of progress than successful delivery.

■ **Practice 10-11** Generate Reports That Demonstrate Progress and Delivery

---

The CI server ought to provide a lot of valuable reports and general information about the project's progress. To anyone interested in gaining insight into the project, the CI server reports communicate that the right things are being done in the right way.

One particularly valuable report lists the commit numbers from the version control system that went into a build. This makes root cause analysis easier because builds are tied back to the change sets relevant to that build. Another source of reporting is that many CI servers generate reports based on information about the builds, such as build times, artifact size, number of passing and failing tests, total lines of code, and other code analysis metrics. These reports and metrics build over time to measure improvement and productivity for continuous integration and overall development. It is important to evaluate this aspect of the CI server or investigate using a tool like Sonar (http://www.sonarsource.org).

Summary

In this chapter you learned about the continuous integration server and lifecycle. You saw how the CI lifecycle begins with a source code check-in and proceeds through to deployment and stability testing.

CHAPTER 11

Code Analysis

This chapter provides an overview of many static and dynamic tools, technologies, and approaches, introducing both general technologies and specific tools with an emphasis on improvements they can suggest and how they can provide continuous, automated monitoring.

Software improvements are the result of a three-phase cycle: Analyze, Improve, and Monitor. Figure 11-1 presents a conceptual model for this cycle. The *Analyze* phase is about understanding the situation. The *Improve* phase is about taking action based on the conclusions of that analysis. The *Monitor* phase involves the recurring activities that prompt further analysis. This cycle is not a rigid methodology of discrete phases but a framework for ongoing software improvement.

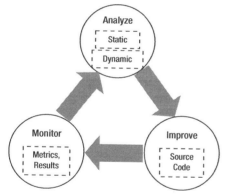

Figure 11-1. The Analyze, Improve and Monitor phases

The system is analyzed in two primary ways: static analysis and dynamic analysis. With *static analysis* the system is evaluated without needing to run the program. This is done by inspecting the source code, the assemblies, or other components of the system. *Dynamic analysis* requires the system to run while the memory usage, performance timings, executed queries, or other profile of the system is captured. Dynamic analysis often takes place by analyzing the data after the run or by comparing two previous runs that took place at different times or under different conditions. An effective Analyze phase points out areas for investigation and improvement.

In the Improve phase source code changes suggested either directly or indirectly in the Analysis phase are made. Improvements to the architecture, design, or other aspects of the system also happen at this point. Tuning, refactoring, and remediation are all implemented within the Improve phase.

The Monitor phase may consist of informal or scheduled code reviews or system testing. Monitoring can be either objective or highly subjective, but the usual outcome is that analysis takes place. For example, if system testing reveals unacceptably slow load times then, as a result, the development team initiates performance analysis. Ideally, there ought to be established metrics and expected results with deviations from the acceptable limits triggering analysis. The best monitoring involves both manual and exploratory review coupled with frequent, structured assessment. The Monitoring phase should use components that are continuous and automated.

The concept of the application lifecycle management (ALM), as presented and discussed in Chapter 2, covers seven important aspects of software development: requirements, design, coding, testing, deployment, maintenance, and project management. These aspects repeat during the stages of any iterative and incremental methodology. As an individual developer or team leader, you will find yourself playing a role, to varying degrees, in each of these aspects of the lifecycle. In this chapter, tools and techniques will be linked to the overall story of ALM by describing which member of the development team would use each tool and technique and at which stage in the lifecycle.

This chapter will introduce and emphasize two specific tools: FxCop and StyleCop. Both of these tools are particularly helpful with respect to maintainability, which is an important theme in this book. The list of practices covered in this chapter is summarized in Table 11-1.

Table 11-1. Code Analysis: Ruthlessly Helpful .NET Practices

	Code Analysis Practice
11-1	Thoroughly Analyze Assemblies Using the FxCop Application
11-2	Fail the Build with *FxCopCmd* for Violations of Required Rules
11-3	Decompile an Assembly to Analyze, Understand, and Troubleshoot
11-4	Use StyleCop to Help Comply with Coding Standards
11-5	Fail the Build with *StyleCop* for Violations of Required Coding Standards
11-6	Use a Differencing Tool to Make File and Folder Differences Obvious
11-7	Find and Address Any Inappropriate Duplication of Code
11-8	Perform Architecture and Design Analysis; Comparing *As-Planned* to *As-Built* Designs
11-9	Run Tests under Code Coverage
11-10	Profile the System's Performance on a Regular Basis
11-11	Examine Database Queries with a Query Profiler
11-12	Incorporate a Flexible Logging Solution to Monitor and Diagnose the Application

---

COMMENTARY

Establishing the Analyze, Improve, and Monitor cycle is not easy and requires time and patience. Both static and dynamic analysis involves knowledge about many specific tools and approaches. The analysis itself demands skill and judgment to separate the important and urgent symptoms from the many indicators of minor improvement. Also, the organization must want the analysis performed. Analysis often takes a back seat to delivering features and functionality—until an acute pain point threatens a delivery date, when there is a sudden interest in profiling, diagnosis, and root-cause analysis.[1] One way to address this dilemma is to investigate and introduce one analysis technique at a time: slowly establish the monitoring of code coverage, metrics and performance numbers; gain experience applying the tools and approaches; communicate the implications of a high cyclomatic complexity, an FxCop error, or virtual memory fragmentation that you discover through ongoing code analysis.

Let's face it: coding style is very personal. Since coding standards are about establishing a coding style and writing code that adheres to a style, meetings and discussions that try to establish a coding standard can result in a lot of conflict. The heart of that conflict is rooted in differences of opinion, where choices are subjective and each has merit and value. Putting together a coding standard document as a project deliverable is rarely worth the investment of time and energy; even when a coding standards document is established, few developers read and follow it and coding standards rarely get past subjective questions.

- What coding style is the easiest to read?

- What coding style is the most straightforward to maintain?

- What coding style do most developers follow?

- What coding style is the team currently following?

Let's be pragmatic and avoid a whole discussion of what the C# coding standards ought to be. Since StyleCop defines a widely-used coding standard that many developers at Microsoft and many C# developers who just want a standard are happy to follow, this chapter assumes the StyleCop coding standard as a baseline.

Case Study

You are a .NET developer at Lender Inc. working on the next generation of the Student Loan Origination System (SLOS) software application.

BACKGROUND

Lender Inc. has engaged Global Contracting (GC), a contract software development company, in a firm fixed-price contract to port the financial module of SLOS from Java to C#; this is called the Financial Rewrite project. Lender Inc. has worked with GC before. GC has a reputation for poor performance, but GC

---

[1] Review the metaphor and consequences of "Technical Debt" described in Chapter 2.

is performing the work because theirs was the only bid that came in under budget. The development team and QA are concerned that the quality of the deliverables will be poor. To address these concerns, Lender's management has insisted that GC sign a contract agreeing to meet strict acceptance criteria and code quality targets. GC is expected to deliver major functionality every week, with nightly code pushes. The source code is built into a single assembly, which is called from within SLOS. When GC pushes source code, Lender's continuous integration (CI) server builds the .NET managed code assembly, Lender.Slos.Financial.dll. Both the source code and the assembly are the project's deliverables.

The contract specifies functionality, performance, and quality acceptance criteria in sufficient detail to satisfy the concerns of QA. The contract specifies that Microsoft's Minimum and Recommended .NET Framework Guidelines must be followed and specifies the StyleCop coding standards as those that GC must follow. Since Lender cannot directly supervise the GC developers, the contract allows Lender to require GC to rework the deliverables, at no cost to Lender, if they do not meet the criteria. There is a catch, however: Lender is barred from using the GC deliverables in production until acceptance is signed off and full payment made.

After 30 days into the 120-day project, QA is on top of the functional quality. All of the Financial Rewrite project features delivered to-date are working properly and as expected. However, the Lender developers are too busy to conduct code reviews and the quality of the source code is a big unknown. Since GC usually hires inexperienced software developers, there is a concern that the GC developers are writing bad code. Performance is also a concern.

The SLOS project manager has made it clear: unless there is a significant problem, management is not going to fight with GC to improve quality. QA is not reporting functionality issues. Any delay in GC's delivery is a delay in Lender delivering SLOS. As a result, the PM agrees to only confront GC if an issue relates to one of the following:

- Likely to impact the end-user.

- A code quality issue has been raised and continues to be a problem.

- Three new violations per week.

The technical lead wants to evaluate the GC deliverables from the perspective of code metrics, non-functional requirements, coding standards, and following the .NET Framework Guidelines. The goal is to analyze the source code and the Lender.Slos.Financial.dll assembly to find specific violations to take up with the project manager. In addition, the analysis should find any issues likely to impact the end-user. Also, the approach needs to work with the CI server to monitor the deliverables; if GC violates any previously raised issues the build ought to break.

Your plan is to use static and dynamic analysis tools to assess the situation and find issues to take to the project manager. You start this analysis by

- Using FxCop to enforce the .NET Framework Guidelines

- Using StyleCop to enforce the coding standards

- Using Visual Studio Code Metrics to compute code metrics

- Using Visual Studio to profile performance and memory usage

Your plan also includes monitoring within the build process, breaking the build if there are any violations of already raised issues.

Static Analysis

Static analysis looks at the code and the assemblies while they are "at rest." Static analysis does not require the program to run. For source code, static analysis is able to determine how well the code follows a set of coding standards. For assemblies, static analysis determines how well the assemblies follow accepted rules for .NET managed code. When the code or the assemblies do not meet expectations the result is a list of violations that reference the standard or rule that is violated. These rules, guidelines, recommendations, and standards come from various sources that may include the following:

- Microsoft's .NET Framework Design Guidelines
- C# coding standards
- Code quality formula
- System architecture and design documents

The purpose of static analysis is to answer important questions about how well the software is built. These questions may include the following:

- Is the code easy to read and maintain?
- Is the complexity of the code under control?
- Do the assemblies perform well?
- Is the code dependable and secure?
- Are best practices and system design objectives being followed?
- Does the system have the desired structure?

Static analysis takes either the source code or the assemblies as input for analysis. Based on these inputs the tool evaluates one or more of the following aspects:

- Adherence to library development guidelines
- Readability, maintainability, and coding standards
- Code quality metrics
- As-built design, structure, and dependencies

MSDN offers the Design Guidelines for Developing Class Libraries for development focused on building .NET reusable libraries.[2] Frameworks and assemblies intended to reach a broad number of .NET developers should follow these guidelines. FxCop is a tool that performs this analysis.

---

[2] The .NET Framework guidelines are presented in Krzysztof Cwalina and Brad Abrams, *Framework Design Guidelines: Conventions, Idioms, and Patterns for Reusable .NET Libraries, Second Edition* (Upper Saddle River, NJ: Addison-Wesley Professional, 2008).

Coding standards are intended to improve readability, consistency, and maintainability. StyleCop defines a widely-used coding standard. StyleCop is a static analysis tool that provides developers an effective way to follow the coding standard. It also gives projects a way to customize and report violations of the coding standard.

There are many tools available to calculate code metrics for your .NET code. If you have Visual Studio 2010 Ultimate or Premium then you already have the means to calculate code metrics. These tools provide a way to monitor code quality as part of the build process.

Static analysis tools that evaluate the system architecture and design reveal the structure, design, and dependencies of the built system. The analysis work involves matching up the system design as it is built to the intended design. The individual developer uses static analysis while coding to ensure that the development work is consistent with the design objectives. The team leader uses static analysis to review and monitor the team's development work against design objectives. Improvements come by resolving the differences and making decisions about whether to conform to the design or change the design to reflect a better choice.

Assembly Analysis

After the source code is built it is possible to explore and analyze compiled .NET assemblies. The processes of assembly inspection, disassembling, and decompiling generally describe the techniques to explore and analyze assemblies. It is useful to examine assemblies for the purposes of analysis to support the following:

- Investigate a compiled assembly and use rules to determine if guidelines are violated.

- Inspect an assembly to browse classes, methods, and properties, and decompile to equivalent C# code.

One approach is to disassemble the assembly file by reading the bytes and converting the bytes into the Microsoft intermediate language (IL). In effect, this reverses the packaging actions of Ilasm.exe. Within the program database (PDB) file are mappings between IL and source code, names of local variables, and other source-level debugging information. Even without the PDB, a decompiler can parse the IL, reverse-engineering it into statements and blocks, and ultimately translating it into C#, or some other higher-level language.

FxCop

The Visual Studio Code Analysis tool, available in Ultimate and Premium editions and through Team Foundation Server, can reveal potential quality issues in the code.[3] There are many rules organized into rule sets targeted to specific goals, such as enforcing best practices for maintainable code. This static code analysis facility is integrated into these versions of Visual Studio and Team Foundation Server. For those who do not use Visual Studio Ultimate or Premium then Microsoft's FxCop application is available. If the build server is not Team Foundation Server then FxCopCmd can run this analysis within build and CI processes. Both the Visual Studio Code Analysis tool and FxCop are founded upon a body of guidance that is generally referred to as the .NET Framework Guidelines.

Microsoft developed the .NET Framework Design Guidelines for Developing Class Libraries to help develop better .NET software internally. The guidelines were published and the Microsoft tool that

---

[3] Learn more about analyzing code by using Code Analysis at MSDN: `http://msdn.microsoft.com/en-us/library/dd264939.aspx`.

checked compliance to the guidelines, FxCop, was also made available. Initially, the FxCop application was a stand-alone tool set. Now, available in Visual Studio 2010 Ultimate and Premium editions under the project Code Analysis tab, in the project's properties. After a .NET managed code assembly is built, either Code Analysis or FxCop inspects the assemblies to determine if any of the configured rules are violated.

The latest version of FxCop, both an application and a command-line tool, can be used for analysis outside Visual Studio and as part of the automated build processes. The latest version of the FxCop setup program is part of the Microsoft Windows SDK for Windows 7 and .NET Framework 4 version 7.1 (see the Introduction for details on pulling out the FxCop setup).

This section is not intended to walk you through FxCop and explain how to use the application; there are books and Internet postings with good examples and walkthroughs describing how to use FxCop. The focus of this section is on using FxCop as part of a code analysis, improvement, and monitoring strategy. For example, FxCopCmd generates a report that can be used to monitor violations and fail the build if critical violations occur.

■ **Note** If you are not familiar with the FxCop application, take some time to learn more about FxCop. Appendix A provides a list of resources for learning and using FxCop.

For the SLOS project, the plan is to create two FxCop projects. One project is configured to reveal all violations based on the rules defined by Microsoft's Minimum and Recommended .NET Framework Guidelines.[4] The second targets only the Lender.Slos.Financial.dll assembly developed by GC and uses only the rules that have already been raised by the project manager. These raised rules are part of the mandatory rules that GC must follow.

■ **Practice 11-1** Thoroughly Analyze Assemblies Using the FxCop Application

---

The FxCop application provides a way to understand the broad condition of the managed code assemblies and various ways to drill into the details of each rule violation. The FxCop desktop application allows you to define a project and select the target assemblies to analyze. You can specify the rules that ought to be followed, specific to your project. You can run the analysis to reveal and explore the violations occurring within the project. You can evaluate the violations and report or suppress the violations based on their priority and significance to the project. Project priority and significance are important; for some projects, for example, globalization rules may be critical. On the Financial Rewrite project they are not.

FxCop provides both a tool to analyze the software and detailed guidance on where and how to improve the source code. It provides the means to monitor the situation with reports and metrics. Many CI servers provide the facilities to display FxCop output as html reports. However, there are real challenges to using FxCop within the build process. The objective is to fail the build if the critical rules are violated.

---

[4] MSDN provides the Microsoft Minimum Recommended Rules Code Analysis Rule Set: http://msdn.microsoft.com/en-us/library/dd264893.aspx.

■ **Practice 11-2** Fail the Build with FxCopCmd for Violations of Required Rules

---

With brownfield applications it is not realistic to fail the build when any FxCop violation occurs.[5] There are simply too many rules in which the priority and significance vary widely from rule to rule, from project to project. However, "mandatory" rules can be established that, if violated, ought to fail the build. Even early in a greenfield project, not every FxCop rule should be mandatory; some are simply not relevant to that project. MSDN provides guidance on various rule sets, such as basic correctness and extended design. It is best to take a wide-reaching set that includes all potentially relevant rules. As the project proceeds, specific rules will become voluntary as the priority and significance decrease. You can still track violations of the voluntary rules in a separate FxCop project, but only allow mandatory rule violations to fail the build. The mandatory rules should include

- Rules that are critical to the project and focus on important problems

- Rules where violations have been resolved and recurrence needs to stop

- Relevant and significant rules that are currently not being violated

For the SLOS project, the plan is to create an FxCop project that targets only the Lender.Slos.Financial.dll, which is developed by GC. The mandatory rules that the project uses are those rules that have been raised as an issue. This project starts with the first three rules reported to GC by the project manager and slowly grows, adding in new rules week-by-week as the mandatory rules that GC must follow are detailed. Once all the rules currently violated are configured in the FxCop project file then all the remaining rules in the Microsoft Minimum Recommended Rules Code Analysis Rule Set are added. Throughout this time, the FxCop project file is used by the command-line tool to analyze the targets and generate the report.

The real trick comes in failing the build when only the mandatory rules are violated. By design, the command-line tool is intended to automate the analysis and reporting performed by FxCop. However, FxCop does not evaluate the output; it reports. FxCop cannot interpret the relevance and significance of the project's rules. Thankfully, the primary FxCop output is an XML file, which the build script can evaluate and then fail the build if FxCop reports mandatory rule violations.

For the remainder of this section, let's walk through and discuss the general approach to failing the build when mandatory rules are violated.

WALKTHROUGH: FAILING THE BUILD FOR FXCOP VIOLATIONS

When FxCop is opened, the project is defined by selecting the Targets to analyze. For the Financial Rewrite project there is only one target assembly, Lender.Slos.Financial.dll.

1. To begin, launch FxCop and choose Project ➤Add Targets …

2. Add the Lender.Slos.Financial.dll assembly by browsing to the folder containing the assembly. The result is shown in Figure 11-2.

---

[5] Brownfield application development ought to have a "technical debt" reduction plan as described in Chapter 2, including arrangements to reduce FxCop violations over time.

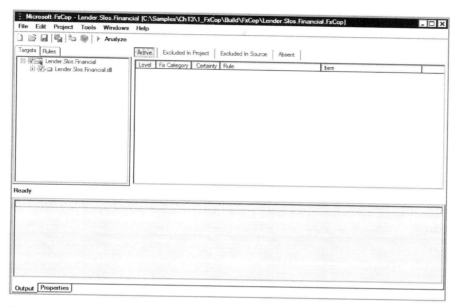

Figure 11-2. *The FxCop target assembly* `Lender.Slos.Financial.dll` *added to the project*

3. To set the project options, select Project ➤ Options ...

4. In the first tab (General), provide a project name of Lender.Slos.Financial. Within the "Save messages" area uncheck the checkbox next to Active. Unchecking this option prevents the active violations from being saved to the project file. This is shown in Figure 11-3.

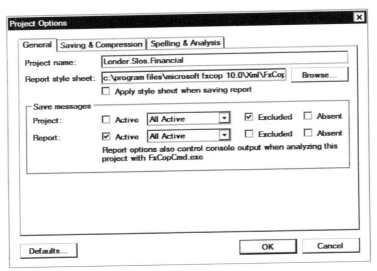

Figure 11-3. The General options tab in FxCop Project Options dialog box

■ **Note** The second tab on the Project Options dialog is Saving & Compression. No changes are needed on this tab.

5. In the third tab (Spelling & Analysis), change the project options to those shown in Figure 11-4.

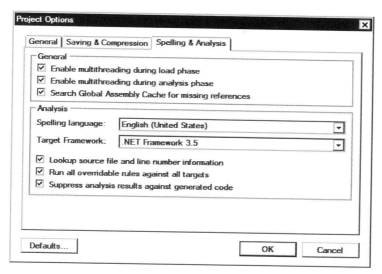

Figure 11-4. The Spelling & Analysis options tab in FxCop Project Options dialog box

6. Now that the FxCop project options are set, press the OK button.

7. Save the FxCop project using the File   Save As ... menu. Save the FxCop project file in the *C:\Samples\Ch11\1_FxCop\Build\FxCop* folder with the filename *Lender.Slos.Financial.Mandatory.FxCop.*

8. Run the analysis by selecting Project   Analyze from the menu. The results are shown in the results pane within the Active tab.

9. Expand the `Lender.Slos.Financial.dll` target to reveal the class within the assembly.

10. Within the Active area, scroll down the list of violations to the "Rethrow to preserve stack detail" violation near the bottom of the list, which is shown in Figure 11-5.

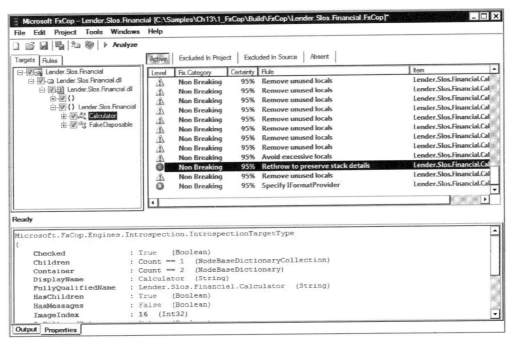

Figure 11-5. The "Rethrow to preserve stack detail" violation in the Calculator class

11. Double-click the "Rethrow to preserve stack detail" violation to view the Message Details including the violation Level and Source. The violation details are shown in Figure 11-6.

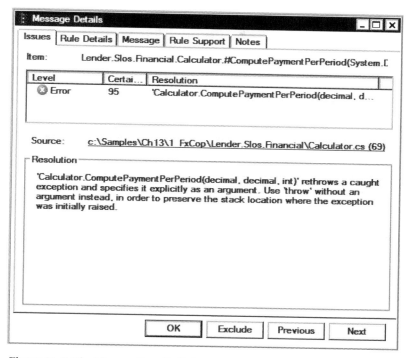

Figure 11-6. The Message Details dialog for the "Rethrow to preserve stack detail" violation

For the Financial Rewrite project let's select three rules as the "mandatory" rules. These violations have been taken up with GC and GC must now follow these rules. The first group of three mandatory rules is listed in Table 11-2.

Table 11-2. Mandatory Rules Selected for the Financial Rewrite Project

CheckId	Level	Category	Description
CA1065	Error	Design	Do not raise exceptions in unexpected locations.
CA1809	Warning	Performance	Avoid excessive locals.
CA2200	Error	Usage	Rethrow to preserve stack details.

Only these mandatory rules should be selected in the FxCop project's Rules tab. Start by deselecting all the rules. Find the three mandatory rules—rules are sorted alphabetically within a category—and select each of the three rules.

Since only these three rules are selected, they are the only active violations, as shown in Figure 11-7.

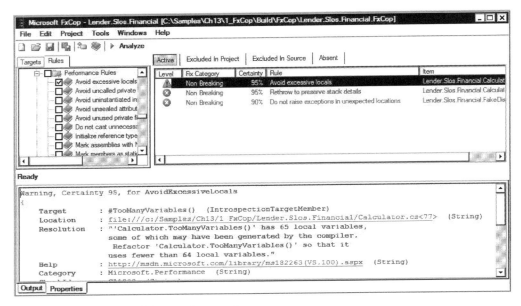

Figure 11-7. *Violations of the mandatory rules*

Save the FxCop project and exit the application.

This new FxCop project is now narrowly focused on just the three mandatory rules. The build script is now able to use FxCopCmd to use this project file to analyze the Lender.Slos.Financial.dll assembly against the mandatory rules.

The next thing to complete is calling FxCopCmd from within the build script. Within the sample code the *runner.msbuild* file has a target named FxCopAnalysis. This target can process the set of preferred and mandatory FxCop projects defined in the FxCopAttribute item group.

```
<Target Name="FxCopAnalysis" DependsOnTargets="Preconditions" >
    <Message Text="Processing FxCopXmlReport file '%(FxCopAttribute.ProjectFile)'" />

    <Exec Condition="Exists('%(FxCopAttribute.ProjectFile)')"
          Command="&quot;$(FxCopRoot)\FxCopCmd.exe&quot; ↵
/project:%(FxCopAttribute.ProjectFile) /fo /out:%(FxCopAttribute.XmlOutput)"

          WorkingDirectory="." />

</Target>
```

Running the FxCopAnalysis target generates one or more XML reports. The build script can use the XML output to determine if any mandatory rule set violations exist.

In the sample *runner.msbuild* file there is the FxCop task that inspects the XML output file specified in the FxCopMandatoryXmlOutput property. This technique combines the use of XPath and the XmlRead task from the MSBuild Community task library, which is covered in Chapter 9, to count the violations. Here is a snippet of the build script that inspects the mandatory XML output:

```
<Target Name="FxCop"
        DependsOnTargets="FxCopAnalysis"
        Condition="Exists('$(FxCopMandatoryXmlOutput)')"
        >
    <XmlRead ContinueOnError="True"
            XmlFileName="$(FxCopMandatoryXmlOutput)"
            XPath="string(count(//Issue[@Level='CriticalError']))"
            >
        <Output TaskParameter="Value"
                PropertyName="FxCopCriticalErrors"
        />

    </XmlRead>
...

    <Error Text="FxCop encountered $(FxCopCriticalErrors) Critical Errors"
           Condition="$(FxCopCriticalErrors) &gt; 0"
           />
...

/>
```

The sample code is under the *C:\Samples\Ch11\1_FxCop* folder and provides a working example of using this approach for the Financial Rewrite project.

By using the FxCop application together with FxCopCmd in the build process the complete Analyze, Improve, and Monitor cycle is achieved. Both monitoring goals are achieved: the CI server can report the FxCop violations for all relevant rule sets and the build script can fail the build when violations of mandatory rules occur. This is a powerful approach for brownfield application development where slow and steady improvement and remediation is accomplished by gradually addressing rule violations and building up a mandatory rule set.

Just beyond the scope of this section, it is important to note that FxCop can be extended with custom rules.[6] For example, a custom rule can enforce design rules, such as no source code from the persistence-layer assembly is allowed to directly call any method in a presentation-layer assembly. There are quite a few static analysis tools that look for quality- and security-related problems. Since it does not follow logic across method calls (intra-procedural analysis), FxCop is one of the simplest of its kind. For more powerful tools see Microsoft Code Analysis Tool .NET (CAT.NET), the HP Fortify tools, and other static analysis tools that look for quality- and security-related problems across the application.

---

[6] Learn more about writing custom FxCop rules at http://www.binarycoder.net/fxcop/html/index.html.

Decompiler

The purpose of using a .NET assembly browser and decompiler is to analyze the packaged deliverables. There are many reasons to use an assembly as the starting point for investigation, including

- Debug an assembly without having the source code.

- Understand an incomplete, unclear, or otherwise inadequately-documented API.

- Compare changes between different versions of assemblies.

- Recover lost source code.

- Determine how well the code obfuscator has disguised the code.

▓ **Practice 11-3** Decompile an Assembly to Analyze, Understand, and Troubleshoot

---

In some situations there may be two versions of an assembly. Perhaps one is exhibiting a defect and the other is not. In this case, a decompiler is helpful to compare and contrast the two versions of the assembly. This analysis can often lead to understanding the differences that cause the defect in one version but not the other.

For a variety of reasons, on many brownfield enhancement and legacy maintenance projects the source code for an assembly is no longer available. An assembly decompiler provides the means to reverse-engineer the code that underlies the assembly. Also, if rewriting that assembly is the goal, then the assembly's *de facto* requirements can be understood by browsing the assembly.

Decompilers have broad application in many aspects of ALM. A developer can decompile a third-party assembly that is inadequately documented during coding to properly develop a feature using that assembly. To resolve deployment problems, the team leader can use a decompiler to compare different versions of assemblies to iron out why the software is having an issue. A developer can use a decompiler to recover lost source code in order to write an entirely updated implementation of an important module, without having to start from scratch.

The .NET managed code assemblies represent a significant part of a software system's deliverables. Assembly analysis is an effective way to adopt the Analyze, Improve, and Monitor cycle with respect to these important deliverables. Table 11-3 provides a list of decompilers that might be worth evaluating.

Table 11-3. Tool Choices: .NET Assembly Browsing and Decompiling

Product	Description	Terms	More Info
.NET Reflector	A widely-used .NET assembly browser and decompiler from Red Gate Software. It has add-ins and years of experience and expertise behind it. Note, the Diff add-in allows you to compare two assemblies.	Commercial	www.reflector.net

Product	Description	Terms	More Info
dotPeek	A new .NET assembly browser and decompiler from JetBrains. It is a free-of-charge tool from the makers of ReSharper and other popular developer productivity tools.	Free	`www.jetbrains.com/decompiler`
ILSpy	A new free and open-source .NET assembly browser and decompiler from SharpDevelop. It is promoted as a free alternative to .NET Reflector.	Free, Open Source	`wiki.sharpdevelop.net/ILSpy.ashx`
JustDecompile	A new .NET decompiler from Telerik. It is a free-of-charge tool designed to enable easy .NET assembly browsing and decompiling.	Free	`www.telerik.com/products/decompiling.aspx`

Source Analysis

This practice area relates to focusing on source code quality. Not code quality in the sense of how well the code meets functional requirements, but in the sense of non-functional quality attributes, such as readability, conciseness, and maintainability. Without regard for its "fitness to a purpose," source analysis tries to answer the question: How well is the source code written? There are many subjective answers and opinions to this question. There are, however, guiding principles that are widely accepted and generally hold true across many software systems. Perhaps it is easier to gain buy-in to source code analysis by focusing on the undesirable outcomes and negative characteristics that are the alternative:

- Inconsistently written code is harder to read and understand.

- Dense and complex code is difficult to maintain.

- Inappropriate dependencies violate the design objectives.

- Copied-and-pasted code is a frequent source of bugs.

- Spaghetti code is a nightmare for developers to enhance.

Developers often talk of the importance of reducing technical debt and cleaning up "bad smells" in code. Source analysis raises the visibility of potential problems related to unintentionally incurring technical debt and preventing "bad smells" from lingering once they surface in source code.

StyleCop

There are many tools available that perform automated code review. These tools help you figure out where the project's coding standards are not being followed in source code. For the purposes of this book and the discussion in this section the focus is on only one tool: the Microsoft-developed StyleCop. The power of free software and the integration with Visual Studio make StyleCop a pragmatic choice.

StyleCop is a free source code–analysis tool for C# developers.[7] Initially developed by Microsoft, the governance and coordination of the StyleCop project was turned over to the .NET community as a CodePlex project. StyleCop integrates well into Visual Studio and warns developers when coding standards are not followed. If you have the ReSharper productivity tool, StyleCop integrates and provides options for code cleanup and feedback while writing code, to further help adhere to the coding standard.

StyleCop defines a widely-used coding standard that many C# developers who just want a standard are happy to follow.[8] Since the standards enforced by StyleCop are not likely to exactly match your team's style preferences, StyleCop provides an effective way to turn off, change, or customize the coding standards within an organization or on a project-by-project basis.

Coding standards are about establishing a coding style and writing code that adheres to that style. The intention of establishing and adhering to coding standards is to make the source code

- Easier to read

- Straightforward to maintain

The coding standards ought to align with the coding style that the source code is currently following and that most developers want to follow. However, for many organizations the coding standards vary from project to project and from developer to developer. A coding standard document is difficult to establish. Even developers with the best of intentions will not strictly follow coding standards. Coding habits are hard to break and differences of opinion persist. Any focus on following and enforcing coding standards should not come at the cost of lost productivity and delayed delivery of functionality.

▓ **Practice 11-4** Use StyleCop to Help Comply with Coding Standards

---

Some of the rules found in the StyleCop coding standards are minor style preferences, while others address a significant readability or maintainability concern. On a scale of 1 to 10, you might rate one standard a 2 or 3 while another person would rate it a 9 or 10. In effect, the coding standards can be divided into non-mandatory and mandatory categories. Let's call these non-mandatory coding standards the preferred or voluntary coding standards. The voluntary standards are the agreed-to coding standards that should be followed, but violations of voluntary coding standards should not break the build. By contrast, mandatory coding standards must be followed and violations need to break the build.

▓ **Practice 11-5** Fail the Build with StyleCop for Violations of Required Coding Standards

---

[7] More information on the StyleCop project is available at http://stylecop.codeplex.com.
[8] "A Brief History of C# Style" can be found at
http://stylecop.codeplex.com/wikipage?title=A%20Brief%20History%20of%20CSharp%20Style.

Using StyleCop to check coding standards presents a dilemma. StyleCop offers the either-or option; either all coding standard violations are warnings or all the violations are errors. You want StyleCop to issue warnings when voluntary coding standards are not followed and errors when mandatory standards are violated. The team's developers voluntarily heed the warnings to adhere to the non-mandatory coding standards. However, when a developer violates a mandatory coding standard then the build needs to break. In this section you learn one way to effectively resolve the dilemma.

When working in brownfield or legacy codebase it is not practical to have StyleCop break the build for every violation that exists in the source code, mandatory or non-mandatory. This is also the case in the Financial Rewrite project. In the Financial Rewrite project, the goal is to bring a few issues to the project manager and let the PM raise the issues with GC. After those few coding standards are raised, break the build if those specific coding standards are violated again in the next code push. In effect, the only mandatory coding standards are those that have been raised as an issue by the PM. In this way, slowly and steadily, specific coding standards are raised and moved from the voluntary category to the mandatory category.

WALKTHROUGH: STYLECOP CUSTOM MSBUILD TASK

To accomplish this StyleCop is going to be called using a custom MSBuild task. This task is based on the code sample provide in the *StyleCopSDK* help file.

1. To begin, open the Lender.Slos.Express.sln file found under the C:\Samples\Ch11\2_StyleCop folder.

2. The *Lender.Build.StyleCop.Tasks* project contains the code for the StyleCopAnalysis class, a custom MSBuild task.

The StyleCopAnalysis class is based on the custom MSBuild task described in the "Creating a Custom MSBuild Task for StyleCop" section of the *StyleCopSDK.chm* file.

There are three additional properties added. The IgnoreVoluntaryRules property is used to determine if all non-mandatory (voluntary) violations should be ignored. The MandatoryRuleIds property holds a list of mandatory rule ids that the StyleCopAnalysis task must never ignore. The third property, AlwaysIgnoredRuleIds, supports a list of rule ids that are trivial and should always be ignored.

```
namespace Lender.Build.StyleCop.Tasks
{

...

    public sealed class StyleCopAnalysis : Task
    {

...

        public bool IgnoreVoluntaryRules { get; set; }

        public string[] MandatoryRuleIds { get; set; }

        public string[] AlwaysIgnoredRuleIds { get; set; }
```

...

There is a new method, the IsViolationIgnored method. It is called from within the OnViolationEncountered event to determine in any raised violation needs to be ignored. The IsViolationIgnored method uses the new AlwaysIgnoredRuleIds and MandatoryRuleIds properties to determine if the violation should or should not be ignored.

...

```
private void OnViolationEncountered(object sender, ViolationEventArgs e)
{
    if (this.IsViolationIgnored(e))
    {
        return;
    }

    ...

}

private bool IsViolationIgnored(ViolationEventArgs e)
{
    if (e == null) throw new ArgumentNullException("e");

    var checkId = e.Violation.Rule.CheckId;

    var alwaysIgnoredRuleIds = this.AlwaysIgnoredRuleIds ?? new string[0];
    var mandatoryRuleIds = this.MandatoryRuleIds ?? new string[0];

    var ignore = this.IgnoreVoluntaryRules;
    if (!ignore)
    {
        if (alwaysIgnoredRuleIds.Any(c => checkId == c))
        {
            ignore = true;
        }
    }

    if (ignore)
    {
        // Do not ignore a mandatory rule
        if (mandatoryRuleIds.Any(c => checkId == c))
        {
            ignore = false;
        }
    }

    return ignore;
}
```

...

The result of these additions is that if the `StyleCopAnalysis` task is called with the proper MSBuild properties then only mandatory rule violations cause the build to fail. In the *runner.msbuild* file, the build target with the name StyleCop calls the `StyleCopAnalysis` task.

```
...

<!-- Define Constants for StyleCop -->
<PropertyGroup>
  <ProjectFullPath>.\Lender.Slos.Financial</ProjectFullPath>
  <DefineConstants>DEBUG;TRACE</DefineConstants>
  <ForceFullAnalysis>True</ForceFullAnalysis>
  <TreatErrorsAsWarnings>False</TreatErrorsAsWarnings>
  <CacheResults>False</CacheResults>
  <OutputFile>$(AnalysisOutputPath)\Lender.Slos.Financial.StyleCop.xml</OutputFile>
  <MaxViolationCount>0</MaxViolationCount>
  <IgnoreVoluntaryRules>True</IgnoreVoluntaryRules>
  <MandatoryRuleIds>SA1507;SA1107</MandatoryRuleIds>
  <AlwaysIgnoredRuleIds>SA1201</AlwaysIgnoredRuleIds>

</PropertyGroup>

<ItemGroup>
  <SourceFiles Include="**\*.cs" />

</ItemGroup>

<Target Name="StyleCop">
  <StyleCopAnalysis ProjectFullPath="$(ProjectFullPath)"
                    SourceFiles="@(SourceFiles)"
                    ForceFullAnalysis="$(ForceFullAnalysis)"
                    DefineConstants="$(DefineConstants)"
                    TreatErrorsAsWarnings="$(TreatErrorsAsWarnings)"
                    CacheResults="$(CacheResults)"
                    OutputFile="$(OutputFile)"
                    MaxViolationCount="$(MaxViolationCount)"
                    IgnoreVoluntaryRules="$(IgnoreVoluntaryRules)"
                    MandatoryRuleIds="$(MandatoryRuleIds)"
                    AlwaysIgnoredRuleIds="$(AlwaysIgnoredRuleIds)"
                    />

</Target>

...
```

Now, when the StyleCop target is called in the build script, the `StyleCopAnalysis` task ignores the voluntary rules and throws errors if a mandatory rule is violated. This breaks the build only when a mandatory coding standard is violated.

StyleCop is an effective tool for analyzing the C# source code files to determine if coding standards are followed. In this section, you learned how a custom `MSBuild` task is used to break the build when mandatory coding standards are violated. Using StyleCop, adherence to coding standards is monitored in a continuous and automated way.

Differencing Tools

The purpose of differencing tools is to quickly compare two files or folder structures to isolate and understand the differences. This is an effective way to analyze a change set, and so nearly every version control system provides a way to work with a differencing tool to understand the changes contained in the change set.

Beyond version control, differencing tools have a broader role to play in source code analysis, configuration management, and troubleshooting. Some of the many applications of differencing include

- Performing code reviews

- Comparing the files and folders between deployment environments

- Finding differences in decompiled code between assembly versions

- Troubleshooting configuration differences

Many problems that are difficult to diagnose and detect are revealed by focusing on the differences. Differencing tools quickly and effectively make these differences explicit. A complete and clear understanding of differences helps to analyze the situation and point to resolutions or improvements.

■ **Practice 11-6** Use a Differencing Tool to Make File and Folder Differences Obvious

---

Differencing tools are commonly used in the coding, design, and maintenance aspects of ALM. Individual developers and team leaders can difference the source code files to review the code and find opportunities to comment on or improve the changes. This is especially important to team leaders responsible for overseeing the day-to-day work of many developers. Developers can maintain the software better when it is easier to isolate changes and describe the modifications in a change set.

The important objective is to develop the habit of using a differencing tool to compare and contrast two files and sets of files and folders. Develop knowledge about using differencing to efficiently diagnose problems. Find a tool that works efficiently for you and master this skill. Table 11-4 provides a list of differencing tools that might be worth evaluating.

Table 11-4. Tool Choices: Differencing

Product	Description	Terms	More Info
Beyond Compare	A feature-rich and modestly-priced commercial file and folder comparison tool by Scooter Software. It offers more than differencing, such as synchronize folders and FTP.	Commercial	`www.scootersoftware.com`

Product	Description	Terms	More Info
C# Smart Differencer	A language-aware and relatively expensive differencing tool by Semantic Designs. It is a differencing tool that understands the C# language syntax. It uses a compiler approach, rather than a string matching approach, to minimize false positives.	Commercial	www.semanticdesigns.com
KDiff3	An effective free and open-source differencing tool. It is widely-used as a merge tool for version control.	Free, Open Source	kdiff3.sourceforge.net
WinMerge	An effective free and open-source differencing tool. It is widely-used as a merge tool for version control.	Free, Open Source	winmerge.org

Duplicate Code Finders

The purpose of a duplicate finder is to find duplicate code. The challenge is to separate the coincidental and unimportant duplication from those candidates for refactoring or remediation. For example, most of the C# class files in a project might have the same dozen using statements. This duplication is fine, but the tool might highlight it as duplicate code. In contrast, every class might implement the same one-line method that validates a social security number, which is not reported because a duplication threshold is not met. The point is that finding duplicate code involves both an automated tool to reveal potential duplication and broad code review. Good judgment is needed to improve duplicate code.

▓ **Practice 11-7** Find and Address Any Inappropriate Duplication of Code

---

Duplicate finders are especially helpful for the design and maintenance aspects of ALM. Team leaders can examine the source code files across the software system looking for duplication. Finding duplicates provides opportunities to assign classes a single responsibility by removing cross-cutting or redundant functionality. Similarly, during maintenance the duplicate finders can be used to focus the team leader on finding technical debt that ought to be addressed as part of a maintenance cycle.

Use a duplicate code finder to analyze the source code. Review the output and draw conclusions about inappropriate reuse. Monitor the code base and vigilantly watch for inappropriate duplication of code. Table 11-5 provides a list of duplicate code finders that might be worth evaluating.

Table 11-5. Tool Choices: Duplicate Code Finders

Product	Description	Terms	More Info
CloneDR	A language-aware and relatively expensive duplicate code finder by Semantic Designs. It is a duplicate code finder tool that understands the C# language syntax. It uses a compiler approach, rather than a string matching approach, to minimize false positives.	Commercial	`www.semanticdesigns.com/Products/Clone`
Simian	A lightweight, command-line duplicate code finder that is moderately-priced, available from Simon Harris. Configured as an External Tool, Simian can examine the whole solution from within Visual Studio.	Commercial	`www.harukizaemon.com/simian`
SolidSDD	A feature-rich and higher-priced duplicate code finder by SolidSource. It offers both a rich user interface and a command-line facility for the build process.	Commercial	`www.solidsourceit.com/products/SolidSDD-code-duplication-cloning-analysis.html`
TeamCity Duplicates Finder (.NET)	Available as a duplicate code finder build configuration within JetBrains' TeamCity CI server.	Commercial	`confluence.jetbrains.net/display/TCD65/Duplicates+Finder+%28.NET%29`

■ **Caution** Overzealous efforts to eliminate duplication can lead to coincidental and improper reuse. On one project, a loan application, which has a lot in common with an approved loan, was handled as a "virtual loan" with horrible results. Eliminating code duplication by creating coincidental reuse tends to make the domain model abstract, ill-defined, and hard to understand.

Manual Code Reviews

To this point, the discussion of static code analysis has focused on tools and automated techniques. It is important not to overlook or underestimate the power of manual code reviews. The manual code review engages the individual developer and team leader in ways that bring judgment, experience, and discernment to uncover issues and improve design.

An effective manual code review focuses on all the areas of code analysis that the automated tools and techniques are weak at covering. This analysis should spotlight how the source code does or does not meet the design. The discussion is a transfer of knowledge from the more experienced to the less experienced developers. The experience, expertise, and judgment informs improvements to the coding in ways that go beyond the ordinary and routine analysis, such as following the coding standards, and toward improving coding technique and better design patterns. The manual code review is a communication vehicle that opens up a healthy dialog on the chosen conventions and why adherence is important. The best techniques associated with manual code analysis bring learning and education to the team.

Architecture and Design

The architecture of a software system includes the intended static design of the system. The goals of developing a system's architecture and design often focus on avoiding improper dependency relationships, managing complexity, and following best practices. However, over time, differences arise between how the software is built and how it was intended to be built. It is important to establish the differences and resolve them by making decisions about whether the software ought to conform to the design or the design ought to change because of an explicit choice.

Static analysis tools that evaluate the system architecture and design reveal the structure, design, and dependencies of the built system. The analysis work involves matching up these results to the design principles and rules that had been defined for the software. The static design and processes of the software system are described by the Unified Modeling Language (UML) diagrams shown in Table 11-6.

Table 11-6. The UML Static Design Diagrams

UML Diagram	Description
Class	Shows the classes and interfaces and the relationships between these classes and interfaces
Component	Depicts the static structure, with respect to how various modules couple to form the components that comprise the software
Deployment	Represents the physical deployment of assemblies, executables, and other essential parts, such as configuration and resource files
Use Case	A behavior diagram that provides a graphical overview of the functionality provided by the software
Object	Illustrates a snapshot of the static structure of the software at a specific point in time

Both Use Case and Object diagrams are used to develop, illustrate, and define system requirements and detailed design. The Class, Component, and Deployment diagrams depict the static design of the classes, modules, components, tiers, and assemblies of the system. These diagrams often suggest design rules and the preferred dependency relationships that some static analysis tools can enforce. Also, when these diagrams are not available, then a static analysis tool can be used to evaluate the system by developing diagrams that depict the system's static design as-is. These design-oriented analysis tools are rarely cheap, but they have powerful application for any large-scale system development.

■ **Practice 11-8** Perform Architecture and Design Analysis; Comparing *As-Planned* to *As-Built* Designs

Static analysis tools that specialize in architecture and design can evaluate the software as it is and develop diagrams that depict the implied static design. These static analysis tools provide useful information, such as listed in Table 11-7.

Table 11-7. Static Analysis of Architecture and Design

Information	Description
Code Quality Metrics	Measures of design quality, such as complexity, coupling, maintainability, cohesion, and instability
Dependency Graph	Diagrams that show how one module depends upon another module and the relationships between modules
Treemaps	Diagrams that display a specific measure as a hierarchy of nested rectangles, with the rectangles inside showing the constituent measures

Most static analysis tools that specialize in architecture and design are commercial products. Much of the output from these tools requires experience and expertise to interpret. There are gray areas that require you to discern and judge the appropriate choice of action.

The architecture and design tools and techniques have great application as part of the coding, design, and maintenance aspect of ALM. The technical leader uses these tools and techniques primarily to evaluate and improve the system's overall design and to target key areas for improvement. The team leader can use these tools to work with the developers, identifying technical debt and targeting maintenance development. Individual developers can use code quality metrics to monitor and correct the code they are writing while implementing features and functionality.

Table 11-8 provides a list of design analysis tools worth evaluating. These are relatively expensive tools that are not intended to be used by all members of the development team. The developers involved in high-level design and code quality analysis ought to budget for and investigate all the available options.

Table 11-8. Tool Choices: Architecture and Design

Product	Description	Terms	More Info
Lattix for .NET	An architecture and design analysis tool that includes an easy-to-understand dependency structure matrix (DSM) view. Licensing and pricing available through Lattix's website.	Commercial	www.lattix.com
NDepend	A widely-used and relatively well-priced architecture and design analysis tool. It has broad application in understanding and improved architecture and in enforcing design rules.	Commercial	www.ndepend.com
Structure 101	A well-regarded and relatively well-priced architecture and design analysis tool. It uses cells to clearly present and communicate system architecture.	Commercial	www.structure101.com
Visual Studio 2010 Ultimate	The top-of-the-line Visual Studio version includes architecture and design analysis tools as well as UML modeling, layering, dependency matrix, and code metrics tools.	Commercial	msdn.microsoft.com/en-us/library/dd409365.aspx

Code Metrics

There are many tools available to calculate code metrics for your .NET code. If you have Visual Studio 2010 Ultimate or Premium then you already have the means to calculate code metrics. Many of the architecture and design analysis tools include some ability to calculate code metrics as well.

Although there are many specific metrics, clear-cut design decisions can be made based on the information from a few key indicators.

In the Financial Rewrite project, you decide that a maximum cyclomatic complexity (CC-max) measure under 15 is preferred, if the code has a CC-max under 30 it requires attention but is acceptable, but any code with a CC-max over 30 requires urgent review. Visual Studio offers you the ability to the review of software with regard to CC-max and provides a way to perform this static analysis.

Quality Assurance Metrics

The notion of adopting practices that add to overall improvement is discussed in Chapter 1. The idea is that new practices in one area bring changes for the better to other areas of development. Tracking and analyzing quality assurance (QA) metrics is an excellent example of a practice that brings overall improvement. For example, the number of issues opened by QA testers or by customers for a certain module reveals important information about that module. More often than not, if a module is responsible for a disproportionate number of defects then that module is an error-prone module.[9] Identification of error-prone modules provides developers with the information needed to prompt a code review or module redesign.

To make QA metrics as powerful as possible, the defect tracking system should tie together as many aspects of application lifecycle management as possible. Specifically, every defect should relate to the requirements, design, coding, and deployment. During maintenance the QA metrics help developers and team leaders target sources of technical debt. The defect tracking system needs to include fields that track one or more requirements related to the defect. The defect ought to capture the logical and physical parts of the system related to the defect, such as screens or modules. The version control system needs to integrate with the defect tracking system to allow developers to connect a source code change set to a defect. The result is that the practice of analyzing defect tracking reports can improve overall development. Here are a few defect tracking reports that are particularly helpful:

- *Defects per requirement:* High values for this metric often imply an overly complex or misunderstood requirement.

- *Defects per module:* High values for this metric often imply an inadequate design, missed requirements, too little unit testing, or careless development.

- *Defects per source file:* High values for this metric often imply an overly complex class, a class with too many responsibilities, or a good candidate for refactoring and redesign.

- *Defects per deployment:* High values for a particular deployment or for deployments to a specific target environment provide important evidence of configuration, scalability, and performance issues.

Dynamic Analysis

Dynamic analysis involves running the program and carrying out usage scenarios, automated tests, and creating other interesting conditions. The purpose is to collect information about performance, memory usage, test coverage, or internal program state while the application is running. For example, code coverage could focus on your interest in understanding how much of the code-under-test is visited while all the tests are running. Some of the many questions that dynamic analysis attempts to answer could include:

- What statements does the program spend the most time executing?

- What is the memory usage and what are the opportunities for optimizations?

- What code are my unit tests not testing?

- What is the application state just before an exception is thrown?

- What are the queries the system is sending to the database?

Dynamic analysis gives insight into what the system is doing as it runs and interacts with other systems, such as the database. Dynamic analysis is also tied into the Microsoft Security Development

---

[9] Hard data on the cost of error-prone modules is provided in Steve McConnell, *Rapid Development* (Redmond, WA: Microsoft Press, 1996).

Lifecycle Process Tools. These are testing tools designed to help detect flaws that may expose security vulnerabilities. Just beyond the scope of this section, these verification tools use approaches like input fuzzing, validation, and attack surface analysis to uncover potential problems.[10]

Code Coverage

Code coverage tools measure how completely a program runs as it is running. In common practice, automated tests are what exercise the program so that the code coverage tool can perform its measurements.

In Chapter 8 the subject of automated testing is presented from the perspective of writing effective tests. The tests are written to check the intention of the code. However, the question remains: what code is not covered by tests? This question is broadly answered with a test coverage number, which indicates the percentage of code that is tested when the tests are run. The principle is that a test coverage tool runs the test suite and monitors the code-under-test. The test coverage tool tracks each symbol within the code-under-test and tracks these symbols as they are executed while the code is running. A symbol can be thought of as any point in the code that is a valid breakpoint for the debugger. The percentage of symbols covered is analyzed and calculated. Various code coverage measures are listed in Table 11-9.

Table 11-9. Measures of Code Coverage

Coverage	Description
Class	If the program-running-under-analysis (program) executes code within a class, then the coverage tool counts that class as visited. The coverage tool totals each visited class and computes a percentage of all the classes in the code that were visited during the run.
Method	Every time the program executes a method, the coverage tool counts that visit. The coverage tool computes a percentage of the methods that were visited during the run.
File	This is the percentage of source files with code that contains code executed during the run.
Statement	If the program executes a statement, then the visit is counted. A percentage is calculated representing the percentage of statements visited during the run.
Symbol	Every time the program executes a symbol in the code, the coverage tool counts that visit toward the percentage of the total symbols executed.
Branch	A branch is any logic-branch in the code; for example, one if statement represents the branching logic for a code block. Every time the test code executes code within a branch, it counts that visit toward the percentage of total branches executed.

---

[10] To read more about the Microsoft Security Development Lifecycle Process Tools see http://www.microsoft.com/security/sdl/adopt/tools.aspx.

■ **Practice 11-9** Run Tests under Code Coverage

Code coverage tools are used as part of the coding, design, testing, and maintenance aspects of ALM. These tools provide the individual developer valuable feedback when writing automated tests. With code coverage, the developer finds the uncovered branches, exception scenarios, and corner-cases. The team leader uses these tools to gauge progress against code coverage objectives. When correctness is important to a critical module, the team leader can monitor and insist that code coverage reach as close to 100% as is practicable. Similarly, improving code coverage is a measurable maintenance goal to target as part of a reduction in technical debt.

Table 11-10 provides a list of code coverage tools worth evaluating. Although there are not too many choices available today, more and more new CI and developer productivity tools are emphasizing code coverage. Take the time to research and evaluate all your options.

Table 11-10. Tool Choices: Code Coverage

Product	Description	Terms	More Info
dotCover	A new and moderately priced code coverage tool by JetBrains. Integrates well into Visual Studio and works with the ReSharper test runner. A command-line utility is available and dotCover is built into the TeamCity CI server.	Commercial	www.jetbrains.com/dotcover
NCover	A widely-used feature-rich code coverage and reporting tool. It is relatively high-priced, but is well-regarded, very established and capable. It is capable of handling large and challenging code coverage situations.	Commercial	www.ndepend.com
OpenCover	A free and open source code coverage tool for .NET. It is a command-line utility that performs statement-coverage analysis and generates XML output. There is a report generator tool.	Free, Open Source	github.com/sawilde/opencover/wiki
VS 2010 Premium and Ultimate	Versions of Visual Studio that provide support for Visual Studio Test projects to run under code coverage. Limited information about using VS code coverage outside of the Microsoft testing framework.	Commercial	msdn.microsoft.com/en-us/library/dd409365.aspx

Performance Profiling

The purpose of performance profiling is to understand the performance characteristics of the software while it is running. Often the performance profiling is motivated by a performance problem; for example, during system testing when a page is taking too long to load. Other indicators include errors and system failures. With a sense of urgency the performance profiler is used to diagnose and debug the problem. However, a lot of time is lost learning how to use the profiler and interpret the results.

The pressure of performance profiling in a crisis situation is an all too common event. Performance profiling can and should be a part of ongoing monitoring activities during development. The Analyze phase of the cycle ought to include running the performance profiler while the system is run under scenarios that range from normal to heavy usage. This dynamic analysis is likely to suggest improvements that prevent problems. As improvements are made, performance monitoring helps detect new issues that prompt further analysis.

■ **Practice 11-10** Profile the System's Performance on a Regular Basis

---

There are two essential ways that performance is profiled:

- *Sampling:* At specified intervals the profiler looks at the top of the program's call stack and determines the active method. The profiler tracks each method that is active and counts the number of times it is active.

- *Instrumentation:* A special build of the software contains statements that help collect timing information at the start and finish of a method. The profiler tracks how long each method takes to execute.

Sampling does not require a special build of the application but is less precise. Instrumentation offers more information; however, an instrumented build is needed to provide the detail. Visual Studio Ultimate and Premium versions include these performance profiling tools, which allow you to perform early and frequent performance analysis. If you have one of these versions of Visual Studio, you can investigate your software's performance today. The sample code for this chapter includes the PeopleTrax project in the *C:\Samples\Ch11\4_Performance* folder. This is a sample application used in MSDN documentation and walkthroughs of the Visual Studio Team System 2010 Profiling Tools. Take some time to investigate the MSDN Walkthrough and other tutorials on profiling applications with Visual Studio.

Profiling techniques are often used as part of the design, testing, and maintenance aspects of ALM. When requirements and expectations are clearly not being met, individual developers ought to profile those aspects of the system as part of coding. Technical leaders use profiling tools and techniques to evaluate the entire system's performance to ensure the architecture is meeting objectives. Individual developers use profiling tools and techniques to properly resolve performance issues found during testing. Together the team leader and developers use profiling to target performance problems that can be addressed during maintenance.

Like performance profiling, memory profiling is often motivated and initiated after symptoms point to a memory problem. Understanding and optimizing an application's memory resource usage can prevent serious problems from occurring in the first place. An overview of the memory used by the application and regular monitoring are able to detect memory difficulties before they are found during system testing.

Query Profiling

Database tuning is too often done as a reaction to poor query performance. When a performance problem is likely rooted in querying the database, a profiler can help you to understand and diagnose the problem. Some of the symptoms that a query profiler helps to reveal include

- Repeatedly querying the same table
- Long-running or inefficient queries
- Queries generated by the LINQ provider
- The lack of appropriate indexes
- Indexes not being used

The Analyze phase reveals symptoms of problems with querying the database. Since the symptoms are revealed by the analysis, current or potential problems can be diagnosed. Improvements, such as caching or indexes, are prescribed to increase efficiency. Ongoing and regular monitoring prompts further analysis to address any new symptoms that arise.

■ **Practice 11-11** Examine Database Queries with a Query Profiler

---

Table 11-11 provides a list of query profilers. One of them is probably relevant to the project you are working on today. There are certainly other query profiling tools worth evaluating; you are encouraged to investigate all options.

Table 11-11. Tool Choices: Query Profiling

Product	Description	Terms	More Info
Entity Framework Profiler	A query profiler that examines the interaction between the system and the database.	Commercial	`efprof.com`
LINQPad	This is a LINQ evaluation tool that helps to understand and develop LINQ queries. The LINQPad Pro and Premium versions require the purchase of a license.	Free	`www.linqpad.net`
NHibernate Profiler	A query profiler that examines the interaction between the system and the database.	Commercial	`nhprof.com`
SQL Server Profiler	A widely-used, feature-rich query profiling tool that is part of the Microsoft SQL Server Performance Tools.	Microsoft SQL Performance Tools	`msdn.microsoft.com/en-us/library/ms181091.aspx`

Logging

Logging is a very powerful way to troubleshoot difficult problems. Unfortunately, many software applications are built to only include error or exception logging. One of the goals of the logging approach ought to include support for dynamic analysis by providing the ability to capture activity and internal system state. In this way, logging is a form of instrumentation.

Good logging solutions are neither heavy nor intrusive. The logging configuration needs to be flexible enough so that error and exception logging is configured under normal situations, but if the need arises then with a configuration change the logging behavior changes to write more detailed information into the log. Here are some specific rules to follow:

- Do not make logging build configuration–dependent. That is, both Debug and Release configurations should have the logging facility so that production systems can perform logging.

- Always allow the logging level to be set or overridden through configuration.

- Carefully consider the logging level every time a logging method is called. Since logging has performance implications, avoid unwarranted logging with critical, error, and warning levels.

■ **Practice 11-12** Incorporate a Flexible Logging Solution to Monitor and Diagnose the Application

---

Logging tools have broad application across many aspects of ALM, including coding, testing, deployment, and maintenance. The individual developer uses logging while coding and debugging features and functionality to dynamically watch and understand the state of the system. During QA testing the developers are provided important problem-solving information from the logs. Otherwise, even if you find problems, they will be very hard to reproduce and fix. During smoke, stability, and performance testing this information is very useful. After deployment, the developers use the information in the logs to pinpoint, diagnose, reproduce, and resolve issues that are often only seen in the deployed system.

There are a number of logging solutions available for .NET applications. However, there is a portable logging abstraction project, called Common.Logging. It allows you to perform logging to a well-defined abstraction layer and then select a specific logging implementation at runtime. The decision on what logging library to use is deferred until deployment through the use of configuration and Common.Logging plugins. These plugins proved support for various logging facilities, such as

- System.Console

- System.Diagnostics.Trace

- Log4Net

- NLog

- Enterprise Library Logging

More information on Common.Logging is available at http://netcommon.sourceforge.net. The reference documentation is available online at http://netcommon.sourceforge.net/documentation.html.

Somewhat related, the software system ought to incorporate a solid framework for defect reporting by QA testers and by customers. An effective logging solution provides a mechanism so that the defect reporting includes data such as the full stack trace of the exception and the list of loaded modules, including their version numbers, when the application crashed.

Summary

In this chapter you learned about the Analyze, Improve, and Monitor cycle of activities that form a conceptual model for software improvement. Also covered were the two broad areas of code analysis, static analysis and dynamic analysis. In the static analysis section you learned how this approach looks at the source code and assemblies without running the program. In the dynamic analysis section you learned how sampling and instrumentation allow the tool to capture information about the program while it runs.

This chapter brings together many of the .NET practice areas presented and discussed in Chapter 2. These topics include application lifecycle management, security analysis, and recommended patterns and practices. In many ways, code analysis is the application of the better .NET practice areas through active analysis, improvement, and monitoring.

CHAPTER 12

Test Frameworks

This chapter covers the topic of test frameworks. In a broad sense, a test framework is a technology or set of tools that supports automated software testing. Most developers are familiar with one of the code-driven test frameworks, which are commonly referred to as unit testing frameworks. In this chapter, you will learn about the four most popular unit testing frameworks. Another important component to any test framework is the test runner. You will learn about a variety of test runners, from the minimalist runners to those that are well-integrated into Visual Studio. This chapter also provides an overview of the xUnit test pattern and explains how each of the unit testing frameworks discussed fits the pattern.

Later in this chapter you will learn about other test frameworks. These include mock object frameworks, database testing with NDbUnit, user interface testing frameworks, and acceptance testing frameworks. Specific practices are highlighted to emphasize how test frameworks offer .NET developers more effective testing and better test methodologies. Table 12-1 lists the ruthlessly helpful practices related to test frameworks.

Table 12-1. Test Frameworks: Ruthlessly Helpful Practices

	Practice
12-1	Use the Test Runner to Debug Both the Test Code and the Code-Under-Test
12-2	Purchase a Visual Studio Add-In Test Runner to Achieve Greater Productivity
12-3	Use a Mock Object Framework to Provide Stub and Mock Functionality
12-4	Use an Isolator to Fake Difficult and Pernicious Dependencies
12-5	For Database Testing, Ensure That the Database State Is Consistent Before Each Test
12-6	Acceptance Test with Business Specifications and Behaviors, Not Test Scripts
12-7	Develop a Purpose-Built Acceptance Testing Framework to Monitor Key Business Logic

COMMENTARY

During the course of my professional development work I have written test code using the four most popular unit testing frameworks: NUnit, MbUnit, MSTest, and xUnit.net. I have seen how each unit testing framework introduced new concepts, extensions, and provided better functionality.

NUnit offers significant advantages in the way it is widely supported by third-party test runners, code coverage tools, and continuous integration servers. MbUnit brings many excellent features to unit testing and is well integrated with the Gallio Automation platform. MSTest and the Microsoft Visual Studio Unit Testing Framework offer excellent integration with both Visual Studio and Team Foundation Server, offering comprehensive application testing. The xUnit.net framework offers extensibility and performance that makes it well-suited to many automated testing applications.

My rationale for presenting all four of these unit testing frameworks is to give you the information you need to appreciate each of them. I expect that this information will help you to select the one or more .NET unit testing frameworks that are useful to you, your team, and your organization.

Unit Testing Frameworks

The fundamental component of code-driven testing is the unit testing framework. Broadly speaking, these testing frameworks are known as *xUnit*[1] test frameworks because they generally fit the xUnit test pattern. The xUnit test pattern is described a little later in this chapter. For now, the main point is that the purpose of these unit testing frameworks is to provide facilities that help do the following:

- Identify the test method
- Identify the test classes and fixtures
- Provide constructs with the means to
  - Perform data-driven tests
  - Perform pre-test setup and arrangement
  - Perform post-test teardown and cleanup
  - Perform test-fixture setup and teardown
  - Handle tests that expect an exception
- Provide constructs that support
  - Making assertions
  - Skipping or ignoring tests
  - Categorizing tests

---

[1] Martin Fowler provides a nice background on xUnit at http://martinfowler.com/bliki/Xunit.html.

The unit test framework helps developers write tests that are effective and can endure as the system evolves.

This chapter will focus on four unit test frameworks: NUnit, MbUnit, MSTest, and xUnit.net. These are the most popular unit test frameworks for .NET development. Each of these unit test frameworks offers a somewhat different approach and benefits to unit testing software. Table 12-2 provides a description of these widely-used .NET unit testing frameworks.

Table 12-2. Popular .NET Unit Test Frameworks

Framework	Description	More Information
NUnit	Free, open source xUnit-based test framework, which was originally ported from JUnit. It is actively enhanced, widely used, and supported by many testing tools and platforms. NUnit is so widely used it is considered the de facto standard unit testing framework for .NET development.	www.nunit.org
MbUnit	Free, open source xUnit-based test framework that brings many great ideas to unit testing. It is closely associated with the Gallio test automation platform. The semantics of MbUnit v3 and NUnit v2.5.x are very similar and are both very straightforward.	www.mbunit.com
MSTest	Part of Microsoft Visual Studio Unit Testing Framework, MSTest is not an xUnit-based test framework. Since the MSTest framework is part of the Microsoft testing toolset, it is widely used and supported. MSTest is well suited to integration testing and to use within the Visual Studio and Team Foundation Server product suites.	msdn.microsoft.com/en-us/library/dd264975.aspx
xUnit.net	Free, open source xUnit-based test framework. The xUnit.net test framework is well regarded as it is considered faster and more original than the other unit test frameworks. The xUnit.net developers and fans make many compelling arguments in favor of this framework.[2]	xunit.codeplex.com

Test Runners

A test runner is an application that performs the tests. The .NET test runners typically load one or more test assemblies and recognize the test methods written with the unit test framework. This set of test methods is often referred to as the test suite.

As the test suite runs, the runner indicates progress and status when each test method does the following:

---

[2] See "Why did we build xUnit.net?" at http://xunit.codeplex.com/wikipage?title=WhyDidWeBuildXunit.

- Executes successfully

- Fails to meet the constraint of an assertion

- Fails because an error occurs

- Is skipped, ignored, or inconclusive

Test runners differ in that some provide a graphical user interface (GUI) while others are a console application. The GUI runner is intended to provide a visual interface so that the person running the test can see the tests execute, monitor the results, and interact with the test runner. The console runner is intended to provide command-line execution of the test suite with the general goal of automating the test run. Both types of test runners are important in the development of a complete and comprehensive set of automated tests.

NUnit GUI and Console Runners

The NUnit test framework is widely used and supported by many third-party tools, such as continuous integration servers, coverage tools, and Visual Studio add-ins. All of the examples in Chapter 8 were written using the NUnit framework. This section starts with the assumption that NUnit is the framework you have selected to write test code. In order to remain focused on the topic of the test runner, it also assumes that the test code is already written. To follow along with the sample code, open the _Lender.Slos.sln_ file, found in the _Samples\Ch12\1_NUnit_ folder, from within Visual Studio. Rebuild the solution to ensure that all the code builds properly.

With the unit tests code written, the challenge is to run the test code through a test runner. NUnit provides a Windows graphical user interface (GUI) as a part of NUnit. This program is a Windows forms application named _nunit.exe_ (or _nunit-x86.exe_). If NUnit is installed then it is available through a program or desktop shortcut. Otherwise, it can be found within the NUnit installation folder, under the _bin_ folder. A screenshot of the NUnit GUI is shown in Figure 12-1.

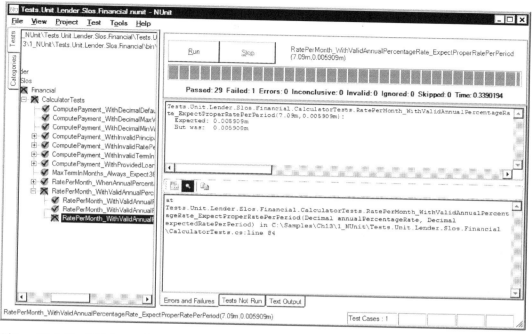

Figure 12-1. *The NUnit graphical user interface (GUI)*

The NUnit documentation provides a complete description of how to use the NUnit GUI runner.[3] To keep things brief, this section is limited to the essential information and a basic orientation. With the NUnit GUI application running, select the File ➤ Open Project ... menu item. Navigate to the *Samples\Ch12\1_NUnit\Tests.Unit.Lender.Slos.Financial* folder and open the *Tests.Unit.Lender.Slos.Financial.nunit* project file. Press the Run button.

Notice the tree view on the left-hand side of the screen; this is the list of tests found in the *Tests.Unit.Lender.Slos.Financial.dll* assembly. The list of tests is the test suite. There is one failing test, which is shown in Figure 12-1. When you select the failing test in the tree, the right-hand side of the screen provides detail about that failing test on the Errors and Failures tab. It is clear that the test expected the value of 0.005909, but since the actual value is 0.005908, the test failed. In addition, the Errors and Failures tab shows the stack trace, which helps reveal the line of code that caused the test to fail. Change the expected value for the third test case from 0.005909 to 0.005908, which is provided to the RatePerMonth_WithValidAnnualPercentageRate_ExpectProperRatePerPeriod method. Rebuild the solution and return to the NUnit GUI runner. Run the tests again and all of the tests should pass.

The NUnit GUI runner is straightforward to run from outside of Visual Studio. However, for debugging in Visual Studio with the Start Debugging menu (*F5 debugging*), it is certainly a lot better to run the NUnit GUI runner as part of the debugging session. You accomplish this by changing the project settings for the *Tests.Unit.Lender.Slos.Financial* project in Visual Studio. You can follow along by

---

[3] For more information see http://www.nunit.org/index.php?p=nunit-gui&r=2.5.10.

referring to the sample code under the *Samples\Ch12\1_NUnit* folder. To start, open the properties window for the test project from Visual Studio's Solution Explorer. Select the Debug tab. This is shown in Figure 12-2. In the Start Action area, make the change to "Start an external program" with the *nunit.exe* program selected. Also, in the Start Options the "Command line arguments" should have the relative path to the *Tests.Unit.Lender.Slos.Financial.nunit* project file. Save the Visual Studio project.

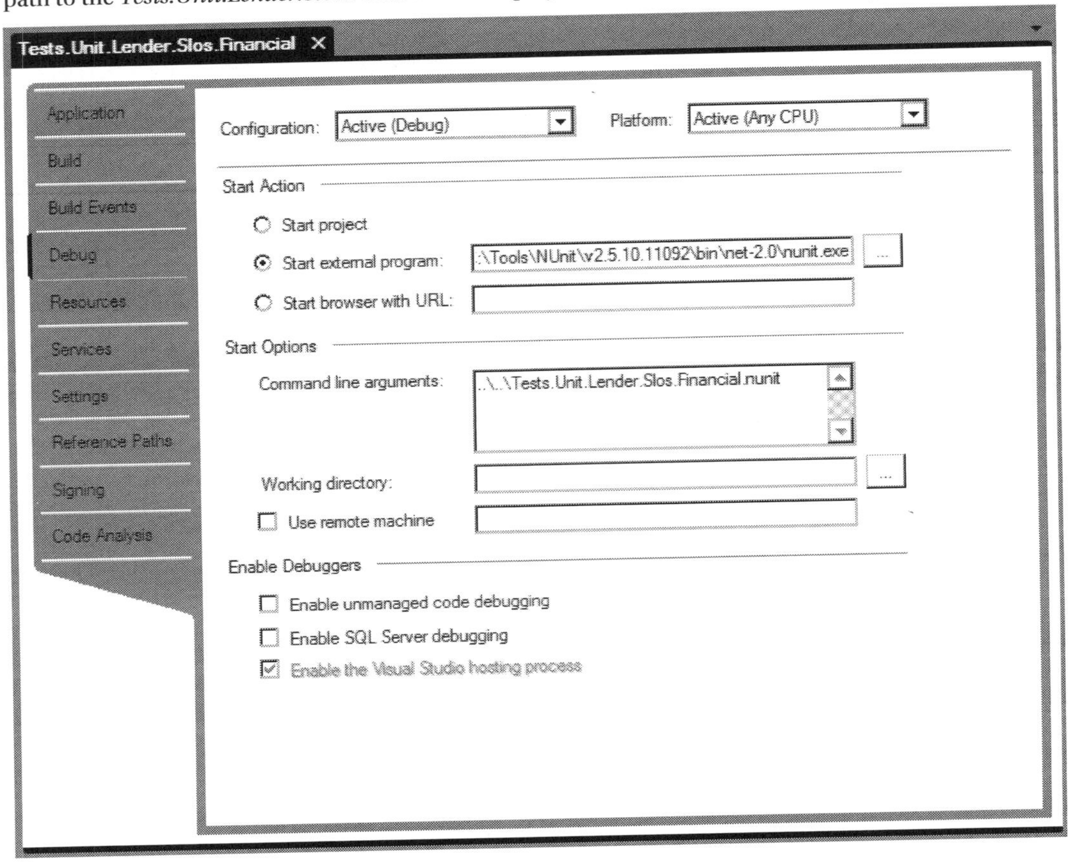

Figure 12-2. Configuring the Visual Studio debugger to run NUnit GUI

Once Visual Studio is configured to run the NUnit GUI runner for debugging, performing F5 debugging launches the NUnit GUI runner. While the NUnit GUI is running tests, breakpoints in the test code and the code-under-test are hit when they are reached.

■ **Practice 12-1** Use the Test Runner to Debug Both the Test Code and the Code-Under-Test

An alternative to running the NUnit GUI runner is the console runner. This is the *nunit-console.exe* program found under the NUnit *bin* folder. The NUnit console runner affords you the opportunity to automate the task of running testing and provides many command-line options.[4] Within Visual Studio the NUnit console can be run using the External Tool feature available under the Tools menu within Visual Studio. Figure 12-3 illustrates how to configure the NUnit console runner as an external tool.[5]

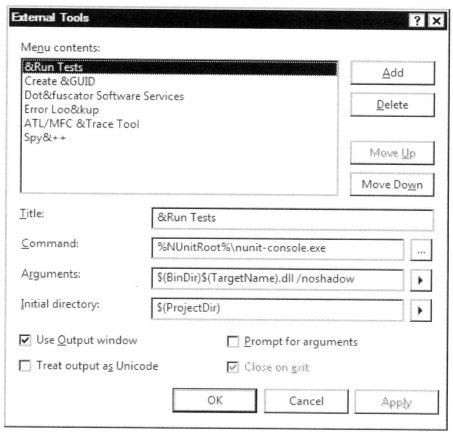

Figure 12-3. Configuring Visual Studio external tools to run NUnit console

---

[4] For more information see http://www.nunit.org/index.php?p=consoleCommandLine&r=2.5.10.
[5] This configuration assumes that you created an environment variable named NUnitRoot that points to the proper NUnit folder, for example, C:\Tools\NUnit\v2.5.10.11092\bin\net-2.0.

Once configured as an external tool, the NUnit console is run from Visual Studio by selecting the newly added Run Tests menu item under the Tools main menu. The results of the NUnit console are output to the Visual Studio Output window, as shown in Figure 12-4.

```
Output
Show output from: Run Tests
NUnit version 2.5.10.11092
Copyright (C) 2002-2009 Charlie Poole.
Copyright (C) 2002-2004 James W. Newkirk, Michael C. Two, Alexei A. Vorontsov.
Copyright (C) 2000-2002 Philip Craig.
All Rights Reserved.

Runtime Environment -
   OS Version: Microsoft Windows NT 6.1.7600.0
   CLR Version: 2.0.50727.4963 ( Net 2.0 )

ProcessModel: Default    DomainUsage: Single
Execution Runtime: v4.0
............................F
Tests run: 30, Errors: 0, Failures: 1, Inconclusive: 0, Time: 0.1470085 seconds
  Not run: 0, Invalid: 0, Ignored: 0, Skipped: 0

Errors and Failures:
1) Test Failure : Tests.Unit.Lender.Slos.Financial.CalculatorTests.RatePerMonth_WithVali
      Expected: 0.005909m
  But was:  0.005908m

at Tests.Unit.Lender.Slos.Financial.CalculatorTests.RatePerMonth_WithValidAnnualPercenta
```

Figure 12-4. Output from running NUnit console as an external tool

What you have learned up to this point is the minimalist's way to integrate test runners with Visual Studio. For the NUnit unit test framework, the GUI and console runners are provided for free. In the next section, you will look at the prospect of buying a commercial product that offers more integration with Visual Studio.

ReSharper Test Runner

This section continues with the premise that you have selected NUnit as your testing framework. Now, you are looking for a test runner that is well-integrated into Visual Studio to achieve greater developer effectiveness and productivity. The Visual Studio add-in test runners provide that boost. They make it very easy to run a single unit test or a subset of unit tests from a context menu, toolbar, and other places in Visual Studio. The results are displayed within purpose-built Visual Studio windows. Having the output right there helps you analyze the test results and navigate to the test code or code-under-test, whenever there is a failing test. This brings unit testing front and center within the Visual Studio IDE. This is a big help to the developer because the workflow to write test code, run test code, and resolve issues is more efficient and the cycle time is much shorter.

For unit tests written with the MSTest framework, the Visual Studio product provides many of these facilities, which we will cover in the next section. This section is about commercial test runners, most of which are Visual Studio add-ins, that focus on both supporting multiple unit testing frameworks (especially NUnit, MbUnit, MSTest, and xUnit.net) and providing "right-click access" to running tests from within Visual Studio. Let's take a closer look at one of these products: ReSharper.

ReSharper is a Visual Studio extension product from JetBrains (www.jetbrains.com). In Chapter 6, you learned that ReSharper is a general tool that provides code inspections and refactoring functionality. Another major feature of ReSharper is that it provides unit testing support that is well integrated with Visual Studio. It directly supports the NUnit and MSTest frameworks. Plug-ins are available to support MbUnit and xUnit.net.

ReSharper provides many context menus, docking windows, toolbars, sidebar marks, and more.[6] To run unit tests, simply right-click a tests method, test class, test project, or the entire solution, and ReSharper will run the tests defined within that context. For example, to run all the tests within a test project, simply right-click the project node in the Visual Studio Solution Explorer window and the context menu includes the Run Unit Tests choice, as shown in Figure 12-5. ReSharper provides similar context menus throughout the Visual Studio IDE. ReSharper offers many ways to support unit testing such as helping you to debug the test code and the code-under-test by selecting the appropriate context menu item.

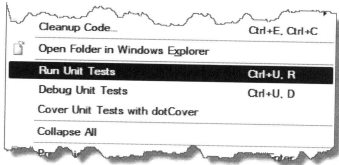

Figure 12-5. ReSharper context menu for running tests

Another significant element that ReSharper adds to the Visual Studio IDE is the Unit Test Explorer window, shown in Figure 12-6. This window allows you to see all the available tests within your solution. This is important because the solution may contain a variety of tests that include unit, integration, surface, performance, and the other types of tests that you learned about in Chapter 8. It is important that the developer run all the tests that are appropriate to the work they are currently performing; just as important, the developer can avoid running tests that involve setup and configuration or are not relevant to their current work.

---

[6] For more information see http://www.jetbrains.com/resharper/features/unit_testing.html.

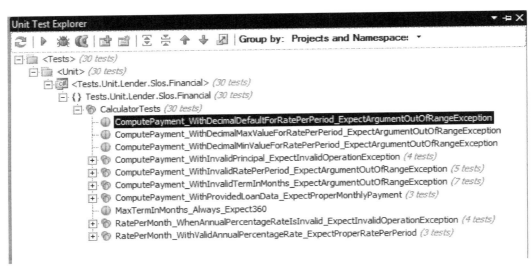

Figure 12-6. ReSharper provides the Unit Test Explorer window within Visual Studio.

When you run tests with ReSharper, a new unit test session is started. There is a Unit Test Sessions window within Visual Studio that allows you to see all the sessions that have run or are currently running. This window is shown in Figure 12-7. The tree provides an effective way to understand how the running test methods fit within the context provided by the test classes. In addition, when there are multiple test cases there is a node added to the tree for each test case. In Figure 12-7, it is clear from the status column that one test failed and the test case node identifies the culprit. By selecting a failed-test node in the tree, the Output tab below reveals the specific reason why that test failed. Notice that the Output tab also provides a stack trace, which is helpful when debugging exceptions thrown from deep in the call stack of a failing test.

■ **Practice 12-2** Purchase a Visual Studio Add-In Test Runner to Achieve Greater Productivity

---

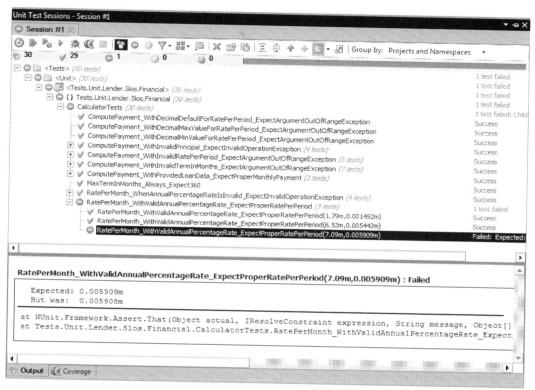

Figure 12-7. ReSharper provides the Unit Test Sessions window within Visual Studio.

As you learned in Chapter 11, JetBrains also sells a .NET code coverage tool, called dotCover. This product integrates well with the unit testing tools of ReSharper. As shown in Figure 12-8, the statement-level coverage is reported within the Coverage tab of the ReSharper Unit Test Sessions window. Bringing code coverage results into the Visual Studio IDE is an important productivity boost for developers writing test code. In effect, dotCover detects when a test covers a particular statement in code and, equally important, identifies and highlights code that is not covered by test code.

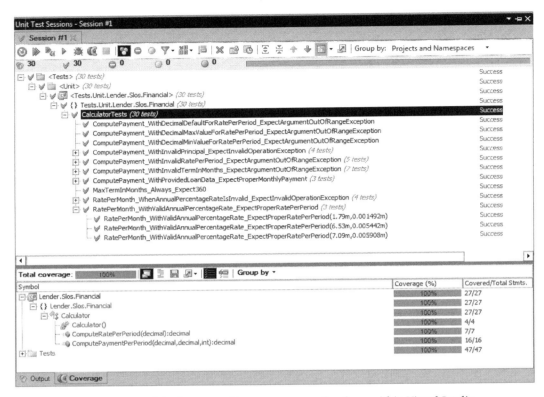

Figure 12-8. ReSharper and dotCover provide coverage reporting from within Visual Studio.

■ **Note** If profiling performance is important to you, ReSharper can allow you to quickly profile performance using its unit test runner from within Visual Studio. This requires an additional purchase and installation of the dotTrace Performance product, which is a .NET profiling tool from JetBrains.

Being productive within Visual Studio with a unit test framework other than Visual Studio Test Framework is a primary reason developers choose a commercial unit test runner that integrates with the Visual Studio IDE. These commercial add-in products also offer a lot more than running tests. Table 12-3 provides a list of products worth evaluating.

Table 12-3. Unit Test Runners for Visual Studio, Which Support Multiple Test Frameworks

Product	Terms	More Info
DevExpress	Commercial	www.devexpress.com/Products/Visual_Studio_Add-in
ReSharper	Commercial	www.jetbrains.com/resharper
TestDriven.NET	Commercial	www.testdriven.net

Visual Studio Test Runner

So far, the premise has been that you and your development team are using the NUnit test framework. Let's switch gears and consider following the "Microsoft way" of developing test code. This means using the Visual Studio Test Framework and the integrated test runner. If you have Visual Studio 2010 Ultimate, Premium, or Professional you can run automated tests from within Visual Studio or from the command line.[7]

Writing tests with the Visual Studio Test Framework does open up a lot of possibilities for running tests from within the IDE. First, there is the Test main menu item. From there, all the tests in the solution can be run, as shown in Figure 12-9.

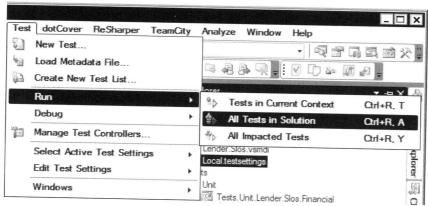

Figure 12-9. Visual Studio test runner main menu

The Visual Studio IDE also includes a Test View window, shown in Figure 12-10. This window allows you to see all the available tests within your solution and to group and select tests. It helps you find the tests that you want to run. This is important so that developers can run only the tests that are appropriate to their current work.

---

[7] For running MSTest from the command line see http://msdn.microsoft.com/en-us/library/ms182486.aspx.

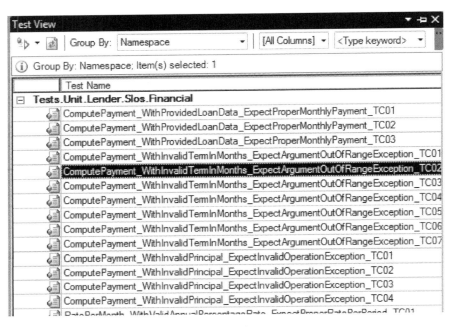

Figure 12-10. The Visual Studio Test View window

After the tests are run, Visual Studio displays the results of the tests in the Test Results window, shown in Figure 12-11. A failing test is quickly identified and the information in the column explains why the test failed. There are toolbar buttons available to further run and debug the tests based on the results.

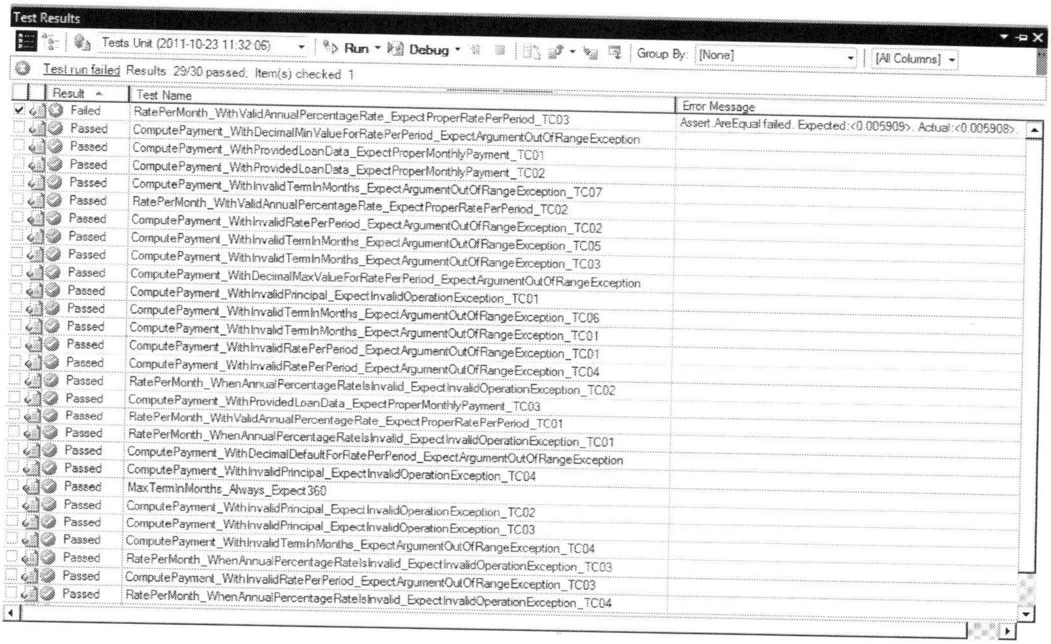

Figure 12-11. *The Visual Studio Test Results window*

Visual Studio test projects include test settings files and the use of diagnostic data adapters. The details are beyond the scope of this book;[8] however it is important to know how to use Visual Studio tests settings to run tests under code coverage.

Within a Visual Studio solution that has a test project there is the *Local.testsettings* file, which runs tests locally without any of the diagnostic data adapters selected. I will briefly point out the steps to add code coverage as a diagnostic data adapter to the sample project found in *Samples\Ch12\3_VisualStudio* folder. To start, open the *Lender.Slos.sln* file in Visual Studio. Within the Solution Explorer window there is a *Local.testsettings* item under the *Solution Items* folder. If you double-click the *Local.testsettings* item, Visual Studio opens the Test Settings window, shown in Figure 12-12. On the left-hand side, select the Data and Diagnostics item. For this selection, you can see that Code Coverage is a choice in the list in the Configure section. Check the Enabled checkbox and press the Apply button.

---

[8] For information on diagnostic data adapters and test settings see http://msdn.microsoft.com/en-us/library/dd286743.aspx.

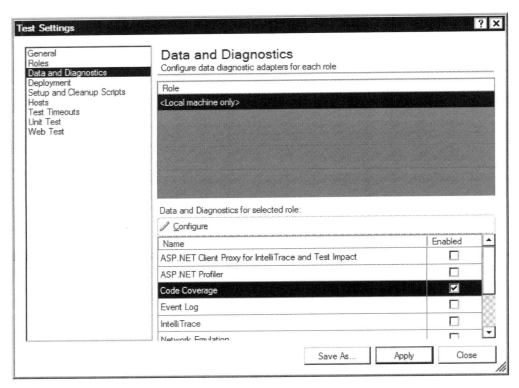

Figure 12-12. Configuring Visual Studio tests to run under code coverage

Once the change is applied, the next thing is to double-click the Code Coverage item in the list. This brings up the Code Coverage Detail window, as shown in Figure 12-13.

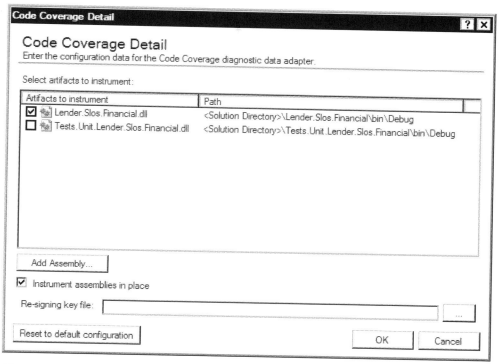

Figure 12-13. Configuring the settings in the Code Coverage Detail window

Within the Code Coverage Detail window the specific configuration for the test settings file are established. Press the OK button to save the configuration. Close the Test Settings window.

With the code coverage settings in place, the Visual Studio Test Runner now runs the tests under coverage and provides the results in the Code Coverage Results window, as shown in Figure 12-14.

Code Coverage Results				
Tests.Unit (2011-10-23 12:03:40)				
Hierarchy	Covered ...	Covered (%...	Not Covered...	
⊟ 🔧 Tests.Unit (2011-10-23 12:03:40}	60	100.00 %	0	
⊟ ⚙ Lender.Slos.Financial.dll	60	100.00 %	0	
⊟ { } Lender.Slos.Financial	60	100.00 %	0	
⊟ ⚙ Calculator	60	100.00 %	0	
◈ .cctor{}	4	100.00 %	0	
◈ ComputePaymentPerPeriod(valuetype System.Decimal,valuetype System.Decimal,int32}	39	100.00 %	0	
◈ ComputeRatePerPeriod(valuetype System.Decimal}	17	100.00 %	0	

Figure 12-14. The Visual Studio Code Coverage Results window

Gallio Test Runner

The Gallio Project is an effort to bring a common and consistent test platform to .NET development. The Gallio Automation Platform provides test runners that run tests for a number of test frameworks, including NUnit, MbUnit, MSTest, and xUnit.net. Gallio includes the command-line runner, called *Echo*, and a Windows GUI named *Icarus*. Because Gallio integrates so many testing tools and approaches it is definitely a platform worth considering if you want a complete and comprehensive testing platform. More information about Gallio and this automation platform for .NET can be found on the Gallio project website at www.gallio.org.

Figure 12-15 shows the Gallio Icarus test runner interface. The list of tests is shown in a tree view on the left-hand side. The test results are summarized in the panel on the right-hand side.

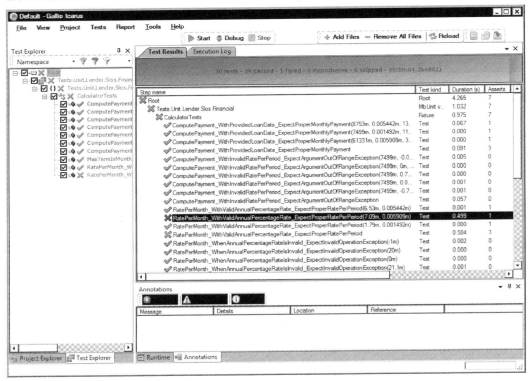

Figure 12-15. *The Gallio Icarus GUI test runner*

Gallio provides a complete execution log that details the output from the test run. An example of the execution log is shown in Figure 12-16, with specific details about one failing test.

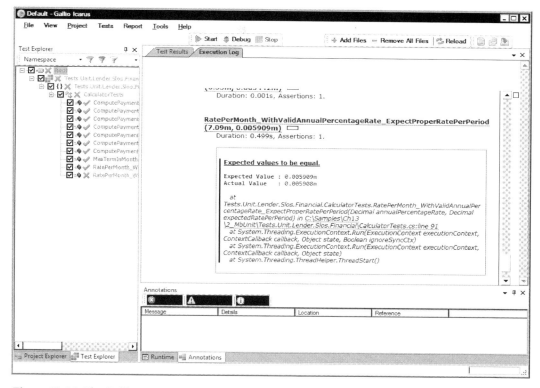

Figure 12-16. The Gallio test runner execution log

xUnit.net Test Runner

The xUnit.net test framework offers a number of significant capabilities. Primary among them is performance. Many developers who work with xUnit.net find that it is a really good framework. It is sometimes referred to as a *lean* framework. Although xUnit.net introduces changes in terminology, it takes a fresh approach and is very flexible. One important virtue is that xUnit.net supports the ability to extend the framework.

The commercial test runners described earlier either support xUnit.net directly or there is a plug-in available. If you are not using a commercial test runner, your basic options are to use the xUnit.net GUI runner, as shown in Figure 12-17, or to use the xUnit.net console runner. Both of these runners come with the framework.

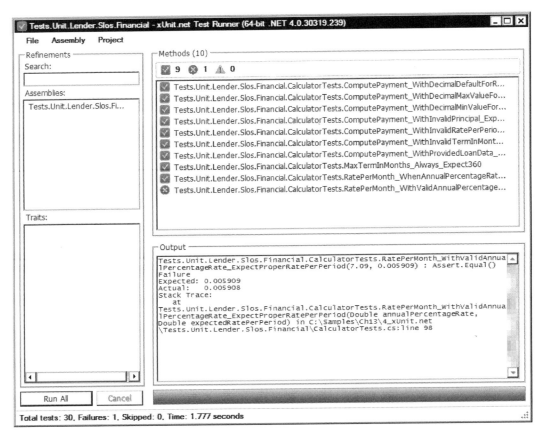

Figure 12-17. *The xUnit.net GUI test runner*

The xUnit.net console runner can be set up to run as an external tool in a manner similar to how the NUnit console is configured, as shown in Figure 12-3. The output from the xUnit.net console runner is shown in Figure 12-18.

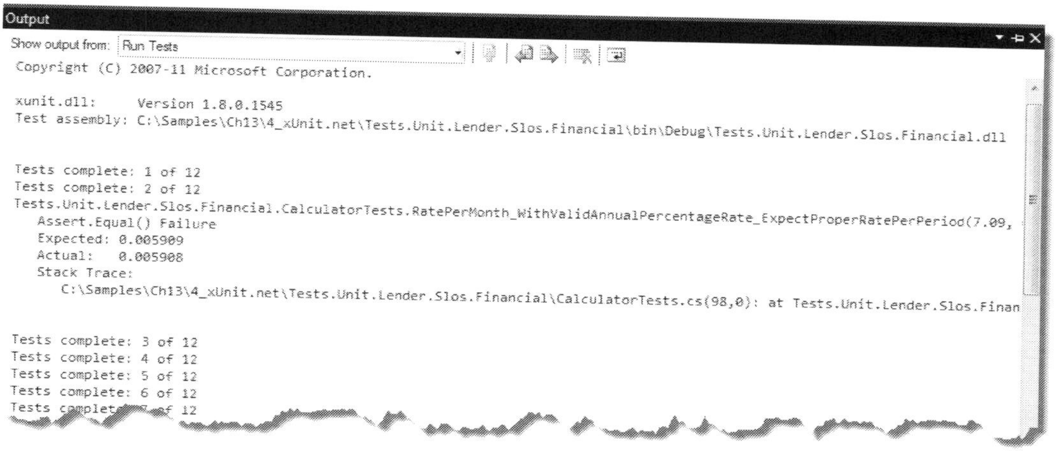

Figure 12-18. Output from running xUnit.net console as an external tool

To this point you have learned about the four test frameworks and various test runners. In the next section I will broadly compare and contrast the test frameworks by examining how they fit into the xUnit test pattern.

XUnit Test Pattern

All xUnit test frameworks share the same basic architecture, referred to as the *xUnit test pattern*.[9] First, there is the execution of one or more individual unit test methods within the test class. Also, before each test method is executed you can define a setup method, which prepares things before the test is run. After each test, a teardown method serves to clean up after the test method. Another feature is that of the test fixture, sometimes known as a test context, which initializes, sets up preconditions, and allocates resources needed to run any of the test methods. The fixture creates a known-good state before the tests run. The fixture also cleans up and disposes of any resources to return the context back to its original state. Let's look at each aspect of the xUnit test pattern in turn.

Identifying the Test Method

Each of the four unit test frameworks, NUnit, MbUnit, MSTest, and xUnit.net, uses an attribute to identify the test methods within an assembly. There is the primary attribute, which identifies a test method that has the basic test method signature. This signature is a public method without arguments that returns void. For example, using the NUnit test framework, the basic test method is defined like this:

---

[9] For more information see http://xunitpatterns.com/XUnit%20Basics.html.

```
[Test]
public void BasicTestMethodSignature()
{
    ...
}
```

When a secondary attribute is used, it identifies test methods that are driven by parameter values or some other source of data. For example, using NUnit a data-driven test is defined like this:

```
[TestCase("How many roads must a man walk down?", 42]
[TestCase("What is your favorite prime number?", 73]
public void ParameterDrivenTestMethodSignature(
    string ultimateQuestion,
    int expectedAnswer)
{
    ...
}
```

Table 12-3 lists the primary and secondary attributes used to identify test methods and data-driven tests with the four unit test frameworks.

Table 12-3. Unit Test Frameworks: Attributes That Identify Test Methods and Data-Driven Tests

Framework	Primary Attribute	Secondary Attributes
NUnit	[Test]	[TestCase],[TestCaseSource],[Theory],[DataPoint] ,[DataPoints]
MbUnit	[Test]	[Row],[CsvData],[XmlData],[CombinatorialTest],[Factory]
MSTest	[TestMethod]	[DataSource]
xUnit.net	[Fact]	[Theory],[InlineData],[ExcelData],[PropertyData]

Identifying the Test Class and Fixture

The goal of unit testing is to run tests in isolation and in a fully-repeatable way. In order to accomplish this it is often necessary to write code that performs before-test tasks, which precede the call to the test method. The test framework will call your before-test method to accomplish the setup. That method establishes the necessary preconditions and initial state required to run one of the test methods within the fixture. The test class and the fixture are basically synonymous.

The idea here is that the method that prepares the preconditions is identified, usually by an attribute, and the unit test framework ensures that that code is run before each test method is run. Similarly, the code that performs the after-test tasks is identified so that the unit test framework runs that method after each test is run, regardless of whether the test passes or fails. Table 12-4 provides the list of attributes or mechanisms of the four frameworks that identify within the test class any before-test or after-test methods.

Table 12-4. Unit Test Frameworks: Identifying Test Class and Fixture Methods

Framework	Test Class	Before-Test	After-Test
NUnit	[TestFixture]	[Setup]	[TearDown]
MbUnit	[TestFixture]	[Setup]	[TearDown]
MSTest	[TestClass]	[TestInitialize]	[TestCleanup]
xUnit.net	n/a	class constructor	IDisposable.Dispose method

Beyond the before-test and after-test methods, the fixture itself provides an environment and a context for the tests. The fixture setup method contains code that must be run before any of the tests in the test class are run. For example, the setup method could allocate resources to be used by all test methods within the test class. Similarly the fixture teardown method contains code that must be called after all the tests in the test class are run. This is important to ensure that the next test class starts with the test environment in a known-good state. The unit test framework supports the goal of creating and disposing of the test class's context through fixture setup and teardown methods. Table 12-5 provides the list of attributes or mechanisms to identify the fixture setup and fixture teardown methods for the four frameworks.

Table 12-5. Unit Test Frameworks: Identifing Fixture Setup and Teardown Methods

Framework	Fixture Setup	Fixture Teardown
NUnit	[TestFixtureSetUp]	[TestFixtureTearDown]
MbUnit	[TestFixtureSetUp]	[TestFixtureTearDown]
MSTest	[ClassInitialize]	[ClassCleanup]
xUnit.net	IUseFixture<T>	IUseFixture<T>

An example may best illustrate how a test runner might use these attributes to execute the test code. Listing 12-1 shows the code for a test class written to use the NUnit test framework. The test class itself is decorated with the TestFixture attribute. Each of these methods is decorated with one of the attributes defined within the NUnit.Framework namespace. These attributes allow the NUnit test runner to determine the methods to execute and the correct order in which to execute them. The basic idea is that the test runner inspects the test assembly to find the test classes and methods using the attributes of the framework.

Listing 12-1. Unit Tests Written to Use the NUnit Test Framework

```
namespace Tests.Unit.Lender.Slos.Financial
{
    using System;

    using NUnit.Framework;

    [TestFixture]
    public class FixtureTests
    {
        [TestFixtureSetUp]
        public void FixtureSetup()
        {
            Console.WriteLine("Fixture setup");
        }

        [TestFixtureTearDown]
        public void FixtureTeardown()
        {
            Console.WriteLine("Fixture teardown");
        }

        [SetUp]
        public void TestSetup()
        {
            Console.WriteLine("Before-test");
        }

        [TearDown]
        public void TestTeardown()
        {
            Console.WriteLine("After-test");
        }

        [Test]
        public void TestMethod_NoParameters()
        {
            Console.WriteLine("Executing 'TestMethod_NoParameters'");
        }

        [TestCase(0)]
        [TestCase(1)]
        [TestCase(2)]
        public void TestMethod_WithParameters(int index)
        {
            Console.WriteLine("Executing 'TestMethod_WithParameters' {0}", index);
        }
    }
}
```

Consider how the NUnit test runner executes the test code in Listing 12-1. The first method that is executed is the FixtureSetup method, which has the [TestFixtureSetup] attribute. It is called before any of the test methods are called.

Before each test method is called the TestSetup method is called, because the NUnit runner detects that it has the [Setup] attribute.

Next, one of the designated test methods is executed. After each test method is executed, the TestTeardown method is called because it is attributed with [TearDown]. This cycle repeats until all the test methods in the fixture are done executing.

The last thing that the NUnit runner does is execute the FixtureTeardown method because it has the [TestFixtureTearDown] attribute. Following is the output from running these unit tests in the NUnit test runner.

```
Fixture setup

***** Tests.Unit.Lender.Slos.Financial.FixtureTests.TestMethod_NoParameters

Before-test

Executing 'TestMethod_NoParameters'

After-test

***** Tests.Unit.Lender.Slos.Financial.FixtureTests.TestMethod_WithParameters(0)

Before-test

Executing 'TestMethod_WithParameters' 0

After-test

***** Tests.Unit.Lender.Slos.Financial.FixtureTests.TestMethod_WithParameters(1)

Before-test

Executing 'TestMethod_WithParameters' 1

After-test

***** Tests.Unit.Lender.Slos.Financial.FixtureTests.TestMethod_WithParameters(2)

Before-test

Executing 'TestMethod_WithParameters' 2

After-test
```

Fixture teardown

The Visual Studio Test Framework works in much the same way as NUnit; the attributes, however, are named differently. Listing 12-2 shows a test class written with the Visual Studio Test Framework. The basic idea remains the same: the test runner inspects the test assembly to find the test classes and methods using the attributes of the framework.

Listing 12-2. Unit Tests Written to Use the Visual Studio Test Framework

```
namespace Tests.Unit.Lender.Slos.Financial
{
    using System.Diagnostics;

    using Microsoft.VisualStudio.TestTools.UnitTesting;

    [TestClass]
    public class FixtureTests
    {
        [AssemblyInitialize]
        public static void AssemblyInit(TestContext context)
        {
            Trace.WriteLine("Test assembly initialize");
        }

        [AssemblyCleanup]
        public static void AssemblyCleanup()
        {
            Trace.WriteLine("Test assembly cleanup");
        }

        [ClassInitialize]
        public static void FixtureSetup(TestContext context)
        {
            Trace.WriteLine("Fixture setup");
        }

        [ClassCleanup]
        public static void FixtureTeardown()
        {
            Trace.WriteLine("Fixture teardown");
        }

        [TestInitialize]
        public void TestSetup()
        {
            Trace.WriteLine("Before-test");
        }

        [TestCleanup]
        public void TestTeardown()
```

```
    {
        Trace.WriteLine("After-test");
    }

    [TestMethod]
    public void TestMethod_NoParameters()
    {
        Trace.WriteLine("Executing 'TestMethod_NoParameters'");
    }

    [TestMethod]
    public void TestMethod_WithParameters_0()
    {
        TestMethod_WithParameters(0);
    }

    [TestMethod]
    public void TestMethod_WithParameters_1()
    {
        TestMethod_WithParameters(1);
    }

    [TestMethod]
    public void TestMethod_WithParameters_2()
    {
        TestMethod_WithParameters(2);
    }

    private void TestMethod_WithParameters(int index)
    {
        Trace.WriteLine(string.Format(
            "Executing 'TestMethod_WithParameters' {0}",
            index));
    }
    }
}
```

Consider how the Visual Studio test runner executes the test code in Listing 12-2. The first method that is executed is the AssemblyInit method, which has the [AssemblyInitialize] attribute. Only one method in an assembly can have this attribute. It is called before any of the test classes are initialized. After this, the execution is very similar to the NUnit runner. The next method that is executed is the FixtureSetup method, which has the [ClassInitialize] attribute. Before each test method is called the TestSetup method is called, because it is decorated with the [TestInitialize] attribute. Then one of the test methods is executed. After each test method is executed the TestTeardown method is called, because it is attributed with [TestCleanup]. This cycle repeats until all the test methods in the fixture are done executing. After all the tests in the class are done, the Visual Studio runner executes the FixtureTeardown method, because it has the [ClassCleanup] attribute. After all tests in the assembly have run, the AssemblyCleanup method is called. Following is the output from running these unit tests in the Visual Studio test runner.

```
Test assembly initialize

Fixture setup

Before-test

Executing 'TestMethod_NoParameters'

After-test

Before-test

Executing 'TestMethod_WithParameters' 0

After-test

Before-test

Executing 'TestMethod_WithParameters' 1

After-test

Before-test

Executing 'TestMethod_WithParameters' 2

After-test

Fixture teardown

Test assembly cleanup
```

In the sample code projects within the appropriate folder, you will find an example of the FixtureTests class written to use each of the four unit test frameworks.

Assertions

Within test code, an assertion is a statement that usually evaluates to true or false. The statement is written in the test method to indicate that the developer believes that the condition ought to be true at that point in the test. If the statement is false then the test is failing and the test framework is expected to record that test as a failed test.

Assertions are the primary way that the developer makes a statement about how the code is intended to work. The assertion is expected to be true and the developer wants the test framework to fail the test when the assertion is false. In effect, this is how the developer communicates with the test framework. For example, if the developer expects that the returned result should not be null, a statement line `Assert.IsNotNull(result)` is written into the test code.

Classic Model of Assertions

The classic model of assertions is to use one of the helper methods of an `Assert` class. Most unit test frameworks provide an assertion helper class with straightforward methods for making assertions. Because the method names are so similar, once you know the method names in one framework it is not hard to figure out the name in another framework.[10] Table 12-6 provides a list of the assertion types with examples from the NUnit unit test framework.

Table 12-6. *Unit Test Frameworks: Classic Assertions*

Assert Type	Description	Examples in NUnit
Utility	Help control the test method evaluation logic.	`Assert.Pass, Assert.Fail`
Conditional	Determine if a test condition is or is not met.	`Assert.True, Assert.False,` `Assert.IsNull,` `Assert.IsNotNull`
Equality	Determine whether the two arguments are equal.	`Assert.AreEqual`
Comparison	Determine how the two arguments compare.	`Assert.Greater,` `Assert.GreaterOrEqual,` `Assert.Less,` `Assert.LessOrEqual`
Identity	Determine if the object instances are the same or not the same instances.	`Assert.Same,` `Assert.AreNotSame`
Type	Determine if an object is an instance of or assignable from a type.	`Assert.IsInstanceOfType,` `Assert.IsAssignableFrom`

Within the frameworks there are more helper classes that support additional test method assertions. In NUnit these helper classes include `StringAssert`, `CollectionAssert`, and `FileAssert`.

Constraint-Based Assert Model

The constraint-based assert model was introduced to NUnit in version 2.4. This model uses a single `That` method of the `Assert` helper class for all assertions.[11] This one method is passed an object and a

---

[10] Here is a comparison of the assertion method names in different frameworks: http://xunit.codeplex.com/wikipage?title=Comparisons#assertions.
[11] For more information see http://www.nunit.org/index.php?p=constraintModel&r=2.4.1.

constraint to perform the assertion. It can use one of the NUnit "syntax helper" classes to provide the constraint. For example, one of the syntax helpers, Is.EqualsTo, is shown in Listing 12-3. Many developers prefer this style of writing assertion statements.

Listing 12-3. Unit Test Frameworks: Constraint-Based Assertions

```
[Test]
public void Load_WithValidFile_ExpectProperData()
{
    // Arrange
    var expectedData = "{BEB5C694-8302-4397-990E-D1CA29C163F1}";
    var fileInfo = new System.IO.FileInfo("test.dat");

    var classUnderTest = new Import();

    // Act
    classUnderTest.Load(fileInfo);

    // Assert
    Assert.That(expectedData, Is.EqualTo(classUnderTest.Data));
}
```

One big advantage to the constraint-based model is that you can implement custom constraints by writing a class that implements the IConstraint interface. Charlie Poole compares and contrasts the two assert models in a blog posting at http://nunit.net/blogs/?p=44.

Mock Object Frameworks

Chapter 8 discussed the need for fakes, stubs, and mocks. In the automated testing examples from that chapter the Moq framework is used to illustrate the application of a mock object framework.

■ **Practice 12-3** Use a Mock Object Framework to Provide Stub and Mock Functionality

---

Generally speaking, a mock object framework dynamically generates a fake object, which is either a stub or mock, as the test code runs. This eliminates the need for you to write a fake implementation of an interface or create a fake subclass. Using one of these frameworks saves a lot of time and provides many features that are tedious to write into handwritten fake implementations.

Dynamic Fake Objects with Rhino Mocks

Rhino Mocks is a dynamic mock object framework for.NET development. Rhino Mocks is a straightforward way to dynamically generate fake objects that implement the specified interface or are derived from the specified type. In this section we will look at using Rhino Mocks to dynamically create fake objects that implement an interface.

It is important to know that Rhino Mocks has some limitations to what it cannot fake. Those limitations include the fact that it cannot

- Intercept calls to non-virtual instance properties and methods
- Create a mock object from a private interface
- Create a mock object from a sealed class

The sample code for this section is found within the *Samples\Ch12\5_RhinoMocks* folder. The goal here is to test the Student class, which is found under the Lender.Slos.Model namespace. As you learned in Chapter 8, the internal constructor is called to create an instance of the Student in the test code. This constructor is shown in Listing 12-4. The Rhino Mocks framework is used to generate the fake repository objects that this constructor requires.

Listing 12-4. The Student Class Constructor

```
public class Student
{
    private readonly IRepository<IndividualEntity> _individualRepo;
    private readonly IRepository<StudentEntity> _studentRepo;

    ...

    internal Student(
        IRepository<IndividualEntity> individualRepo,
        IRepository<StudentEntity> studentRepo)
    {
        _individualRepo = individualRepo;
        _studentRepo = studentRepo;
        HighSchool = new School();
    }
...

}
```

The test code that tests the Save method of the Student class is shown in Listing 12-5. Testing the code's interaction with the repositories is not the goal of this test method; therefore, the Rhino Mocks framework is used to generate stub objects.

Rhino Mocks provides the MockRepository static class as a primary way to write arrange-act-assert pattern test methods. In Listing 12-5 the call to the MockRepository.GenerateStub<IRepository<IndividualEntity>>() method dynamically generates an object that implements the IRepository<IndividualEntity> interface. This object, which is now in the stubIndividualRepo variable, is later passed to the Student constructor. The next line adds a stub-expectation to this stubIndividualRepo object by providing a lambda expression to the Stub method. What this expression is telling the stub object is to expect a call to the Update method and the arguments can be any object of type IndividualEntity. In this way, the stub object is now dynamically primed to receive a call to the Update method.

Listing 12-5. Using Rhino Mocks to Generate Stub Repositories

```
[Test]
public void Save_WithAnExistingStudentImproperlyCreated_ExpectInvalidOperationException()
{
    // Arrange
```

```
var today = new DateTime(2003, 5, 17);

const int ExpectedStudentId = 897931;

var stubIndividualRepo = MockRepository.GenerateStub<IRepository<IndividualEntity>>();
stubIndividualRepo
    .Stub(e => e.Update(Arg<IndividualEntity>.Is.Anything));

var stubStudentRepo = MockRepository.GenerateStub<IRepository<StudentEntity>>();
stubStudentRepo
    .Stub(e => e.Retrieve(ExpectedStudentId))
    .Return(null);
stubStudentRepo
    .Stub(e => e.Create(Arg<StudentEntity>.Is.Anything))
    .Return(23);

var classUnderTest =
    new Student(stubIndividualRepo, stubStudentRepo)
    {
        Id = ExpectedStudentId,
        Today = today,
        DateOfBirth = today.AddYears(-19),
    };

// Act
TestDelegate act = () => classUnderTest.Save();

// Assert
Assert.Throws<InvalidOperationException>(act);
}
```

The next stub object that is created is the stubStudentRepo. The setup here involves two methods. The first is the Retrieve method, which is set up to return null. The second is the Create method, which is set up to return 23. Since the goal is to have the Save method throw an exception when it is called, the setup for the Create method returns 23. This ensures that the returned value won't equal the ExpectedStudentId value of 897931. These two Rhino Mocks fake objects allow the call to the Save method to proceed to the point when the exception is thrown, which is exactly what you want. In effect, these stubs stand in for the repositories that the Student class uses so that they behave the way the test wants them to behave.

Let's switch over to interaction testing using a mock object instead of a stub. In Listing 12-6, the mockIndividualRepo object is generated from the call to the Rhino Mocks framework's MockRepository.GenerateStrictMock<IRepository<IndividualEntity>>() method. There are two things to notice. First, the variable name uses the *mock* prefix instead of *stub*. This is so you remember that this fake object is used for interaction testing. Second, the generation method that is called is named GenerateStrictMock. The *strict* behavior means that any method calls that are not expected cause an exception. In effect, any unexpected interaction results in a failed test, which is what you want. The opposite of strict behavior is *loose* behavior. Generally speaking, you should use strict behavior so that the test method does not pass when unexpected interactions should fail the test. Loose behavior can hide flaws in the test code or the code-under-test.

Listing 12-6. Using Rhino Mocks to Generate a Mock Repository for Interaction Testing

```
[Test]
public void Save_WithAnExistingStudent_ExpectIndividualDalUpdateIsCalledOnce()
{
    // Arrange
    var today = new DateTime(2003, 5, 17);

    const int ExpectedStudentId = 897931;
    var studentEntity = new StudentEntity { Id = ExpectedStudentId, };

    var stubStudentRepo = MockRepository.GenerateStub<IRepository<StudentEntity>>();
    stubStudentRepo
        .Stub(e => e.Retrieve(ExpectedStudentId))
        .Return(studentEntity);

    var mockIndividualRepo = MockRepository
        .GenerateStrictMock<IRepository<IndividualEntity>>();
    mockIndividualRepo
        .Expect(e => e.Update(Arg<IndividualEntity>.Is.Anything))
        .Repeat
        .Once();

    var classUnderTest =
        new Student(mockIndividualRepo, stubStudentRepo)
        {
            Id = ExpectedStudentId,
            Today = today,
            DateOfBirth = today.AddYears(-19),
        };

    // Act
    classUnderTest.Save();

    // Assert
    Assert.AreEqual(ExpectedStudentId, classUnderTest.Id);
    mockIndividualRepo.VerifyAllExpectations();
}
```

In Listing 12-6, the line after the mockIndividualRepo object is generated sets the expectation for interaction with the mock. This expectation is set with a call to the Expect method, passing in a lambda expression. The expression conveys that the Update method is expected to be called. For this setup, the argument passed to the Update method can be any object. The next part is the Repeat property, which is set to expect that Update will be called once and only once.

At this point, the test method proceeds as a regular test method. It is not until the last line of the test method that expectations are verified. When the VerifyAllExpectations method is called on the mockIndividualRepo object, the mock object framework verifies the interactions. If the expectations set during arrangement are all met, this statement does not throw an error. However, if the expectations were not met, the Rhino Mocks framework throws an exception and the test fails.

Mock object frameworks are an effective way to dynamically generate stubs and mocks. These frameworks provide an effective mechanism to quickly establish stub object behavior that allows the test code to focus on creating the conditions that the test is trying to create. In addition, these frameworks provide mechanisms to verify that the code-under-test is interacting with dependencies in the proper and expected way.

Test in Isolation with Moles

In Chapter 2 you learned about Microsoft Research and the Pex and Moles project. The Moles framework allows Pex to test code in isolation so that Pex is able to automatically generate tests. The goal of isolation testing is to test the code-under-test in a way that is separate from dependencies and underlying components and subsystems. This section looks at how to use Moles to write tests in isolation.

▨ **Practice 12-4** Use an Isolator to Fake Difficult and Pernicious Dependencies

▨ **Note** This section refers to sample code in the *Samples\Ch12\6_Moles* folder. The sample code is based on the *Unit Testing with Microsoft Moles* tutorial that comes with the Moles documentation.[12]

The Import class in Listing 12-7 depends on the FileSystem class. This FileSystem class is an external dependency that is difficult to fake with some of the mock object frameworks like Moq and Rhino Mocks. The reason is that the class-under-test is directly calling a static method named ReadAllText from within the Load method. The calling of a static method tightly couples the class-under-test to this class.

Listing 12-7. The Import Class Is the Class-Under-Test

```
public class Import
{
    public string Data { get; private set; }

    public void Load(System.IO.FileInfo fileInfo)
    {
        Data = FileSystem.ReadAllText(fileInfo);
    }
}
```

---

[12] This tutorial is available also at http://research.microsoft.com/en-us/projects/pex/molestutorial.pdf.

In this section, assume that you want to write a unit test for the Load method; also assume that rewriting the Import class is not an option. Within the FileSystem class the static method ReadAllText is defined, as shown in Listing 12-8. Since a static method like this one is not easy to fake with some mock object frameworks, the first approach might be to take an automated integration testing approach.

Listing 12-8. The Static Method ReadAllText

```
public static class FileSystem
{
    public static string ReadAllText(
        System.IO.FileInfo fileInfo)
    {
        if (fileInfo == null) throw new ArgumentNullException("fileInfo");

        if (fileInfo.Exists)
        {
            return System.IO.File.ReadAllText(fileInfo.FullName);
        }

        return null;
    }

    public static void WriteAllText(
        System.IO.FileInfo fileInfo,
        string contents)
    {
        if (fileInfo == null) throw new ArgumentNullException("fileInfo");

        System.IO.File.WriteAllText(fileInfo.FullName, contents);
    }
}
```

The test code shown in Listing 12-9 includes a before-test and an after-test method to create the file and delete the file that ReadAllText needs. This allows the test code to find the file and properly perform the test. This approach is not isolated: if the file is not created as part of the setup it cannot work.

Listing 12-9. Automated Integration Testing of the Import.Load Method

```
public class ImportTests
{
    private const string FileName = "temporary.dat";

    private const string Data = "{BEB5C694-8302-4397-990E-D1CA29C163F1}";

    [SetUp]
    public void TestSetup()
    {
        System.IO.File.WriteAllText(FileName, Data);
    }

    [TearDown]
    public void TestTeardown()
```

```
    {
        if (System.IO.File.Exists(FileName))
        {
            System.IO.File.Delete(FileName);
        }
    }

    [Test]
    public void Load_WithValidFile_ExpectProperData()
    {
        // Arrange
        var fileInfo = new System.IO.FileInfo(FileName);

        var classUnderTest = new Import();

        // Act
        classUnderTest.Load(fileInfo);

        // Assert
        Assert.AreEqual(Data, classUnderTest.Data);
    }
}
```

It is not hard to imagine a situation where the internals of some method-under-test cannot be accommodated by the test or fixture setup and teardown. For example, the method-under-test might call a web service or interact with a temperamental or sensitive legacy system. In order to mock static and non-virtual methods in isolation you need a mock object framework like Moles that can create an object that stands in for the FileSystem class and allows the call to the WriteAllText method to be faked.

The sample code in the *Samples\Ch12\6_Moles\Begin* folder contains the *Lender.Slos.sln* file. To follow along with this example, open the solution in Visual Studio. The test code is in the *Tests.Unit.Lender.Slos.DataInterchange* project. The test class ImportTests is written to perform the integration test shown in Listing 12-10. Rebuild the solution and the Load_WithValidFile_ExpectProperData test method should pass.

Expand the References node under the *Tests.Unit.Lender.Slos.DataInterchange* project, within the Solution Explorer window. There is a reference with the name *Lender.Slos.DataInterchange*. Since this assembly contains the implementation of the FileSystem class, this is the assembly that needs to be *moled*. Right-click the *Lender.Slos.DataInterchange* assembly and the context menu should contain an option to Add Moles Assembly. Select this option and rebuild the entire solution. (See Figure 12-19.)

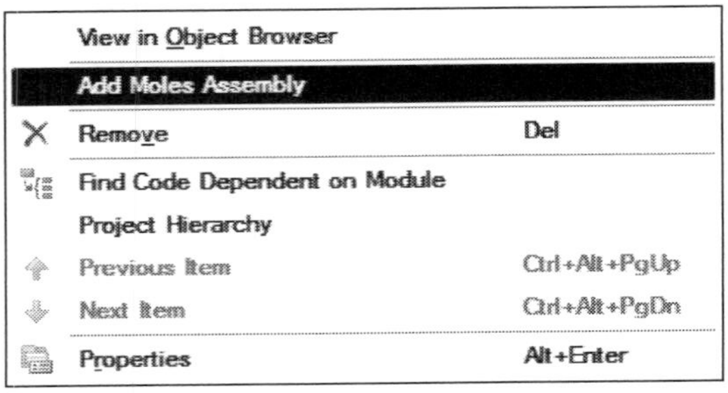

Figure 12-19. Use Moles to create a code-generated stub type.

After the rebuild is successful there will be a new assembly reference named *Lender.Slos.DataInterchange.Moles* in the References section of the *Tests.Unit.Lender.Slos.DataInterchange* project. This new assembly is the moled version of the *Lender.Slos.DataInterchange* assembly.

By convention, the moled class name is the same name as the class it stands in for, with the letter M prefixed. For example, `FileSystem` class has a corresponding mole class name of `MFileSystem`.

With the mole assembly in the test project, the test method is now written as shown in Listing 12-10. Be advised, there are two new namespaces needed:

```
using Lender.Slos.DataInterchange.Moles;
using Microsoft.Moles.Framework;
```

The `MolesContext.Create` method is how the Moles framework provides the context for the test. This using block wraps the entire test method. In the arrangement section, the `MFileSystem` class includes the `ReadAllTextFileInfo` delegate, which is used to establish the expected behavior when the `ReadAllText` method is called. The completed sample code is found under the *Samples\Ch12\6_Moles\End* folder.

Listing 12-10. *Unit Test the* `Import.Load` *Method in Isolation with Moles*

```
public class ImportTests
{
    [TestCase("1FBF377361CD.dat", "{BEB5C694-8302-4397-990E-D1CA29C163F1}")]
    [TestCase("A72498755DD2.dat", "{4E9C15FD-5966-4F69-8263-16E11F239873}")]
    public void Load_WithValidFile_ExpectProperData(
        string filename,
        string data)
    {
        using (MolesContext.Create())
        {
            // Arrange
            var expectedData = data;
            var fileInfo = new FileInfo(filename);

            MFileSystem.ReadAllTextFileInfo = info =>
                {
                    Console.WriteLine("filename: {0}", info.Name);
                    Assert.IsTrue(info.Name == filename);
                    return data;
                };

            var classUnderTest = new Import();

            // Act
            classUnderTest.Load(fileInfo);

            // Assert
            Assert.AreEqual(expectedData, classUnderTest.Data);
        }
    }
}
```

The NUnit test runner cannot directly run this test. It needs to run using the *moles.runner.exe*, which provides the Moles framework context. For this sample, run the *moles.runner.exe* program configured as an external tool as shown in Figure 12-20. The Command entry is `%MolesRoot%\moles.runner.exe`.[13] The Arguments entry is `$(BinDir)$(TargetName).dll /runner:"%NUnitRoot%\nunit-console.exe"`.

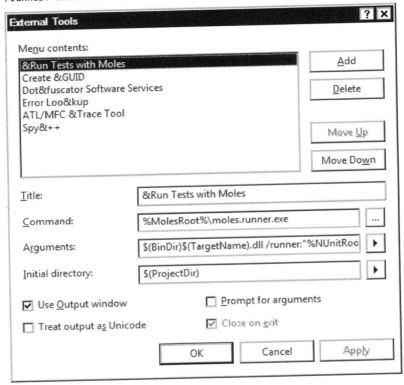

Figure 12-20. Configuring the Visual Studio external tool entry to run Moles

Make sure you are in the *Tests.Unit.Lender.Slos.DataInterchange* project and select Run Tests with Moles from the Visual Studio Tools menu. The Moles runner executes the tests and the output is written to the Output window, as shown in Figure 12-21.

---

[13] This assumes that you created an environment variable named MolesRoot that points to the proper Moles folder; for example, `C:\Program Files\Microsoft Moles\bin`.

```
Output
Show output from:  Run Tests with Moles                              [icons]
Microsoft Moles Runner v0.94.51023.0 -- http://research.microsoft.com/moles -- .NET v4.0.30319
Copyright (c) Microsoft Corporation 2007-2010. All rights reserved.

instrumenting...started
NUnit version 2.5.10.11092
Copyright (C) 2002-2009 Charlie Poole.
Copyright (C) 2002-2004 James W. Newkirk, Michael C. Two, Alexei A. Vorontsov.
Copyright (C) 2000-2002 Philip Craig.
All Rights Reserved.

Runtime Environment -
   OS Version: Microsoft Windows NT 6.1.7600.0
   CLR Version: 4.0.30319.239 ( Net 4.0 )

ProcessModel: Default    DomainUsage: Single
Execution Runtime: Default
.filename: 1FBF377361CD.dat
.filename: A72498755DD2.dat

Tests run: 2, Errors: 0, Failures: 0, Inconclusive: 0, Time: 0.6760676 seconds
   Not run: 0, Invalid: 0, Ignored: 0, Skipped: 0
```

Figure 12-21. Output from running Moles as an external tool

In Figure 12-21, the output writes the file name as the runner executes the test. This is because the ReadAllText method is executing the delegate method defined in the arrangement of your test code. It is obvious from the output that the Moles framework uses the MFileSystem stand-in object instead of a FileSystem object when the test code runs. The test method is now isolated from the file system and you are able to write test code in your arrangement that verifies that the code-under-test works as intended.

■ **Note** An excellent alternative to Moles is the *Typemock Isolator* mock object framework.[14] Like Moles, it supports isolation testing of non-virtual instance methods, non-public methods, sealed classes, static classes, and more. Since it is a commercial product, be prepared to make the case for purchasing Typemock.[15]

Database Testing Frameworks

A database is often a major component of many software systems. To have complete confidence in the system, the entire data access layer (DAL) needs to be tested as an integrated whole with the database. This is especially true for object-relational mapping (ORM) technologies like Entity Framework and

---

[14] For more information see http://www.typemock.com/isolator-product-page.
[15] You can read a comparison of Typemock, Moles, and Moq at http://blog.devdungeon.com/a-business-case-for-typemock-isolator/.

NHibernate. Once an integration testing database is in place, a big challenge is keeping the data in the database in a known-state before executing a test. A database testing framework can provide the capability to effectively arrange the data in the database before and after a test method runs, which ensures that the database's state is consistent for the execution of each test.

■ **Practice 12-5** For Database Testing, Ensure That the Database State Is Consistent Before Each Test

---

This section looks at the NDbUnit database testing framework.[16] This framework is based on DbUnit, which is used for Java development. NDbUnit is free and open source. Here are some key concepts and features to know about NDbUnit:

- Relies on a .NET DataSet schema file (XSD) to govern its interaction with the database

- Operates on only the subset of tables defined in the XSD schema file

- Loads data from an XML file that adheres to the XSD constraints defined by the XSD schema file

- Supports the following database servers:

  - Microsoft SQL Server 2005 and 2008, from Enterprise to CE

  - OLEDB-supported databases

  - SQLLite

  - MySQL

  - Oracle

■ **Note** This section refers to sample code in the *Samples\Ch12\7_NDbUnit* folder. It is adapted from the NDbUnit web site's step-by-step tutorial.[17]

The sample code is found in the *Samples\Ch12\7_NDbUnit* folder. Open the *Lender.Slos.sln* file in Visual Studio to follow along with the examples.

Before working with NDbUnit, a test database must be created and available to run the tests against. You should have already created the *Lender.Slos* database as part of running the samples for Chapter 8. If not, refer to the instructions on creating the database found in the *Samples\Ch08* folder.

---

[16] The NDbUnit project site is found at http://code.google.com/p/ndbunit/.
[17] For more information see http://code.google.com/p/ndbunit/wiki/QuickStartGuide.

A crucial element to running NDbUnit is the creation of the .NET DataSet schema definition file. MSDN provides a walkthrough on how to create a DataSet with the Visual Studio DataSet designer at http://msdn.microsoft.com/en-us/library/ms171897(v=VS.100).aspx. Here is an overview of creating and DataSet from within Visual Studio:

1. To start, right-click the *Data* folder under the *Tests.Unit.Lender.Slos.Dal* project.

2. Select the Add New Item … from the context menu.

3. In the Add New Item window there is a Data template named DataSet. Provide the name as *ExampleDataSet.xsd*. Press the Add button. This adds the DataSet file to the project and opens the designer window.

4. Browse to the *Lender.Slos* database from the Server Explorer in Visual Studio.

5. Drag the Individual table from the Server Explorer into the DataSet designer surface, which adds it to the DataSet definition.

6. Save and close the DataSet designer.

■ **Note** The Visual Studio .NET DataSet designer support files, such as ExampleDataSet.xsc, ExampleDataSet.xss, and ExampleDataSet.designer.cs, are not used by NDbUnit. You can exclude the DataSet from the project, remove these files, and just include the *ExampleDataSet.xsd* file in the project.

In the sample code, the DataSet schema file is named *Lender.Slos.DataSet.xsd* and is found under the *Samples\Ch12\7_NDbUnit\Tests.Unit.Lender.Slos.Dal\Data* folder. This schema only defines one table in the database, the Individual table.

Since NDbUnit loads data from an XML file, the next step is to create the XML data file. The contents of the *IndividualDalTests_Scenario01.xml* file are shown in Listing 12-11. Each Individual element defines one row that NDbUnit needs to insert into the database table. Within each Individual element are the elements that define the data that belongs in each column.

Listing 12-11. The XML Data Used to Populate the Individual Table

```xml
<?xml version="1.0" standalone="yes"?>
<Lender xmlns="http://tempuri.org/Lender.xsd">
  <Individual>
    <Id>1</Id>
    <LastName>Roosevelt</LastName>
    <FirstName>Theodore</FirstName>
    <MiddleName />
    <Suffix />
    <DateOfBirth>1858-10-27</DateOfBirth>
  </Individual>
  <Individual>
    <Id>3</Id>
    <LastName>Smith</LastName>
```

```
    <FirstName>John</FirstName>
    <MiddleName>Q</MiddleName>
    <Suffix>Sr.</Suffix>
    <DateOfBirth>2011-01-01</DateOfBirth>
  </Individual>
  <Individual>
    <Id>5</Id>
    <LastName>Truman</LastName>
    <FirstName>Harry</FirstName>
    <MiddleName>S</MiddleName>
    <Suffix />
    <DateOfBirth>1884-05-08</DateOfBirth>
  </Individual>
</Lender>
```

Now turn to the test code in Listing 12-12. The IndividualDalTests class defines the test fixture. The first method to look at is the FixtureSetup. It is here where the SqlDbUnitTest object is instantiated based on the connection to the test database and stored in the _database field. As part of the fixture setup the XML schema file is read and the XML data file is read. Now, the NDbUnit framework is prepared to load the data whenever a call is made to load this data.

With the FixtureSetup method called, the unit test framework calls the TestSetup method before any test method is executed. It is from the TestSetup method that the NDbUnit method is called to perform the database operation. This one statement clears the Individual table and reloads it with the XML data, resetting the identity column to match the values in the XML data:

```
_database.PerformDbOperation(DbOperationFlag.CleanInsertIdentity);
```

Before any and all test methods defined in the IndividualDalTests class are called, the unit test framework calls the TestSetup method. This method performs the database operation that clears the Individual table and reloads it with the XML data, resetting the identity column to match the values in the XML data. In this way, each of the test methods begins with the Individual table in the same known-good state.

Listing 12-12. The IndividualDalTests Class Working with NDbUnit to Set the Database's State

```
using NDbUnit.Core;
using NDbUnit.Core.SqlClient;

using NUnit.Framework;

public class IndividualDalTests
{
    private const string ConnectionString =
    @"Data Source=(local)\SQLExpress;Initial Catalog=Lender.Slos;Integrated Security=True";

    private INDbUnitTest _database;

    [TestFixtureSetUp]
    public void FixtureSetup()
    {
        _database = new SqlDbUnitTest(ConnectionString);

        _database.ReadXmlSchema(@"..\..\Data\Lender.Slos.DataSet.xsd");
```

```
        _database.ReadXml(@"..\..\Data\IndividualDalTests_Scenario01.xml");
    }

    [TestFixtureTearDown]
    public void FixtureTeardown()
    {
        _database.PerformDbOperation(DbOperationFlag.DeleteAll);
    }

    [SetUp]
    public void TestSetup()
    {
        _database.PerformDbOperation(DbOperationFlag.CleanInsertIdentity);
    }

    ...

}
```

An example of a test method in the IndividualDalTests class is shown in Listing 12-13. Each of the three test cases passes because NDbUnit populated the Individual table with the records that the test method expects.

Listing 12-13. Test Method That Calls the Retrieve Method

```
[TestCase(1, "Roosevelt")]
[TestCase(3, "Smith")]
[TestCase(5, "Truman")]
public void Retrieve_WithScenarioDataInDatabase_ExpectProperLastName(
    int id,
    string expectedLastName)
{
    // Arrange
    var classUnderTest = new IndividualDal(ConnectionString);

    // Act
    var actual = classUnderTest.Retrieve(id);

    // Assert
    Assert.NotNull(actual);
    Assert.AreEqual(expectedLastName, actual.LastName);
}
```

User Interface Testing Frameworks

As discussed in Chapter 8, the benefits of a fully automated integration testing environment for stability and regression testing usually outweighs the effort it takes to set everything up and get it working together. Many developers and testers feel, for very good reason, that user interface (UI) testing is a necessary part of fully automated integration testing. However, UI test automation requires a significant investment in startup costs, development, and maintenance effort.[18]

Except for Windows services and embedded systems, most software systems are developed to interact with an end user. The user interacts with a user interface in a way that can be difficult to test. It is the role of a user interface testing framework to simulate and automate the user interactions with the application. In this way, the test code can compare the actual results to the expected results to determine if the software is working as intended.

Web Application Test Frameworks

Writing automated user interface tests for web applications presents a number of significant challenges. Consider the common approach of automating the hosting of the application in a web server and automating the testing through a web browser. To fully automate this through a continuous integration server requires automated deployment to the web server. The automated test framework needs to be able to open the browser and navigate to the landing page. There could be a login and other pages that need to load just to get to the page where the first test method runs. This work is the heart of the effort needed to establish the Smoke testing infrastructure you learned about in Chapter 8.

At the heart of web application test frameworks is browser automation, which simulates a human using the browser through software. For example, you programmatically navigate to a page, enter data into a field, and click a button. The actions that happen through the browser are then compared to the expected response, which could be a validation message on the page or a new record you expect to see in a database. There are many choices and the tools and technologies offer a variety of supported browsers and different approaches. Table 12-7 provides a list of widely-used web application test frameworks worth evaluating.

Table 12-7. Web Application Test Frameworks

Framework	Description	More Information
Lightweight Test Automation Framework	The Lightweight Test Automation Framework is used by the Microsoft ASP.NET QA Team to automate browser testing. Tests are written in any .NET language to run tests in Microsoft Internet Explorer, Mozilla Firefox, Apple Safari, and Opera.	`aspnet.codeplex.com/wiki page?title=ASP.NET%20QA`
Selenium	Selenium is a free and open-source suite of tools that helps you to automate and control web browsers through a testing framework. Selenium supports many browsers, operating systems, programming languages, and testing frameworks.	`seleniumhq.org`
WatiN	WatiN is a free and open-source suite of tools that helps you automate your application testing in Internet Explorer and Firefox. It integrates with .NET unit test frameworks, such as NUnit, MbUnit, and xUnit.net.	`watin.org`

---

[18] Read more about UI test automation at `http://gojko.net/2010/04/13/how-to-implement-ui-testing-without-shooting-yourself-in-the-foot-2/`.

Windows Forms and Other UI Test Frameworks

Windows Forms, Windows Presentation Foundation (WPF), Flash, Silverlight, and other UI technologies present different challenges when testing the applications that use them. Some of the challenges of deploying and running the application are different than those found in browser automation. Many of the challenges are technical, such as having the test code select an item from a third-party dropdown list. Finding the right UI testing framework depends on so many factors that the only effective strategy is for you and your team to perform proof-of-concept prototyping and feasibility study to find an approach that is effective. Table 12-8 provides a list of widely-used UI test frameworks worth evaluating.

Table 12-8. Windows Forms and Other UI Test Frameworks

Framework	Description	More Information
NUnitForms	NUnitForms is a free and open-source NUnit extension for automating the testing of Windows Forms applications.	`nunitforms.sourceforge.net`
Ranorex	Ranorex offers commercial testing tools for the automated testing of Windows and web applications. It supports automating tests of Windows Forms, WPF, Flash, and Silverlight applications.	`www.ranorex.com`
Silverlight Toolkit	The Silverlight Toolkit supports automated Silverlight testing that allows unit tests to run in the browser.	`silverlight.codeplex.com`
White	White is a free and open-source project developed to hide the complexity of testing with the Microsoft UI Automation platform. It supports automating tests of Windows Forms, WPF, and Silverlight applications.	`white.codeplex.com`

Acceptance Testing Frameworks

In the broadest sense, acceptance testing is a series of tests that determine if the requirements and features of a software system are met. At some point in the development process a decision is made as to whether the software is ready. If the software does not meet the acceptance criteria then it is rarely put into production. The software must fulfill a set of minimum and essential requirements and must have all the necessary features. A formal acceptance phase methodically tests the software to determine if the software meets all the objectives, after which a decision is made as to whether the software is or is not acceptable. An informal acceptance phase relies on the decision-makers' judgment, based on what they know or don't know about the readiness of the system. Whether formal or informal, software that meets the acceptance criteria is the ultimate goal of the development team; it is the destination. To arrive at that destination the development team needs a navigation system to keep them on course. An acceptance test framework helps establish a navigation system to guide the team toward their ultimate goal: software that ships.

The goal of an acceptance test framework is to integrate the effort of customers, analysts, developers, and testers. For example, the customer describes the high-level need or desire for a new feature. The analyst works to understand, expand, and advance that information as a set of detailed requirements which are complete, clear, and consistent. The developers then take the detailed requirements and implement the software. The testers verify that the software meets the requirements. So, where does the acceptance test framework come in? The acceptance test framework is fed through examples and scenarios. The customer provides high-level, general examples of how the new feature is specified to work. These examples communicate conditions, outcomes, behaviors, and results.

These scenarios are fed into the framework as acceptance tests. The analyst may provide more detailed and elaborate scenarios, especially for exception handling, which are fed into the framework. The developers write software that satisfies the requirements and are explicit in these scenarios. The testers continue to feed test cases and scenarios as special cases, exceptions, and missing requirements are uncovered. The acceptance test framework provides a way to evaluate the software against the acceptance criteria.

The acceptance test framework ought to serve the goal of automating the acceptance testing. The advantages of automated acceptance testing include

- Keeping developers focused on the entire set of features and requirements

- Performing feature verification and regression testing

- Collecting metrics that are used to measure progress toward the desired results

- Providing guidance and direction based on acceptance criteria

Testing with Specifications and Behaviors

The primary goal of using specifications and behaviors to perform acceptance testing is to reach a common understanding between the analysts and the developers on the conditions and expected outcomes of the test cases. The key is to find a language that the analyst can use for behavior specifications that both the developer and the acceptance testing framework can also use to verify the software. It is a common language for everyone to work together and provide complete, clear, and consistent system behavior and requirement expectations.

■ **Practice 12-6** Acceptance Test with Business Specifications and Behaviors, Not Test Scripts

---

Too many people view automated testing as the execution of testing scripts. It is very important to understand and appreciate the difference between a test script and a specification.[19] The primary distinction is that test scripts are instructions fed to the testing framework, while a specification is a well-structured set of explicit statements about the requirements. A script focuses on the means and the methods of testing, while a specification focuses on conditions, outcomes, and results. Perhaps the biggest distinction is that analysts and product owners often do not take full ownership and responsibility for test scripts. These scripts are often tedious to read and rarely make explicit statements about requirements and behaviors.

Table 12-9 provides a list of widely-used acceptance test frameworks that use specifications as the underlying driver of acceptance testing.

---

[19] The Concordian site describes the differences between writing test scripts and specifications: http://www.concordion.org/Technique.html.

Table 12-9. Acceptance Test Frameworks

Framework	Description	More Information
FitNesse	Free and open-source framework that specifies requirements through wiki pages. The wiki markup describes the specification in a structured way.	`fitnesse.org`
SpecFlow	Free and open-source framework that specifies behaviors in the Gherkin language. Gherkin uses a *Given-When-Then* sentence structure to specify behaviors.	`specflow.org`
Concordion .NET	Free and open-source framework that works with the Gallio testing platform using a Concordion adapter plug-in. Specifications are written into an HTML file that matches to a test fixture that Gallio runs.	`code.google.com/p/concordion-net`

Business-Logic Acceptance Testing

Often software systems are built around a set of business rules. For example, a fixed-asset accounting system has the depreciation calculation engine as a central component of the software. The requirements for this module are governed by the generally-accepted accounting principles (GAAP) and the tax accounting rules and regulations. The analysts work hard to write detailed requirements for the developers to use to build the calculation engine. Also, testers work hard to write test cases and scenarios to verify and validate that the calculation engine is developed properly. The correctness and completeness of the business logic is central to determining if the software is acceptable. The developers benefit when the test cases that the analysts and testers provide feed an automated acceptance testing framework.

Situations like this exist in many domains, such as payroll systems, life insurance, banking, benefit systems, and many more. The important point is that automated acceptance testing does not have to involve the entire system working as an integrated whole. It can be used to continuously verify and validate a single business-logic module independent of the user interface, database, or any other part of the system. This is crucial when the acceptance of this module is at the very foundation of accepting the entire system.

To continue with the fixed-asset accounting system example, the analyst could use an Excel spreadsheet to develop detailed test cases and scenarios. This could be one spreadsheet providing one scenario in a structured format that has specific values for each of the input variables and calculates the expected results. The acceptance test framework is built to read the spreadsheet, provide the parameters to the depreciation engine, and verify that the engine calculates the expected results. Over time the analyst and testers work together to build a complete and comprehensive set of spreadsheets that cover all the acceptance criteria through test cases and scenarios. The challenge is to create a purpose-built acceptance test framework that takes the spreadsheet as input, arranges the module properly, performs the calculations, and then asserts that the actual results match the expected results.

■ **Practice 12-7** Develop a Purpose-Built Acceptance Testing Framework to Monitor Key Business Logic

A purpose-built acceptance testing framework can be a very effective tool for the development team to monitor and control the correctness and completeness of the business-logic modules. This approach is built upon the features provided by a unit testing framework, discussed earlier in this chapter. The fixture is responsible for providing the acceptance data to the test case with the test code performing the specific arrangement, actions, and assertions that carry out the acceptance test.

Summary

In this chapter you learned about the detailed features of testing frameworks, including NUnit, MbUnit, MSTest, and xUnit.net. You also learned about mock object frameworks, especially the stubbing and the interaction testing facilities they provide. This chapter included a discussion of NDbUnit and how to use this database testing framework to control the state of the database. You also learned about some available options for UI testing frameworks and acceptance testing.

In Chapter 13 the topic of the many biases and aversions that impact the adoption of new and different practices is discussed.

CHAPTER 13

Aversions and Biases

This chapter is about the tendencies of many people to keep better practices from being adopted. As human beings, we see the world, not as it is, but as we perceive it to be. If our eyes and mind could not deceive us then optical illusions would not work.[1] To explain the success of optical illusions, there are two basic theories:

- *Physiological Illusions:* Effects that are based on the manner by which things are sensed, which influences or changes our perceptions.

- *Cognitive Illusions:* Effects that are based on the manner by which things are judged, thought about, or remembered, which influences or changes our perceptions.

Although physiological illusions are interesting, it is not a topic we will cover in this chapter. It is unlikely that someone is opposing a better practice because they are literally seeing stars. The more relevant topic relates to the mental processes that influence and impact the adoption of better practices. More specifically, there are two ways cognitive perception often thwarts new or different practices:

- *Aversion:* Reluctance of an individual or group to accept, acknowledge, or adopt a new or different practice as a potentially better practice.

- *Bias:* Tendency or inclination of an individual or group to hold a particular view of a new or different practice to the detriment of its potential.

In the case of an aversion, the developer or team is not interested in the practice. In the case of a bias, the developer or team does not hold a fair or complete understanding of the practice. Some would argue that an aversion is simply a very strong bias. However, the distinction is important in that people are usually more willing to talk about practices that they are biased against. If there is an unwillingness to consider a change in practice then it is an aversion. If it is ambivalence, skepticism, uneasiness, or worry then there is likely a bias that needs to be overcome. It is important to know how to approach either an aversion or a bias.

Nobody wants to have food they cannot stand shoved down their throat, even if they are told it is "healthy." People often have an aversion to new or different practices for some reason; ultimately the reason may not turn out to be a good one, but it is still a reason. With the exception of exigent circumstances, such as a life and death situation, the worst way to deal with an aversion is to force the better practice upon the individual or group. In almost all cases, it is best to start by listening. Assume there are good reasons that you do not know about. Focus on finding those reasons. Not surprisingly, many good practices are made better by information that those that oppose the change in practice. They cannot articulate their concerns, and so, they have an aversion. You can benefit from knowing what they

---

[1] This site has a lot of great optical illusions: http://www.123opticalillusions.com/.

know or what they are reluctant to tell you. Do not expect to convince them to support the change, but you should fully convince them that you understand and appreciate their concerns.

In the case of a bias, the way to deal with the bias depends on the strength and nature of the bias. If it is a mild confusion then a brief explanation may be enough to eliminate the bias. Sometimes a little training is all that is needed. Other times you need to make a strong case in a group presentation. The goal is to make a persuasive case by cultivating a change in knowledge, skill, or attitude.

In the broadest sense, this chapter describes cognitive biases. These are observable behaviors that are studied in both cognitive science and social psychology. Experiments have shown that the information that is actually taken in by a person depends on that person's assumptions, aversions, biases, and preconceptions.[2] In other words, people cannot always see the evidence that is right in front of them. People tend to perceive what they expect to perceive. This is a bias that impacts people evaluating evidence. Researchers find biases in decision-making, thinking, interacting, and remembering. There are many, many cognitive biases and this chapter cannot provide practices to help you cope with *every* one of them. Instead, this chapter introduces a dozen aversions and biases and provides practices to help cope with those twelve, which are listed in Table 13-1. The hope is that by understanding how cognitive bias impacts changes in practice that you can learn to identify, cope with, and manage those biases.

Table 13-1. Coping with Aversions and Biases: Ruthlessly Helpful .NET Practices

	Strategy
13-1	Use Evidence to Support Better Practices That Reduce Undesirable Outcomes
13-2	Keep Notes As Problems and Events Occur to Provide Perspective During Retrospectives
13-3	Identify Specific Individuals and Approach Them About Improving Their Personal Practices
13-4	Make Incremental Positive Changes to Improve the Status Quo
13-5	Show the Balanced Picture of Desirable and Undesirable Qualities of Current Practices
13-6	Do Not Assume That Everyone Has the Same Skills and Abilities
13-7	Raise Awareness About the Negative Situations That Are Being Ignored
13-8	Relying on Past Luck to Prevent Future Problems Is Really Pressing Your Luck
13-9	Try Out a New or Different Practice to Clear Up Missing Information
13-10	Point Out Multiple Aspects to Broaden the Focus During Decision Making
13-11	Highlight Present Payoffs to Promote Incremental Improvement
13-12	Collect Anecdotes About the Problems Others Have Experienced to Prepare for Disaster

[2] This fascinating book covers many cognitive biases: Richards J Heuer, *Psychology of Intelligence Analysis* (Washington, DC: Center for the Study of Intelligence, Central Intelligence Agency, 1999).

Group-Serving Bias

There is a natural tendency for people to take credit for successes and distance themselves from failures. For the individual this is called a self-serving bias and for a group it is group-serving bias.[3] A development team would like to believe that what the team is doing is leading to success and that the problems and issues are caused by situations or circumstances beyond the control or influence of the team. This bias can inhibit the team from adopting better practices because they would have to first acknowledge that they bear some responsibility for the issues. The message they are resistant to hear is, "We could have done things better."

For example, a team of developers writes a lot of code under severe schedule pressure, and so there is little or no unit testing before the system is released to the quality assurance (QA) testers. The developers are happy to take credit for their productivity and extraordinary effort. However, the QA testers soon find that the system is not stable and that important functionality is incomplete or incorrect. The system is not working as intended. In this example, the evidence clearly shows that the software was deployed for QA to test before it was ready. At this point, the developers could acknowledge that more unit and integration testing on their part would have found these issues before QA testing began.

If the entire project understood and accepted that the developers were delivering an unstable and incomplete system then the responsibility is shared by the entire project team. If, on the other hand, the developers ignored or misrepresented the situation then the developers must bear the responsibility for releasing the system to QA before it was ready. The reality is often somewhere between these two extremes. The better practice is to not release the software to QA until the developers are convinced that the software is stable enough to test and that there are no significant showstopper issues.

▪ **Practice 13-1** Use Evidence to Support Better Practices That Reduce Undesirable Outcomes

---

There is often clear evidence that mistakes were or are being made and that things could be done better. Better practices are premised on the idea that mistakes can be avoided and that there are better ways to do things. Use that evidence to point to the better practices. In this section's example, the developers could have insisted that they needed time to determine if the system was ready for QA testing. They could have established a set of unit and integration tests. They could have worked with QA to establish the minimum and essential criteria that determines if the software is ready to be tested. The important practice here is to avoid the self-serving bias and look to the evidence that a better set of practices can lead to better outcomes.

Rosy Retrospection

It is nice to look back on an issue, mistake, or event and believe that it was not as bad as it seemed. People are biased to have a rosy memory and regard the past as being less negative or more positive than it really was.[4] When the problem came up, the situation may have been dire, but now that events are seen in retrospect, the problem is minimized. It is understandable that for unpredictable and uncontrollable events this helps people overcome the trauma of the event. Few people want to

---

[3] For more information see http://en.wikipedia.org/wiki/Self-serving_bias.
[4] For more information see http://en.wikipedia.org/wiki/Rosy_retrospection.

remember just how bad things were. However, if the event was preventable, this bias is unhelpful. The message is, "In retrospect, the problem was not that bad, so we can get through it if it happens again."

This tendency blocks many better practices from being adopted. Continuous integration is a practice that helps to avoid the long and difficult late-integration cycles that many development projects face. Too many developers forget how catastrophic late integration is. Instead of clearly remembering the difficulties involved, developers can rationalize the situation during a retrospective meeting. Late integration is described as an unavoidable obstacle that was overcome and will be overcome in the next iteration or a future project.

▪ **Practice 13-2** Keep Notes As Problems and Events Occur to Provide Perspective during Retrospectives

---

Jot down short notes on the pain-points and problems that are occurring as they are occurring. These notes help during retrospective meetings because they recall the real and serious concerns that underlie the issue. They help make the problems clearer and get people to focus on avoiding the preventable problems of the past by adopting better practices.

Group-Individual Appraisal

In some organizations, a manager scolds an entire department for the action or inaction of one or two individuals. The classic example is an e-mail that reprimands everyone in the organization for not submitting their timesheets on time. Those who submit their timesheets on time ignore the e-mail because it does not apply to them. Ironically, the many who do not turn in their timesheets on time also ignore the e-mail. Individuals are likely to think that nobody in the department is turning in their timesheet on time, and so assume their behavior is the norm. Individuals in the department ultimately attribute the poor appraisal to the entire department, not to themselves.

In the realm of software development, a team leader can gather the team and explain that the defect rate is unacceptably high. The team leader hopes that the one or two developers who are writing buggy code get the message and improve. This rarely works because those individual developers do not see themselves as responsible for the team's high defect rate.

▪ **Practice 13-3** Identify Specific Individuals and Approach Them About Improving Their Personal Practices

---

In this example, it would be better if the team leader talked to the individual developer directly about the unacceptably high defect rate. That developer needs to know that their individual performance is a problem for the team. Letting the developer know that their personal practices are expected to improve offers an opportunity to teach better practices.

Status Quo and System Justification

People become comfortable with the way things are. They like the status quo. Alternative ways of doing things are disparaged.[5] The existing state of affairs is familiar and a source of predictability. People have developed habits and have come to know what to do and how to do them. There is a bias toward justifying, defending, and supporting the status quo. Any disruption to the status quo is opposed, sometimes blocked. Some people cannot rationally discuss a new or different practice simply because it represents a change to the way things have always been done. The message is, "Do not introduce change because any change is disruptive and bad."

Some development environments have become entrenched in their practices and processes. One example is manual deployments. Perhaps a developer copies the files to the target server and changes the configuration settings. All the evidence shows that the manual deployments are error prone because the manual steps are regularly misapplied. Since some developers are careful and some are not, there is a lot of unevenness in the quality and reliability of the deployments. However, this is the way deployments have always been done. Nobody wants to adopt an automated deployment solution, in large part, because it changes the status quo.

■ **Practice 13-4** Make Incremental Positive Changes to Improve the Status Quo

---

People are afraid that if the status quo is destroyed they will be lost. A better message is one that focuses on bringing forth a slightly better status quo. The new status quo ought to keep all the benefits of the old status quo and introduce a few incremental improvements. In the case of the manual deployments, there could be a command file that copies the files to the target server. The developer still sees that the files go to the proper folders. That command file could also run an MSBuild script that sets all the configuration settings. Again, the developer reviews the values to double-check that the script works properly. The message is that only the tedious and error-prone parts of the task are improved without reducing the developer's involvement. The results from these incrementally better practices are more consistent and reliable deployments.

Illusory Superiority

Many people like to think that the way they are doing things is just as good, if not better, than some other way. In other words, there is an overestimation of the desirable qualities and an underestimation of the undesirable qualities, referred to as illusory superiority.[6] The message is, "The practice that we follow is superior to another new or different practice."

An example of this can be seen with regards to automated code analysis. Some team leaders feel that group code reviews are the only appropriate form of code analysis. To be sure, there are many desirable benefits of reviewing the source code as a group. Those benefits are undeniable. However, team code reviews do have undesirable qualities, as well. For one, they take up a significant amount of time. For another, they often do not occur frequently enough or cover enough of the source code. Most significantly, they can get bogged down in topics like coding standards and guidelines that the

---

[5] For more information see http://en.wikipedia.org/wiki/System_justification.
[6] For more information see http://en.wikipedia.org/wiki/Illusory_superiority.

automated code analysis tools readily identify. In other words, the group covers matters that should already be settled and ends up wasting time remediating preventable problems.

■ **Practice 13-5** Show the Balanced Picture of Desirable and Undesirable Qualities of Current Practices

---

The goal is to always keep things in perspective. Current practices should not be justified by ignoring the undesirable qualities of that practice. With manual code reviews, the practice can be enhanced by automated code analysis. For example, prior to the team getting together to review the code, the developer is expected to meet all the coding standards and guidelines that the automated code analysis tool is configured to find. Yes, exceptions may be warranted, and they should be brought to the attention of the group. In this way, the code review does not focus on the mundane and settled issues, but remains focused on the quality of the solution and the implementation of the design. The better practice is to recognize that undesirable qualities of current practices can be improved by new and different practices.

Dunning-Kruger Effect

A person with a lot of experience and expertise can make the assumption that others have the same understanding and skills that they have. This incorrect calibration of what others know is part of the Dunning-Kruger effect.[7] Experts can be biased to believe that if they know something then everyone else ought to know it as well. There is a mistaken assumption that their specialized knowledge is common knowledge. This can make them a weak advocate for better practices when faced with opposition or hesitation from others. Their bias leads them to believe that their detractors, who are assumed to be equally informed, have good reasons to oppose them. In many cases, this is simply not true.

For example, a developer who has been unit testing code for ten years has acquired a lot of experience. If they read widely and keep on unit testing then they bring the experience and expertise of others. This aptitude, skill, and knowledge justifies their strongly-held position that unit testing is a beneficial practice. Another less experienced developer, who has limited experience unit testing, might view the practice as unproductive and unhelpful. The experienced advocate wrongly assumes that his or her colleague is equally skilled, and therefore, does not promote the practice of unit testing. An opportunity to benefit from the experience and expertise of the more senior developer is lost.

■ **Practice 13-6** Do Not Assume That Everyone Has the Same Skills and Abilities

---

Start with the premise that everyone has different experiences, skills, and abilities. Assume that, knowing what you know, they would be likely to support the better practices you advocate. This approach suggests building a proof-of-concept, having a trial period, running a pilot project, or designing a training exercise. The goal is to get everyone closer together on the evidence as to whether the practice is better or not better. The most important thing is to focus on knowledge transfer and better practices through experience and know-how.

---

[7] For more information see http://en.wikipedia.org/wiki/Dunning%E2%80%93Kruger_effect.

Ostrich Effect

All too often, people ignore an obviously negative situation instead of dealing with it straight on. Like the proverbial ostrich, they bury their head in the sand to avoid the dire circumstances that surround them.[8] The implications of facing the situation may be too painful to deal with and sometimes they hope that by ignoring the situation it will improve on its own. Others may believe that by not recognizing the negative situation they cannot be held accountable for not resolving it. This message is, "If I do not see the problems, I do not have to deal with the problems."

An example of the ostrich effect in software development is security and threat assessment. Software vulnerabilities are a growing problem; however, all too many developers are not involved enough in dealing with security and minimizing vulnerabilities. Developing systems that are "secure by design" requires that those developers who design and build the software are actively assessing the security of the software. Ignoring security and not worrying about vulnerabilities and threats cannot lead to secure designs. No aspect of the software is improved by ignoring the potential or existing problems that lie within that aspect of software development.

■ **Practice 13-7** Raise Awareness About the Negative Situations That Are Being Ignored

---

The security development lifecycle is all about thinking through the security implications of decisions at every step of development. One example is the practice of threat modeling. Through this practice the design is considered from a threat vulnerability perspective so that potential negative situations are revealed. With the information that comes from threat modeling, designs can then be improved. In general, directly confronting current and potential negative situations is one of the most effective ways to prevent problems and adopt better practices.

Gambler's Fallacy

To the person who plays the lottery with the same numbers every day there is often the mistaken assumption that their odds improve each time their numbers are not chosen as the winning numbers. The biased belief that past events influence future probabilities is the gambler's fallacy.[9] The odds of winning are always the same and are not influenced by past events. Similarly, past luck does not influence future luck. When it comes to resisting new and different practices that prevent problems there can be some of the gambler in all of us. The message is, "We have avoided any problems so far, so let's assume we will continue to avoid problems."

This can be seen in software development when important practices are ignored only because problems have not yet occurred. For example, the uninitiated developer may not like reversion control. They prefer to operate on their own development environment free from the constraints of the version control system. They do not regularly check in their code or get the latest code from the other developers. They rely on the fact that, since they have always been able to manage things this way, they can continue to operate in this way. When their luck runs out and the problems come from late integration, lost changes, or worse problems, it is their unwise decision not to follow best practices that is to blame.

---

[8] For more information see http://en.wikipedia.org/wiki/Ostrich_effect.
[9] For more information see http://en.wikipedia.org/wiki/Gambler%27s_fallacy.

▪ **Practice 13-8** Relying on Past Luck to Prevent Future Problems Is Really Pressing Your Luck

---

Direct and unambiguous communication is very important to adopting a better practice. It must be made clear that not following a practice that prevents problems is unwise and unacceptable. Any past luck developers have had not following the practice needs to be quickly forgotten. The project's gamblers need to stop gambling to ensure that better practices are consistently followed.

Ambiguity Effect

When there is ambiguity or missing information there is a tendency to avoid a direction, practice, or option. It may be a better practice, however, simply because there is not enough information; there is a bias against the potentially better practice.[10] People are uncomfortable with ambiguity, but that should not mean a new or different practice is to be avoided. It means the practice needs to be understood, investigated, and appreciated. Once the uncertainty is cleared up then it can be recognized as a helpful practice or discarded as an unhelpful practice.

There is a lot of ambiguity that surrounds unit testing. Some developers avoid unit testing simply because they have more questions than answers. They avoid the practice because they do not know where to start or how to proceed. The same is true for other new and different practices that offer a lot of promise but present a lot of uncertainty as well.

▪ **Practice 13-9** Try Out a New or Different Practice to Clear Up Missing Information

---

Often a little experience or a short tutorial on a better practice can fill in the missing information that is holding back adoption. Other times the team needs to try out the practice for a short period of time just to clear up some vagueness and doubt. This is especially true when their reluctance relates to feasibility and practicality. In the case of unit testing, many developers have found that unit testing is helpful and improves their overall productivity. This is true once they have experienced the benefits of problem prevention and early defect resolution. It is the simple act of trying out a potentially better practice that fills in the missing pieces and convinces the team to adopt the practice.

Focusing Effect

There is a tendency, called the focusing effect, for people to put too much emphasis on one aspect of a problem or event during decision making.[11] Often there are many contributing factors that influence things; however, many people search for or focus on one in particular. Since there is a singular focus, this bias can lead to a situation where the important impacts of the other aspects are ignored.

When investigating a significant problem, the focusing effect bias can lead people to search for just one root cause. In actual fact, there may be many contributing factors to the problem. Each of the contributing factors created the conditions or caused the actions that led to the problem. The problem-

---

[10] For more information see http://en.wikipedia.org/wiki/Ambiguity_effect.
[11] For more information see http://en.wikipedia.org/wiki/Focusing_effect.

solving effort ought to lead to more than one recommended change; however, only one aspect is seriously considered. Instead of a set of better practices being selected, only one is selected. Sometimes, no change in practice is recommended because the one aspect that was investigated is an unavoidable aspect. It is better to review all the contributing factors of a problem because a better practice can change the conditions and prevent the problem.

▨ **Practice 13-10** Point Out Multiple Aspects to Broaden the Focus During Decision Making

---

It is usually better to assume that there are multiple reasons that a problem or event occurred. There are usually multiple conditions that existed at the time the problem occurred. There are multiple actions that happened or failed to happen that contributed to the problem. Expand the focus to multiple causes as a way to reveal many more new and different practices that can improve the situation.

Hyperbolic Discounting

Risk and reward are not always considered in a rational way. Add in the element of time delay and the tendency is to favor the immediate reward, even though the delayed reward will be greater. This is the cognitive bias that underlies hyperbolic discounting.[12] Given two options that have the same risk, many people prefer a smaller reward that they can realize today rather than wait for a larger reward that comes later on. A payoff today is enjoyed today, but a future payoff requires the person to wait to enjoy it.

Understanding this bias is applicable to best practices in the idea of incremental improvement. In software development, better practices are sometimes not adopted because there are several options, and no one option is a clear favorite. Some take a long time to show improvement and require significant effort to get started, but offer huge potential benefits. Others can show immediate results, but the potential benefits are modest. In these cases, the practice that shows the quickest results could be the one to emphasize. The relatively quick rewards that come from the payoff are very gratifying and support further incremental improvement. The decision-makers appreciate the immediate reward of supporting the change.

▨ **Practice 13-11** Highlight Present Payoffs to Promote Incremental Improvement

---

Take time to consider the many better practices that can be implemented. Some are likely to produce immediate or near-term improvements. Those are the practices that have early payoffs and should be promoted. Adopting better practices is an initiative that is helped by incremental, not radical, changes. As each better practice is put into place the rewards of the previously selected practices help keep the initiative active.

---

[12] For more information see http://en.wikipedia.org/wiki/Hyperbolic_discounting.

Normalcy Bias

Too often people do not plan for a problem or event simply because it has never happened to them before. Since they have not had the experience, they are biased against the need to plan for the problem. This is the normalcy bias.[13] Most people plan for eventualities that are expected over the normal course of events. On the other hand, there are unexpected and disastrous events that are out of the ordinary, which many people do not prepare for. Some people refuse to plan for a disaster only because they have not experienced the disaster before.

Today, many companies are experiencing problems related to cyber attacks and hacking. However, some development groups refuse to plan or prepare for these attacks and other threats. Unlike the ostrich effect, the danger is not present, and so it is hard to point to a specific problem that is or has happened. Today things seem normal and calm, but there is a disaster waiting to happen. The better practice is opposed simply because the problem has never happened to them before.

▪ **Practice 13-12** Collect Anecdotes About the Problems Others Have Experienced to Prepare for Disaster

---

Have you read an article that describes how another organization had to cope with a denial of service attack? The stories range from annoying to very ugly.[14] In the news recently, a major corporation sent e-mails to all their customers advising them that their personal information, including credit card information, was compromised. Consider the impact to your organization if they had to let all your users know that their personal data is now in the hands of an intruder. The horrible experiences of others can be a powerful motivator that counteracts the normalcy bias. Collect the anecdotes and experiences of others who have not followed best practices and use that information to support a change in practices.

Summary

In this chapter you learned about the influence that cognitive biases have upon following or changing better practices. Since software development is significantly impacted by individuals interacting, it stands to reason that how an individual or group perceives and thinks about a new and different practice is very important. Now that you have read about the gambler's fallacy, the Dunning-Kruger effect, and the group-serving bias it should be clear that rational argument alone is frequently insufficient to advance a change in practice. You may need to understand the aversion. You may need to counteract a bias.

---

[13] For more information see http://en.wikipedia.org/wiki/Normalcy_bias.
[14] Phil Haack describes his experiences at http://haacked.com/archive/2008/08/22/dealing-with-denial-of-service-attacks.aspx.

APPENDIX A

Resources

This appendix covers the following topics:

- General Software Development
- .NET Guidelines, Patterns, and Practices
- C# Language
- Testing and Test Frameworks
- Debugging and Problem Solving
- Build Automation
- Continuous Integration
- Static Code Analysis
- Dynamic Code Analysis
- Security
- Research Areas
- Miscellaneous

Each topic contains the following resources:

- Books
- Articles
- Guides and Tutorials
- Tools

General Software Development

Books

- Steve McConnell, *Rapid Development* (Redmond, WA.: Microsoft Press, 1996).

- Grady Booch, *Object Solutions: Managing the Object-Oriented Project* (Menlo Park, CA: Addison-Wesley, 1996).

- Kyle Baley, Donald Belcham, *Brownfield Application Development in .NET* (Greenwich, CT: Manning, 2010).

- Michael C. Feathers, *Working Effectively with Legacy Code* (Upper Saddle River, NJ: Prentice Hall Professional, 2007).

- Joachim Rossberg, *Pro Visual Studio Team System Application Lifecycle Management* (New York: Apress, 2008)

- Will Stott, James Newkirk, *Visual Studio Team System: Better Software Development for Agile Teams* (Upper Saddle River, NJ: Addison-Wesley, 2007)

- Microsoft Corporation, *Building Secure Microsoft ASP.NET Applications* (Redmond, WA: Microsoft Press, 2003)

- James Avery, Jim Holmes, *Windows Developer Power Tools* (Sebastopol, CA: O'Reilly Media, Inc., 2006)

Articles

- "The Manifesto for Agile Software Development," agilemanifesto.org.

- Martin Fowler, "Technical Debt," http://www.martinfowler.com/bliki/TechnicalDebt.html.

- Martin Fowler, "Technical Debt Quadrant," http://martinfowler.com/bliki/TechnicalDebtQuadrant.html.

- Jeff Atwood, "Paying Down Your Technical Debt," www.codinghorror.com/blog/2009/02/paying-down-your-technical-debt.html, February 27, 2009.

- Construx Conversations, "Technical Debt," forums.construx.com/blogs/stevemcc/archive/2007/11/01/technical-debt-2.aspx.

- AgileManiac, "Reinvigorated Retrospectives," agilemaniac.com/tag/4ls.

- Microsoft web site, "Microsoft Visual Studio Roadmap," www.microsoft.com/visualstudio/en-us/roadmap.

Guides

- Available at agilemanifesto.org.

- Code Kata: codekata.pragprog.com.

- For a list of wide-ranging brainstorming techniques see celestinechua.com/blog/25-brainstorming-techniques.

- Ward Cunningham Wiki: c2.com/cgi/wiki.

.NET Guidelines, Patterns and Practices

Books

- Krzysztof Cwalina, Brad Abrams, *Framework Design Guidelines: Conventions, Idioms, and Patterns for Reusable .NET Libraries, 2nd Edition* (Upper Saddle River, NJ: Addison-Wesley Professional, 2008). This book contains many best practices for designing reusable libraries for the Microsoft .NET Framework.

- Steve McConnell, *Code Complete* (Redmond, WA: Microsoft Press, 2004).

- Robert C. Martin, *Clean Code: A Handbook of Agile Software Craftsmanship* (Upper Saddle River, NJ: Prentice Hall, 2008).

- Kevlin Henney, *97 Things Every Programmer Should Know: Collective Wisdom from the Experts* (Sebastopol, CA: O'Reilly Media, Inc., 2010).

- Martin Fowler, Kent Beck, *Refactoring: Improving the Design of Existing Code* (Reading, MA: Addison-Wesley Professional, 1999).

- Kent Beck, *Implementation Patterns* (Upper Saddle River, NJ: Addison-Wesley Professional, 2008).

- Adam Freeman, Steven Sanderson, *Pro ASP.NET MVC 3 Framework, Third Edition* (New York: Apress, 2011).

- Books from Microsoft patterns & practices:
  msdn.microsoft.com/en-us/practices/hh124092.

Articles

- Michael Howard, "8 Simple Rules For Developing More Secure Code," msdn.microsoft.com/en-us/magazine/cc163518.aspx, MSDN Magazine, November 2006.

- John Robbins, "Bad Code? FxCop to the Rescue," msdn.microsoft.com/en-us/magazine/cc188721.aspx, MSDN Magazine, June 2004.

- Niraj Bhatt, "MVC vs. MVP vs. MVVM," nirajrules.wordpress.com/2009/07/18/mvc-vs-mvp-vs-mvvm, 2011.

- Martin Fowler, "Inversion of Control Containers and the Dependency Injection pattern," martinfowler.com/articles/injection.html, 2004.

- Elegant Code, "IoC Libraries Compared," elegantcode.com/2009/01/07/ioc-libraries-compared, 2009.

- MSDN Library, "Managed Extensibility Framework (MEF) Overview," msdn.microsoft.com/en-us/library/dd460648.aspx, 2010.

- Ayende@Rahien, "The Managed Extensibility Framework," ayende.com/blog/3611/the-managed-extensibility-framework, 2008.

Guides and Tutorials

- MSDN Library, "Design Guidelines for Developing Class Libraries," msdn.microsoft.com/en-us/library/ms229042.aspx.

- Gendarme Rules: www.mono-project.com/Gendarme.

- StyleCop documentation: stylecop.codeplex.com/documentation.

- Microsoft patterns & practices Developer's Guide: msdn.microsoft.com/en-us/library/ff953181(v=PandP.50).aspx.

- Encodo C# Handbook: archive.msdn.microsoft.com/encodocsharphandbook.

- Microsoft All-In-One Code Framework: 1code.codeplex.com.

- Idesign C# Coding Standards: www.idesign.net.

- CAT.NET Rules: www.microsoft.com/security/sdl/adopt/tools.aspx.

C# Language

Books

- Joseph Albahari, Ben Albahari, *C# 4.0 in a Nutshell* (Sebastopol, CA: O'Reilly Media, Inc., 2010).

- Jon Skeet, *C# in Depth, 2nd Edition* (Greenwich, CT: Manning, 2008).

- Andrew Troelsen, *Pro C# 2010 and the .NET 4 Platform, 5th Edition* (New York: Apress, 2010).

Articles

- Developer Journey, "Code Contracts," http://devjourney.com/blog/code-contracts-part-1-introduction. A very comprehensive treatment of Code Contracts in this 14-part series of blog postings, 2010.

Testing and Test Frameworks

Books

- Roy Osherove, *The Art of Unit Testing* (Greenwich, CT: Manning, 2009).

- Andy Hunt, Dave Thomas, Matt Hargett, *Pragmatic Unit Testing in C# with NUnit* (Raleigh, NC: Pragmatic Bookshelf, 2007).

- Cem Kaner, James Bach, Bret Pettichord, *Lessons Learned in Software Testing: a Context-Driven Approach* (New York: Wiley, 2002).

- James Avery, Jim Holmes, *Windows Developer Power Tools*, (Sebastopol, CA: O'Reilly Media, Inc., 2007)

- Steve Freeman, Nat Pryce, *Growing Object-Oriented Software, Guided by Tests* (Upper Saddle River, NJ: Addison-Wesley Professional, 2009)

- David Astels, *Test-Driven Development: a Practical Guide* (Prentice Hall PTR, 2003).

- Automation

  - James D. McCaffrey, *.NET Test Automation Recipes: a Problem-Solution Approach* (New York: Apress, 2006).

  - Daniel J. Mosley, Bruce A. Posey, *Just Enough Software Test Automation* (Upper Saddle River, NJ: Prentice Hall Professional, 2002).

- Web Testing

  - Jeff McWherter, Ben Hall, *Testing ASP.NET Web Applications* (Indianapolis: John Wiley & Sons, 2011).

  - Alan John Richardson, *Selenium Simplified* (Compendium Developments, 2010).

  - Gojko Adzic, *Test Driven .NET Development with FitNesse*, (London: Neuri, 2008).

Articles

- Agile Data, "Introduction to Test Driven Design (TDD)," `www.agiledata.org/essays/tdd.html`.

- "Arrange Act Assert (3-As) pattern," `c2.com/cgi/wiki?ArrangeActAssert`.

- Will Stott and James Newkirk, MSDN Magazine, "Improve the Design and Flexibility of Your Project with Extreme Programming Techniques," `msdn.microsoft.com/en-us/magazine/cc163982.aspx`, April 2004.

- Codevanced, "Mocking Frameworks Comparison," `codevanced.net/post/Mocking-frameworks-comparison.aspx`.

Guides and Tutorials

- MSDN Library, "Guidelines for Test-Driven Development," `msdn.microsoft.com/en-us/library/aa730844(v=vs.80).aspx`

- Open Source C# Testing Tools: `csharpopensource.com/csharptesting.aspx`

- Open Source Web Testing Tools: `csharpopensource.com/webtesting.aspx`

Tools

- Test Runner:
    - Visual Studio Unit Testing Framework (MSTest): msdn.microsoft.com/en-us/library/ms243147.aspx
    - NUnit: www.nunit.org
    - xUnit.net: xunit.codeplex.com
    - MbUnit: mbunit.com
- Mock Object Framework:
    - Moq: code.google.com/p/moq
    - TypeMock: www.typemock.com
    - NMock 2: sourceforge.net/projects/nmock2
    - Rhino-Mocks: github.com/ayende/rhino-mocks
- Browser Automation
    - Coded UI Test (Visual Studio UI Automation Testing): msdn.microsoft.com/en-us/library/dd286681.aspx
    - Lightweight Test Automation Framework: aspnet.codeplex.com
    - Selenium: seleniumhq.org
    - WatiN: watin.org
- NUnit Test Generator: www.kellermansoftware.com/p-30-nunit-test-generator.aspx
- Pex and Moles: research.microsoft.com/en-us/projects/pex/downloads.aspx
- NDbUnit: code.google.com/p/ndbunit
- MvcIntegrationTestFramework: blog.stevensanderson.com/2009/06/11/integration-testing-your-aspnet-mvc-application
- SMTP Server Emulation for Developers: antix.co.uk/Projects/SMTP-Impostor-an-SMTP-server-for-developers

Debugging and Problem Solving

Books

- Darin Dillon, *Debugging Strategies For .NET Developers* (Berkeley, CA: Apress, 2003).

- Mario Hewardt, *Advanced .NET Debugging* (Upper Saddle River, NJ: Addison-Wesley Professional, 2010).

- John Robbins, *Debugging Microsoft .Net 2.0 Applications* (Redmond, WA: Microsoft Press, 2007).

- Dean L. Gano, *Apollo Root Cause Analysis: A New Way of Thinking* (Richland, WA: Apollonian Publications, 2008).

Articles

- Dean Gano, "Effective Solutions vs the Root Cause Myth," `www.apollorca.com/_public/site/files/Effective%20Solutions%20vs%20Root%20Cause%20Myth.pdf`.

Tools

- Debugging Tools Download: `www.microsoft.com/download/en/details.aspx?id=10640`

Build Automation

Books

- Sayed Ibrahim Hashimi, William Bartholomew, *Inside the Microsoft Build Engine: Using MSBuild and Team Foundation Build*, (Redmond, WA: Microsoft Press, 2011).

- Sayed Ibrahim Hashimi, *Deploying .NET Applications: Learning MSBuild and ClickOnce*, (Berkeley, CA: Apress 2006).

- Mike Clark, *Pragmatic Project Automation: How to Build, Deploy, and Monitor Java Applications* (Raleigh, NC: Pragmatic Bookshelf, 2004).

Articles

- MSDN, "Logging in MSBuild," `msdn.microsoft.com/en-us/library/bb651789.aspx`.

- MSDN, "Well-known Item Metadata," `msdn.microsoft.com/en-us/library/ms164313(v=VS.100).aspx`.

- MSDN, "MSBuild Inline Tasks," `msdn.microsoft.com/en-us/library/dd722601.aspx`.

- Vishal Joshi, "Web Packaging: Creating web packages using MSBuild," `vishaljoshi.blogspot.com/2009/02/web-packaging-creating-web-packages.html`, 2009.

- Andrei Volkov, "How to 'Package/Publish' Web Site project using VS2010 and MSBuild," zvolkov.com/blog/post/2010/05/18/How-to-Publish-Web-Site-project-using-VS2010-and-MsBuild.aspx, 2010.

- MSDN, "How to: Transform Web.config When Deploying a Web Application Project," msdn.microsoft.com/en-us/library/dd465318.aspx.

- Scott Hanselman, "Web Deployment Made Awesome: If You're Using XCopy, You're Doing It Wrong," www.hanselman.com/blog/WebDeploymentMadeAwesomeIfYoureUsingXCopyYoureDoingItWrong.aspx, 2010.

- "Troubleshooting Common MSDeploy Issues," blogs.iis.net/kateroh/archive/2009/06/05/troubleshooting-common-msdeploy-issues.aspx, June 5, 2009.

- Kristina Olson, "Code Download and the Web Deployment Tool (MSDeploy) - Remote Management options,"blogs.iis.net/krolson/archive/2010/01/27/code-download-and-the-web-deployment-tool-msdeploy-remote-management-options.aspx, January 27, 2010.

- Sourceforge, "NAnt Fundamentals," nant.sourceforge.net/release/latest/help/fundamentals.

- Davesquared.net,"Basic .NET builds using Rake," www.davesquared.net/2009/04/basic-net-builds-using-rake.html.

Guides and Tutorials

- MSBuild team blog: blogs.msdn.com/b/msbuild

- Visual Studio blog: blogs.msdn.com/b/visualstudio/archive/tags/msbuild

- Sayed Ibrahim Hashimi blog: sedodream.com

- Mike Fourie blog: mikefourie.wordpress.com

- MSBuild: By Example: en.csharp-online.net/MSBuild:_By_Example

- 7 Steps to MSBuild: brennan.offwhite.net/blog/2006/11/30/7-steps-to-msbuild

- Buck Hodges blog: blogs.msdn.com/b/buckh

Tools

- Build Tools: see Table 10-2

- MSBuild Extension Pack: msbuildextensionpack.codeplex.com

- Community TFS Build Extensions: tfsbuildextensions.codeplex.com

- MSBuild Community Tasks Project: msbuildtasks.tigris.org

- Web Deploy 2.0: www.iis.net/download/webdeploy

- Windows Installer XML (WiX) Toolset: `wix.sourceforge.net`

Continuous Integration

Books

- Marcin Kawalerowicz, Craig Berntson, *Continuous Integration in .NET* (Greenwich, CT: Manning Publications, 2011).

- Paul M. Duvall, Steve Matyas, Andrew Glover, *Continuous Integration: Improving Software Quality and Reducing Risk*, (Upper Saddle River, NJ: Addison-Wesley, 2007).

- John Ferguson Smart, *Jenkins: The Definitive Guide* (Sebastopol, CA: O'Reilly Media, Inc., 2011).

Articles

- The original CI article: `http://martinfowler.com/articles/originalContinuousIntegration.html`.

- Ward Cunningham describes Integration Hell in his wiki: `c2.com/cgi/wiki?IntegrationHell`.

Guides and Tutorials

- JetBrains provides a getting started guide for TeamCity: `http://confluence.jetbrains.net/display/TCD65/Getting+Started`.

- CruiseControl.NET provides installation and getting started guides on their project website: `http://www.cruisecontrolnet.org/projects/ccnet`.

- David Veksler provides a jumpstart for CI with TFS 2010: `http://dotmac.rationalmind.net/2011/03/continuous-integration-with-tfs/`.

- Patrick Weibel provides a Jenkins jumpstart for .NET development: `http://blog.eweibel.net/?p=982`.

Tools

- TFS 2010 Power Tools: `http://msdn.microsoft.com/en-us/vstudio/bb980963`.

- CCNetConfig is a GUI tool to manage CC.NET configuration files: `http://ccnetconfig.codeplex.com/`.

- Continuous Integration servers: see Table 11-2

Static Code Analysis

Books

- Brian Chess, Jacob West, *Secure Programming with Static Analysis* (Upper Saddle River, NJ: Addison-Wesley, 2007).

- Donis Marshall, John Bruno, *Solid Code: Optimizing the Software Development Life Cycle* (Redmond, WA: Microsoft Press, 2009). Chapter 10 provides an overview of code analysis and quality metrics.

Articles

- Scott Hanselman, "Educating Programmers with Placemats - NDepend Static Analysis Poster," `www.hanselman.com/blog/EducatingProgrammersWithPlacematsNDependStaticAnalysisPoster.aspx`, June 2, 2007. Scott Hanselman provides a great overview of the NDepend metrics in this blog post.

- MSDN, "Analyzing Managed Code Quality by Using Code Analysis," `msdn.microsoft.com/en-us/library/dd264939.aspx`.

- CodePlex, "A Brief History of C# Style," `stylecop.codeplex.com/wikipage?title=A%20Brief%20History%20of%20CSharp%20Style`.

- John Robbins, "Bad Code? FxCop to the Rescue," `msdn.microsoft.com/en-us/magazine/cc188721.aspx`, MSDN Magazine, June 2004.

- Anoop Madhusudanan, "Top 5 Common programming mistakes .NET developers must avoid !!" `www.amazedsaint.com/2010/02/top-5-common-programming-mistakes-net.html`, February 8, 2010.

- Jeff Atwood, "Code Smells," `www.codinghorror.com/blog/2006/05/code-smells.html`, May 18, 2006.

Guides and Tutorials

- Visual Studio 2010 Code Analysis Rule Set Reference for Managed Code: `msdn.microsoft.com/en-us/library/dd264925.aspx`

- StyleCop documentation: `stylecop.codeplex.com/documentation`

- JetBrains Code Inspection wiki: `confluence.jetbrains.net/display/ReSharper/Code+Inspection+Wiki`

Tools

- StyleCop: `stylecop.codeplex.com`.

- Gendarme: www.mono-project.com/Gendarme. Gendarme is a rule-based tool to find problems in .NET applications and libraries.

- ReSharper: www.jetbrains.com/resharper/.

- . NET Assembly Browsing and Decompiling (see Table 12-3).

- Differencing: see Table 12-4.

- Duplicate Code Finders: see Table 12-5.

- Architecture and Design: see Table 12-8.

Dynamic Code Analysis

Books

- Michael Sutton, Adam Greene, Pedram Amini, *Fuzzing: Brute Force Vulnerability Discovery* (Upper Saddle River, NJ: Addison-Wesley, 2007).

- Ian Molyneaux, *The Art of Application Performance Testing* (Sebastopol, CA: O'Reilly Media, Inc., 2009). Effective automated performance testing is a big part of dynamic code analysis.

- Microsoft Corporation, J. Meier, *Performance Testing Guidance for Web Applications* (Redmond, WA: Microsoft Press, 2007). This book is available in PDF from Microsoft patterns & practices: http://www.codeplex.com/PerfTestingGuide/Release/ProjectReleases.aspx?ReleaseId=6690.

Articles

- Rahul V. Patil, Boby George, "Tools And Techniques to Identify Concurrency Issues," http://msdn.microsoft.com/en-us/magazine/cc546569.aspx, MSDN Magazine, June 2008 .

Guides and Tutorials

- Terrence Dorsey, "Tools and Techniques for .NET Code Profiling," http://msdn.microsoft.com/en-us/magazine/hh288073.aspx, MSDN Magazine, July 2011.

- Visual Studio 2010 Ultimate, "Testing Application Performance and Stress," http://msdn.microsoft.com/en-us/library/dd293540.aspx.

- Visual Studio 2010 Ultimate, "Creating and Editing Load and Web Performance Tests," http://msdn.microsoft.com/en-us/library/ee923687.aspx

- "Visual Studio 2010 Walkthrough: Run Tests and View Code Coverage," http://msdn.microsoft.com/en-us/library/ms182534.aspx.

Tools

- Performance
    - Microsoft Visual Studio Ultimate and Premium: www.microsoft.com/visualstudio/en-us/products
    - JetBrains dotTrace: www.jetbrains.com/profiler
    - Red Gate Software ANTS Performance Profiler: www.red-gate.com/products/dotnet-development/ants-performance-profiler
    - EQATEC Profiler: eqatec.com/Profiler/Home.aspx
- Code Coverage: see Table 12-10
- Query Profiling: see Table 12-11

Security

Books

- J. D. Meier, *Improving Web application security: threats and countermeasures*, (Redmond, WA: Microsoft, 2003).
- Frank Swiderski, Window Snyder, *Threat Modeling* (Redmond, WA: Microsoft Press, 2004.)

Articles

- Michael Howard, "A Look Inside the Security Development Lifecycle at Microsoft," msdn.microsoft.com/en-us/magazine/cc163705.aspx.
- Microsoft Security Development Lifecycle, "Writing Fuzzable Code," blogs.msdn.com/b/sdl/archive/2010/07/07/writing-fuzzable-code.aspx.
- Microsoft Security Development Lifecycle, "Microsoft Security Development Lifecycle Process Tools," www.microsoft.com/security/sdl/adopt/tools.aspx.
- Michael Howard, "8 Simple Rules For Developing More Secure Code," msdn.microsoft.com/en-us/magazine/cc163518.aspx, MSDN Magazine, November 2006,
- MSDN, "Security in the .NET Framework," msdn.microsoft.com/en-us/library/fkytk30f.aspx.
- Michael Howard, "Threat Models Improve Your Security Process," msdn.microsoft.com/en-us/magazine/dd148644.aspx, MSDN Magazine, November 2008.
- Marcus Ranum, Fred Avolio, "Seven Tenets of Good Security," www.avolio.com/papers/7tenets.html.

- Peter Torr, MSDN Blogs, "High-Level Threat Modelling Process," `blogs.msdn.com/b/ptorr/archive/2005/02/08/368881.aspx`, February 8, 2005.

- Peter Torr, MSDN Blogs, "Guerrilla Threat Modeling," `blogs.msdn.com/b/ptorr/archive/2005/02/22/guerillathreatmodelling.aspx`, February 22, 2005.

- MSDN, "ASP.NET Security," `msdn.microsoft.com/en-us/library/91f66yxt.aspx`.

Guides and Tutorials

- Security and Identity: `msdn.microsoft.com/en-us/library/ee663293(v=VS.85).aspx`

- Secure Coding Guidelines: `msdn.microsoft.com/en-us/library/8a3x2b7f.aspx`

- MSDN Blogs, Security Tools: `blogs.msdn.com/b/securitytools`

- Microsoft Security Development Lifecycle Core Training classes: `www.microsoft.com/download/en/details.aspx?displaylang=en&id=16420`. Microsoft made its four core SDL Training classes available to the public.

- Security How-to Topics: `msdn.microsoft.com/en-us/library/ms172378.aspx`

- Microsoft Security Development Lifecycle (SDL) – Process Guidance: `msdn.microsoft.com/en-us/library/cc307891.aspx`

Tools

- Microsoft Web Protection Library: `wpl.codeplex.com`

Microsoft Research

- Microsoft Research: `research.microsoft.com`.

- DevLabs: `msdn.microsoft.com/en-us/devlabs`.

- Spec#: `research.microsoft.com/en-us/projects/specsharp`

- Automated Test Generation: `research.microsoft.com/en-us/projects/atg`

- Pex and Moles - Isolation and White box Unit Testing for .NET: `research.microsoft.com/en-us/projects/pex`

- Holmes: Automated Statistical Debugging for .NET: `research.microsoft.com/en-us/projects/holmes`

- Code Contracts: `research.microsoft.com/en-us/projects/contracts`

Miscellaneous

Books

- Stephen R. Covey, *Principle Centered Leadership* (New York: Summit, 1991).

- Richards J Heuer, *Psychology of Intelligence Analysis* (Washington, DC: Center for the Study of Intelligence, Central Intelligence Agency, 1999).

- Richard Marcinko, *Leadership Secrets of the Rogue Warrior: A Commando's Guide to Success* (New York: Simon and Schuster, 2000).

- Stephen M. R. Covey, Rebecca R. Merrill, Stephen R. Covey, *The Speed of Trust: The One Thing That Changes Everything* (New York, Simon and Schuster, 2008)

- Fergus O'Connell, *How to Run Successful Projects III: the Silver Bullet* (New York: Addison Wesley, 2001).

- Fergus O'Connell, *The Competitive Advantage of Common Sense: Using the Power You Already Have* (FT Press, 2003).

Articles

- Joel Spolsky, "*A Little Less Conversation,*" www.inc.com/magazine/20100201/a-little-less-conversation.html, Inc. Magazine, Feb 2010.

- Wikipedia, "Cognitive bias," en.wikipedia.org/wiki/Cognitive_bias.

- Wikipedia, "List of cognitive biases," en.wikipedia.org/wiki/List_of_cognitive_biases.

Scorecard

A scorecard is any structured report that helps guide and monitor the activities and actions that relate to an initiative. Steve McConnell created the Software Project Survival Test as a way to score software project management.[1] His test is a scorecard that helps estimate a project's risks and identifies areas for improvement.

In this book, the entire thrust and theme is that you, your team, or your organization is undertaking an initiative to adopt new or different .NET practices. The goal is to achieve positive outcomes through better practices. Having the right scorecard helps in the following ways:

- Establishes a list of valued and relevant practices

- Shows off the practices that are being followed

- Identifies practices that are not being followed

- Helps track and monitor progress

As mentioned in Chapter 1, any choice of a new or different practice ought to be a better practice that is entirely appropriate to your situation. The scorecard presented in this appendix is based on many practices described in the book. The goal is to provide you with an example that is a starting point. Feel free to expand and adapt the scorecard, as appropriate, to suit your circumstances. Certainly cross out any practices that do not make sense or are not applicable. The Excel spreadsheet file *Samples\AppB\DotNetBestPracticesScorecard.xls* is a simple way to track and compute the overall score. To keep things uncomplicated, the scorecard only includes the following practice areas:

- Automated Testing

- Build Automation

- Continuous Integration

- Code Analysis

Within the sections that follow, there are questions that assess the degree to which practices are being followed. Consider each question and provide a score for the answer:

- 5 – Yes, we are completely there.

---

[1] For more information see Steve McConnell, *Software Project Survival Guide* (Redmond, WA: Microsoft Press, 1998).

- 4 – Probably, we are mostly there, or it is almost done.
- 3 – Somewhat, we are making good progress, or there is more to be done.
- 2 – Kind of, we have just started, or there is quite a lot to be done.
- 1 – Planning, we want to start, or it is under investigation.
- 0 – No, not at all.

The section at the end of this appendix explains how to interpret the score.

Automated Testing

To score this practice area, provide a numeric score to the questions in Tables B-1. The numeric score ranges from 0 through 5, as described at the beginning of this appendix.

Table B-1. Scorecard for Automated Testing Practices

Practice Assessment	Score
Is the team focused on writing maintainable test code?	
Has the team adopted an effective naming convention for test code?	
Does the team use the Arrange-Act-Assert (3-As) pattern, or any other effective pattern?	
Does the team write test code as short test methods?	
Does the team avoid writing more than one line of "test action" in the test method?	
Does the team avoid writing more than one "primary assertion" in the test method?	
Does the team avoid explicit typing of local variables in test code?	
Does the team use a "tests context" class to reduce repetition and manage test code complexity?	
Does the team write "test helper" classes to promote reuse?	
Does the team "data drive" the test methods when there are multiple test cases?	
Does the team perform boundary analysis to ensure that tests cover all scenarios?	
Does the team use stub objects to test in isolation?	
Does the team use only one mock object within a test method when testing interaction?	

Add up the scores in Table B-1 and enter the section score in the formula below. There are 13 questions in this section. Take the section score, divide it by 65, and multiply the result by 100 to compute a percentage.

(_____ / 65) * 100 = _____ %
     section score

Build Automation

To score this practice area, provide a numeric score to the questions in Tables B-2. The numeric score ranges from 0 through 5, as described at the beginning of this appendix.

Table B-2. Scorecard for Build Automation Practices

Practice Assessment	Score
Has the team learned the fundamentals of build automation scripting?	
Is the team able to use logging to diagnose build script issues?	
Are the scripts written to use parameters to provide variables and control logic?	
Is the team able to extend the build automation scripts by using task libraries?	
Does the team's build script import common script to promote reuse across projects?	
Does the build script make effective use of the date, time, and duration functions?	
Does the build script update the assembly version to tie it back to the build and revision number?	
Is the build script able to read and write XML data?	
Is the build script able to archive build artifacts?	
Is the build script able to deploy the one set of build artifacts to multiple target environments?	
Does the build script package deliverables using an approach that works for both the team and the customer?	
Does the build script use an approach that makes deployments automated, robust, and reliable?	

Add up the scores in Table B-2 and enter the section score in the formula below. There are 12 questions in this section. Take the section score, divide it by 60, and multiply the result by 100 to compute a percentage.

(_____ / 60) * 100 = _____ %
   section score

Continuous Integration

To score this practice area, provide a numeric score to the questions in Tables B-3. The numeric score ranges from 0 through 5, as described at the beginning of this appendix.

Table B-3. Scorecard for Continuous Integration Practices

Practice Assessment	Score
Does the team use a continuous integration (CI) server?	
Is a rebuild triggered after every source code push?	
Does the CI server start rebuilding with a clean working folder?	
Are the build artifacts organized in an effective manner?	
Does the CI server run all automated tests to confirm that the latest build works as intended?	
Does the CI server perform code analysis monitoring and report failures if violations occur?	
Does the CI server generate full and complete analysis reports for ongoing review?	
Does the CI server package the components and content into one deliverable?	
Is the CI server able to use one script to deploy to any of the target environments?	
Is the CI server able to run automated smoke tests to verify that a deployment is deployed properly?	
Is the CI server able to run stability tests to verify that the deployment is ready for quality assurance testers?	
Is the CI server able to generate reports and keep metrics that demonstrate progress and delivery?	

Add up the scores in Table B-3 and enter the section score in the formula below. There are 12 questions in this section. Take the section score, divide it by 60, and multiply the result by 100 to compute a percentage.

(_____ / 60) * 100 = _____ %
   section score

Code Analysis

To score this practice area, provide a numeric score to the questions in Tables B-4. The numeric score ranges from 0 through 5, as described at the beginning of this appendix.

Table B-4. Scorecard for Code Analysis Practices

Practice Assessment	Score
Is the team thoroughly analyzing assemblies using one or more static code analysis tools?	
Does the build fail when there are violations of required static code analysis rules?	
Is the team able to decompile an assembly if there is a need to analyze, understand, or troubleshoot an issue?	
Does the team use a tool to help everyone comply with coding standards?	
Does the build fail when there are violations of mandatory coding standards?	
Is the team able to use a thorough differencing tool to analyze, understand, and troubleshoot an issue?	
Is the team able to find and address all inappropriate duplication of source code?	
Does the team perform architecture and design analysis to compare as-planned to as-built designs?	
Is the team able to run the automated tests with a code coverage analysis tool?	
Does the build run automated tests with a code coverage analysis tool?	
Is the team able to profile the system's performance?	
Does the team profile the system's performance on a regular basis?	
Is the team able to examine database queries with a query profiler?	
Does the system incorporate a flexible logging solution to monitor and diagnose the system?	

Add up the scores in Table B-4 and enter the section score in the formula below. There are 14 questions in this section. Take the section score, divide it by 70, and multiply the result by 100 to compute a percentage.

(_____ / 70) * 100 = _____ %
    section score

Calculating the Overall Score

To interpret the results you must calculate an overall score. The result is a high-level number that can be used to report and track overall progress. If tracked over the course of a "best practices initiative" this overall score can help management and others quickly see the strides the team is making toward following better practices.

Add up the section scores and enter the total score in the formula below. There are 51 questions in all. Take the total score, divide it by 255, and multiply the result by 100 to compute a percentage.

(_____ / 255) * 100 = _____ %
    total score

Depending on the overall score, there are some comments that can be made. If the team's score is at 80% or above then congratulations are in order. If the team's score is at or above 60% but is below 80% then that is good, although there are improvements to be made. If the score is below 60%, there is much work to do. The good news is that you are motivated to learn and adopt better practices. Further comments are in the breakdown shown in Table B-5.

Table B-5. Score Comments

Overall Score	Comments
90% or above	Excellent. Outstanding achievement. The team has mastered the objectives and is exceeding expectations in all practice areas.
80 - 89%	Very good. Above average achievement. The team has mastered most of the objectives and is meeting expectations in most practice areas. Consider new and different practices that help target areas to improve efficiency and effectiveness.
60-79%	Good. Satisfactory achievement. The team has mastered the basic objectives in the practice areas. Consider new and different practices that are designed to improve those practice areas that need improvement.
40-59%	Needs improvement. This is typical for those just starting to adopt better practices. Focus on understanding the basic objectives the team needs to master in each practice area. Consider new and different practices that help to improve overall efficiency and effectiveness.
Less than 40%	At risk. The team recognizes that there are significant weaknesses in major practice areas. Focus on understanding how not following better practices creates problems and pain points. Consider new and different practices that help with problem prevention.

Index